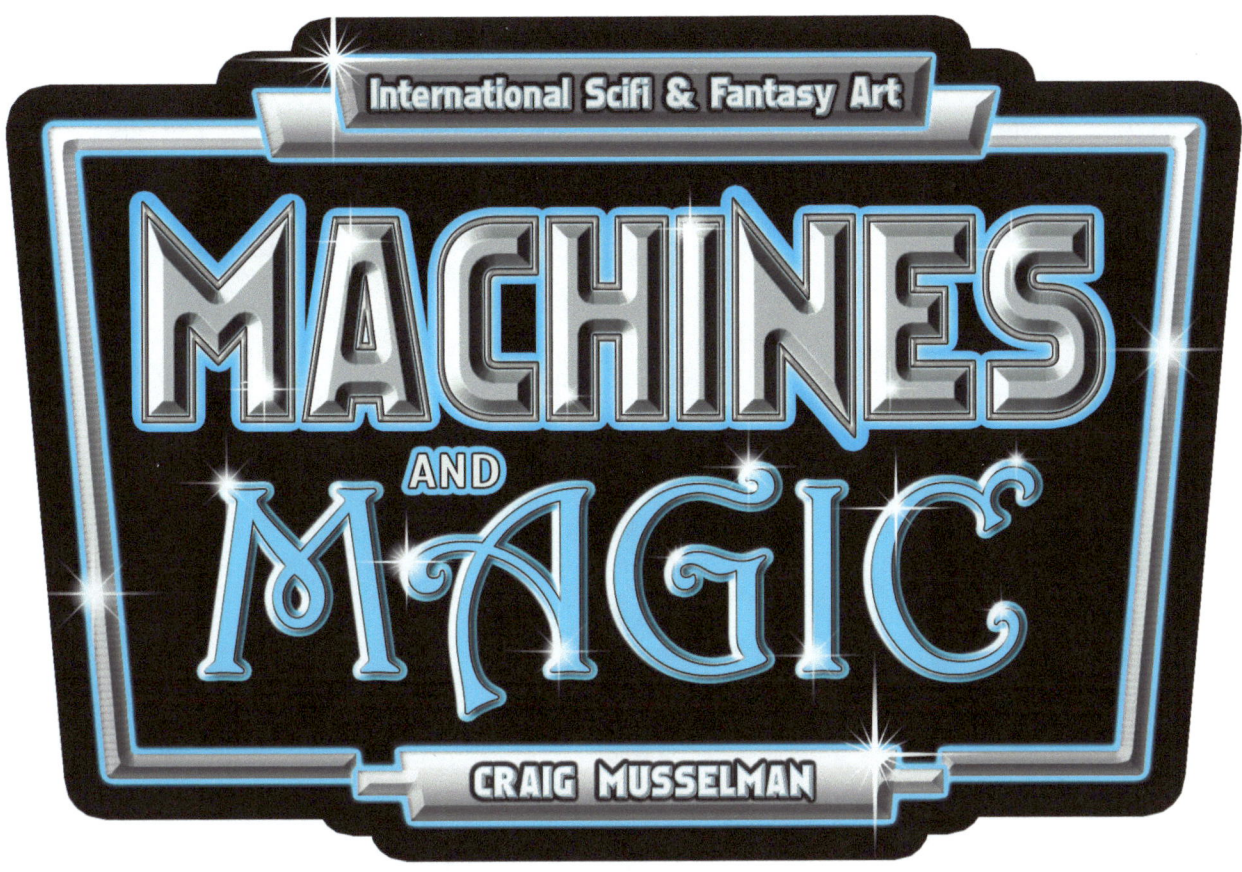

International Scifi & Fantasy Art

MACHINES AND MAGIC

CRAIG MUSSELMAN

FOR LINKS TO PURCHASE THE BOOK OR SUBMIT ART TO THE NEXT VOLUME PLEASE VISIT

MACHINESANDMAGIC.COM

IF YOU ARE AN ARTIST IN A DIFFERENT GENRE VISIT

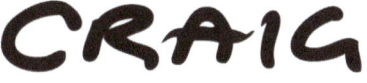

TO SEE IF I AM MAKING A BOOK IN YOUR STYLE

CRAIG

EDITOR

Omnium rerum principia parva sunt - Parva scintilla saepe magnam flamam excitat.

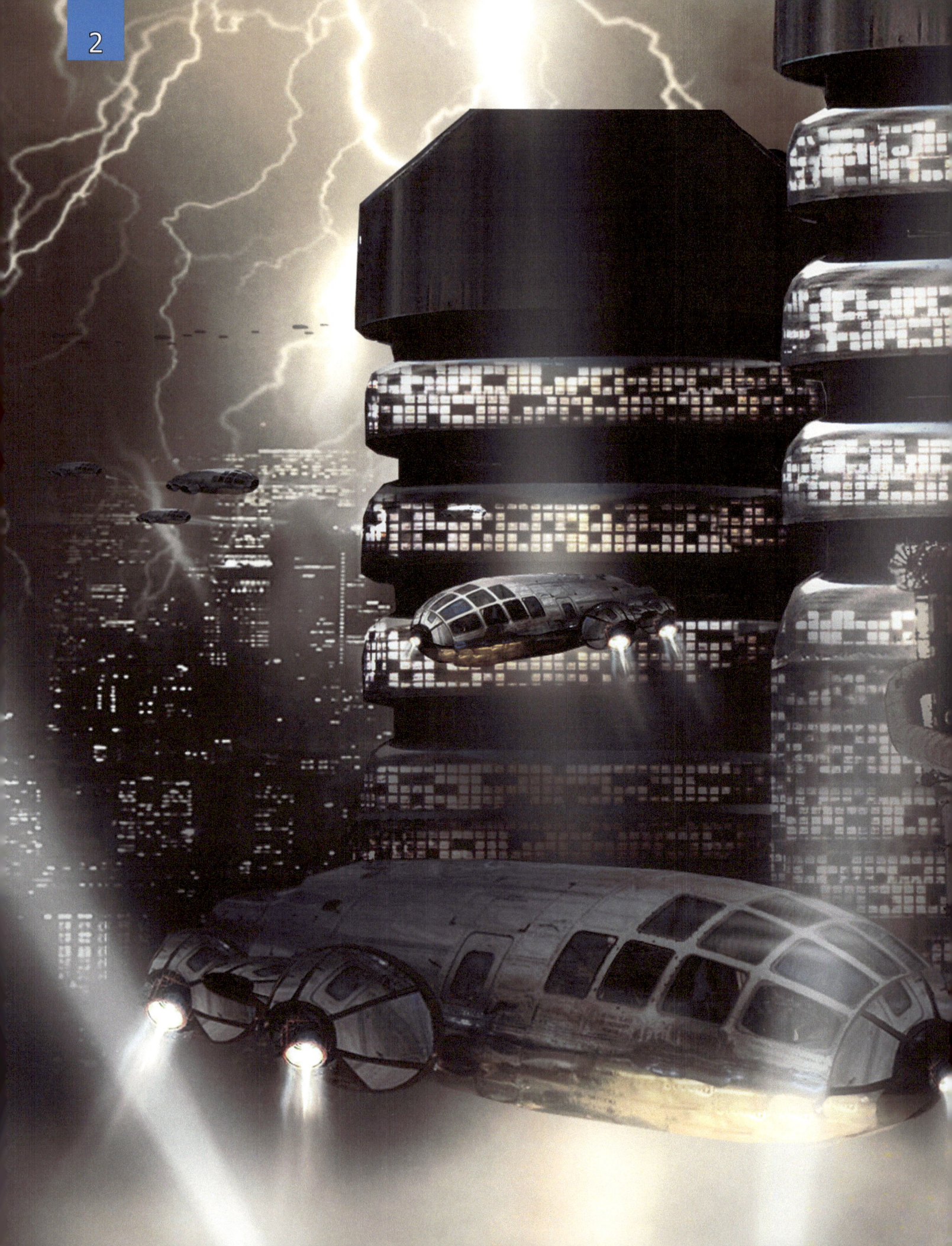

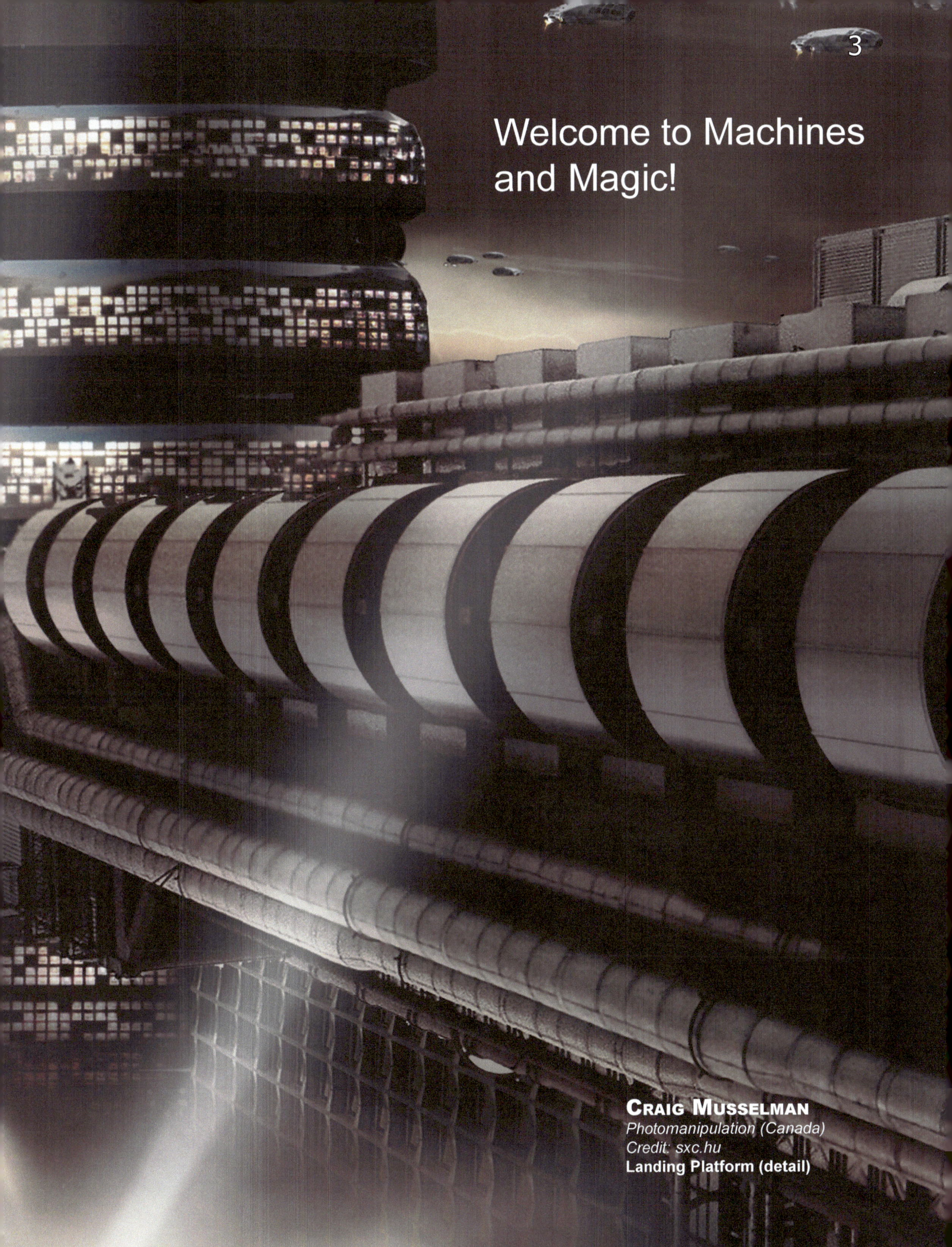

Welcome to Machines and Magic!

CRAIG MUSSELMAN
Photomanipulation (Canada)
Credit: sxc.hu
Landing Platform (detail)

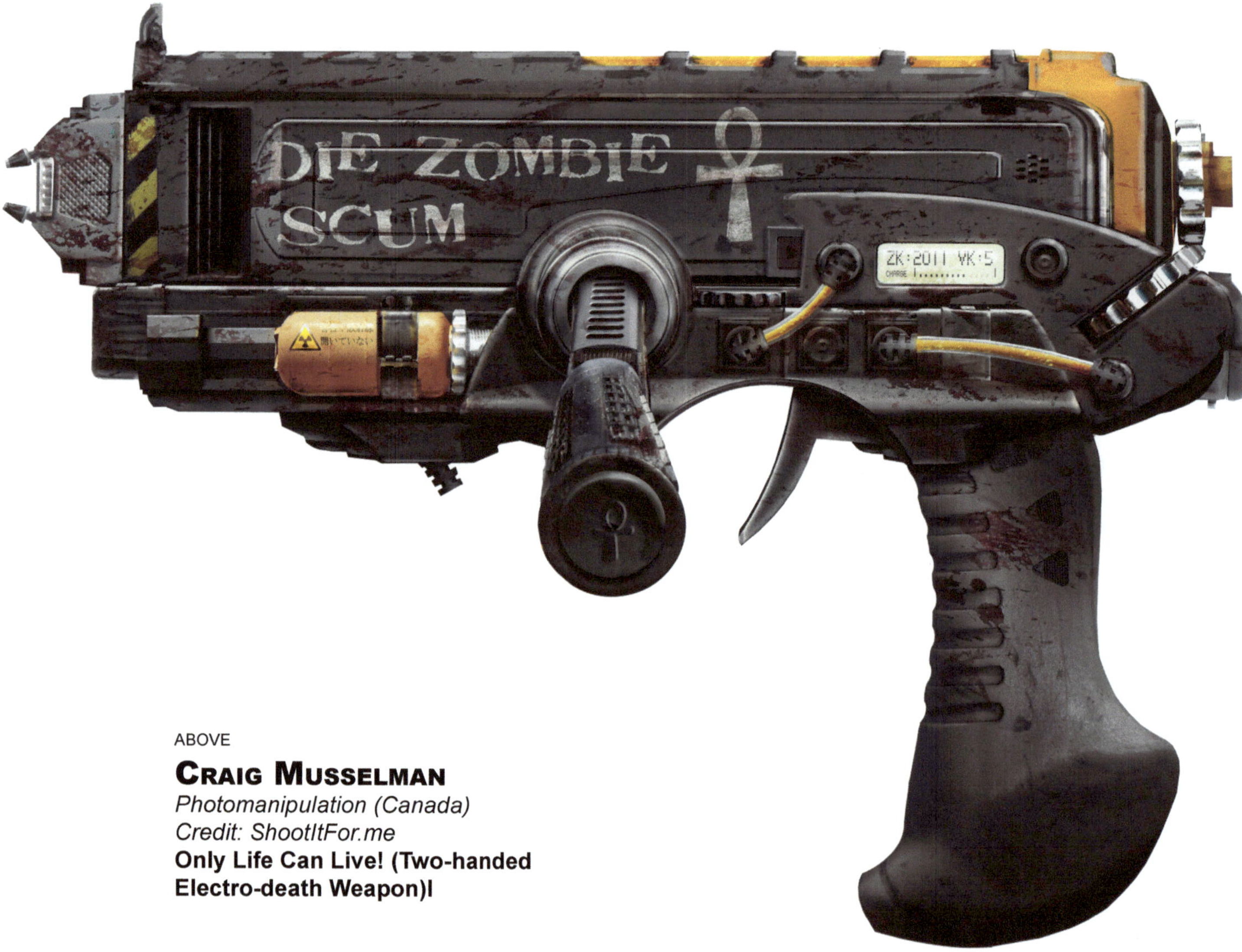

ABOVE

CRAIG MUSSELMAN
Photomanipulation (Canada)
Credit: ShootItFor.me
Only Life Can Live! (Two-handed Electro-death Weapon)l

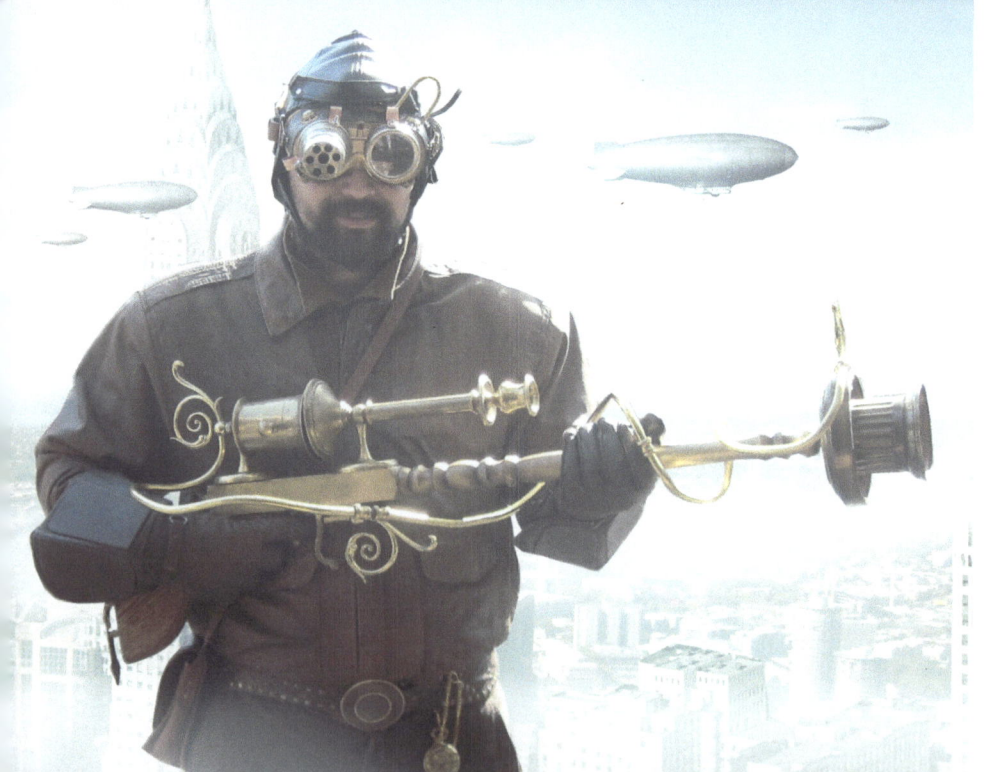

MACHINES AND MAGIC (VOL. 1)

is just a TASTE of the many Science Fiction and Fantasy artists found and recruited by Craig Musselman to compile this fascinating collection of images. Thank you to them!

After taking in the works featured here, it is my hope that you use the listing at the end of the book, or visit the site to contact the artists, praise them, and find out how you can see (and BUY!) more of their work.

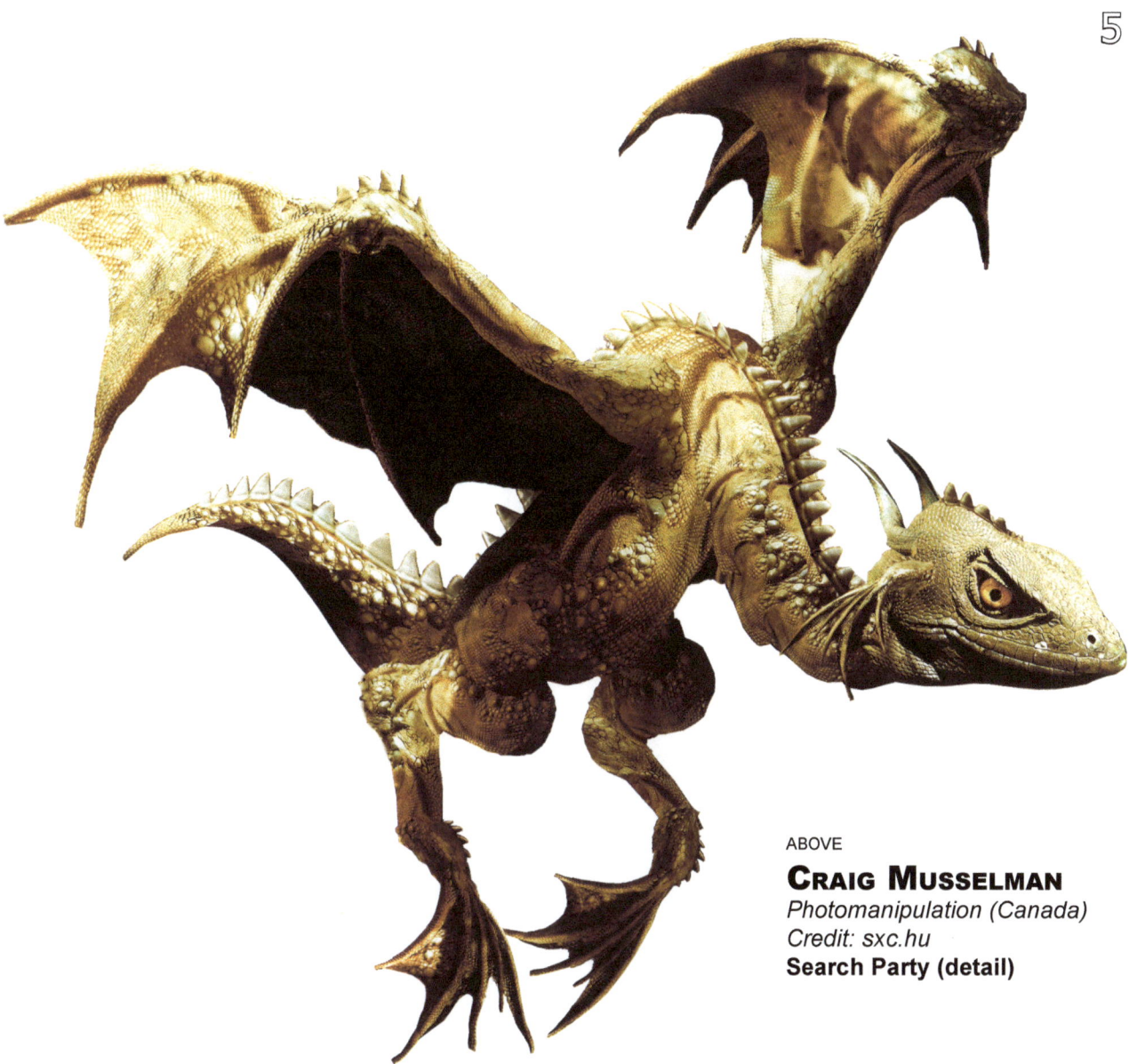

All works (submittted before the deadline) were judged independently by four international artists. I would like to thank the judges for a very difficult task. Their short lists appear first. I have also selected one artist for my editor's choice award which is found in the main section.

CRAIG MUSSELMAN
Editor (pictured far left - as captain Draco Flambeau) is an internationally award winning Artist and Graphic Designer and Physics aficionado, specializing in elaborate digital photomontage works of art, as well prop & costume design. He has been featured in Advanced Photoshop Magazine, ImagineFX Magazine, as well as co-authored a textbook on creative uses of Photoshop with his friends at Photoshop competition website Worth1000.com.

He is also the founder and author of the TalentNextDoor.com series of books on local arts. Look for other books coming soon through his collection of websites: SteampunkArt.ca, RealisticArt.org, ShootItFor.me (his photomanipulation stock site) or CraigMusselman.com for the latest news and emails to submit to, or inquire about the books. For more about THIS book and helpful links visit: MachinesAndMagic.com .

Craig was born in 1970, & lives in Waterloo, Ontario, Canada, with his longtime partner.

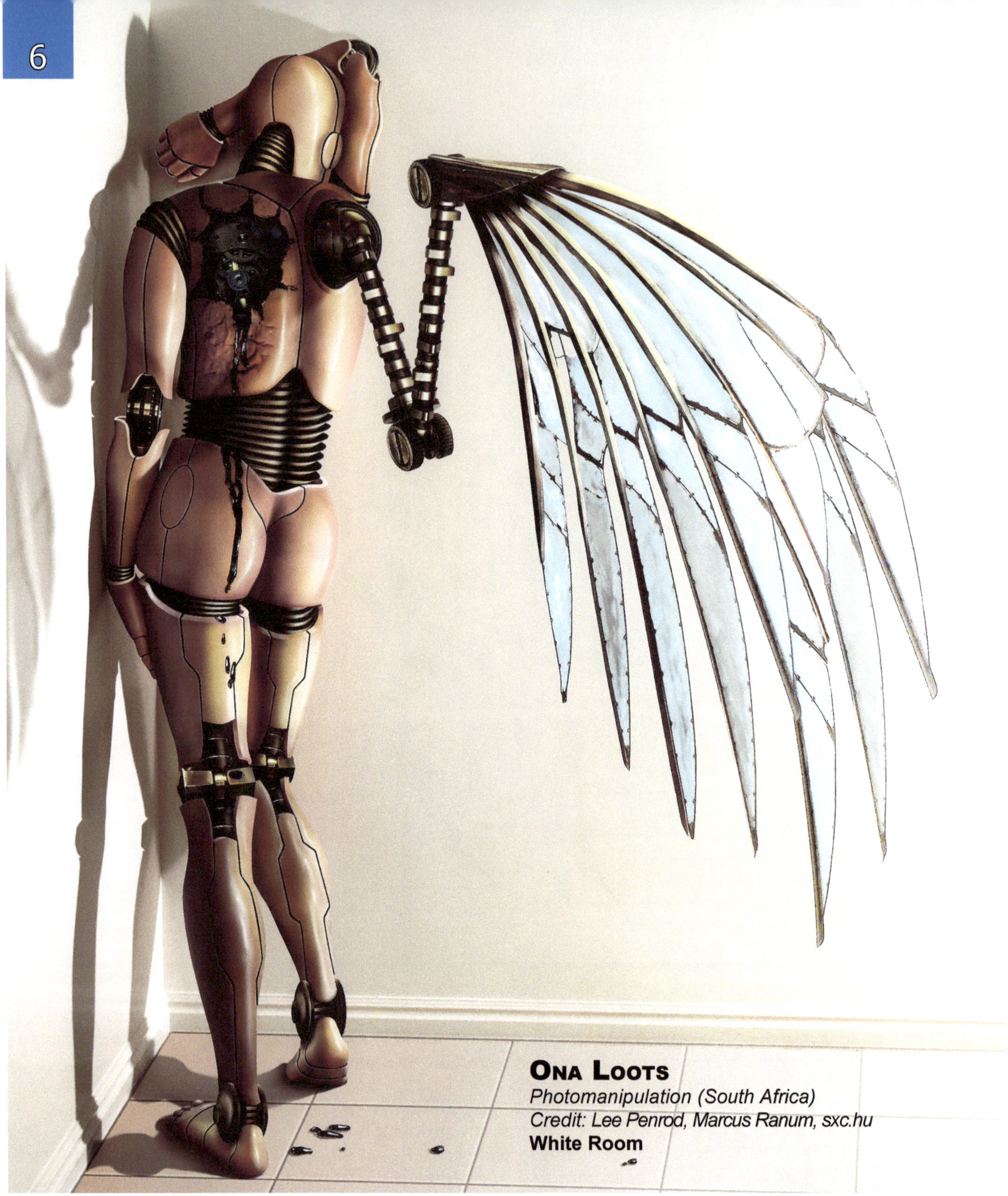

ONA LOOTS
Photomanipulation (South Africa)
Credit: Lee Penrod, Marcus Ranum, sxc.hu
White Room

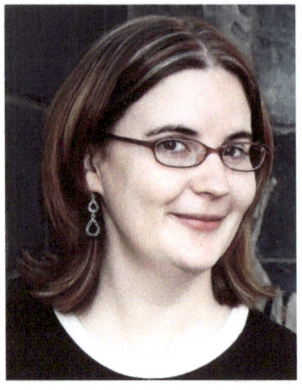

JUDGE

Ona Loots (left) *aka Onany-mous* is our first judge. She is a web designer and illustrator from Pretoria, South Africa. Her amazing photomanipula-tions have been a major force to contend with in online competitions since starting in 2005.

WINNER

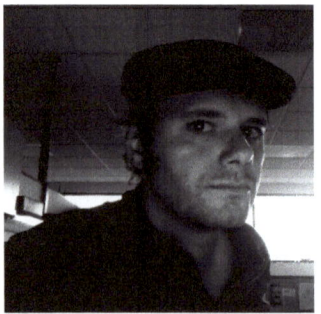

John Petersen (right) is a full-time illustrator and animator from Ames, Iowa. Clients include Crown Publishing, Citadel Press and Gotham Books. This picture came very close to topping TWO judges' lists, for its gritty emotional story.

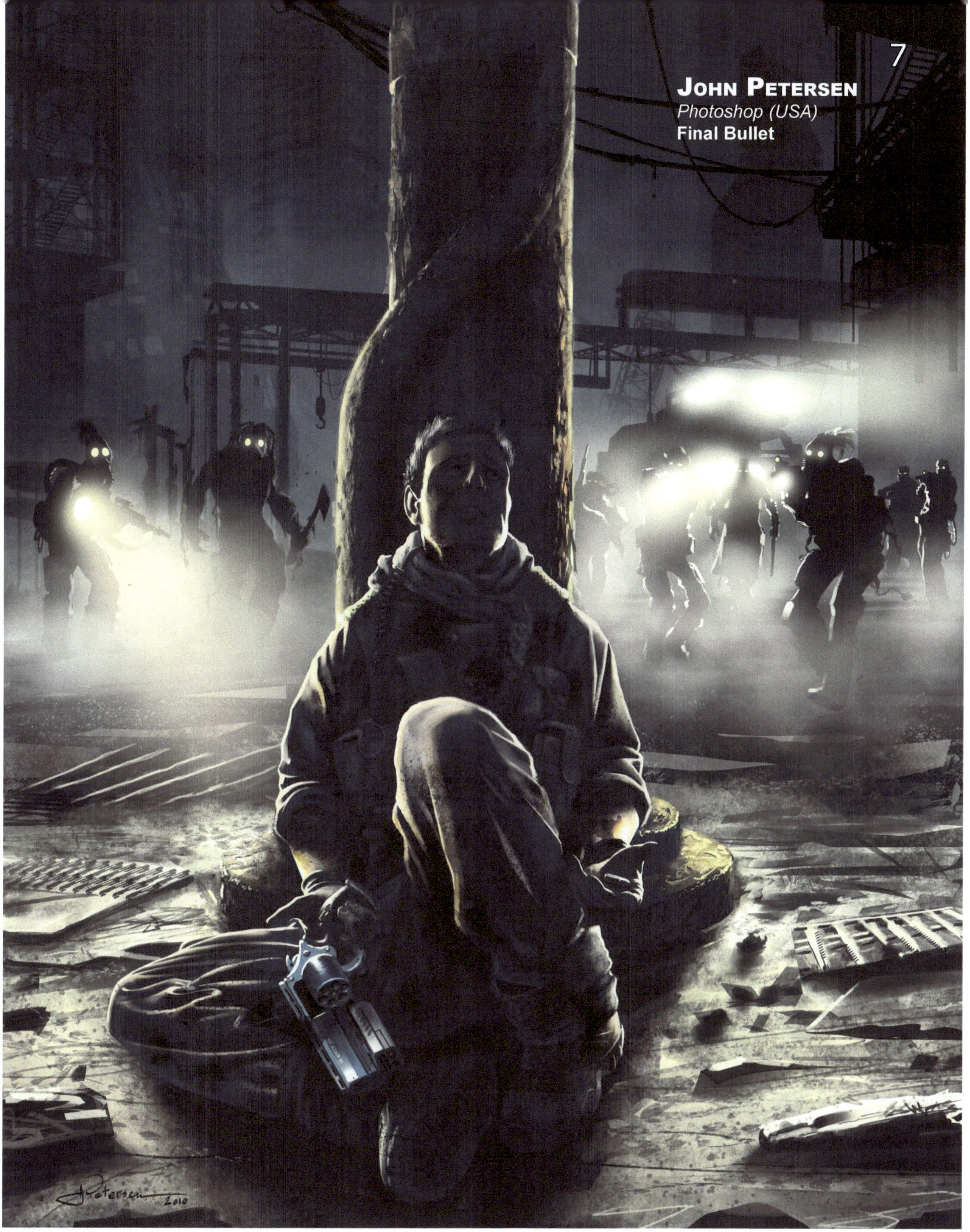

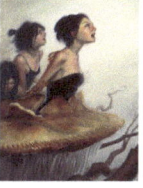

ONA'S SHORT LIST

JOHN PETERSEN "FINAL BULLET"
▶ **Rob Rey** "FOUR AND TWENTY"
▶ **Philip Longson** "MURDER ON THE ROOFTOPS"
▶ **Vincent Lefevre** "BIO PALADIN"
▶ **Vincent Lefevre** "BABY DINO"
▶ **Angel Alonso** "WITCH OF THOUGHT"

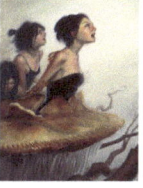
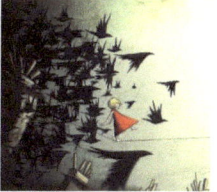
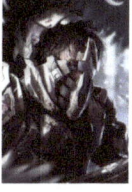
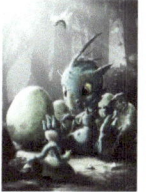
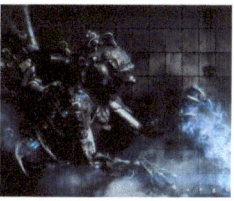

BELOW
JOËL LAROSE
Costume - Silk, Rattan , Rubber (Canada)
Samurai

OPPOSITE
SHICHIGORO-SHINGO
Photoshop (Japan)
Red Line

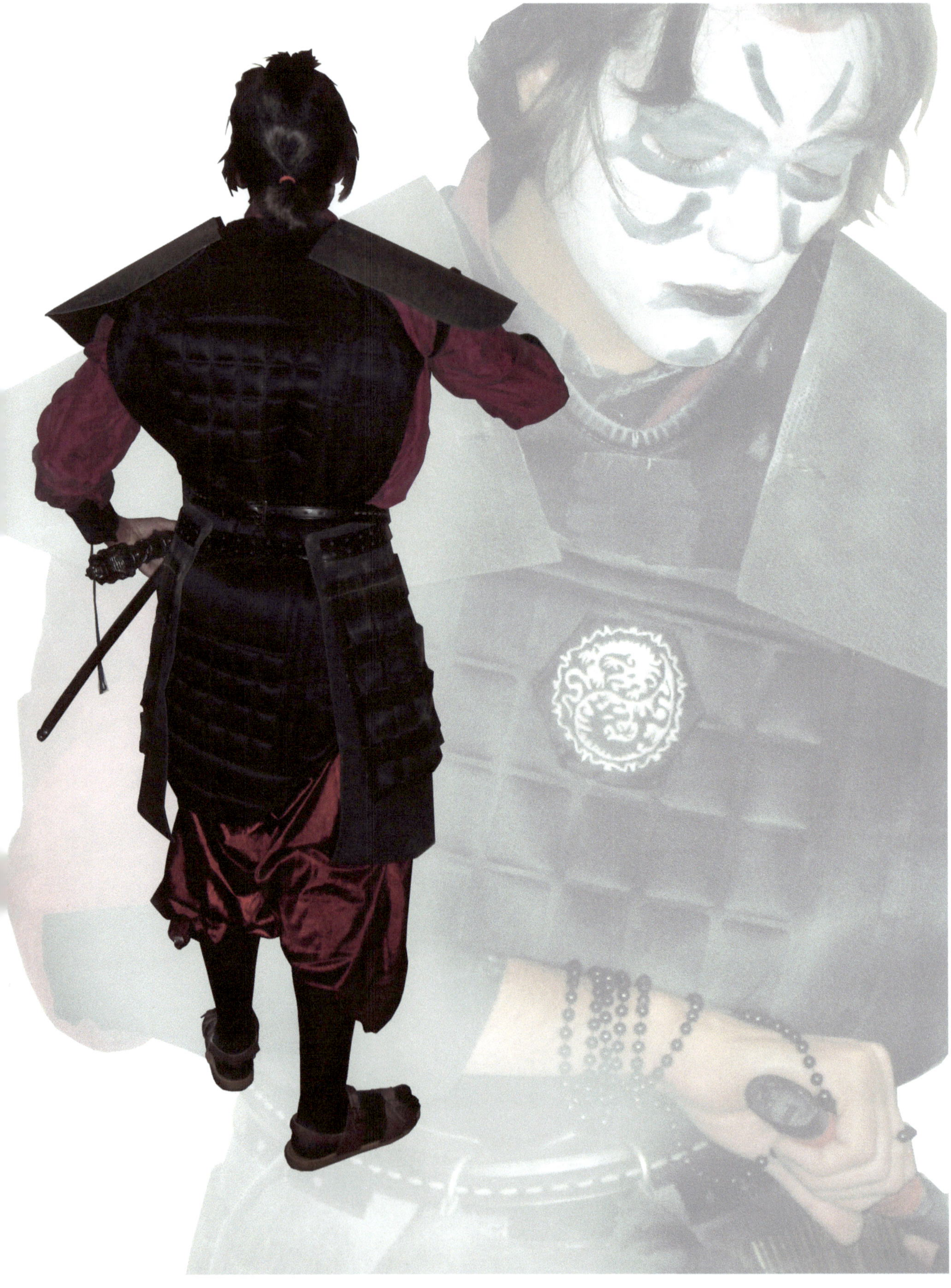

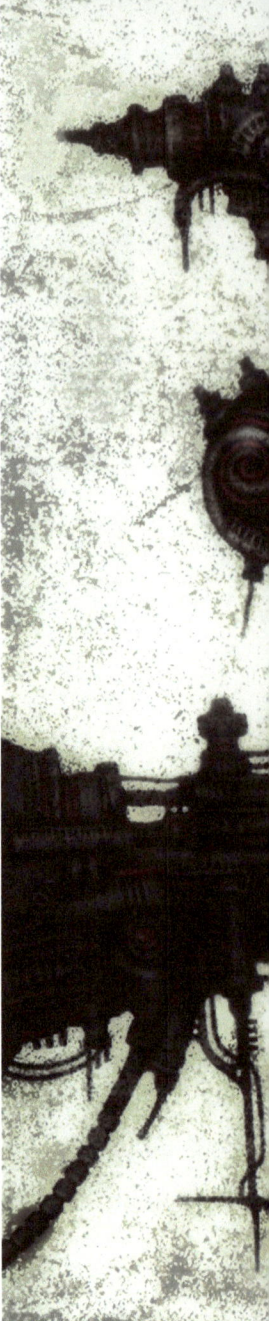

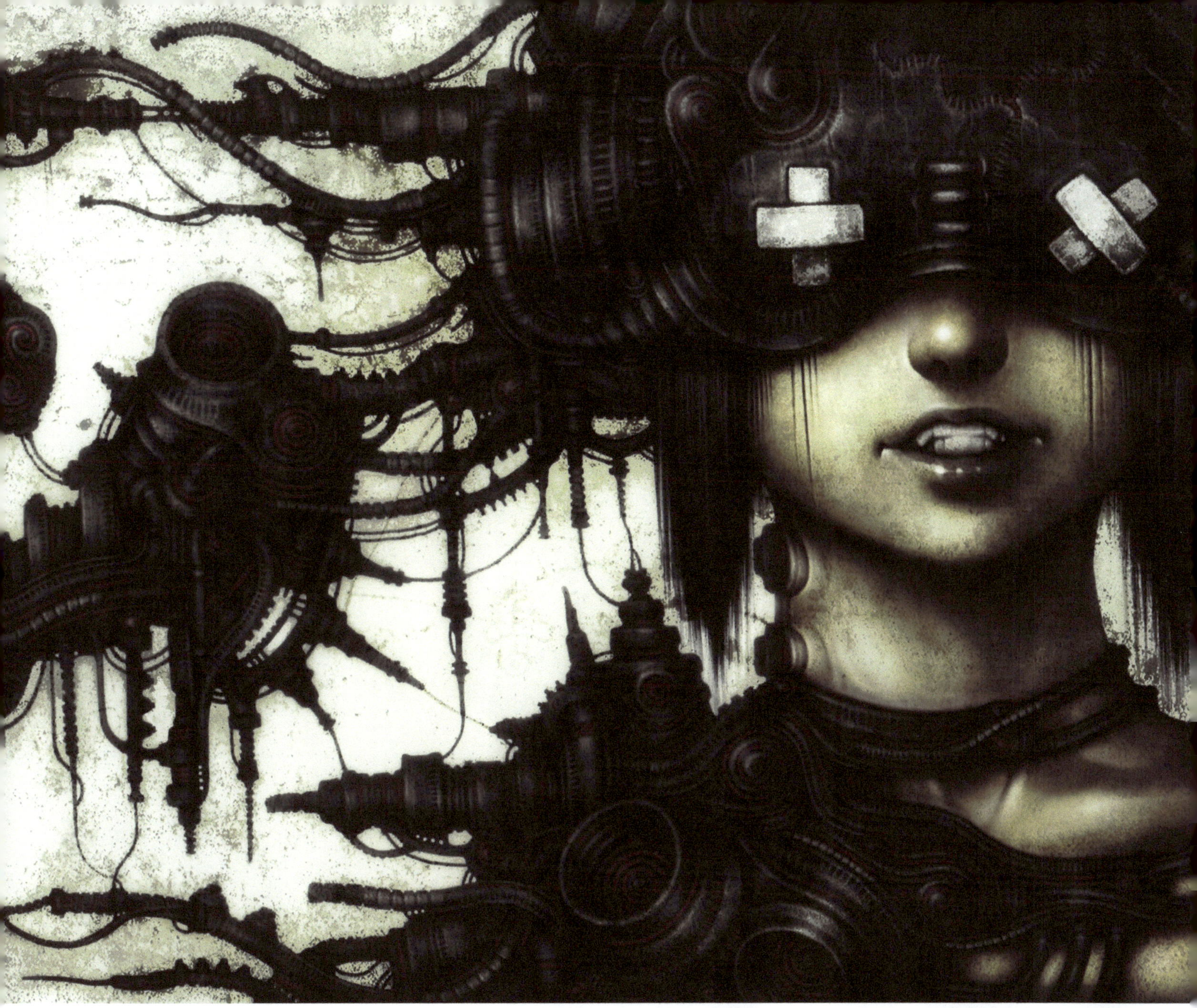

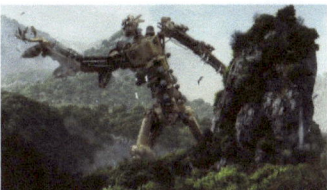

SHICHIGORO-SHINGO
"Redline 3"
- ▶ **Angel Alonso** "THE LOVER LIFE"
- ▶ **Vincent Lefevre** "BABY DINO"
- ▶ **Markus Stadlober** "VIRTUAL FIELD COMMANDER"
- ▶ **Yangtian Li** "LYDIA"

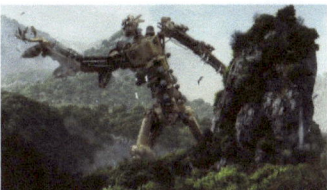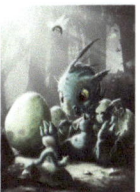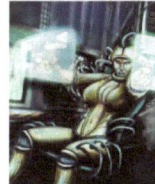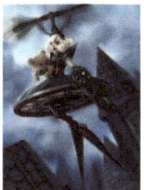

JOËL'S SHORT LIST

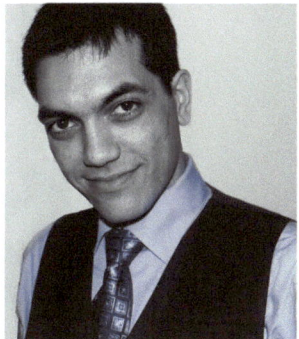

JUDGE

Joël Larose (left) is the partner and muse of the editor who listens calmly to all his frustrations about publishing, and more importantly helps with decisions when late nights have taken their toll. He is a blackbelt martial artist, programs computers, and has extensive knowlege of Tarot symbolism and ancient Japan.

WINNER

Shichigoro-shingo I'm a freelance illustrator based in Japan. I quit work a few years ago, I'm drawing a picture every day now. There are many robots and strange living creatures fused with inorganic substances in my work, but I never imbue these creatures with negative feelings like "unhappiness, sadness, fear, or anger." Although they have a strange look about them, they evoke subtle feelings of "quietness, peace, tenderness, and joy."

shichigoro.com

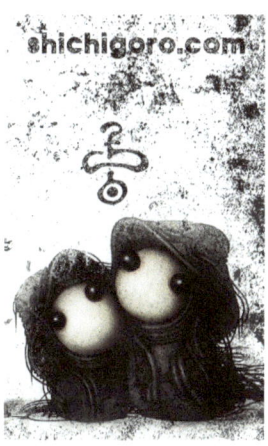

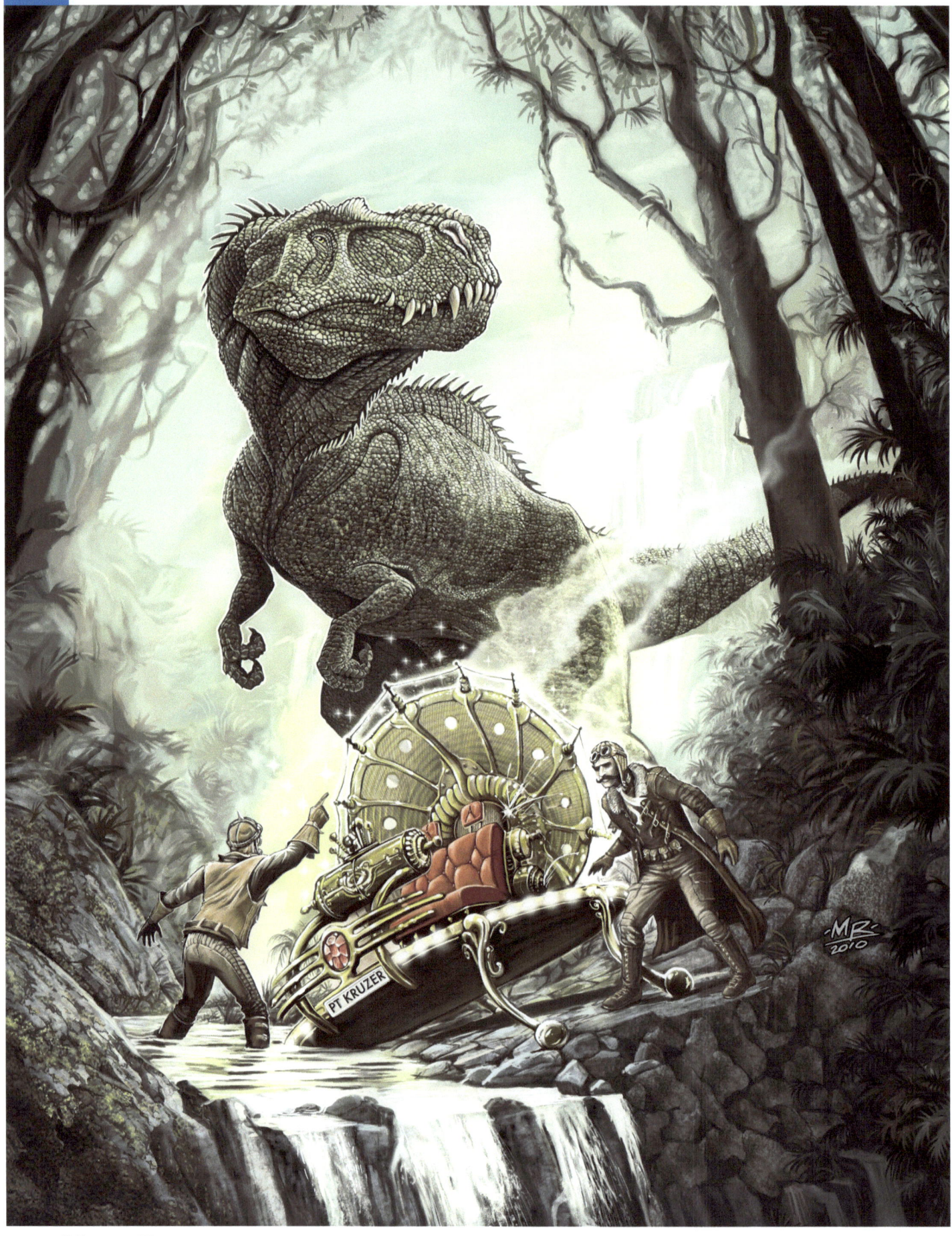

ABOVE **MARK REHKOPF**
Digital (Canada)
Cretaceous Conundrum

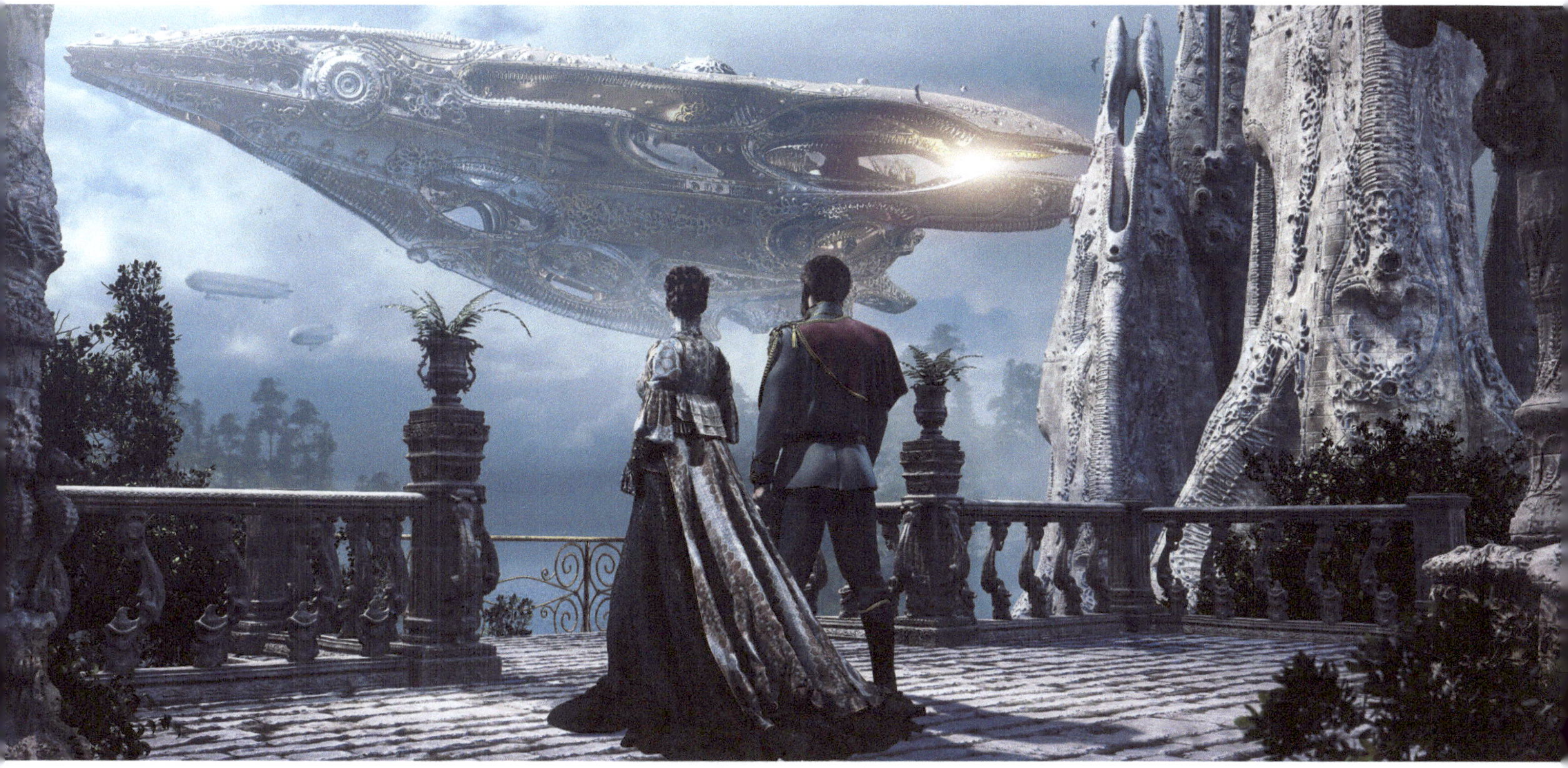

MARK'S SHORT LIST

ANGEL ALONSO
"House Atreides"
▶ **Peter Morbacher** "Valley of Mists"
▶ **Raoul Vitale** "Unrequited"
▶ **Krisztian Balla** "Dungeon Delve"
▶ **Ross Tran** "Everglow"

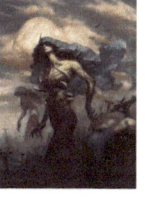 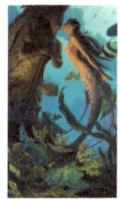 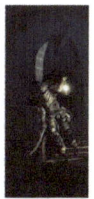 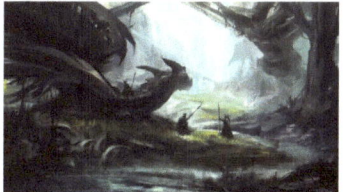

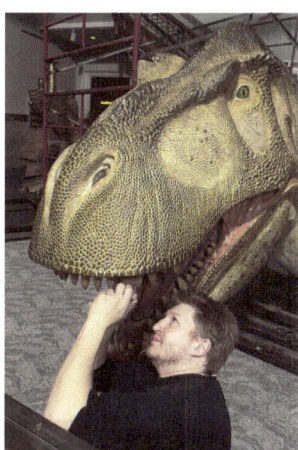

JUDGE

Mark Rehkopf (left) is a diverse freelance artist with over twenty years experience. He works in realism, abstract, comic and cartoon, and all the various stages in between. He has spent the last ten years sculpting life-sized dinosaur exhibits for natural history museums worldwide. Today he concentrates on painting and illustrating for public companies and private collectors. Mark has a penchant for painting wildlife, retro pop art, science-fiction, fantasy, dinosaurs, pin-up girls, and very big rocks !

TOP
ANGEL ALONSO
Digital 3D (Spain)
House Atreides

WINNER

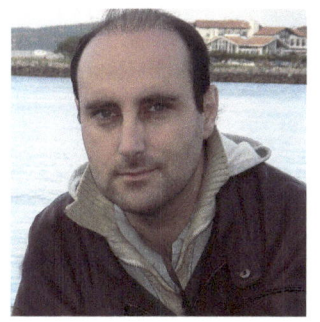

Angel Alonso (right) had three different images appear on three different short-lists. Born in 1967. He lives in Irun, Spain and is married with two children. He started as an illustrator and comic artist, painting with water colors and airbrush.He has 25 years in the field of animation for film and television. He is self-taught in 3D and has done: Art Direction, Concept design, matte painting 2D/3D, compositing and digital FX.

Angel Alonso. Nacido en 1967. Vive en Irun, (España) casado y con dos hijos. Empezo como ilustrador y dibujante de comics, pintando con aquarelas y aerografo. Experiencia: 25 años en el sector de la animacion para cine y television Aprendio 3D, de forma autodidacta.Ha realizado: Direccion artistica, Concept design, matte painter 2D/3D, compositing y FX digitales.

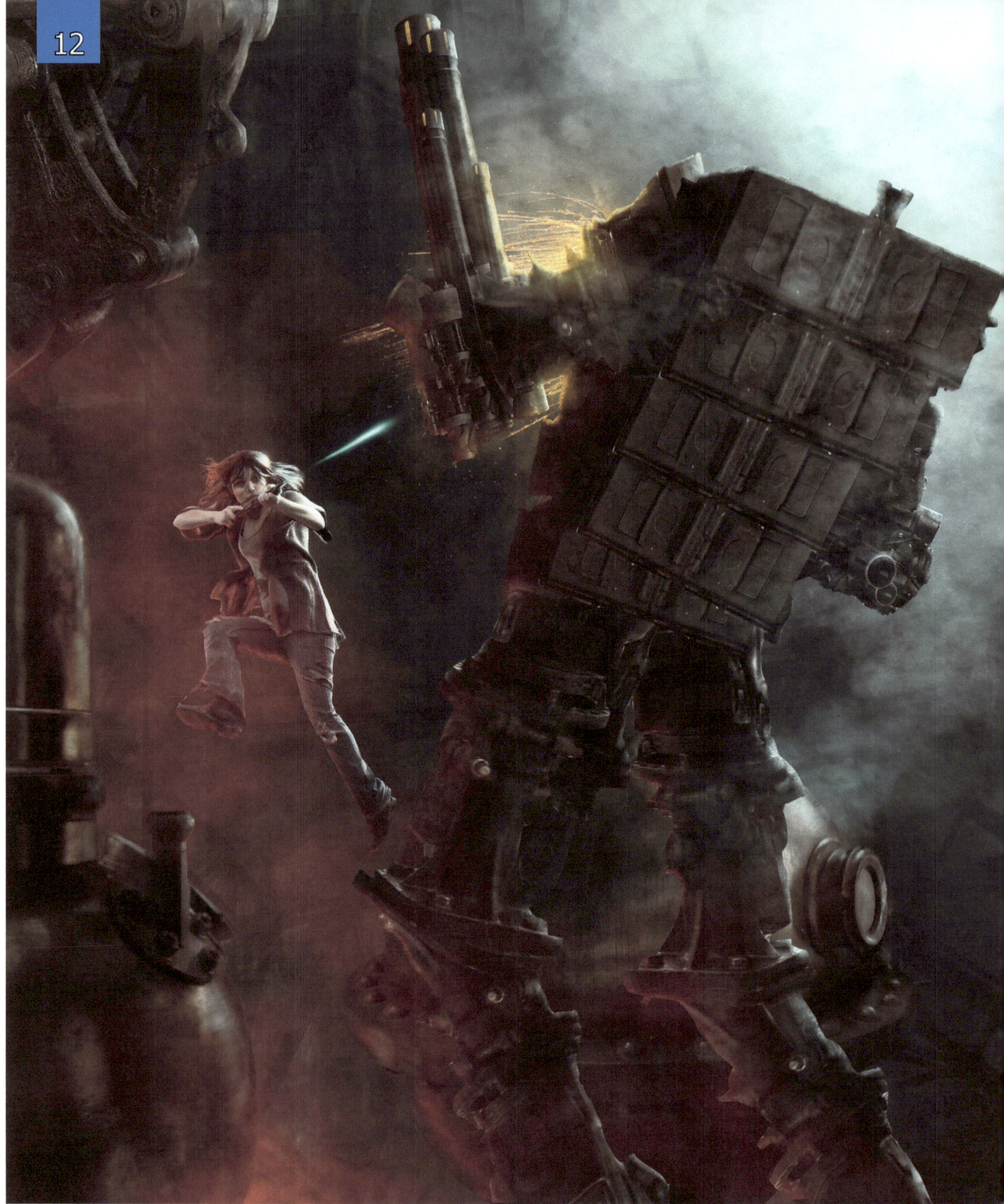

ABOVE

ANGELA TYGERSON ROSS
Photomanipulation (USA)
Credit: Deviantart.com (Tasastock), ShootItFor.me
Outgunned

OPPOSITE TOP

RAOUL VITALE
Oil on masonite (USA)
Scouts

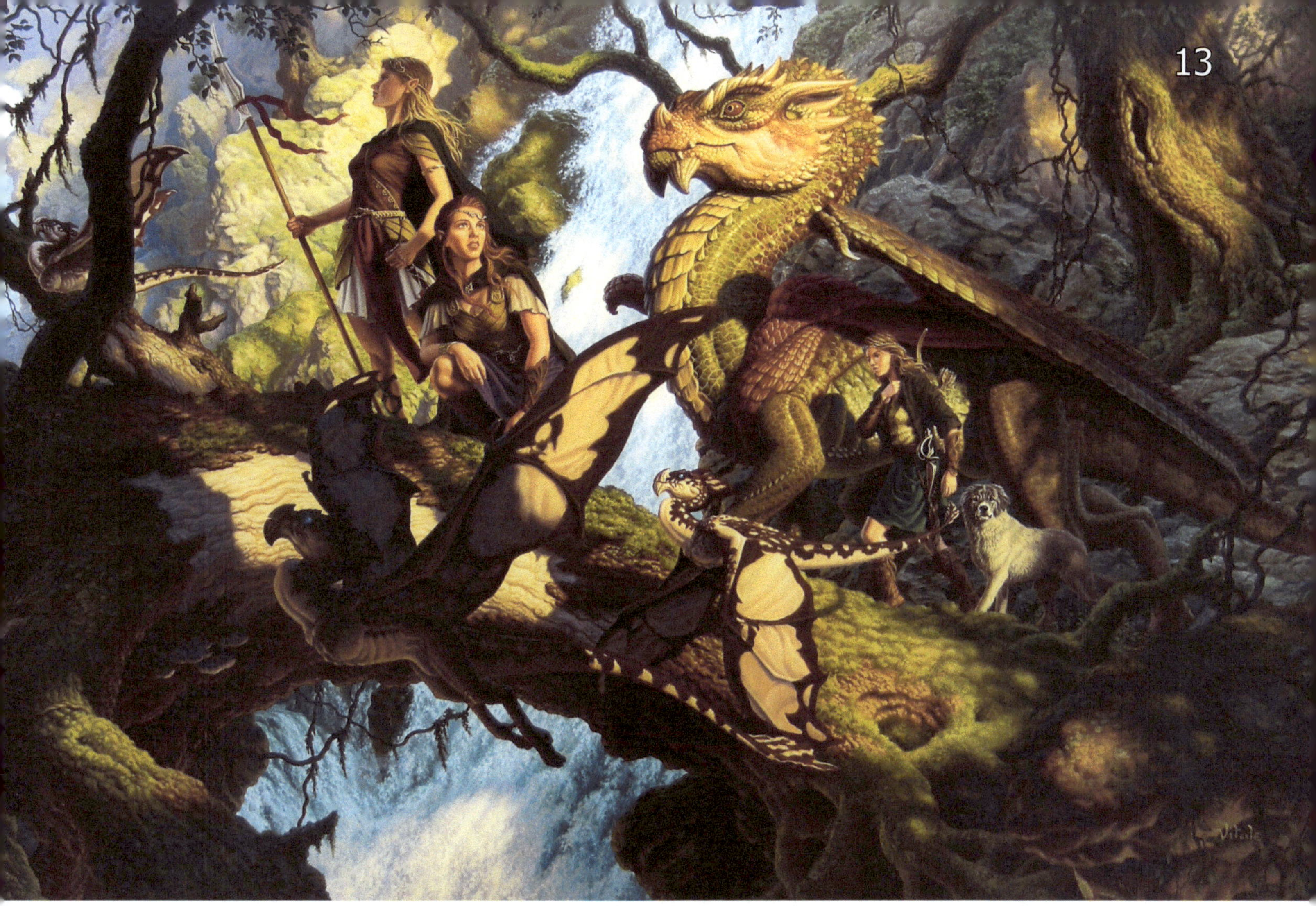

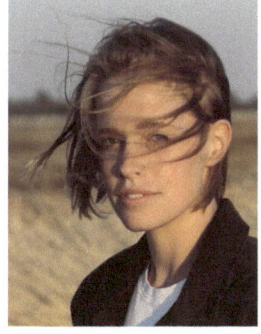

ANGELA'S SHORT LIST

RAOUL VITALE "SCOUTS"

- ► **Raoul Vitale** "WILDLIFE"
- ► **John Petersen** "FINAL BULLET"
- ► **Rob Rey** "LAST STAND"
- ► **David Lecossu** "THE WORM"
- ► **Cathrine Langwagen** "ELEMENTS-FIRE"

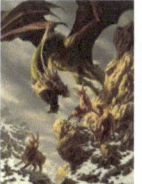 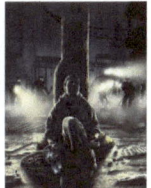 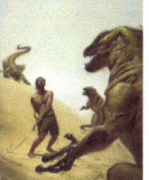 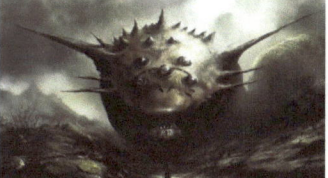 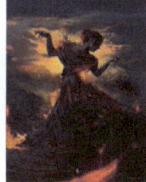

JUDGE

Angela Tygerson Ross (left) is an artist on many levels; from balancing her life as a wife and mother of two, to creating masterful pieces of art. What might surprise you is that her perspective comes from her science background. Since she was young, she was fascinated with light, optical effects, and how things work. In college she studied physics. Now she constantly devises little experiments to figure out how to capture light in her art. Her curiosity about the world inspires each image she creates.

WINNER

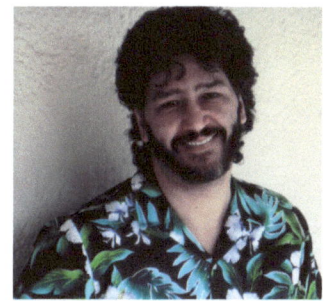

Raoul Vitale (right) is also on multiple short lists. Born in 1955, Raoul began drawing at around the age of three. Not having any formal art training, he learned by trial-and-error. He graduated high school and went to work as a stained glass designer and painter - all the while, his primary goal was to illustrate full time. After leaving the stained glass studio, he began designing and illustrating books, magazines, collectables, and has had opportunities to create commissions for private collectors. Raoul lives in Ohio with his wife and son.

NEAR RIGHT
Michael Mowat
Photoshop Painting (Scotland)
The Charge

OPPOSITE RIGHT
Gabriel Verdon
Photoshop(Canada)
Alexis and the Raven

BELOW
Brent Woodside
Digital (USA)
Roll Initiative!

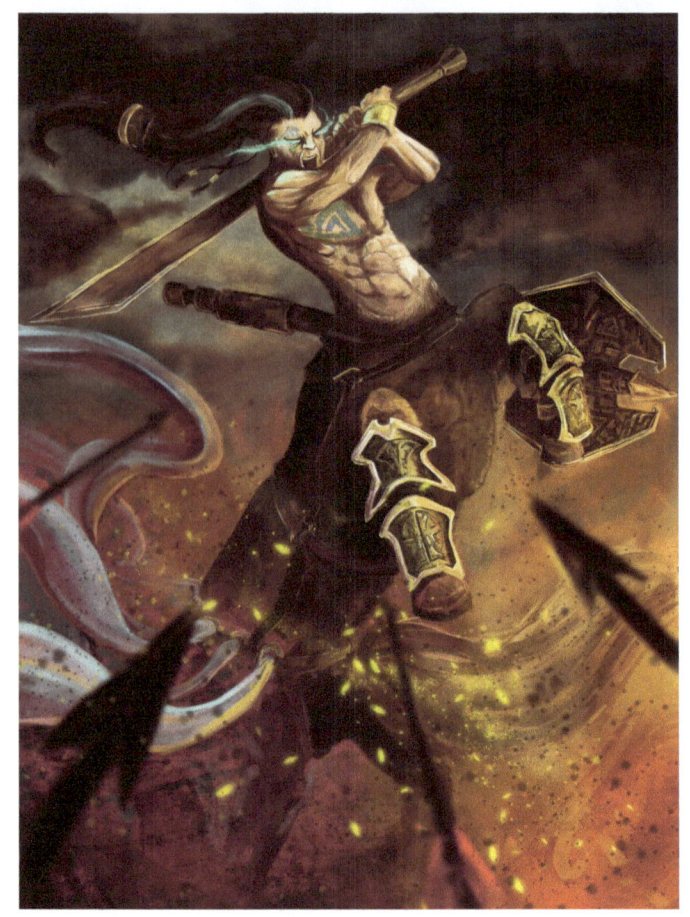

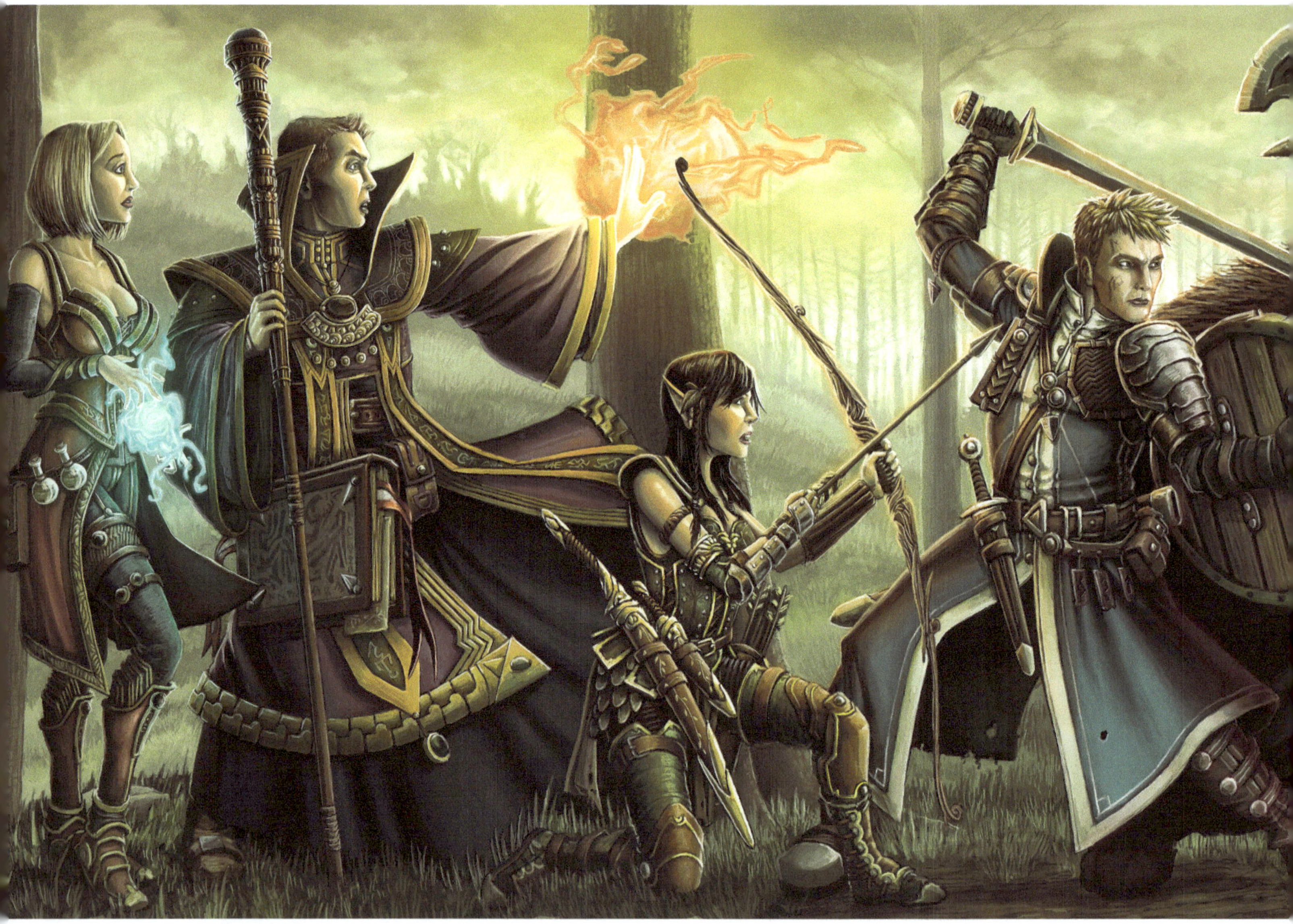

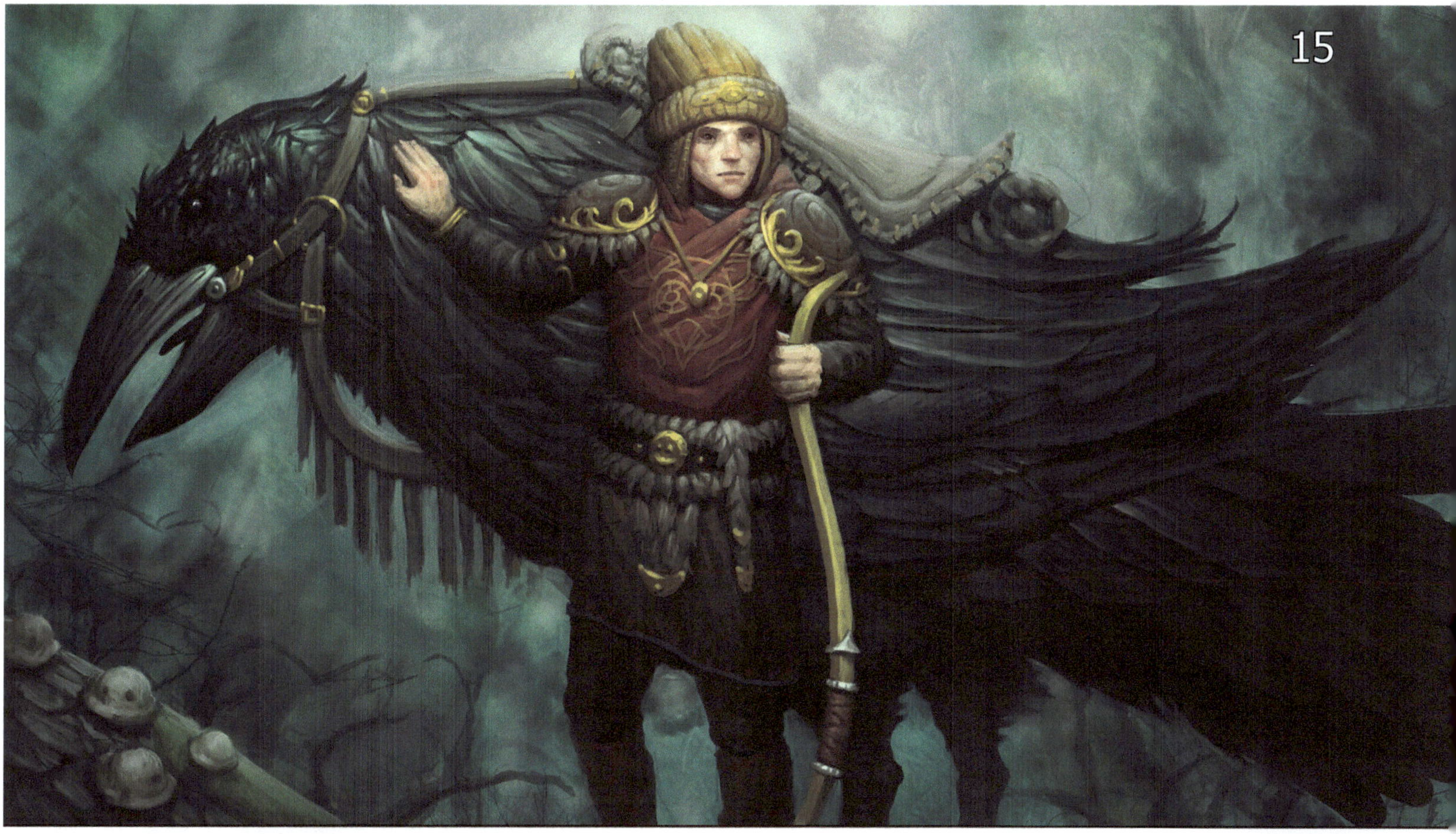

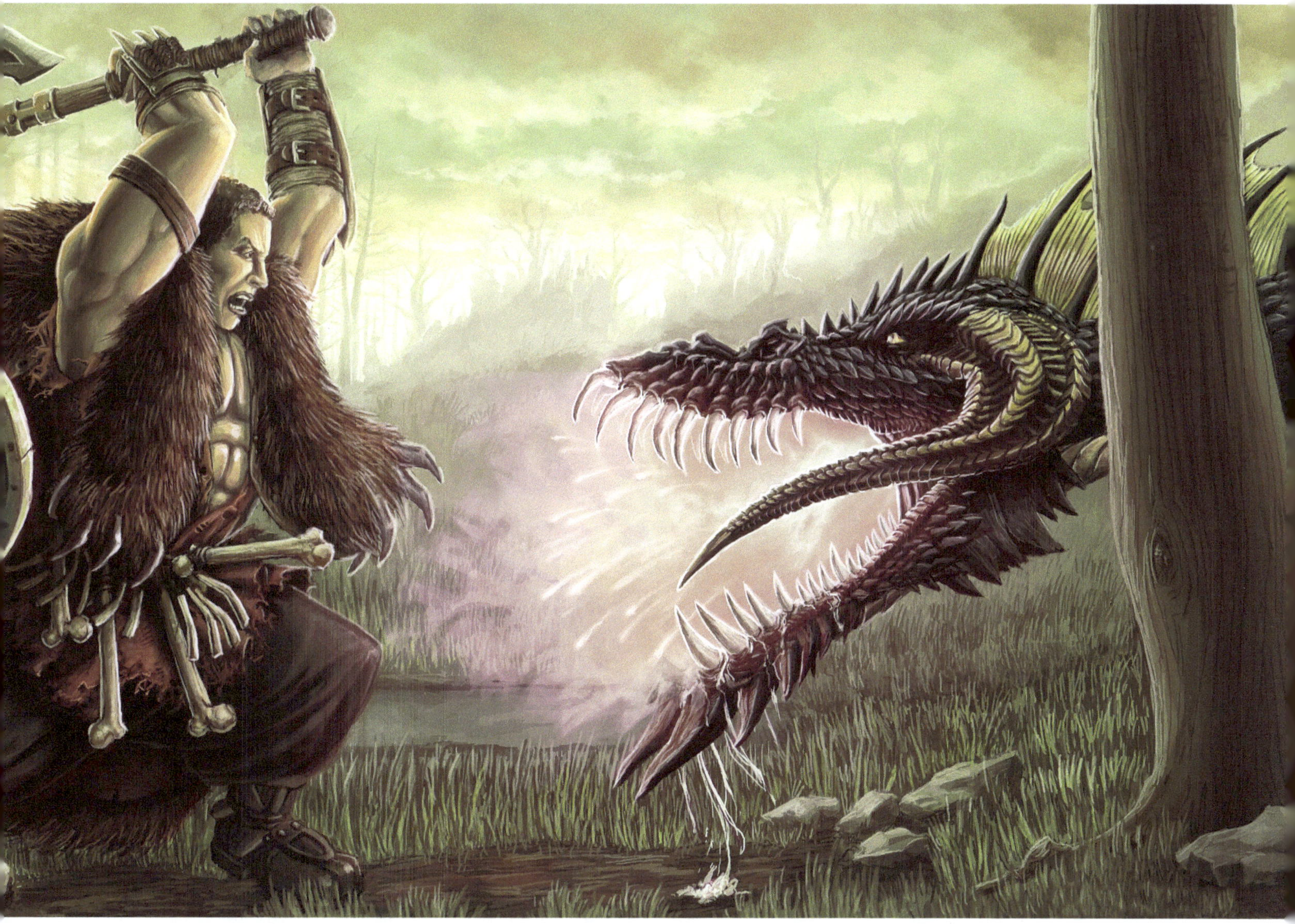

RIGHT
ALEX LYON
Digital (USA)
Cavernous Encounter

BELOW
BRENT WOODSIDE
Digital (USA)
Three Giants

BOTTOM RIGHT
ALEX LYON
Digital (USA)
Temple Raid

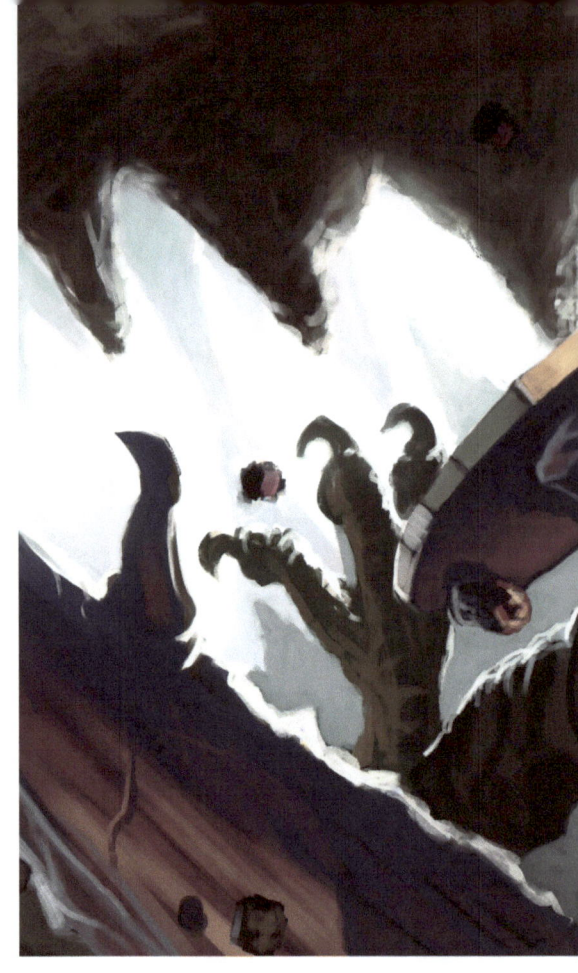

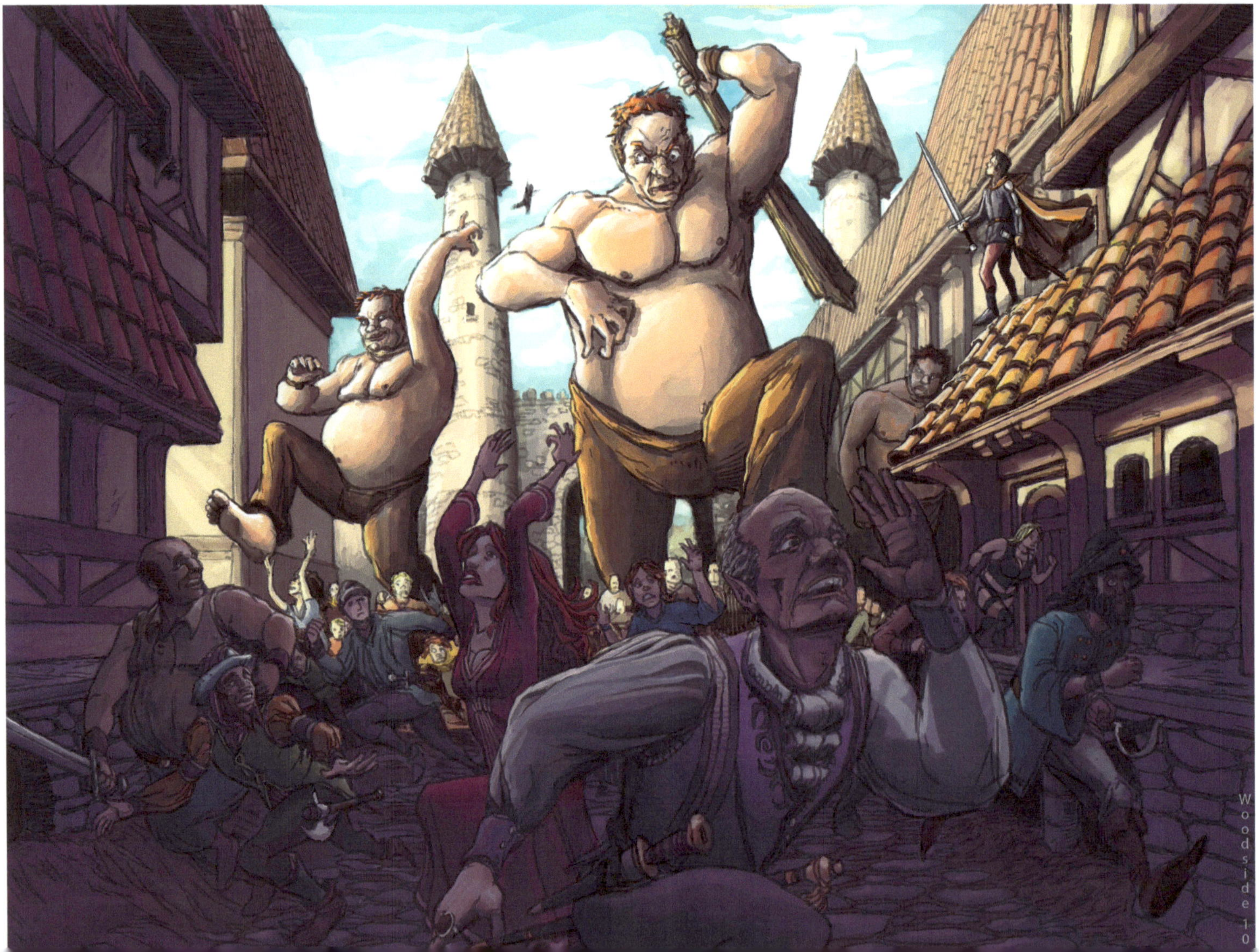

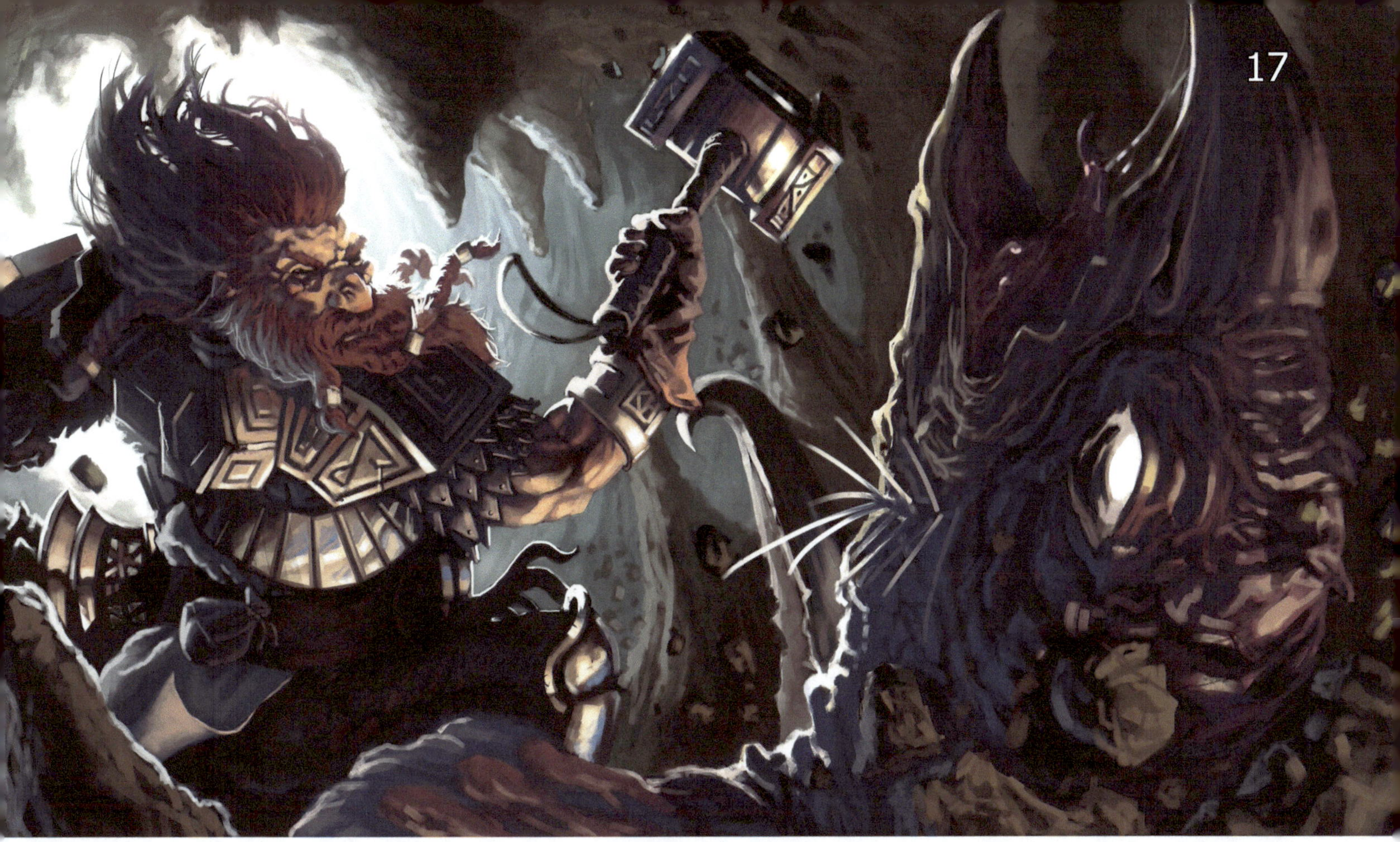

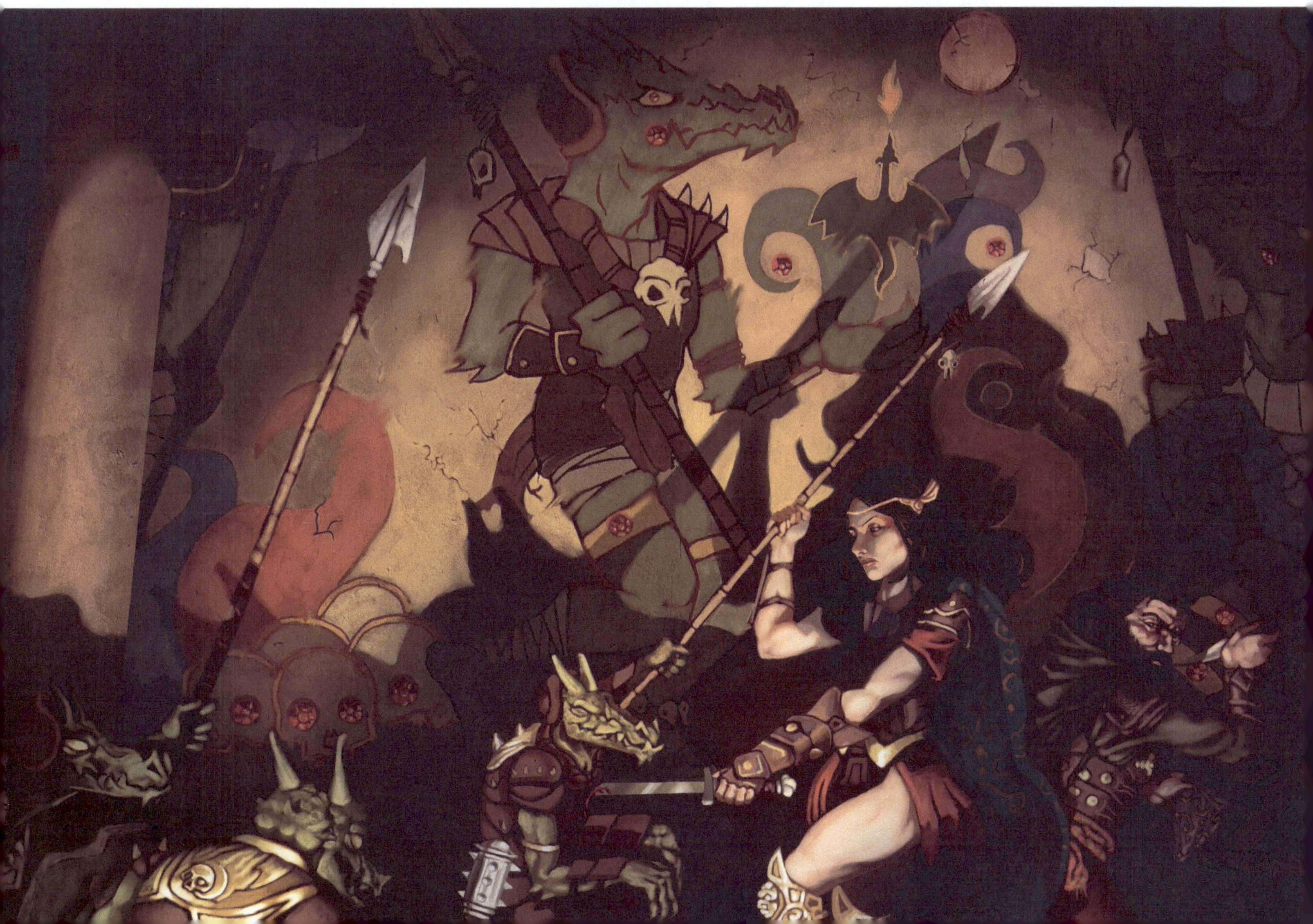

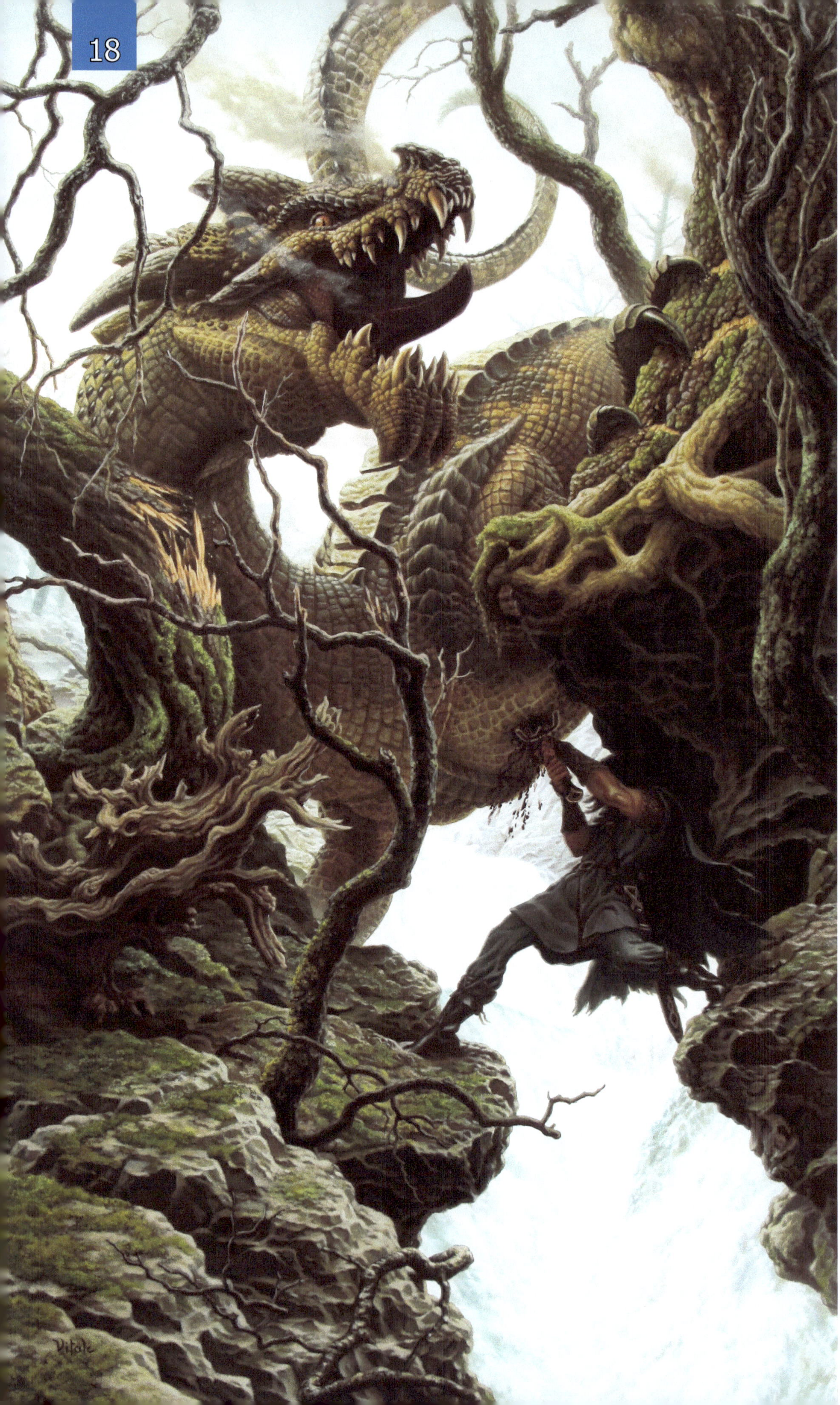

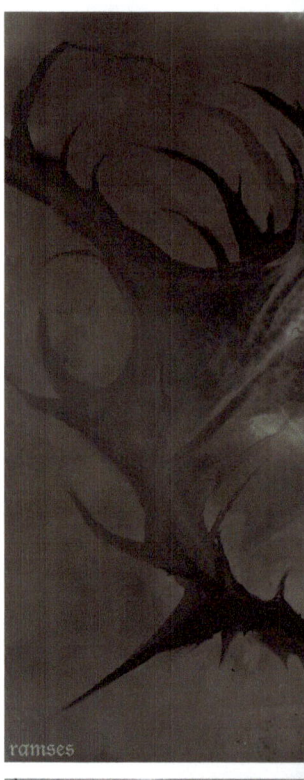

ramses

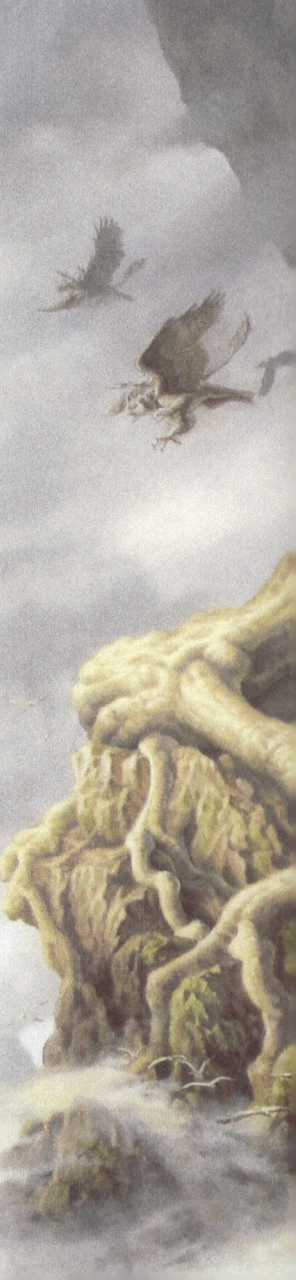

Vitale

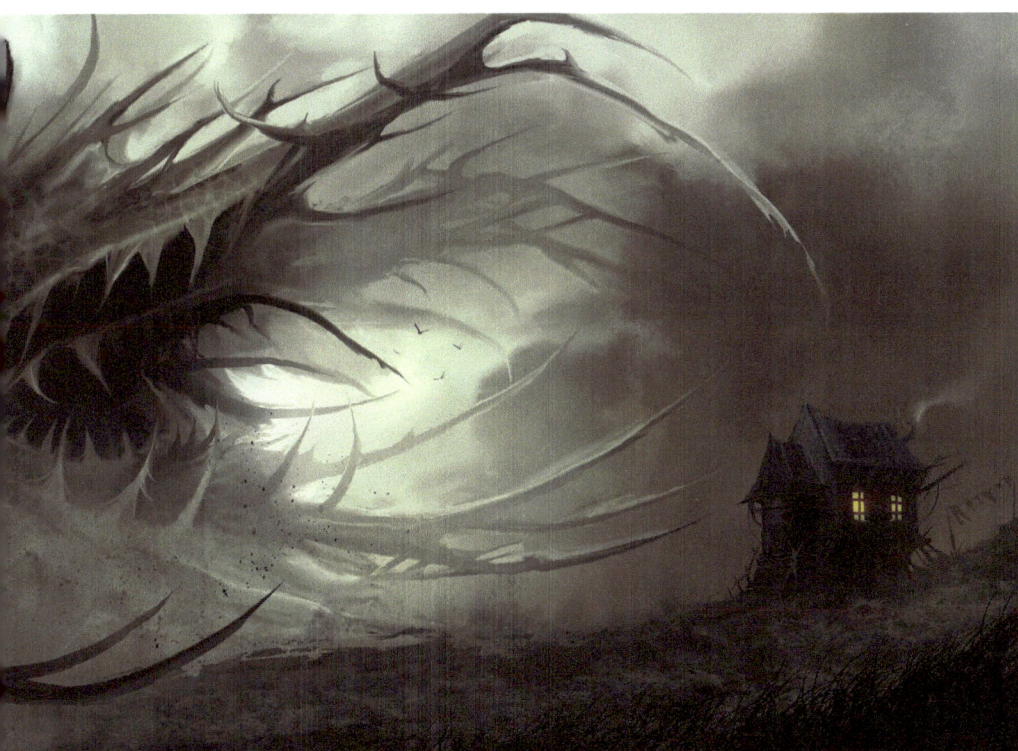

LEFT

RAMSES MELENDEZ
Photoshop (Mexico)
Selkemh Ancient Monster

FAR LEFT

RAOUL VITALE
Oil on masonite (USA)
Turin and Glaurung

BELOW

RAOUL VITALE
Oil on masonite (USA)
Torins Quest

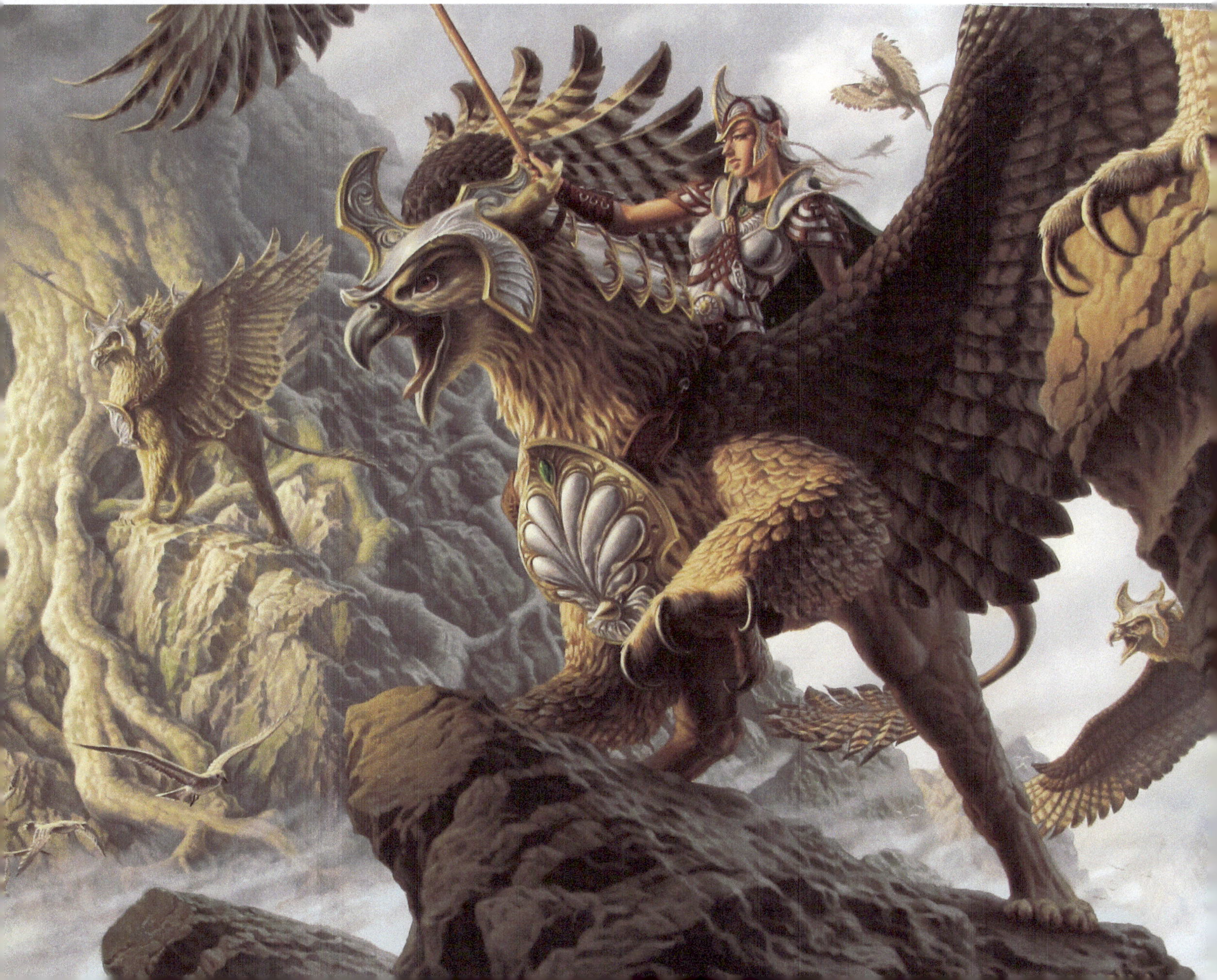

RIGHT

GORDON NAPIER
Digital(UK)
Thalestris

BELOW

DAVID LECOSSU
Photoshop (France)
The Statue

OPPOSITE

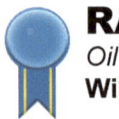

RAOUL VITALE
Oil on masonite (USA)
Wild Life

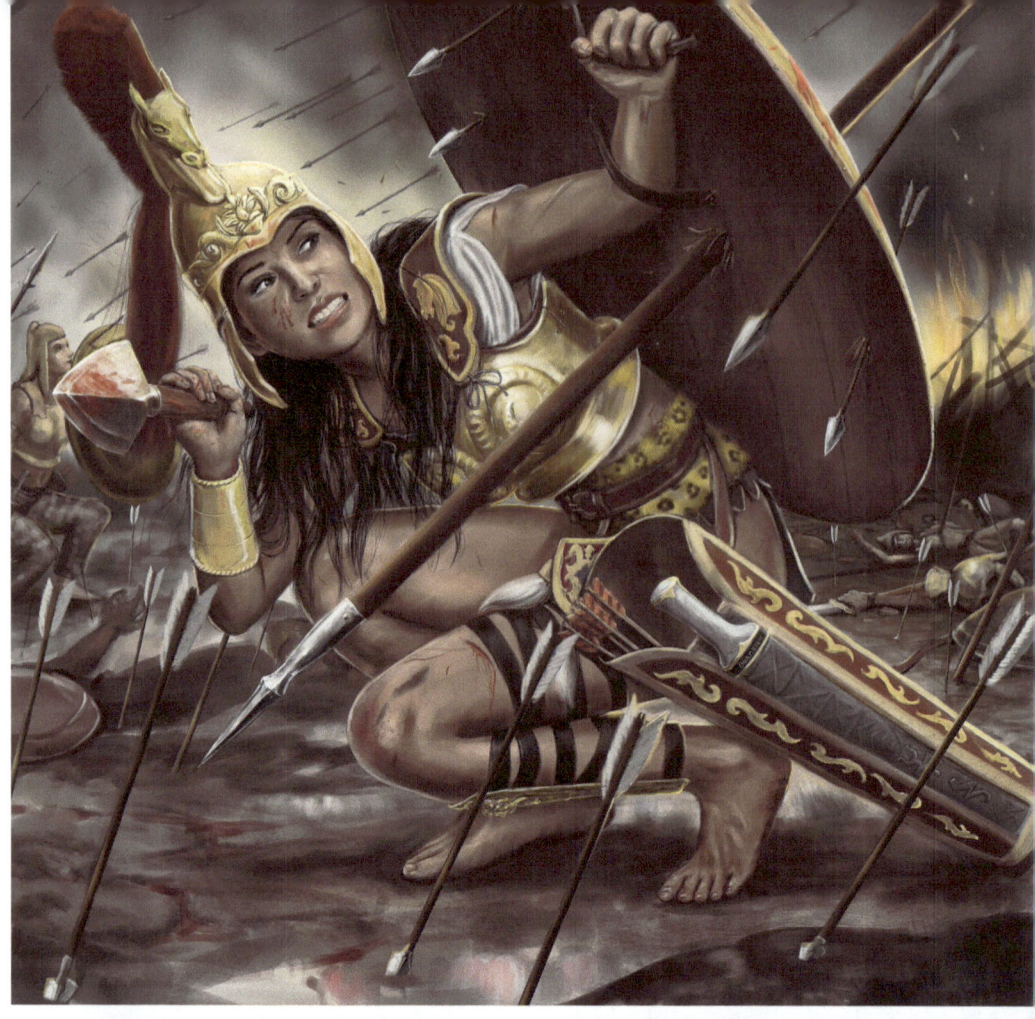

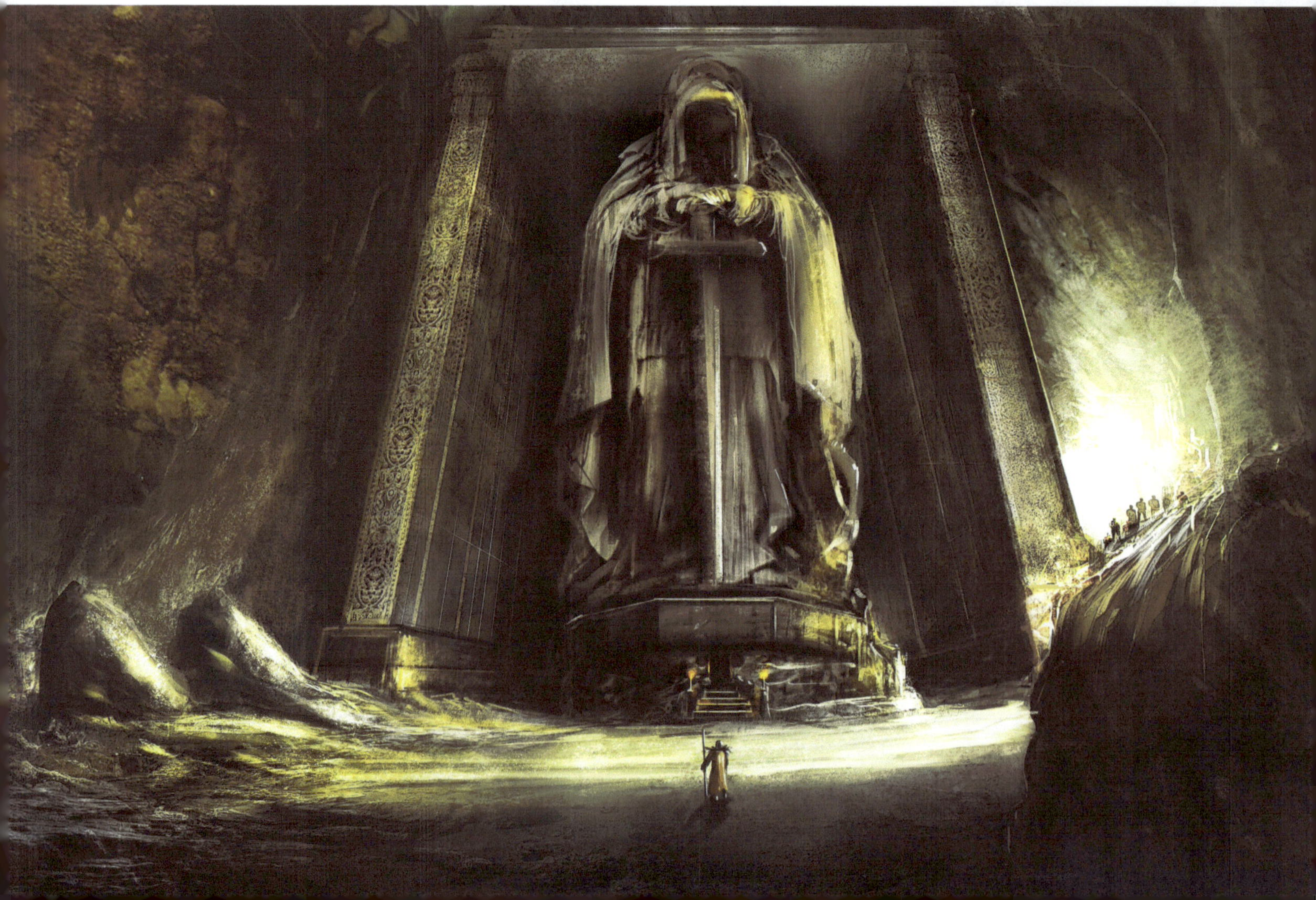

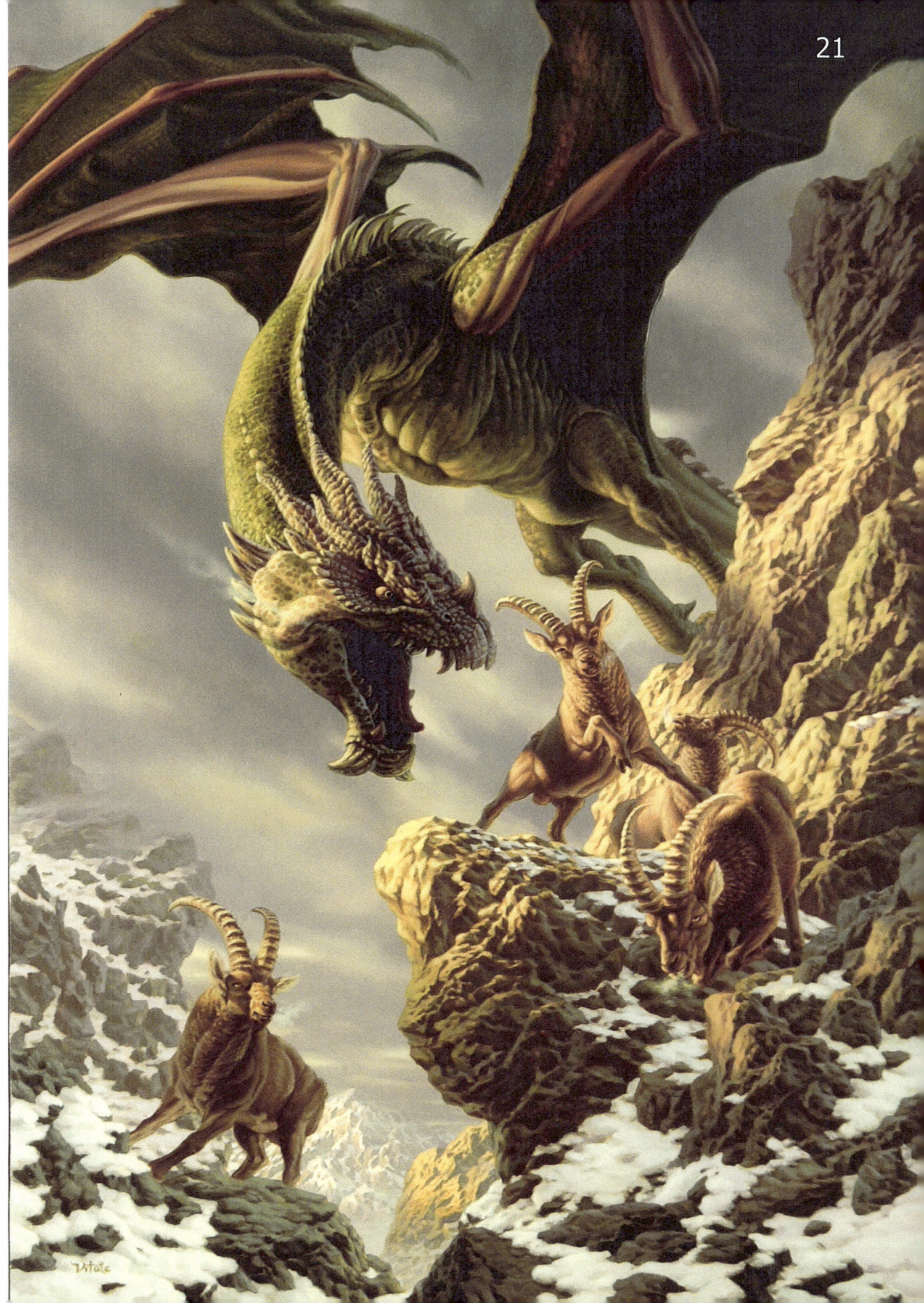

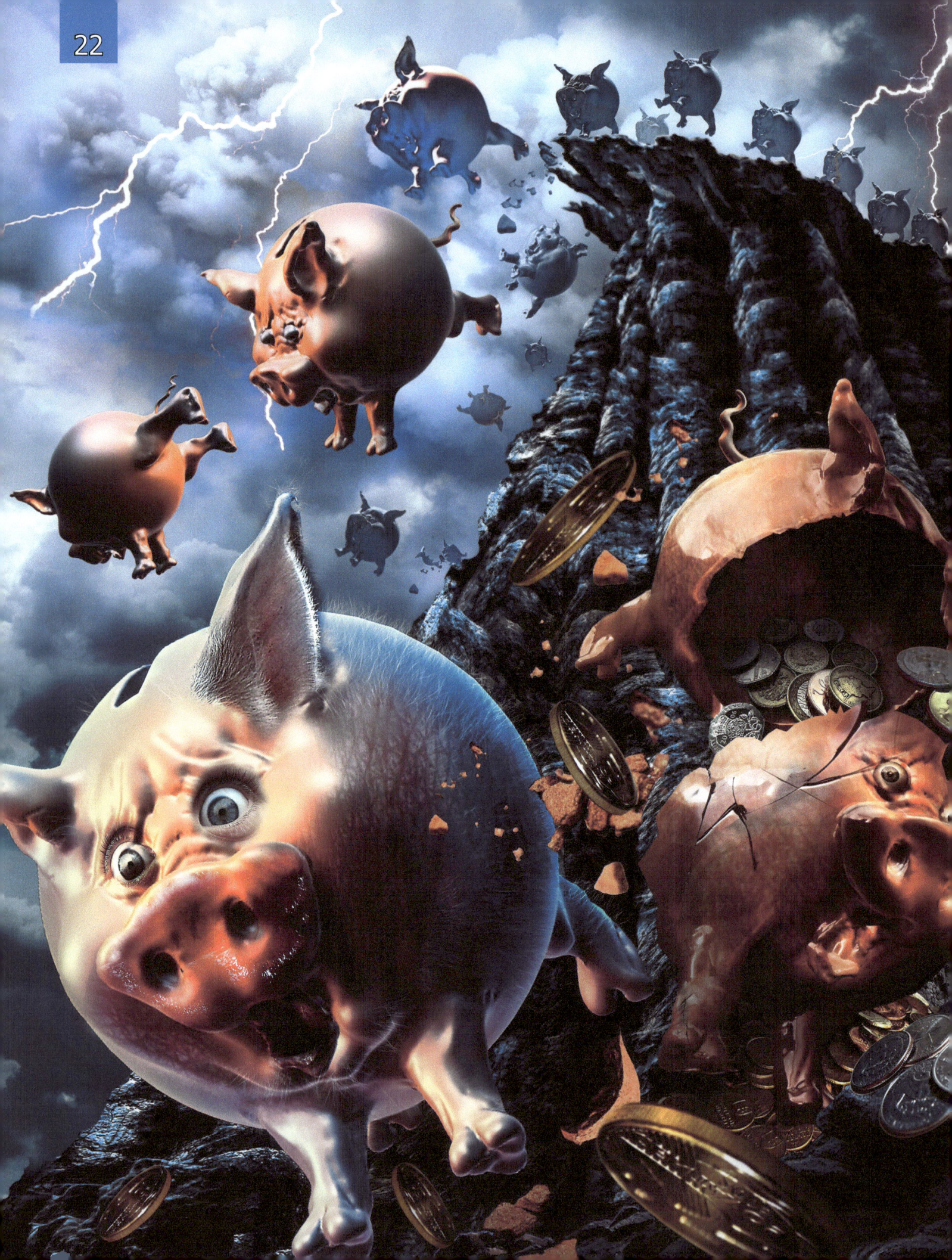

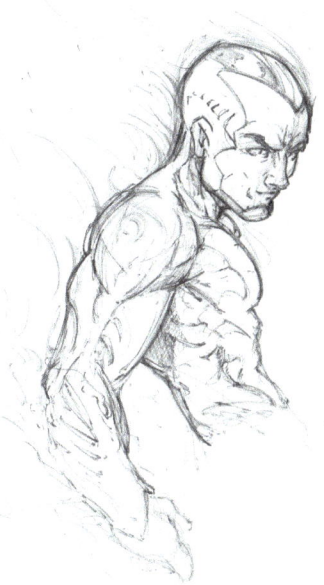

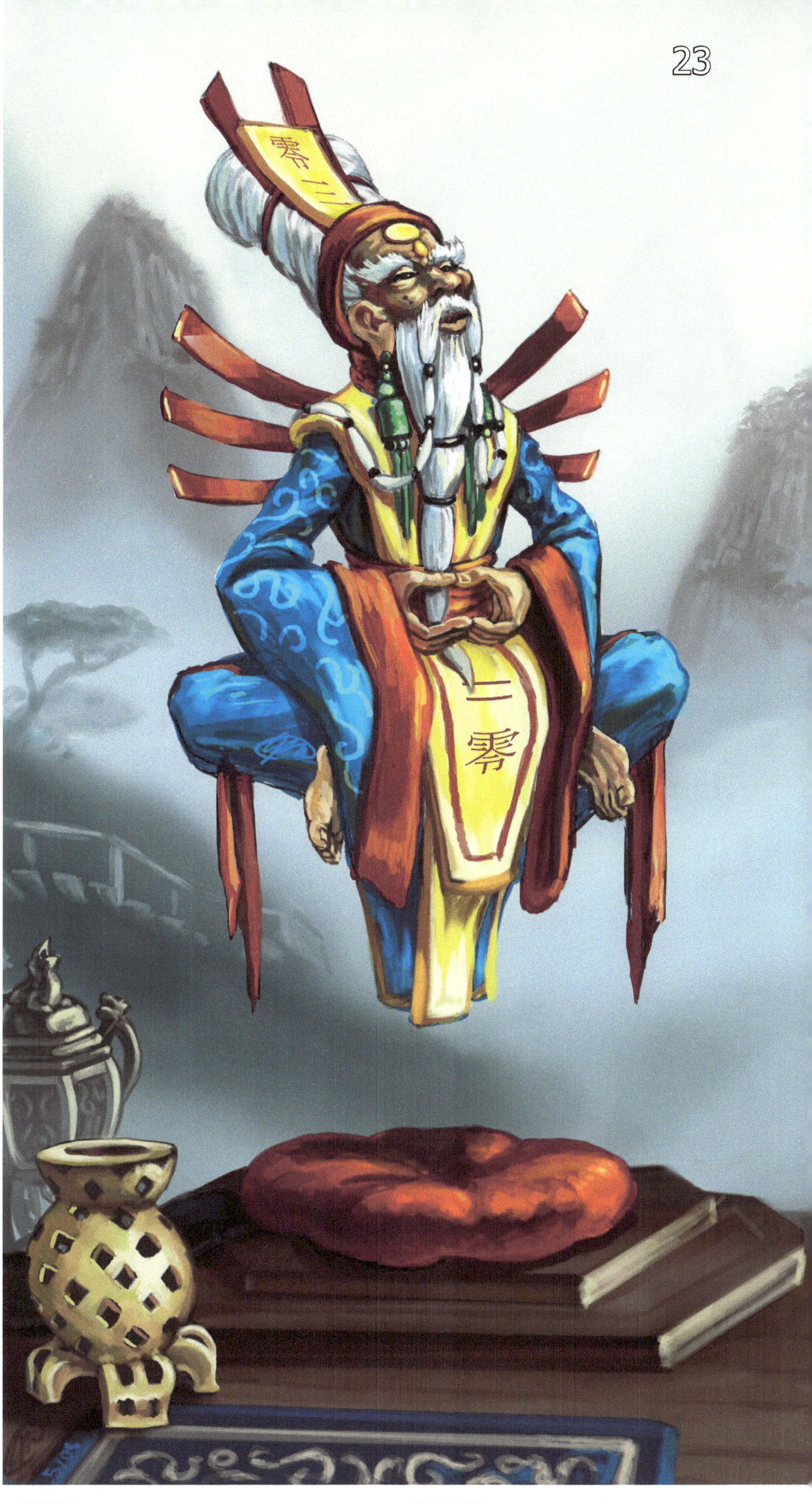

ABOVE
DERRICK UTZ
Pencil (USA)
Burning Man

LEFT
HOWARD VAUSE
Photoshop (England)
Piggy Bankers

RIGHT
JASON MARTIN
Digital (USA)
Sensei

(Overleaf)

FAR RIGHT
PETER MOHRBACHER
Photoshop (USA)
Valley of Mists

MIDDLE
PETER MOHRBACHER
Photoshop (USA)
Fiefdom of Angels

TOP LEFT
PETER MOHRBACHER
Photoshop (USA)
Skyhook

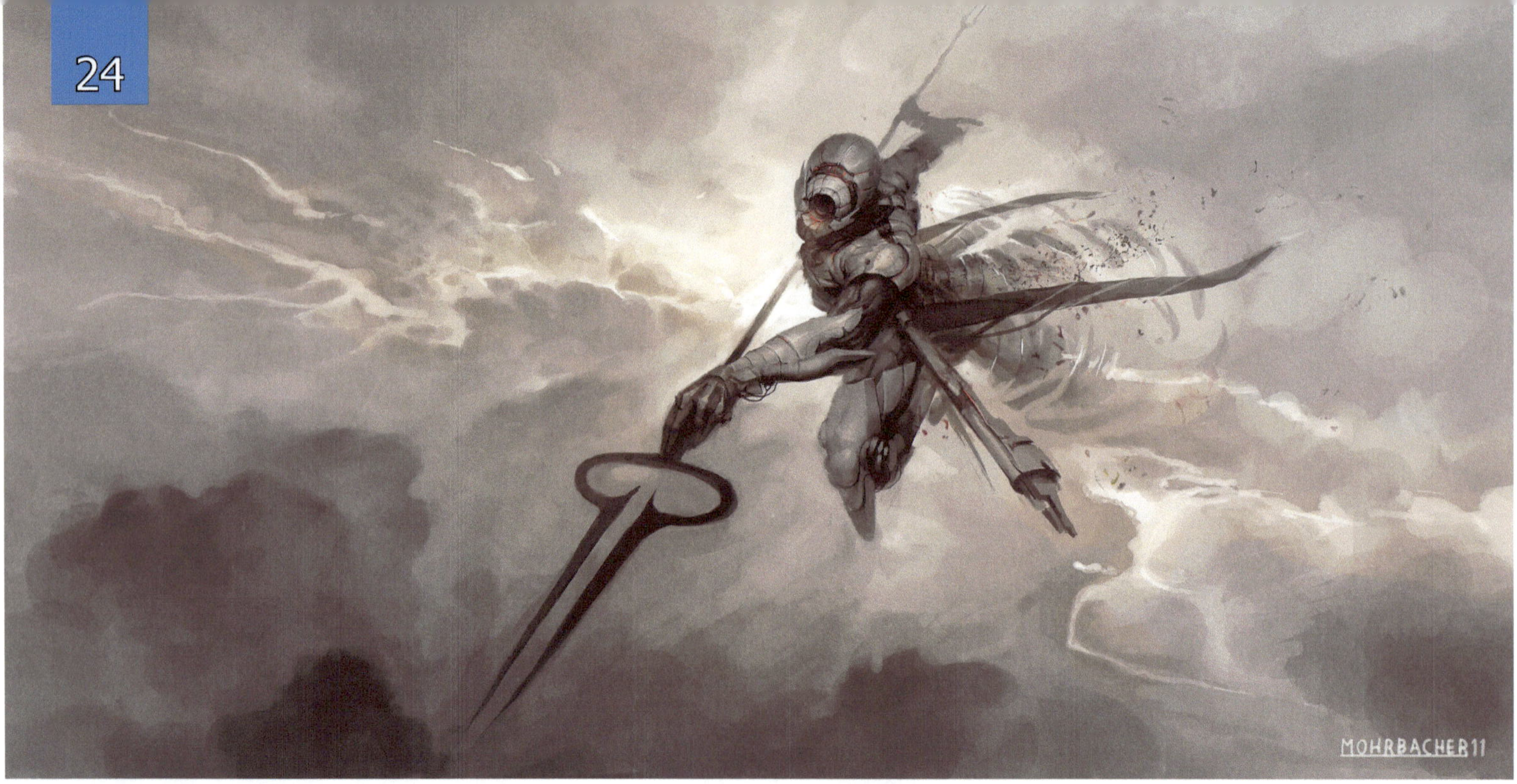

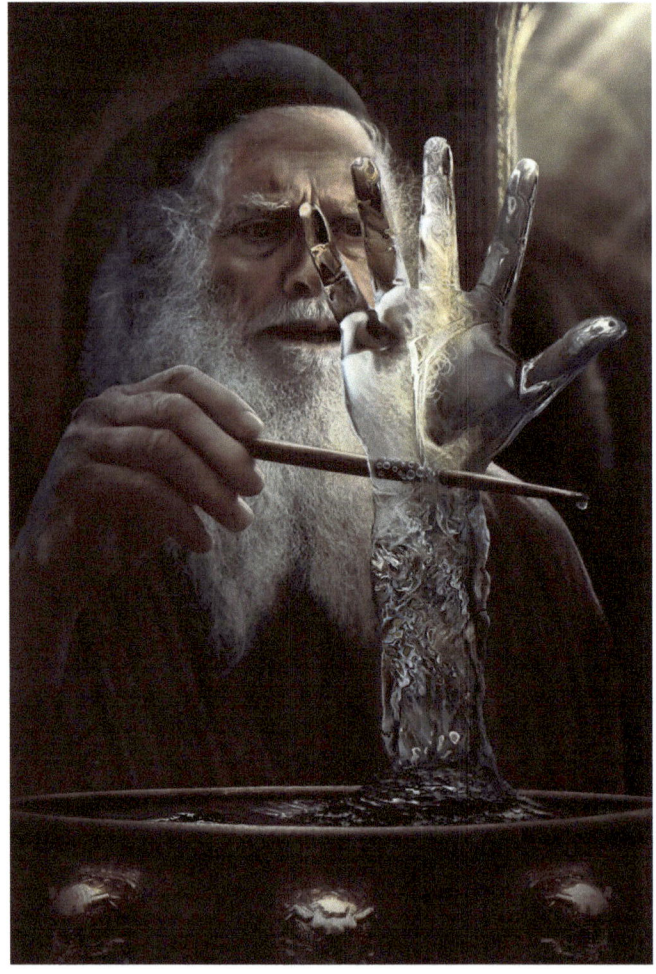

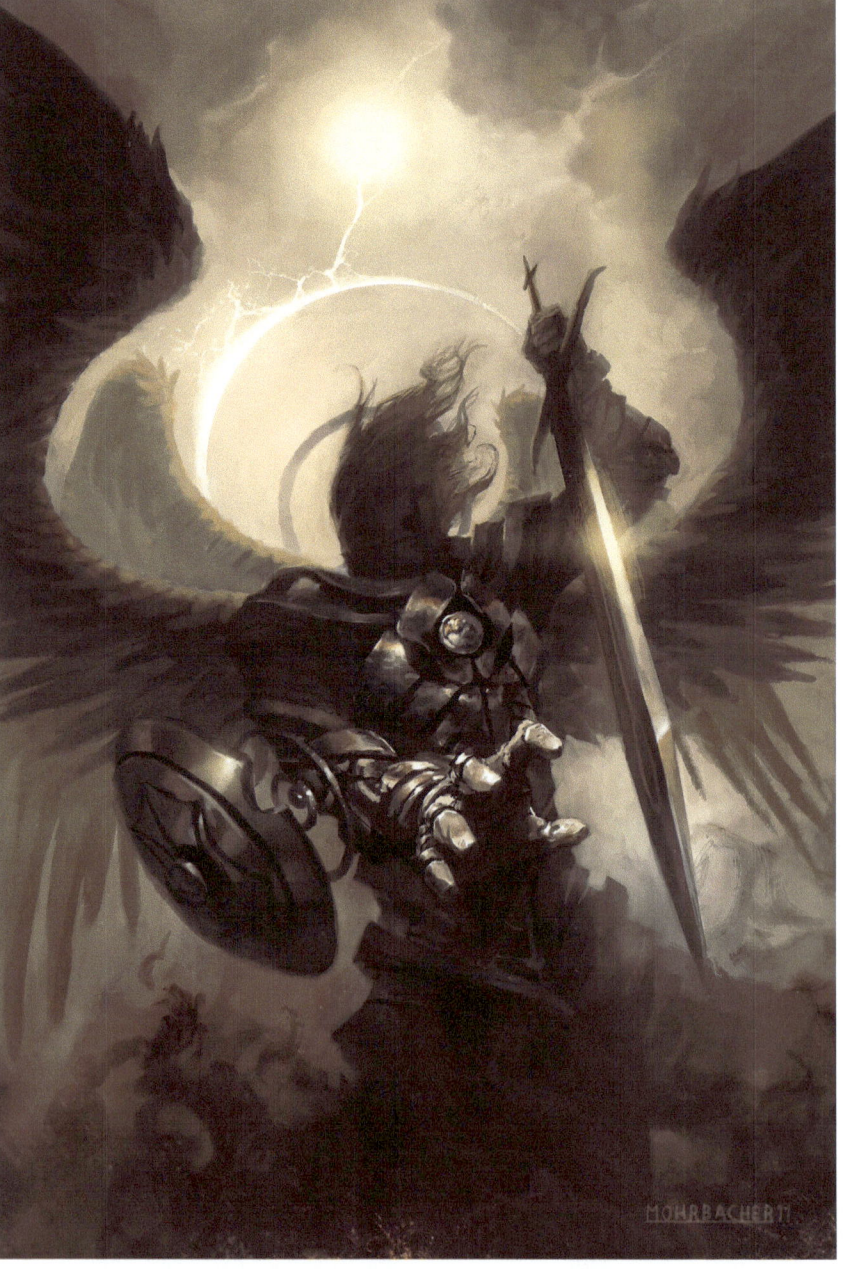

ABOVE

BRIAN KELSEY
Photomanipulation (USA)
The Alchemist

SEE PREVIOUS PAGE FOR CREDITS

PETER MOHRBACHER

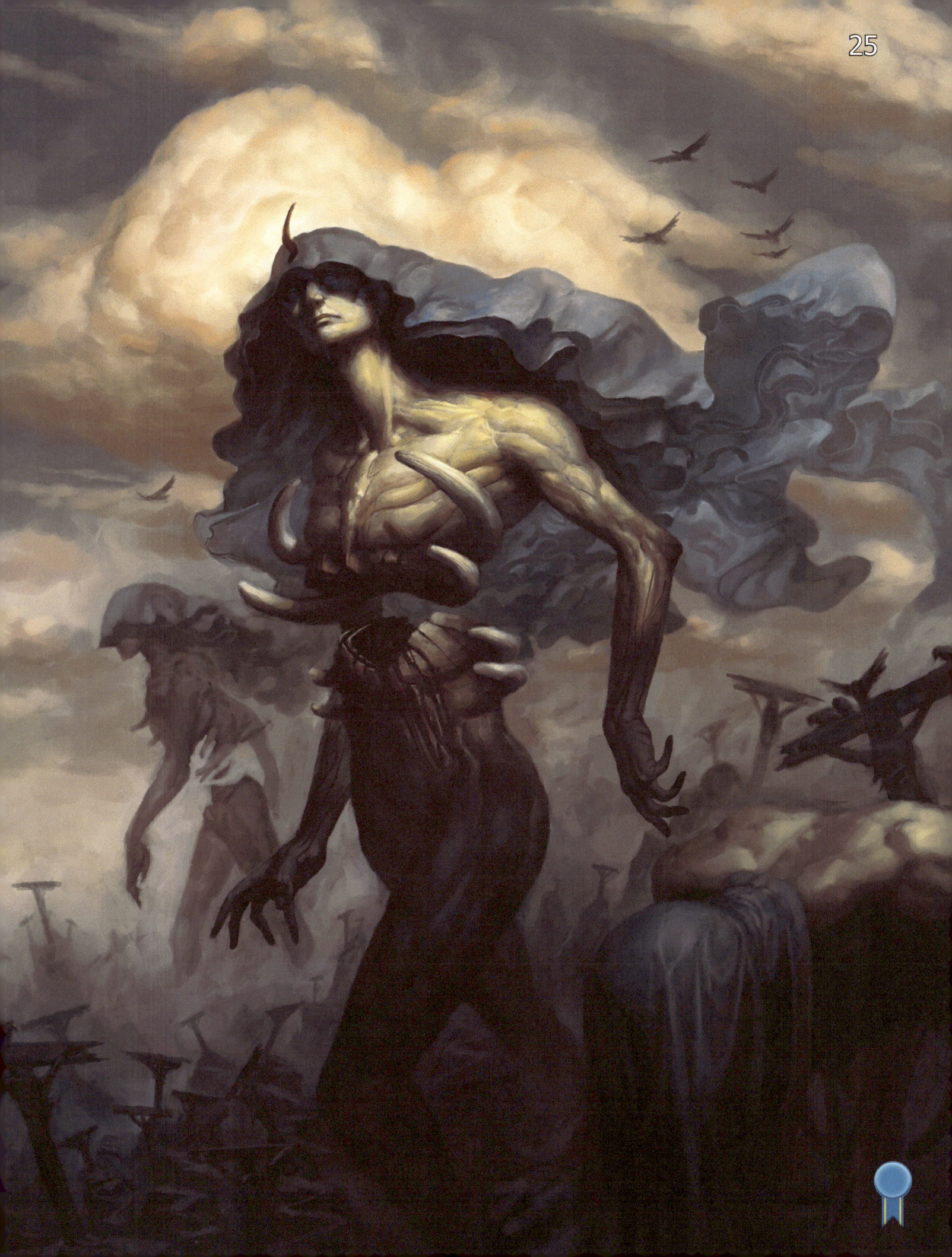

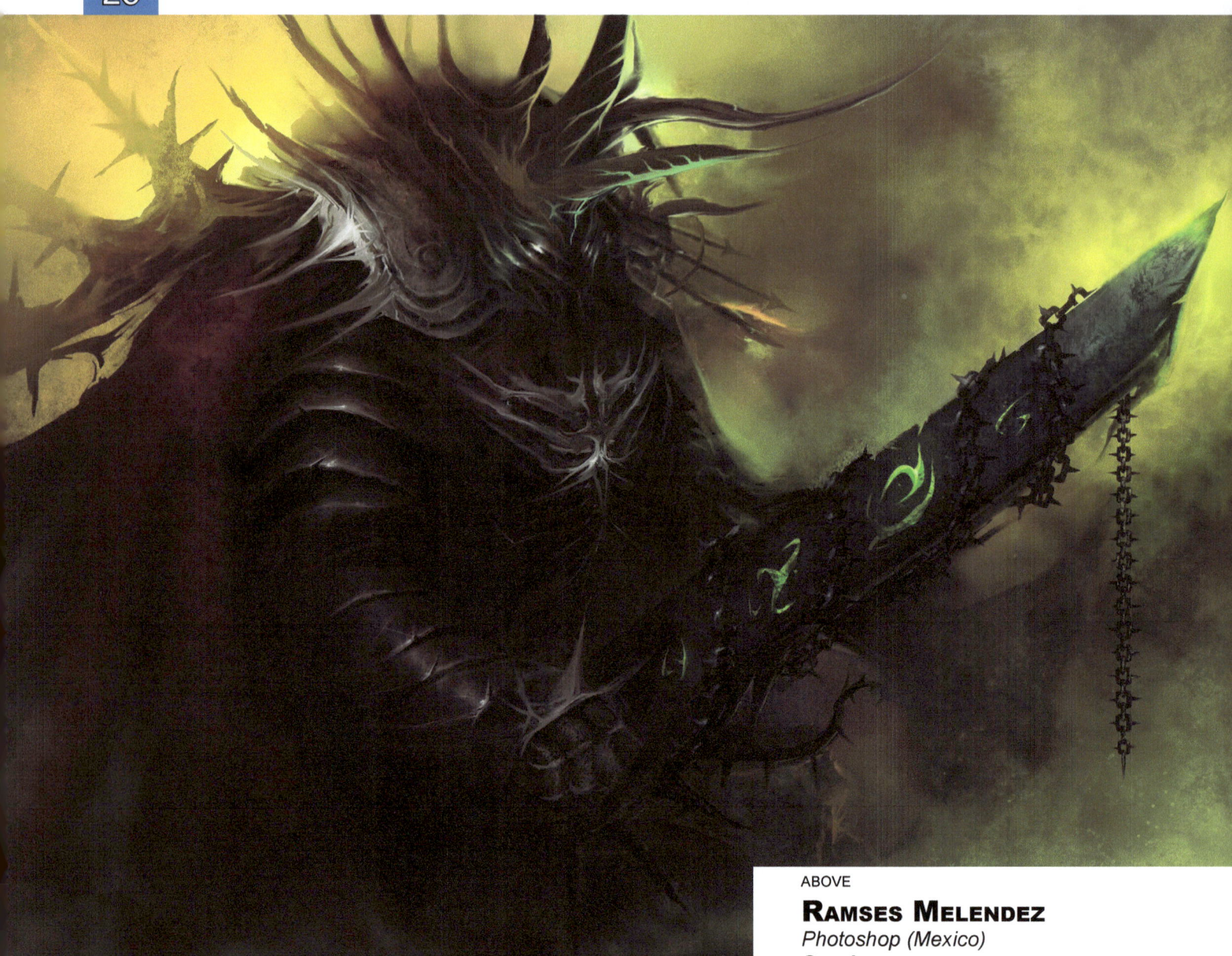

ABOVE

RAMSES MELENDEZ
Photoshop (Mexico)
Gaazh

LEFT

OLIVER WETTER
Photoshop (Germany)
Guardian of Legend

OPPOSITE TOP LEFT

ONA LOOTS
Photomanipulation (South Africa)
Credit: sxc.hu, iStockphoto
Casandra

OPPOSITE TOP RIGHT

IMMAR PALOMERA
Photoshop (USA)
Eowyn and Nazgul

OPPOSITE BOTTOM

JENNIFER GALYE
Photoshop (Canada)
More Than Sibling Rivalry

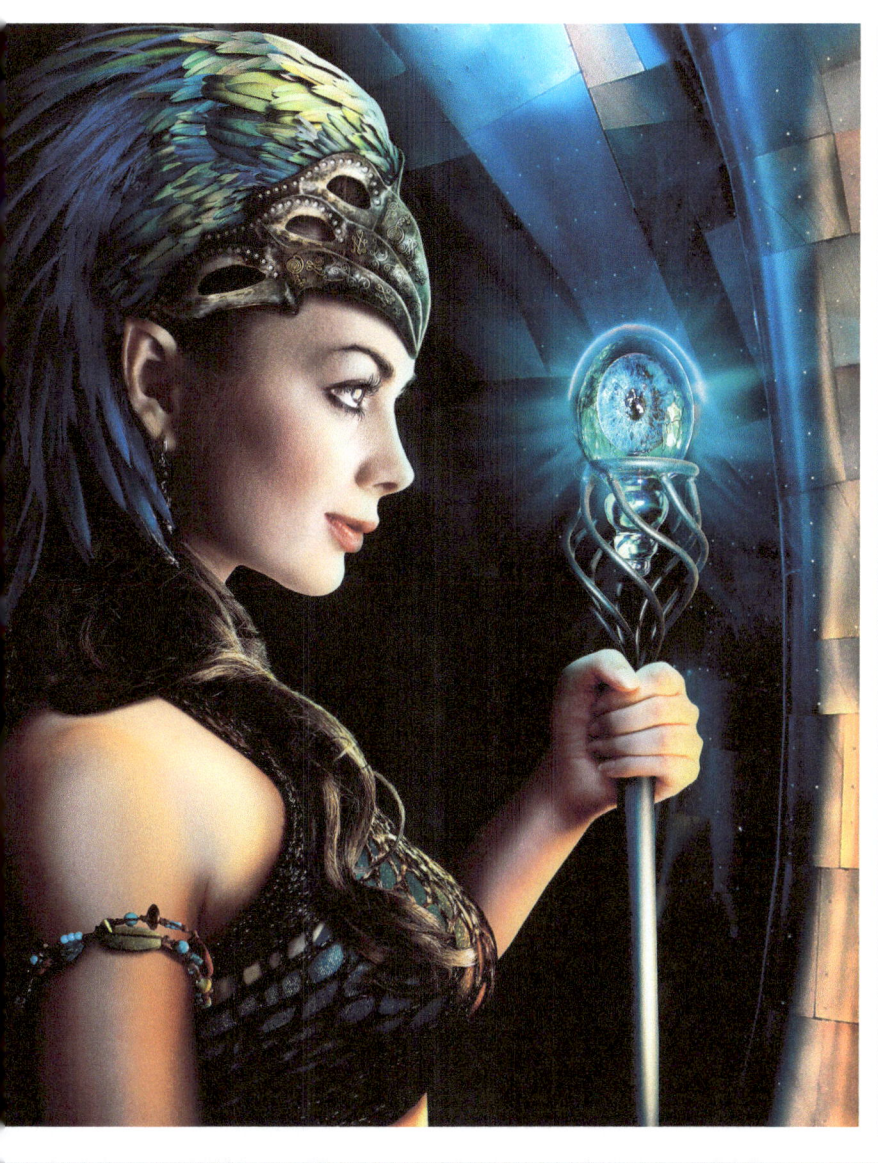

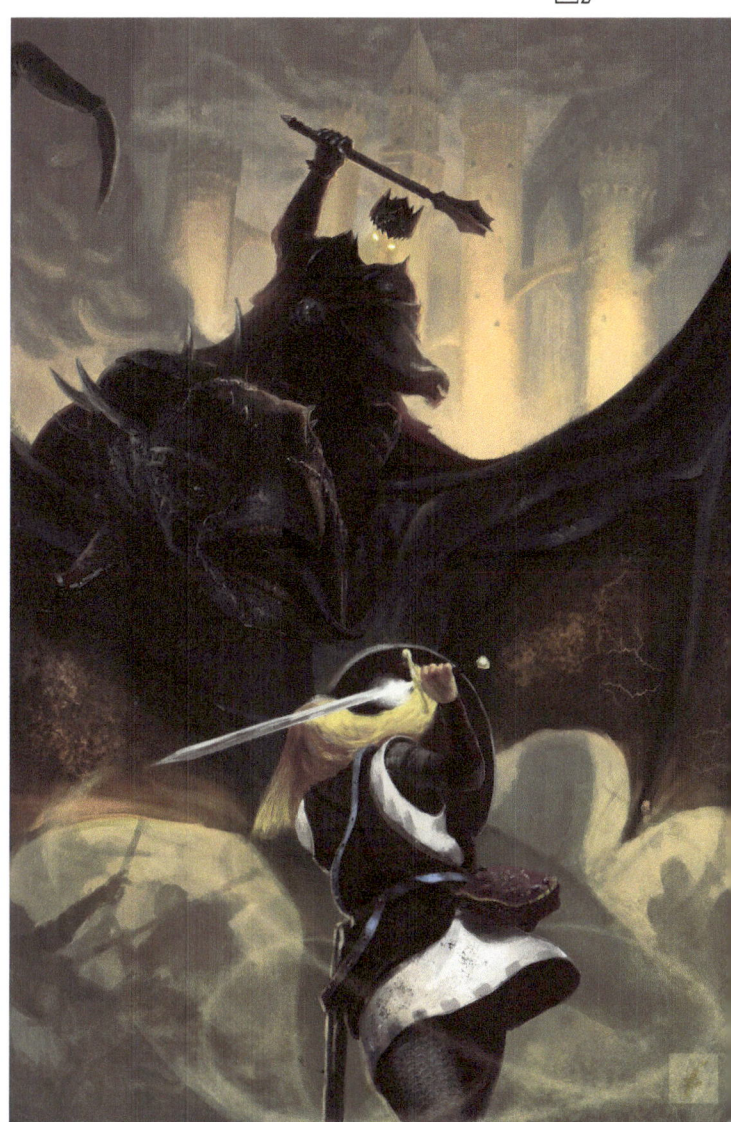

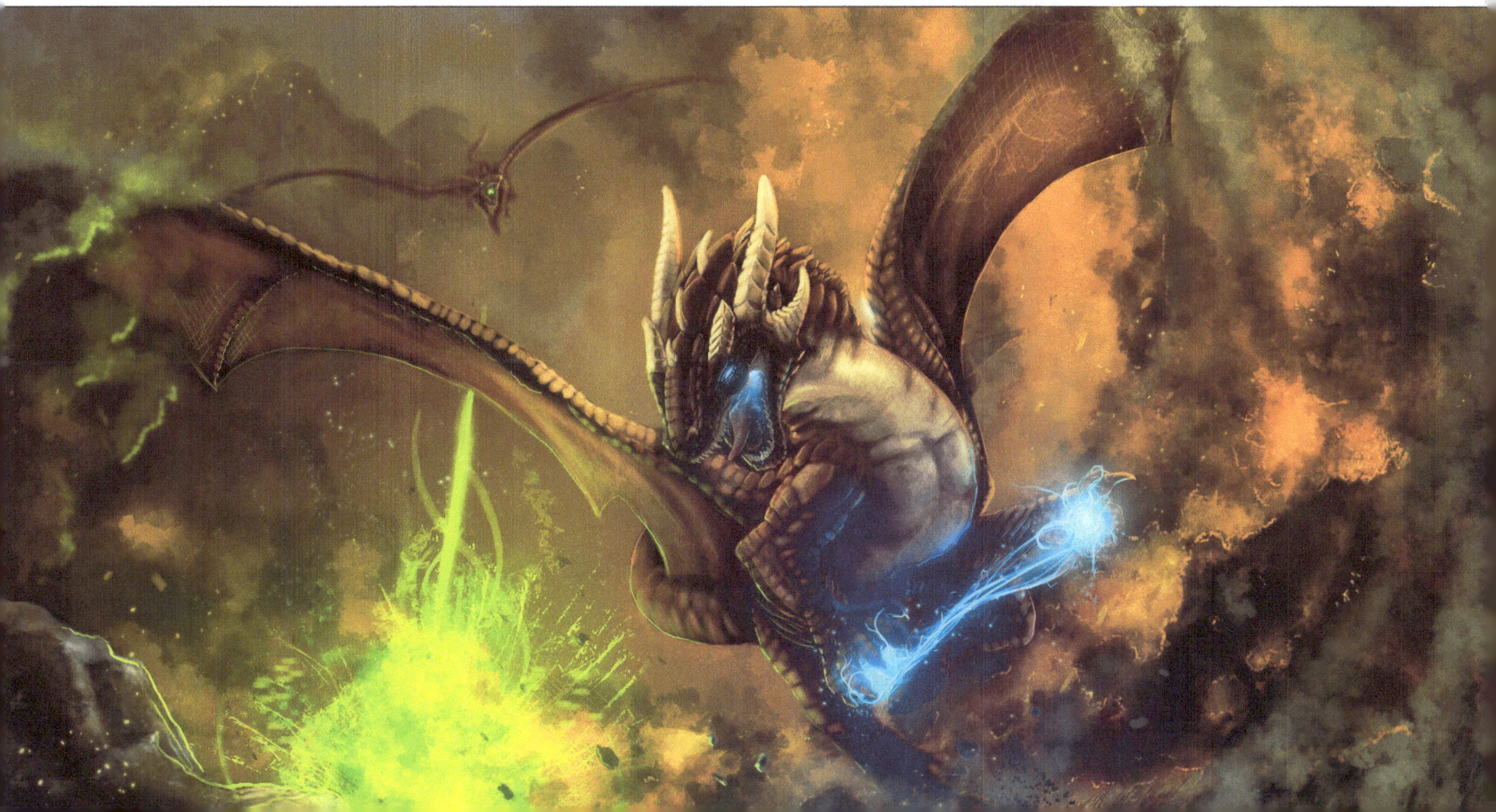

RIGHT

DANIEL OGUIN
Photoshop (USA)
Graveyard Guardian

BOTTOM LEFT

BRENT WOODSIDE
Photoshop (USA)
Woodside Archer

BOTTOM RIGHT

YUKARI MASUIKE
Photoshop (Japan)
Ice Dragon

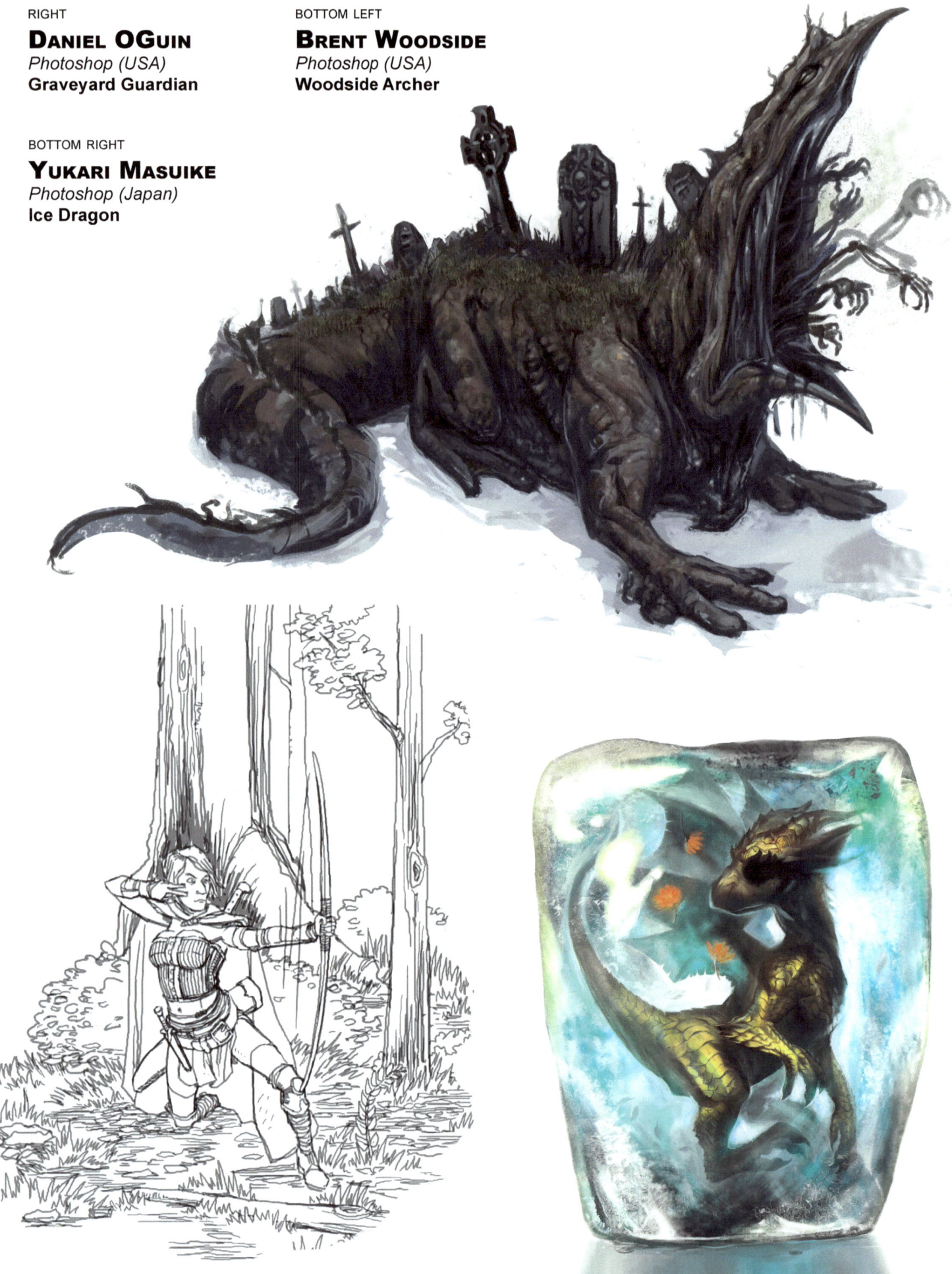

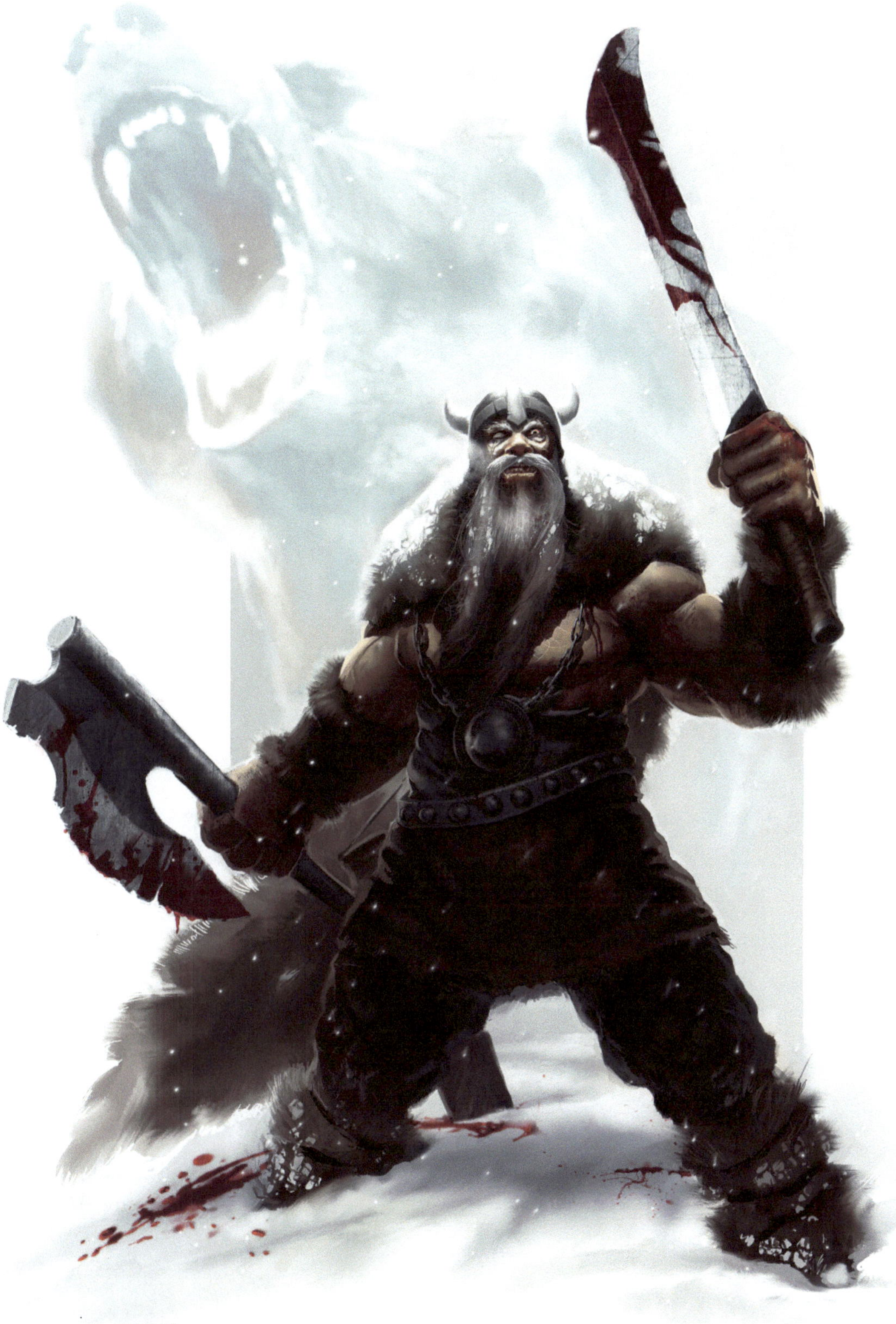

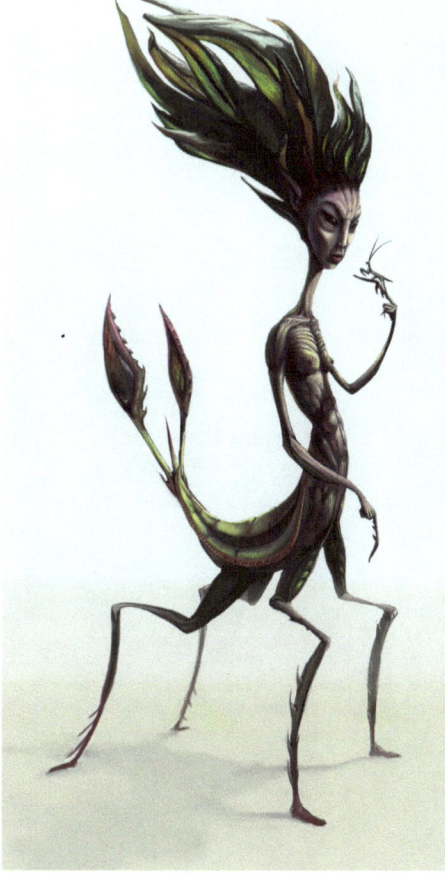

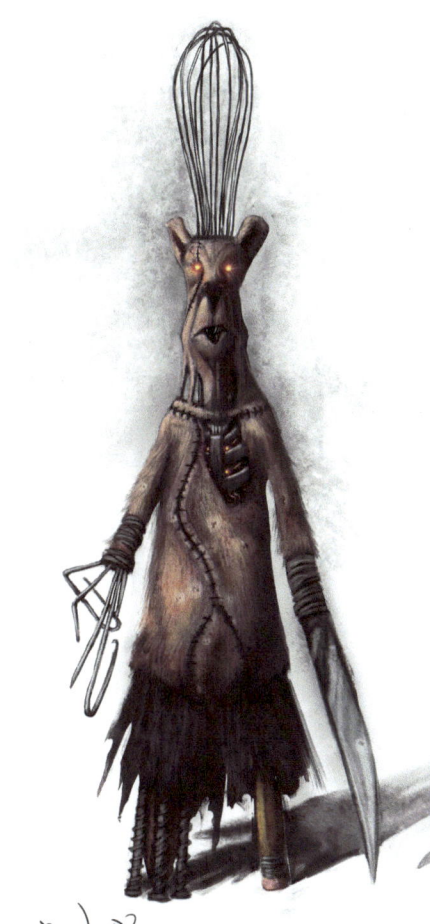

ABOVE

DIMITRI SIRENKO
Photoshop (Canada)
Viking Berserkr

BOTTOM RIGHT

DANIEL OGUIN
Photoshop (USA)
Clips

TOP RIGHT

DANIEL OGUIN
Photoshop (USA)
Ti

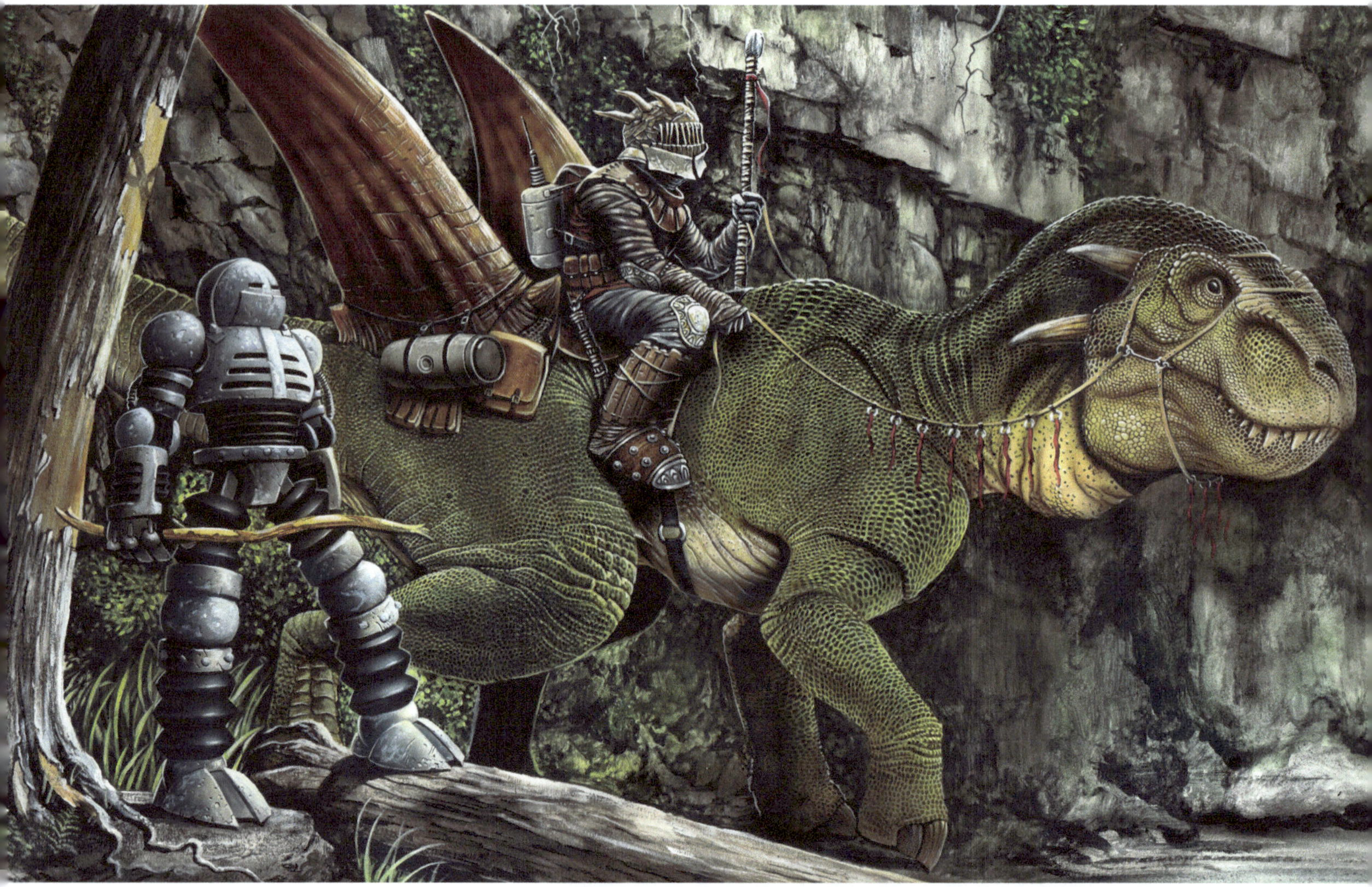

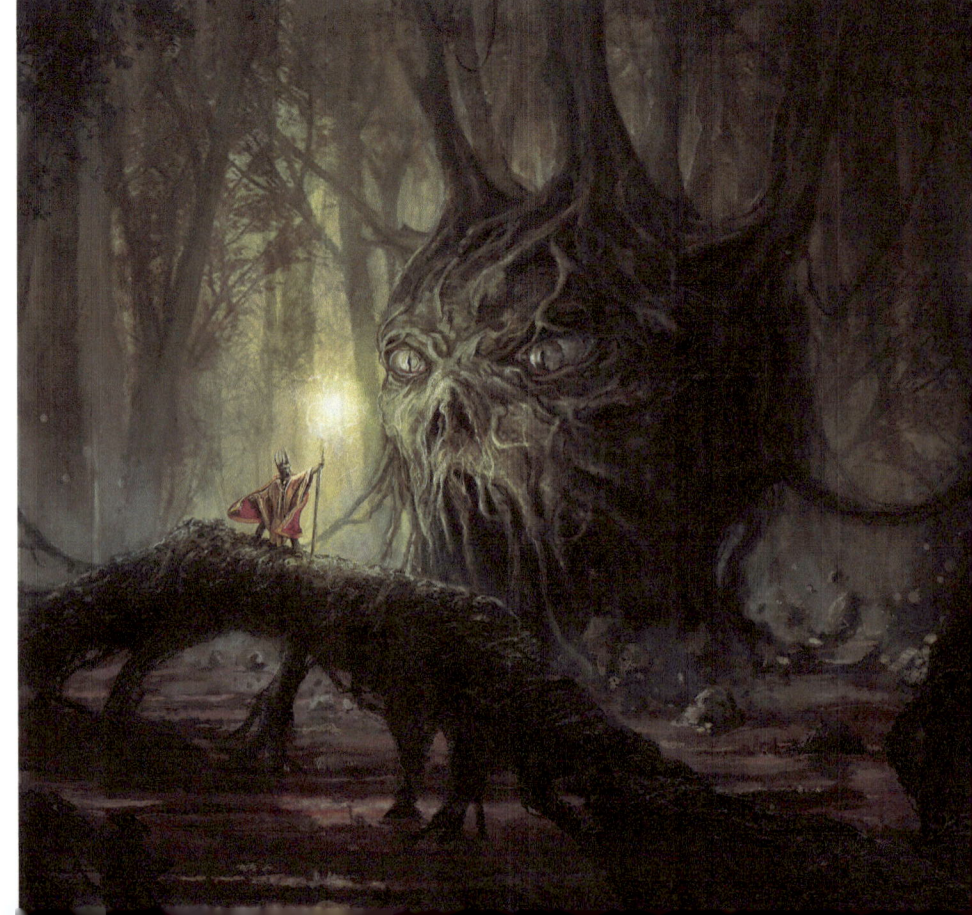

ABOVE
MARK REHKOPF
Digital (Canada)
Journey to Sector 4

LEFT PAGE BOTTOM
LINCOLN RENALL
Photoshop (New Zealand)
The Summoning

OPPOSITE TOP LEFT
RAOUL VITALE
Oil on masonite (USA)
Turin and Glaurung

OPPOSITE TOP RIGHT
LINCOLN RENALL
Photoshop (New Zealand)
Floater

OPPOSITE BOTTOM
ROSS TRAN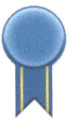
Digital (USA)
Everglow

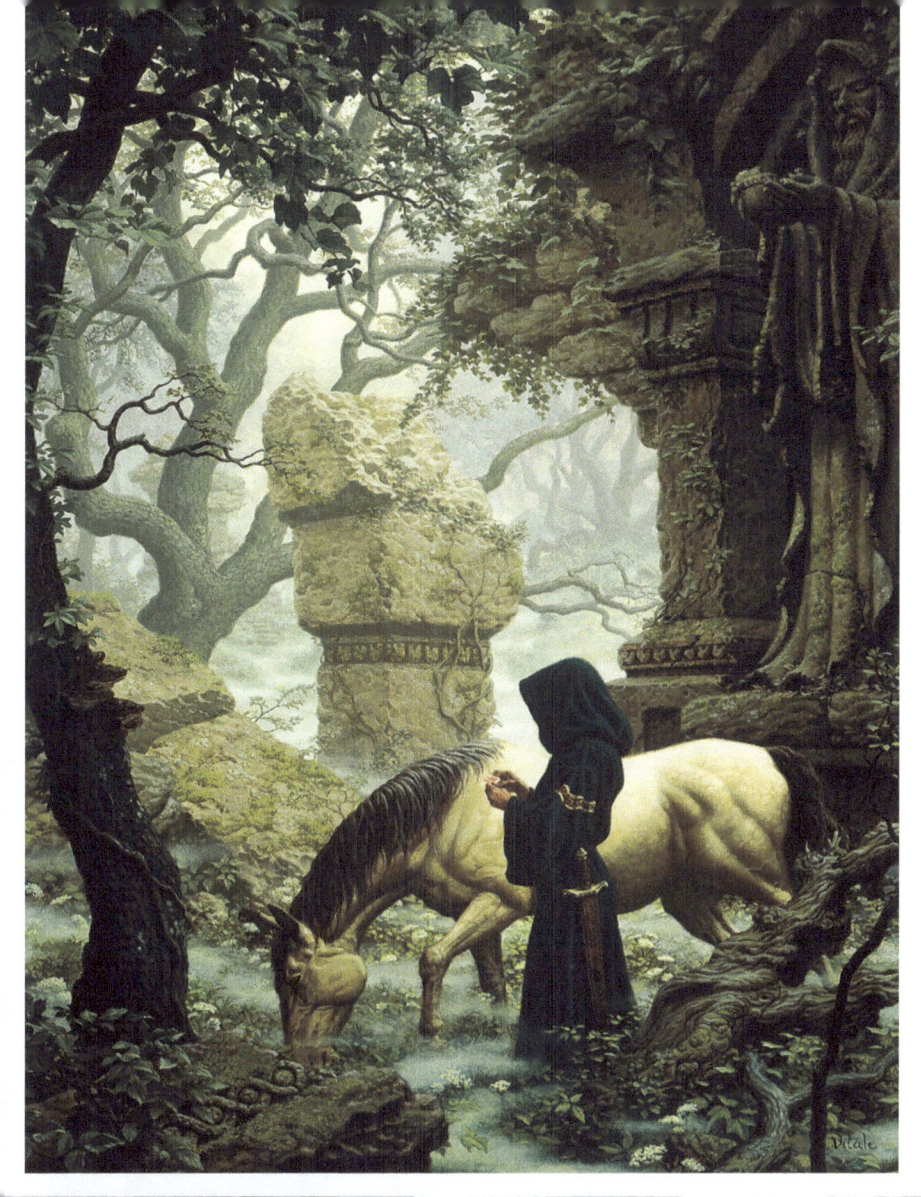

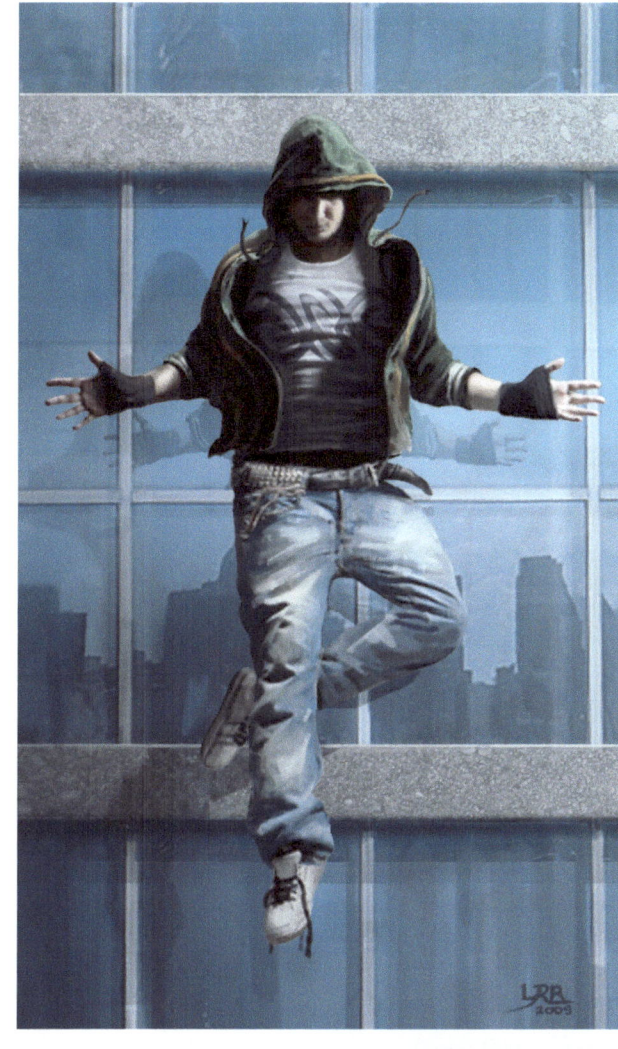

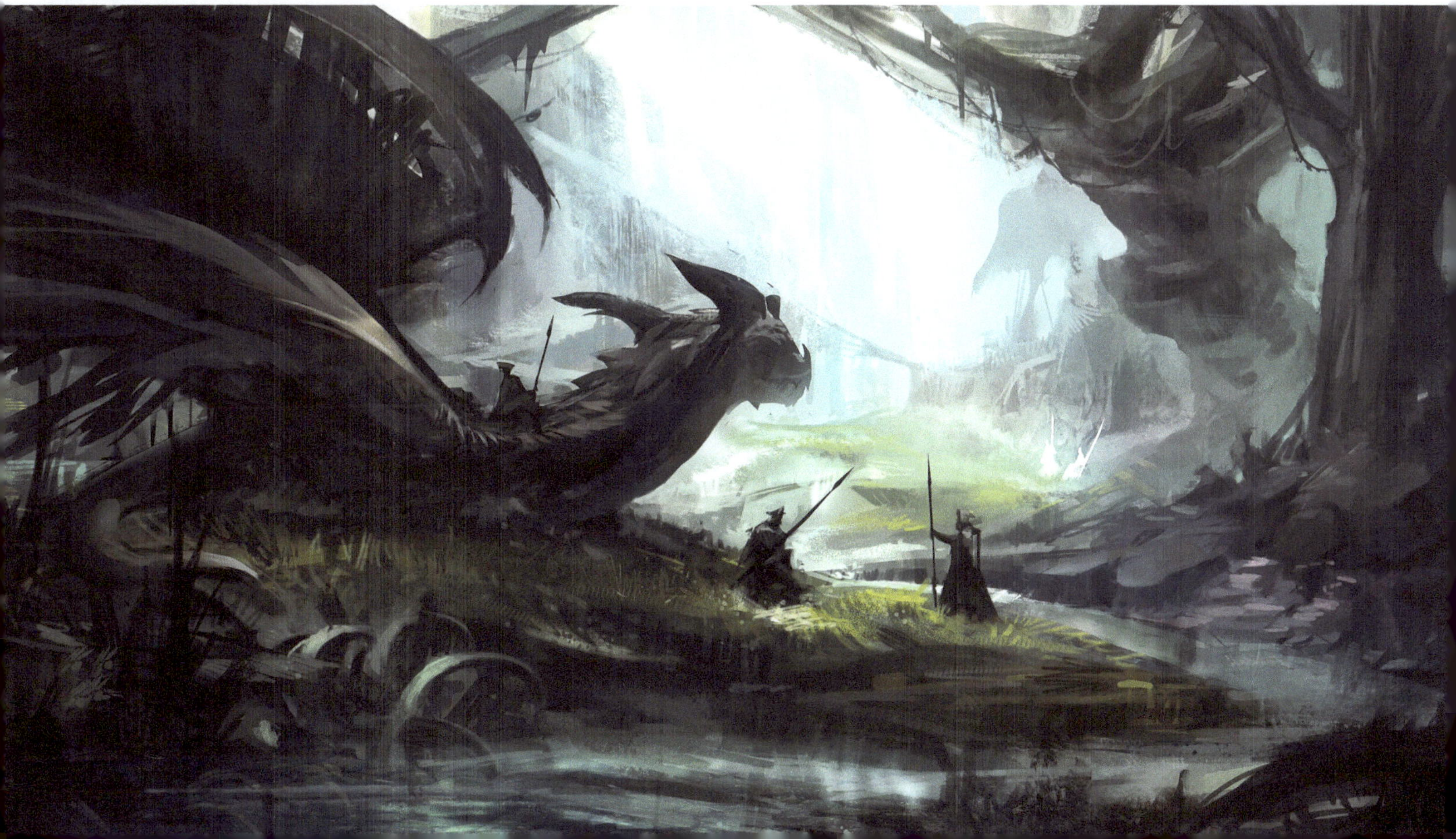

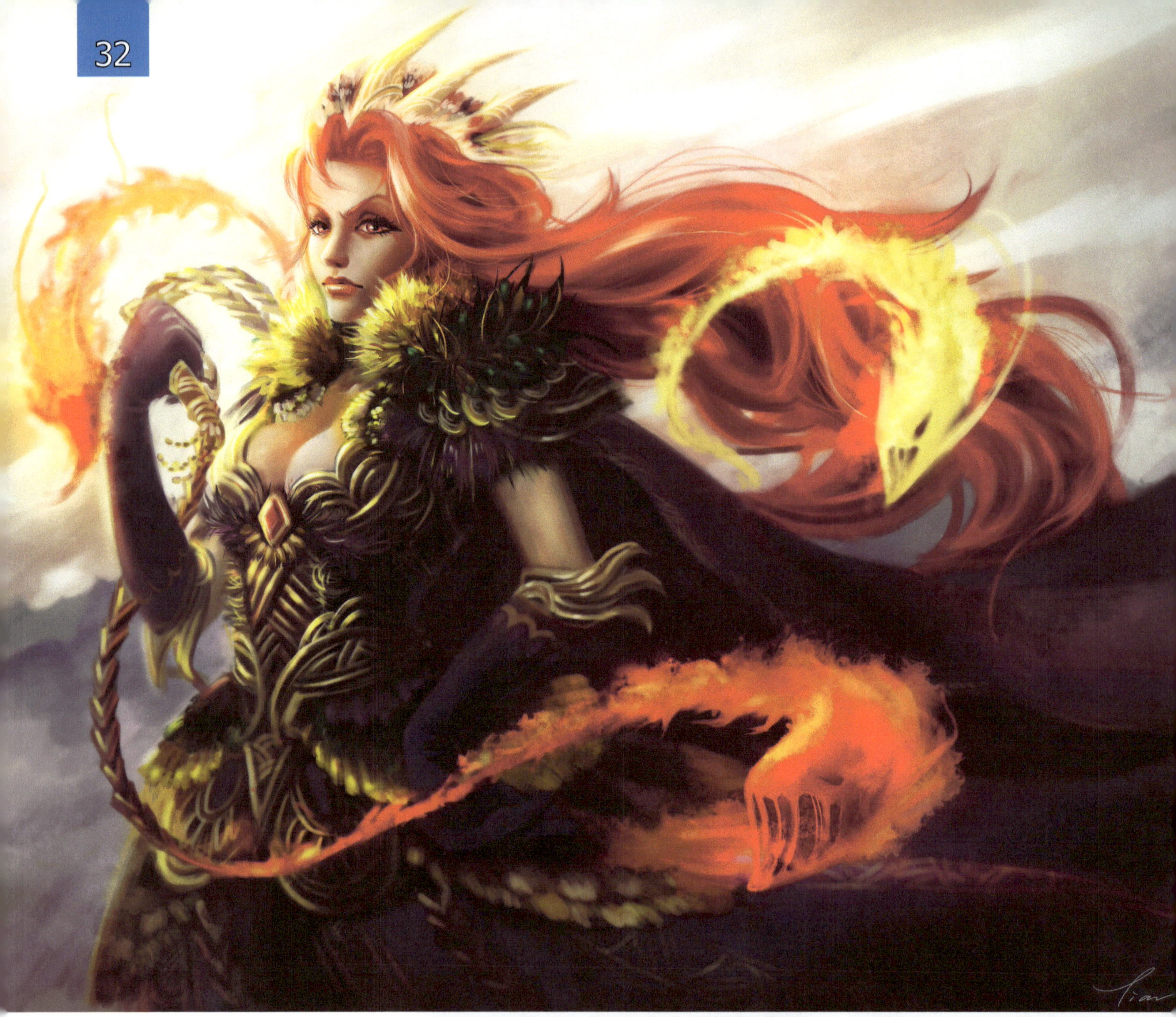

ABOVE
YANGTIAN LI
Photoshop (Australia)
Hera

RIGHT
DIMITRI SIRENKO
Photoshop (Canada)
Goblin's Best Friend

OPPOSITE
SIMON VARISTO
Photoshop Painting (Finland)
Evening Snack

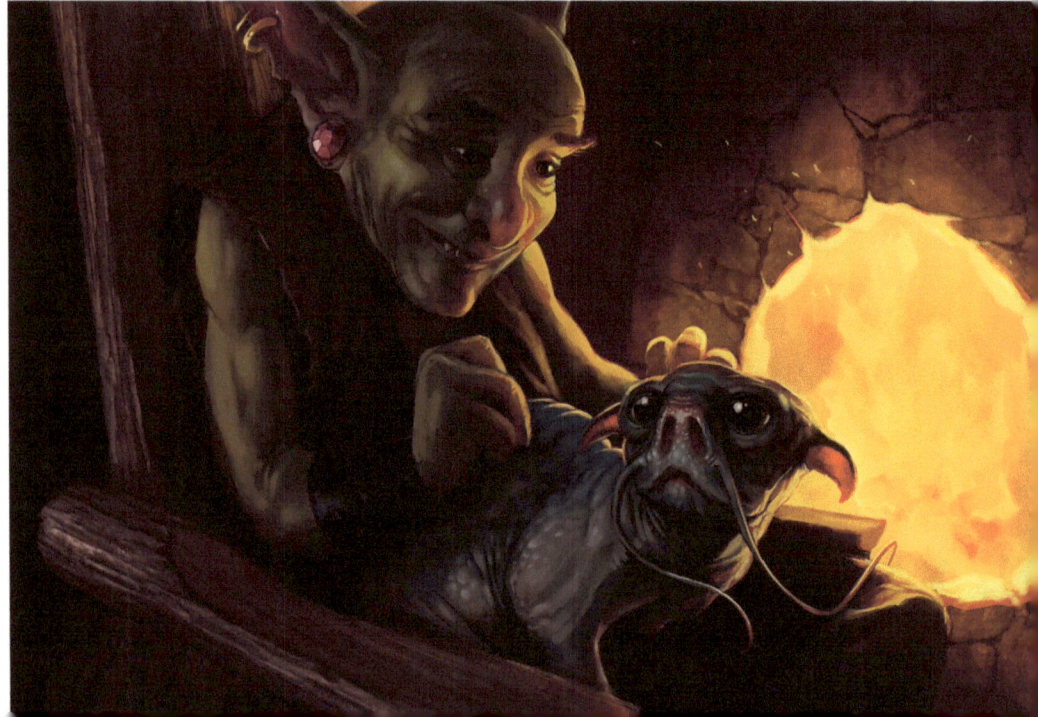

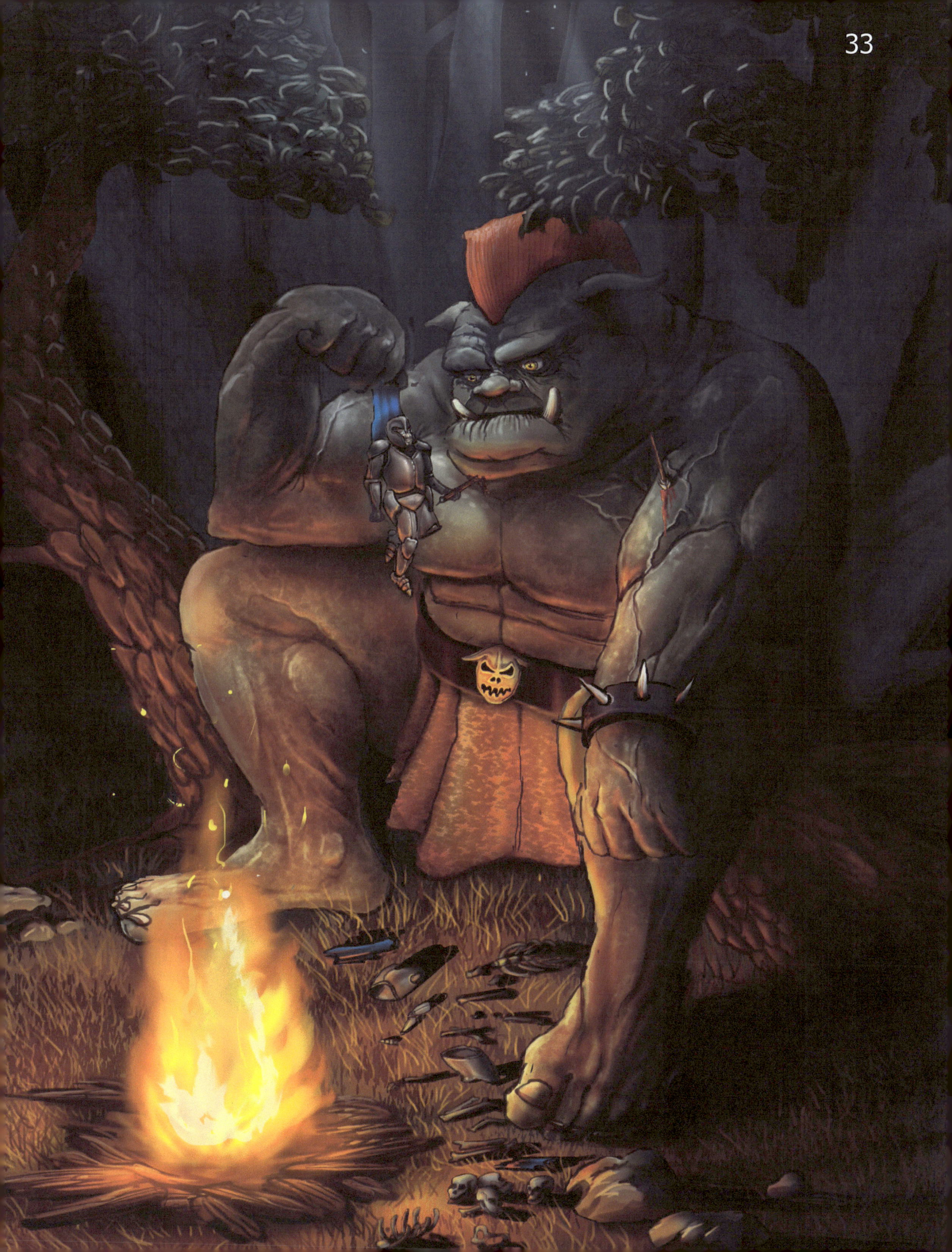

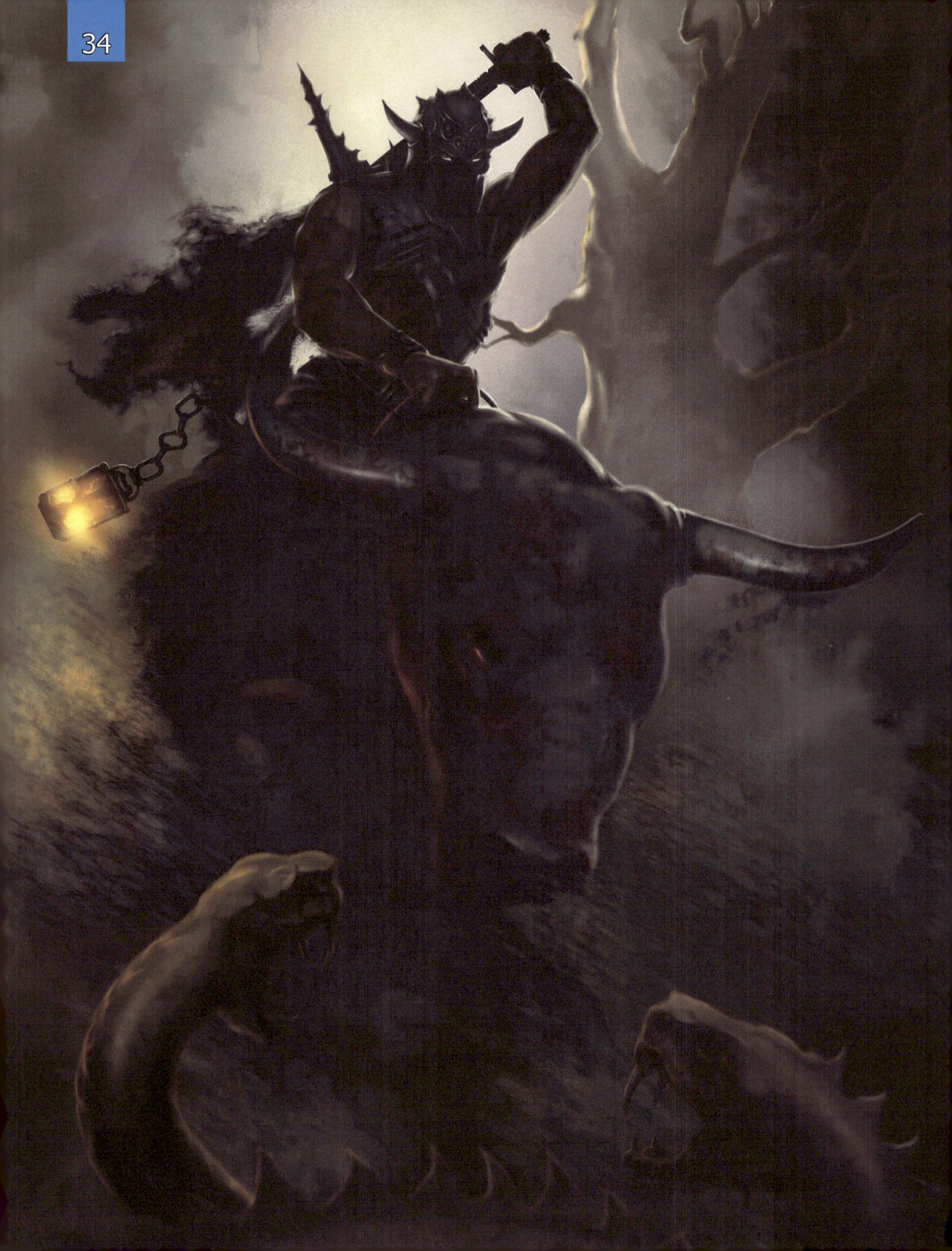

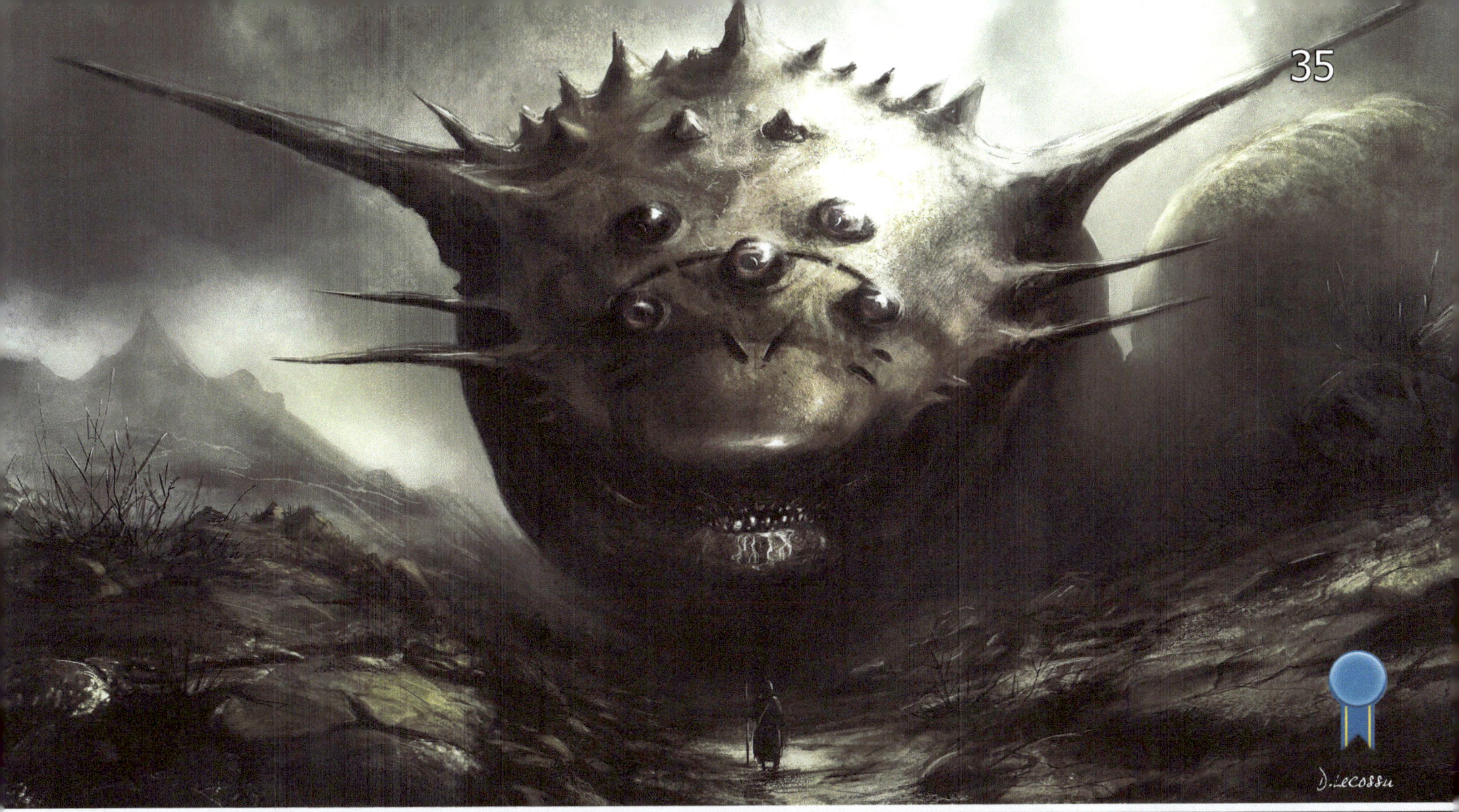

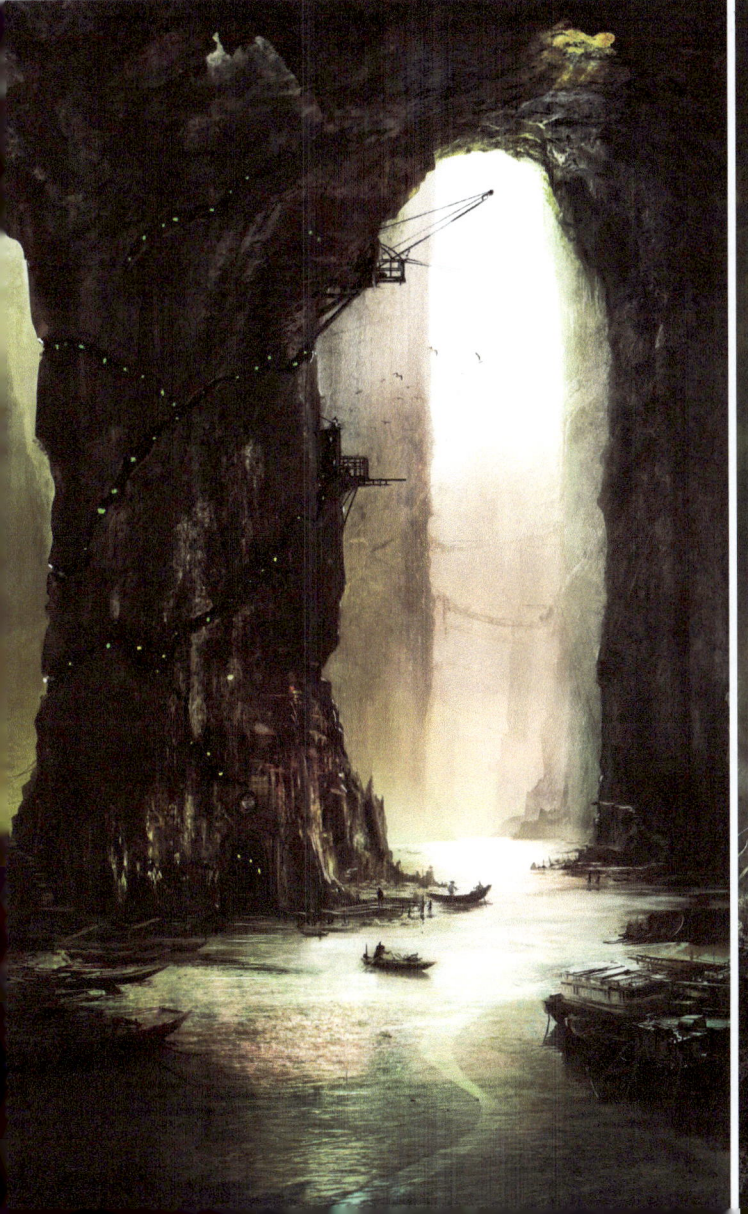

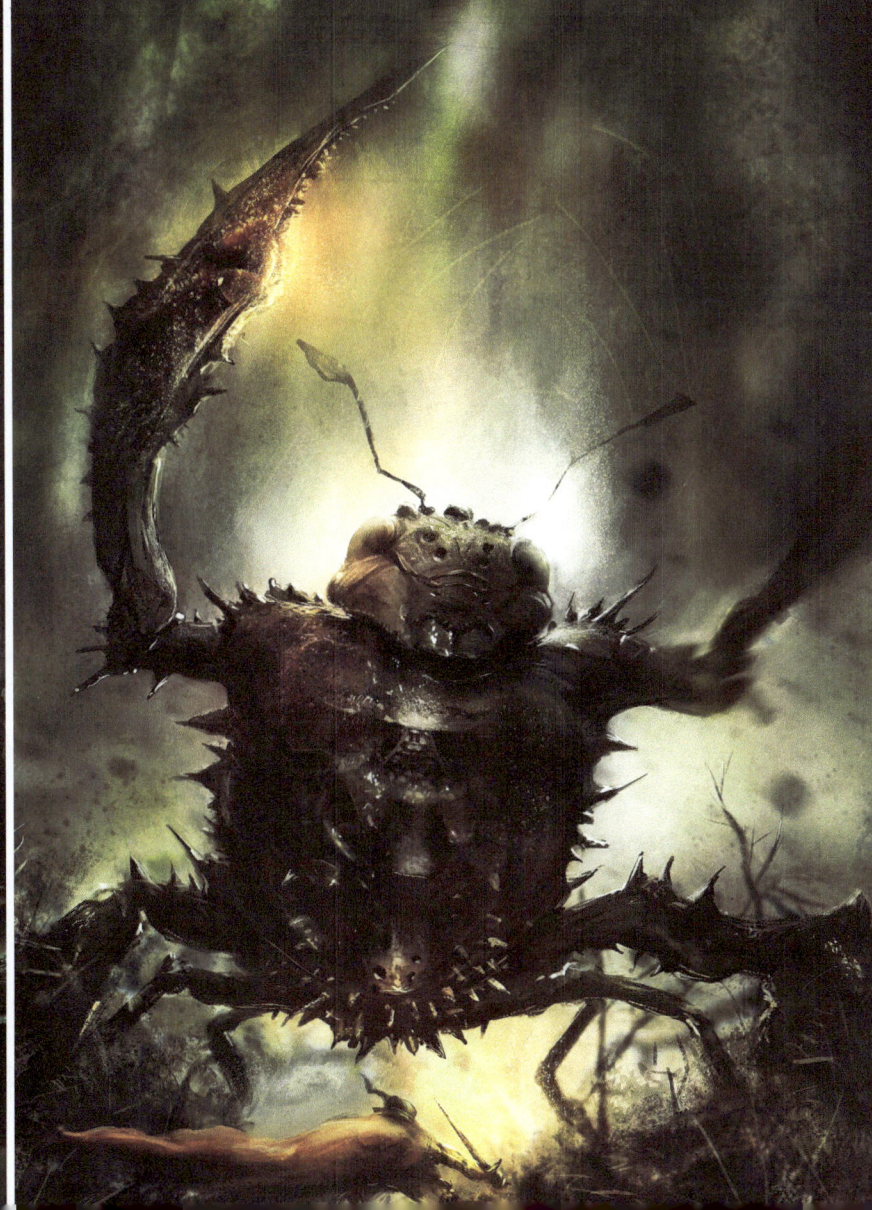

36

(Previous)

LEFT
SIMON ANDERSON-CARR
Digital (Canada)
Bull Fighter

RIGHT PAGE LOWER LEFT
DAVID LECOSSU
Photoshop (France)
Somewhere

RIGHT PAGE LOWER RIGHT
DAVID LECOSSU
Photoshop (France)
Insect

RIGHT PAGE UPPER
DAVID LECOSSU
Photoshop (France)
The Worm

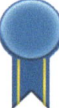

NEAR RIGHT
DANIEL OGUIN
Photoshop (USA)
Hawaiian Warrior

OPPOSITE TOP
ALEX LYON
Digital (USA)
Surviving the Storm

OPPOSITE CENTRE
BRIAN KELSEY
Photomanipulation (USA)
Low Tide

OPPOSITE LOWER RIGHT
WIL OBERDIER
Photoshop (USA)
Aries

OPPOSITE BOTTOM LEFT
DANIEL OGUIN
Photoshop (USA)
Assassin

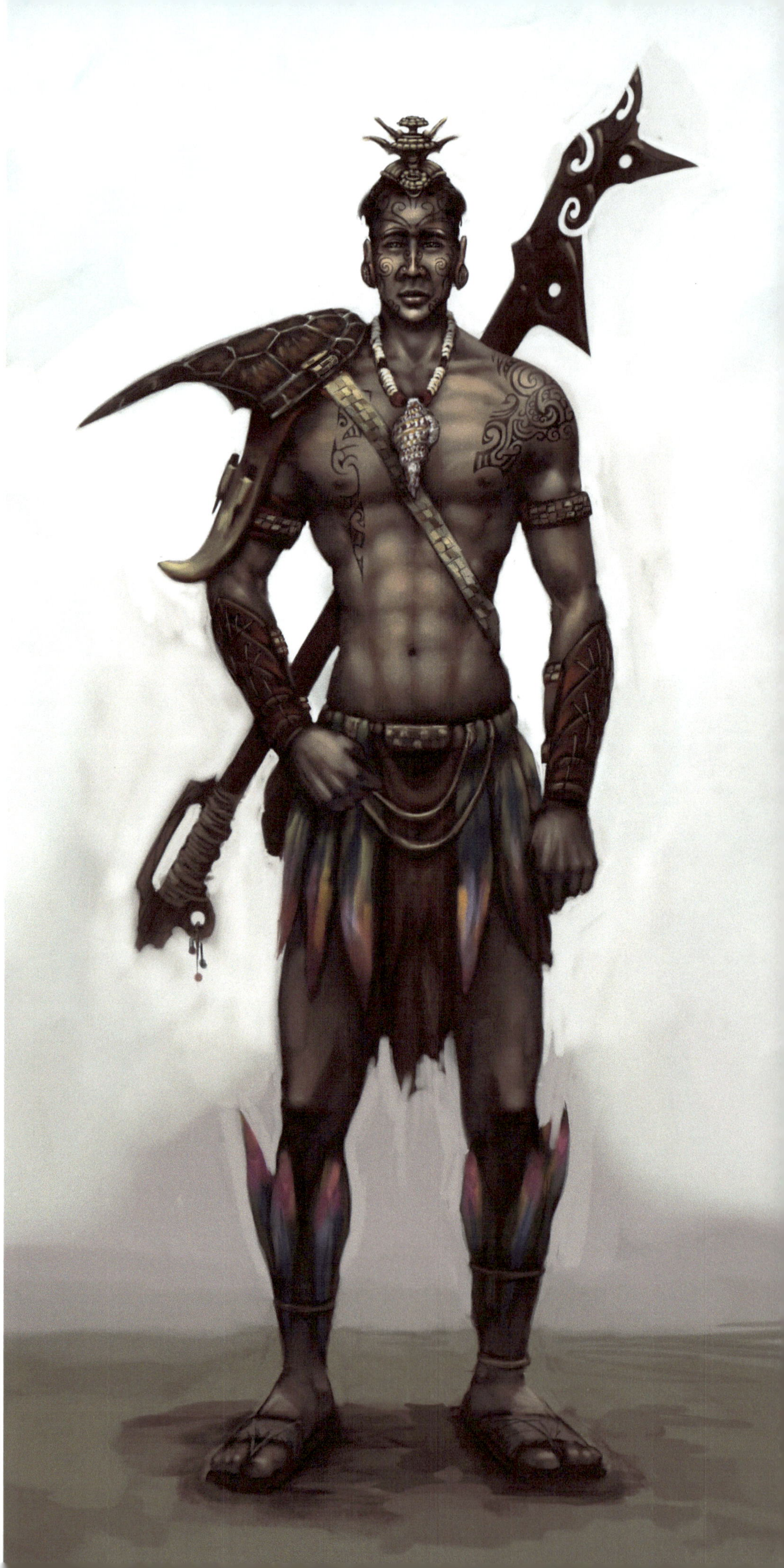

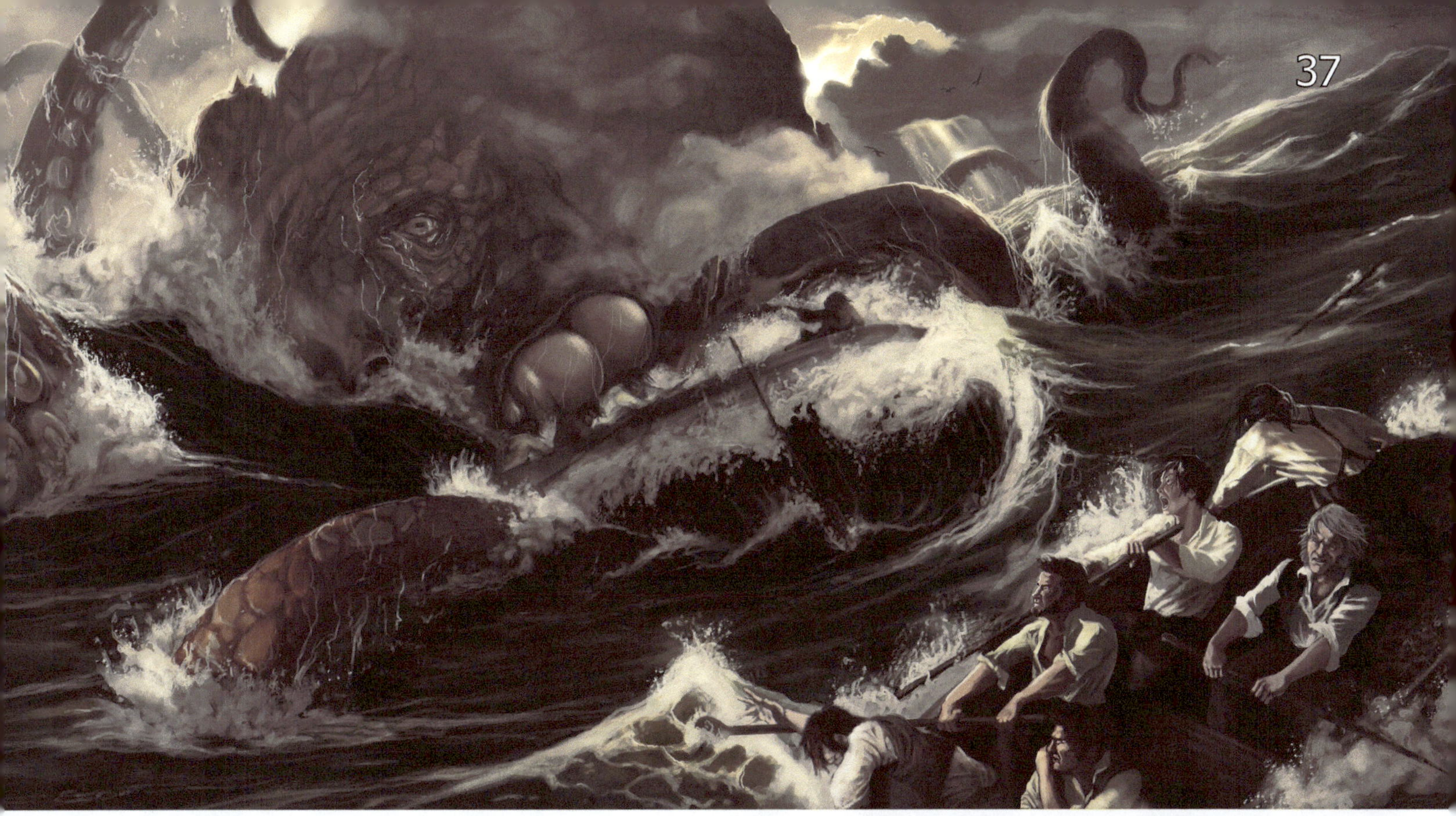

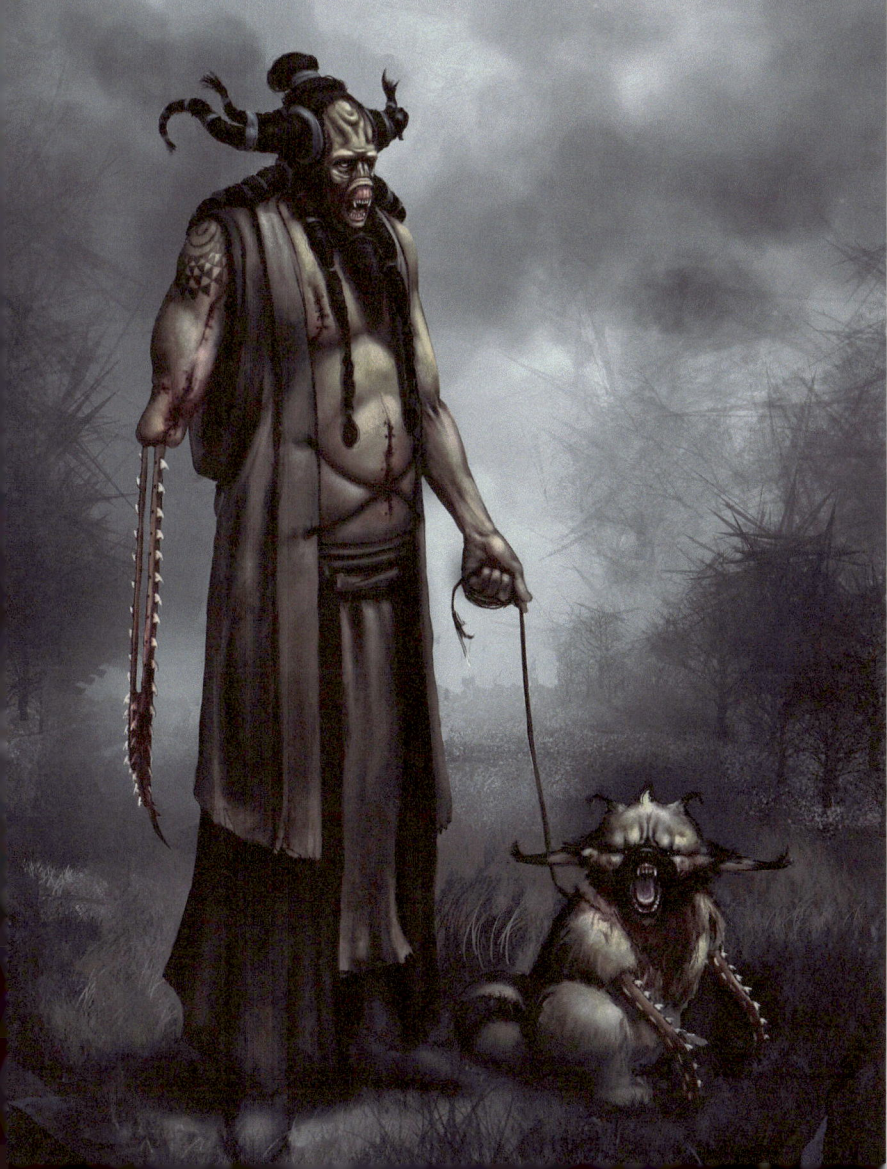

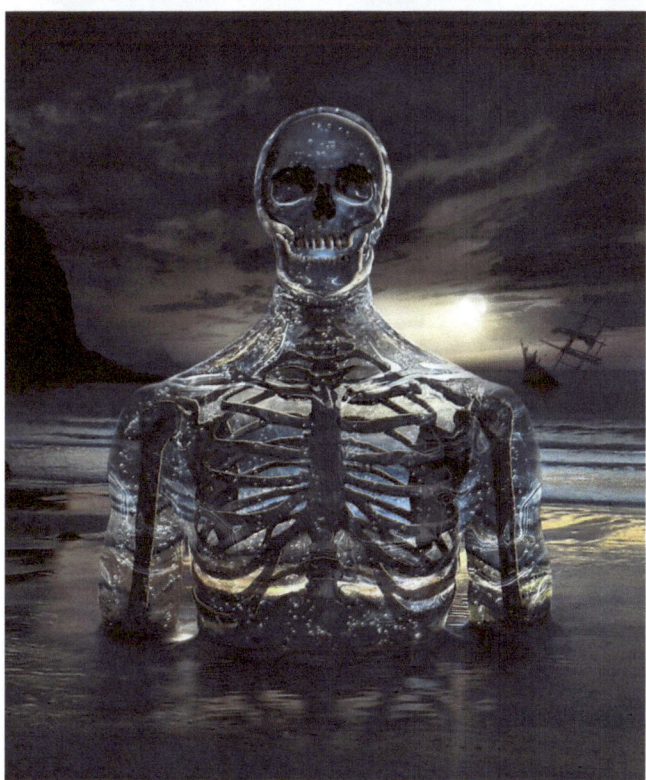

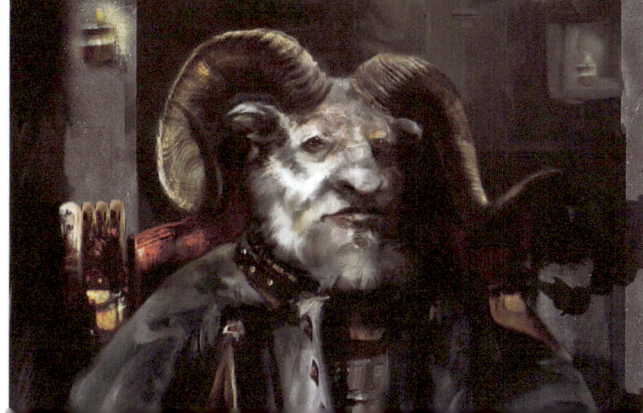

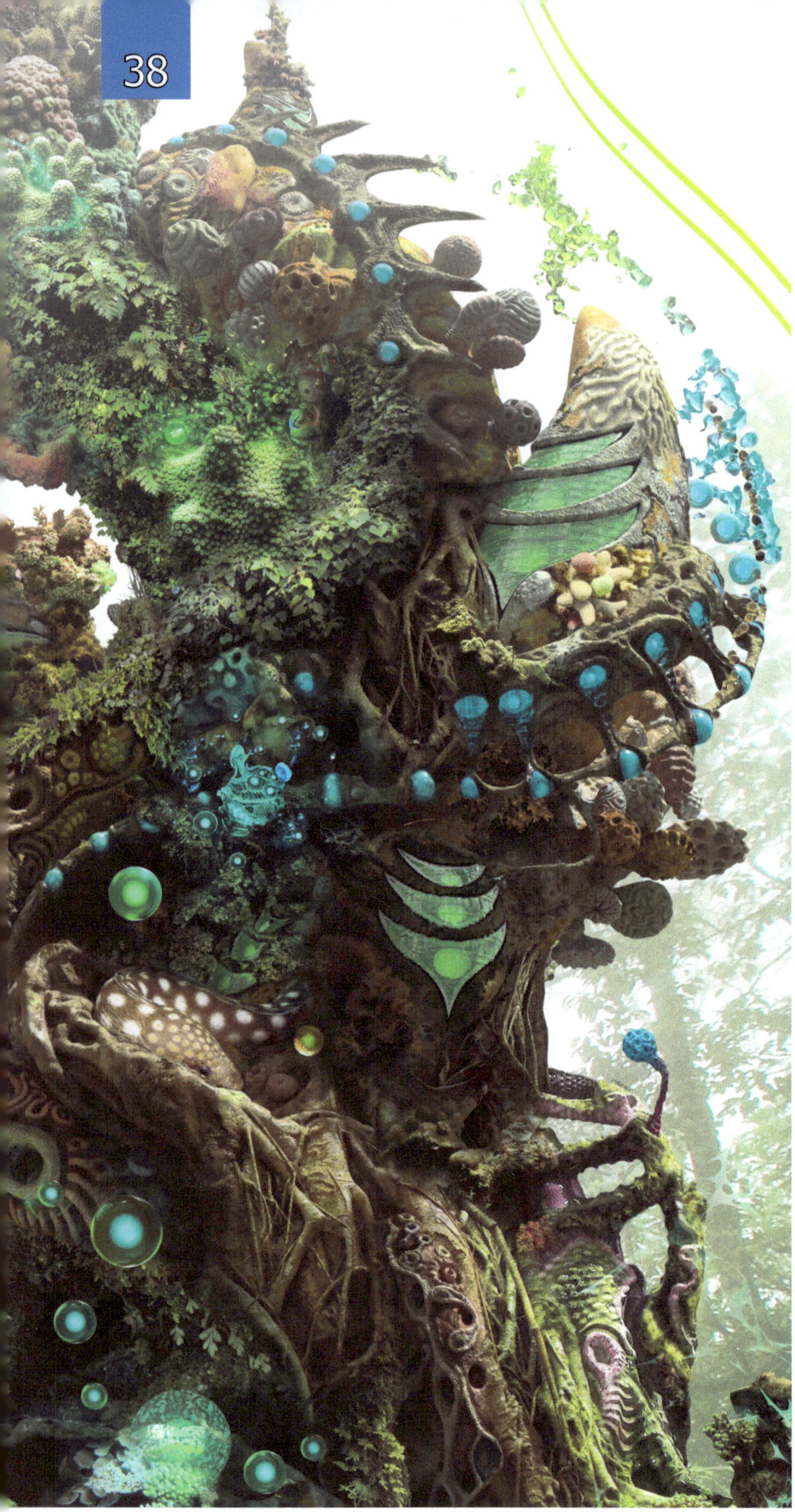

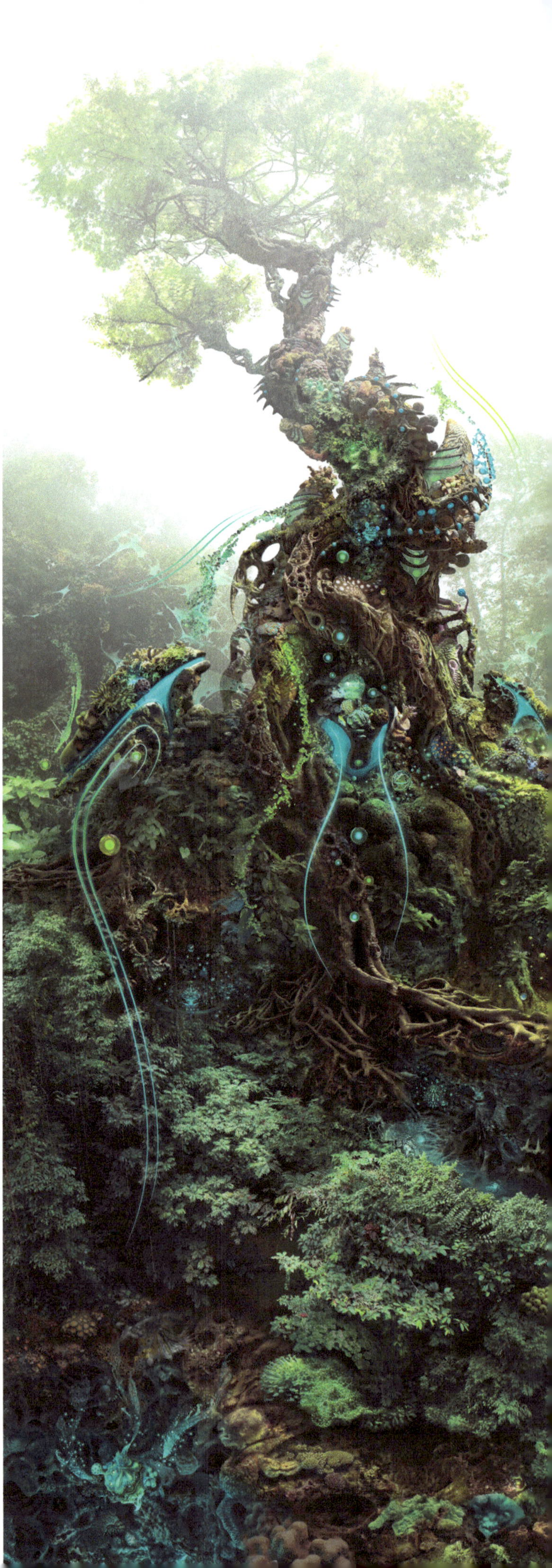

ABOVE
(Detail)

editor's note:
Andy's work is HUGE and is truly worth seeing online:
www.andythomas.com.au

RIGHT
ANDY THOMAS
Photoshop, 3dsmax, Zbrush (Australia)
Cyanide Tree

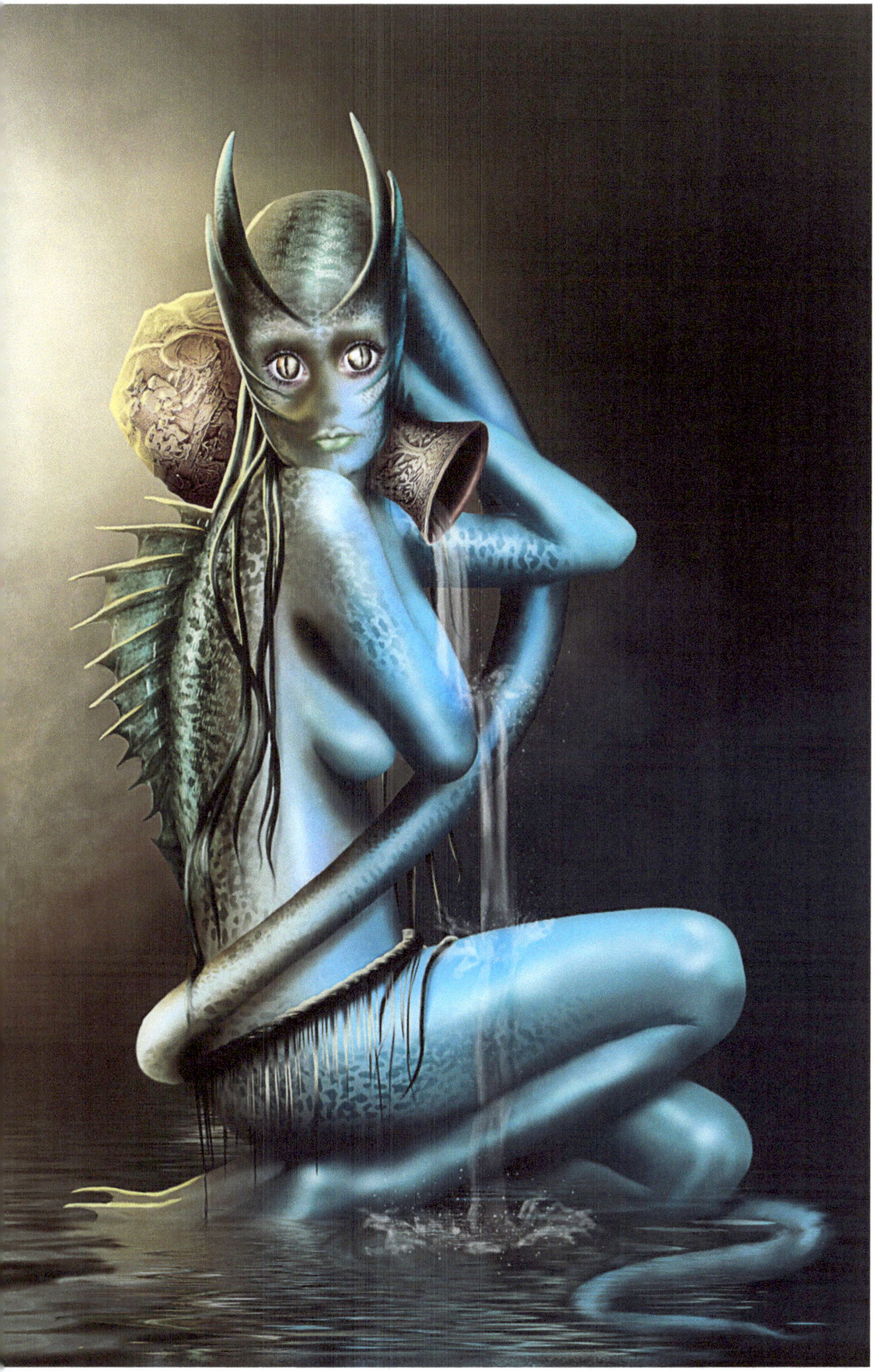

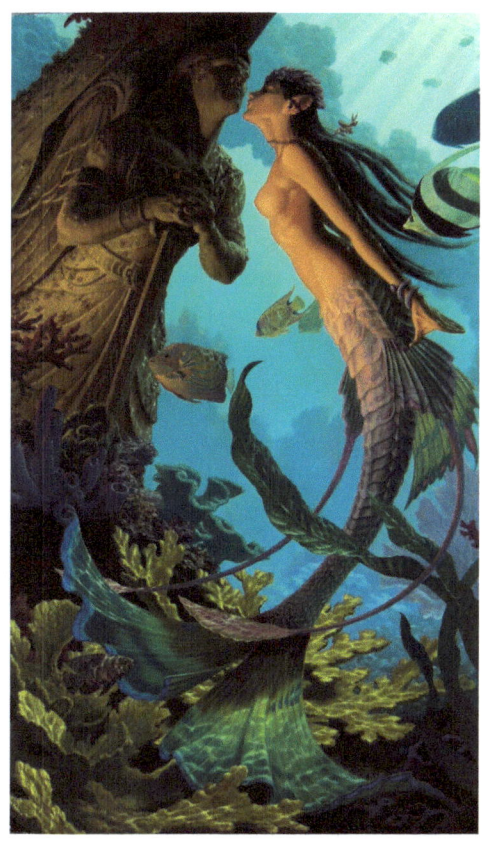

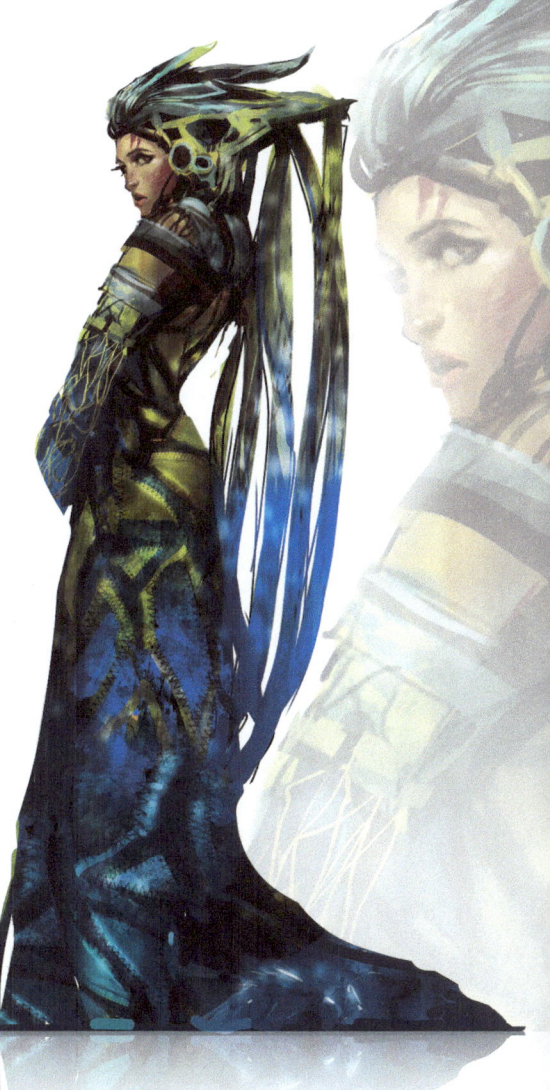

ABOVE
MadameThenadier
Photoshop (The Netherlands)
Aquarius

NEAR RIGHT
Ahmed Aldoori
Photoshop (USA)
Costume Design

TOP RIGHT
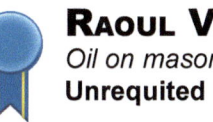
Raoul Vitale
Oil on masonite (USA)
Unrequited

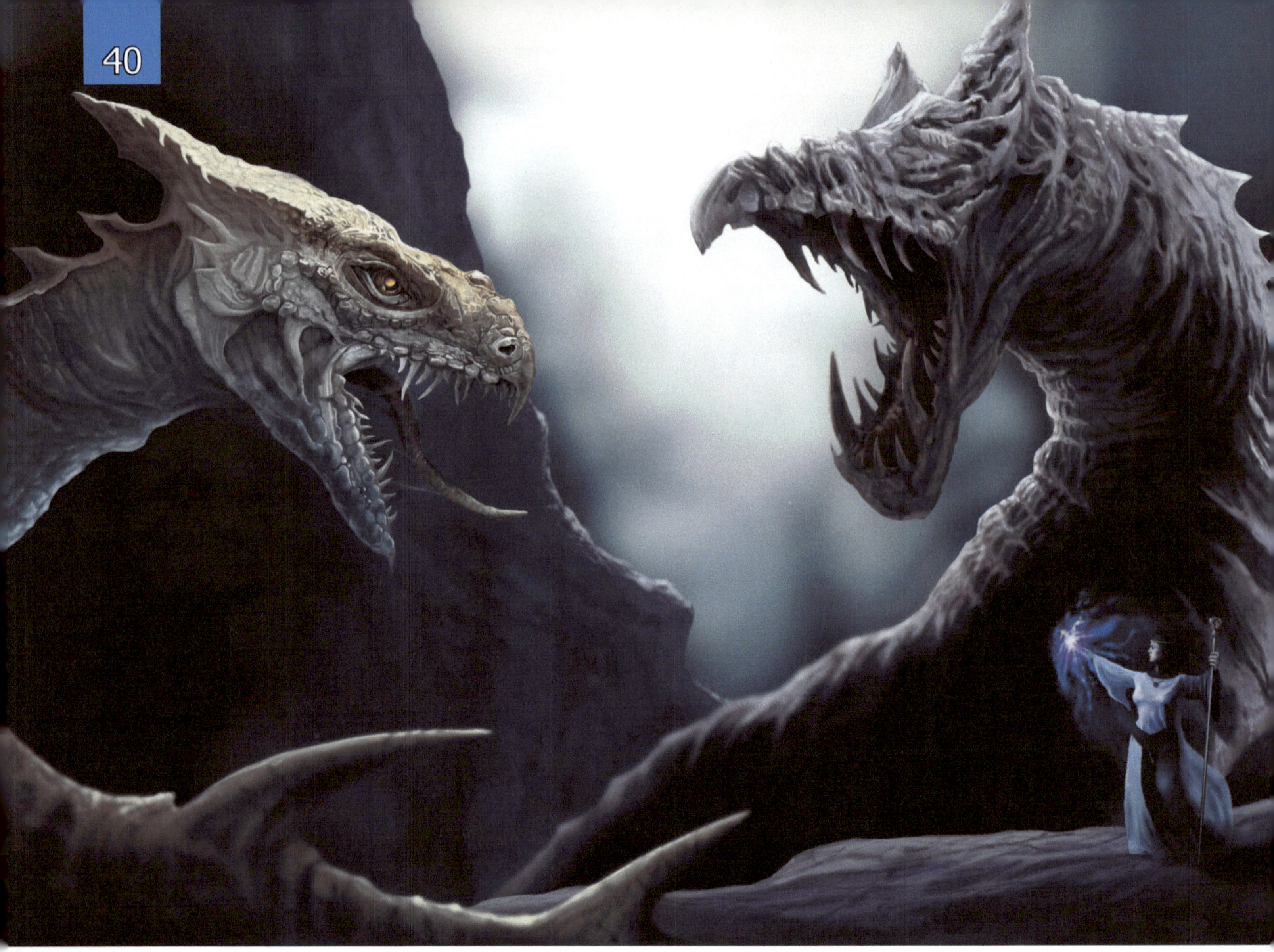

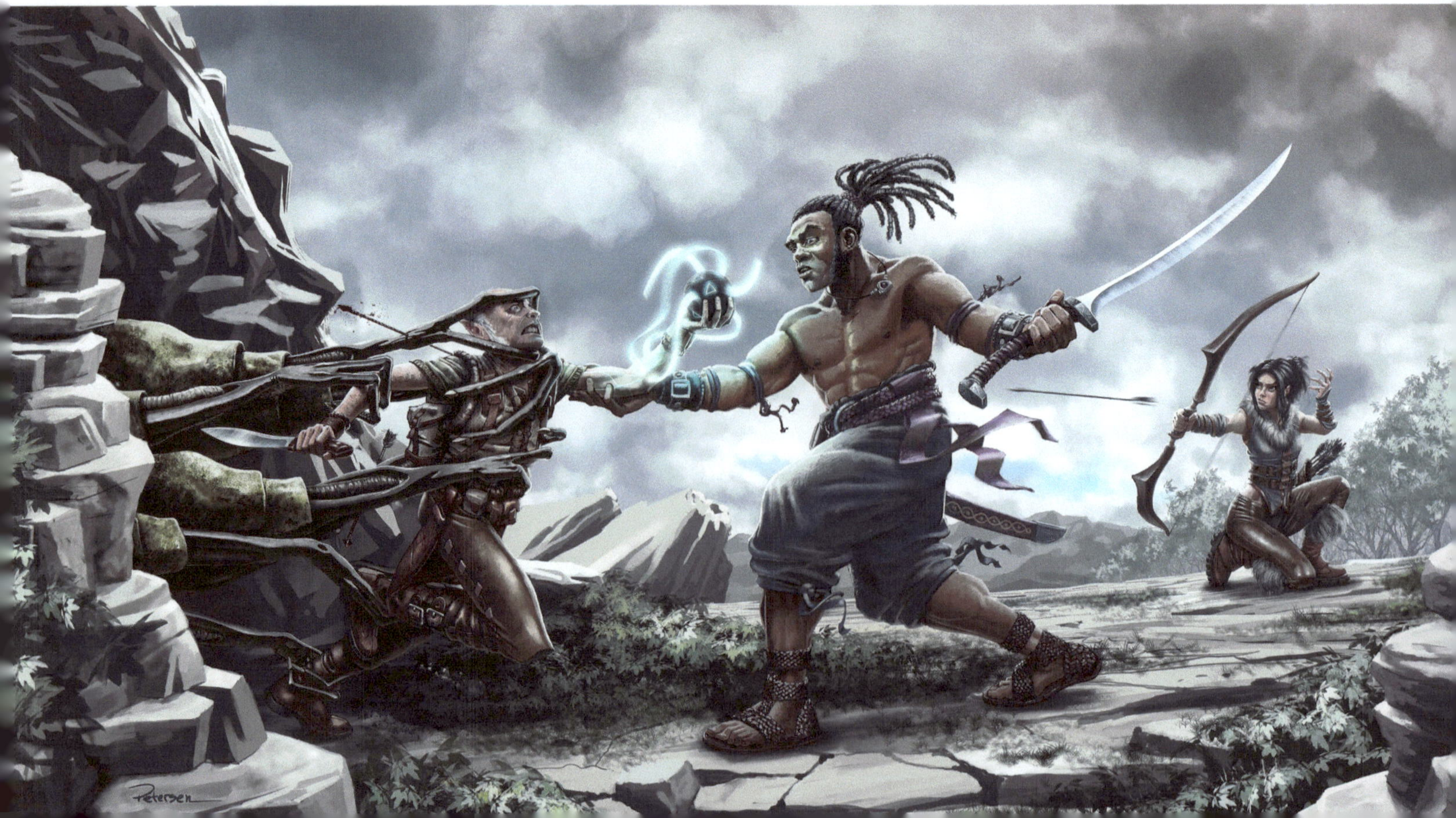
Petersen

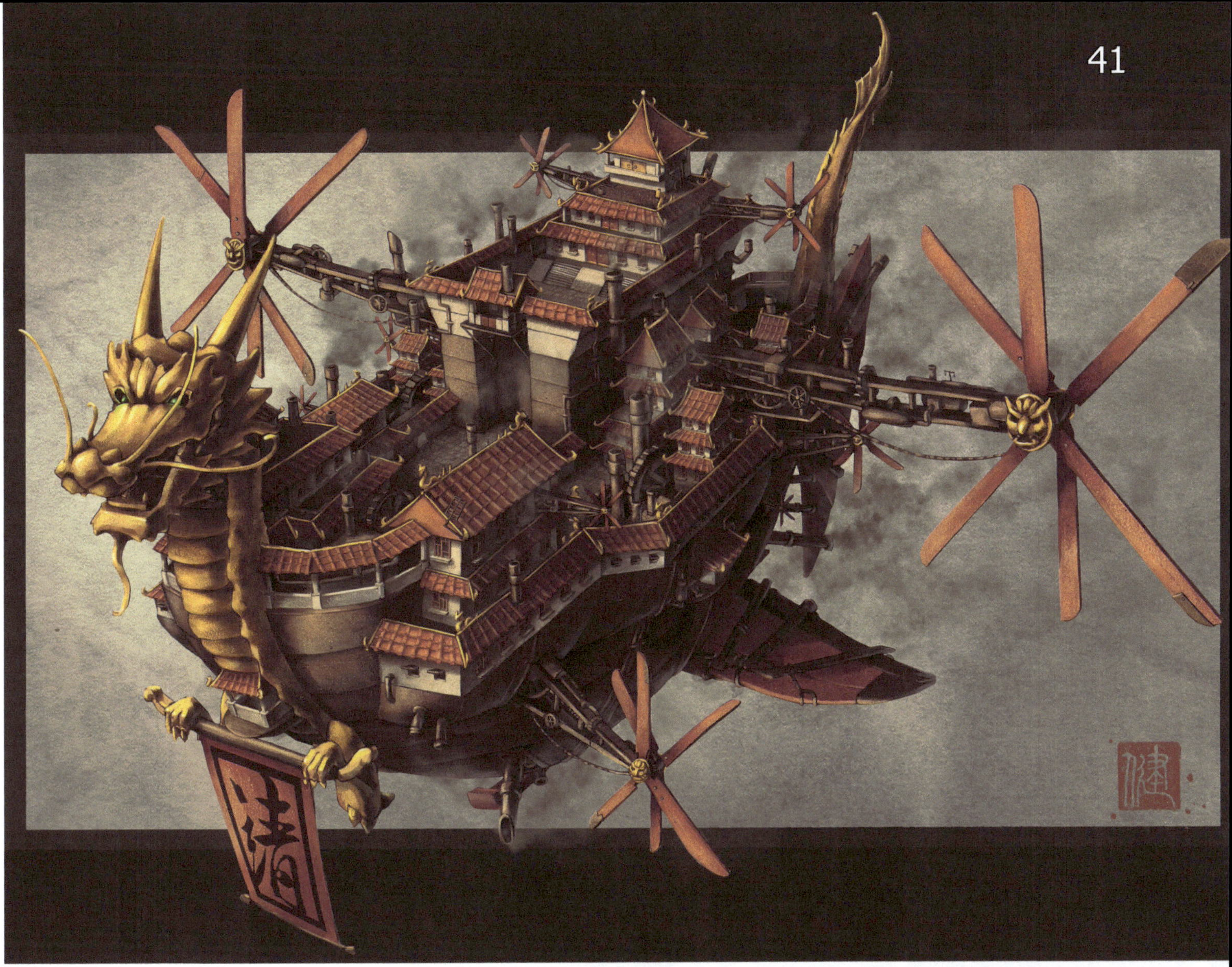

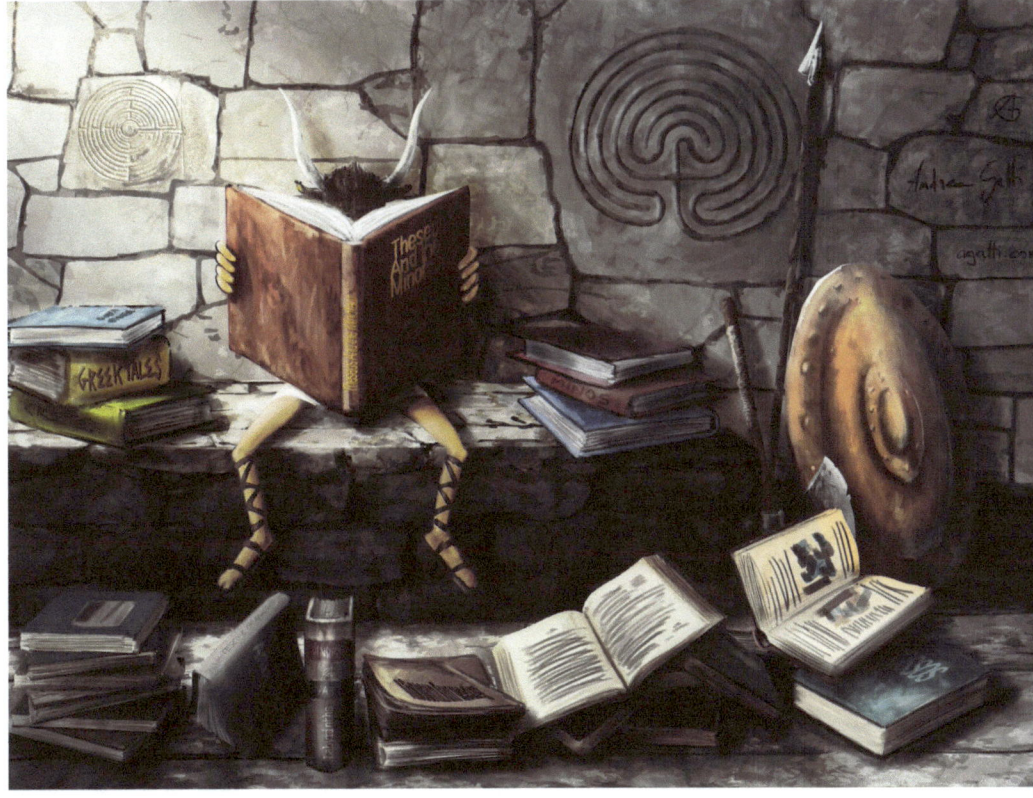

ABOVE

JAMES NG
Pencil, Charcoal, Painter,
Photoshop (Hong Kong/ Canada)
Imperial Airship

RIGHT

ANDREA GATTI
Photoshop (Italy)
Minotauro

OPPOSITE TOP

STEFAN MEISL
Photoshop (Germany)
Clash of Avatars

OPPOSITE BOTTOM

JOHN PETERSEN
Photoshop (USA)
The Artifact

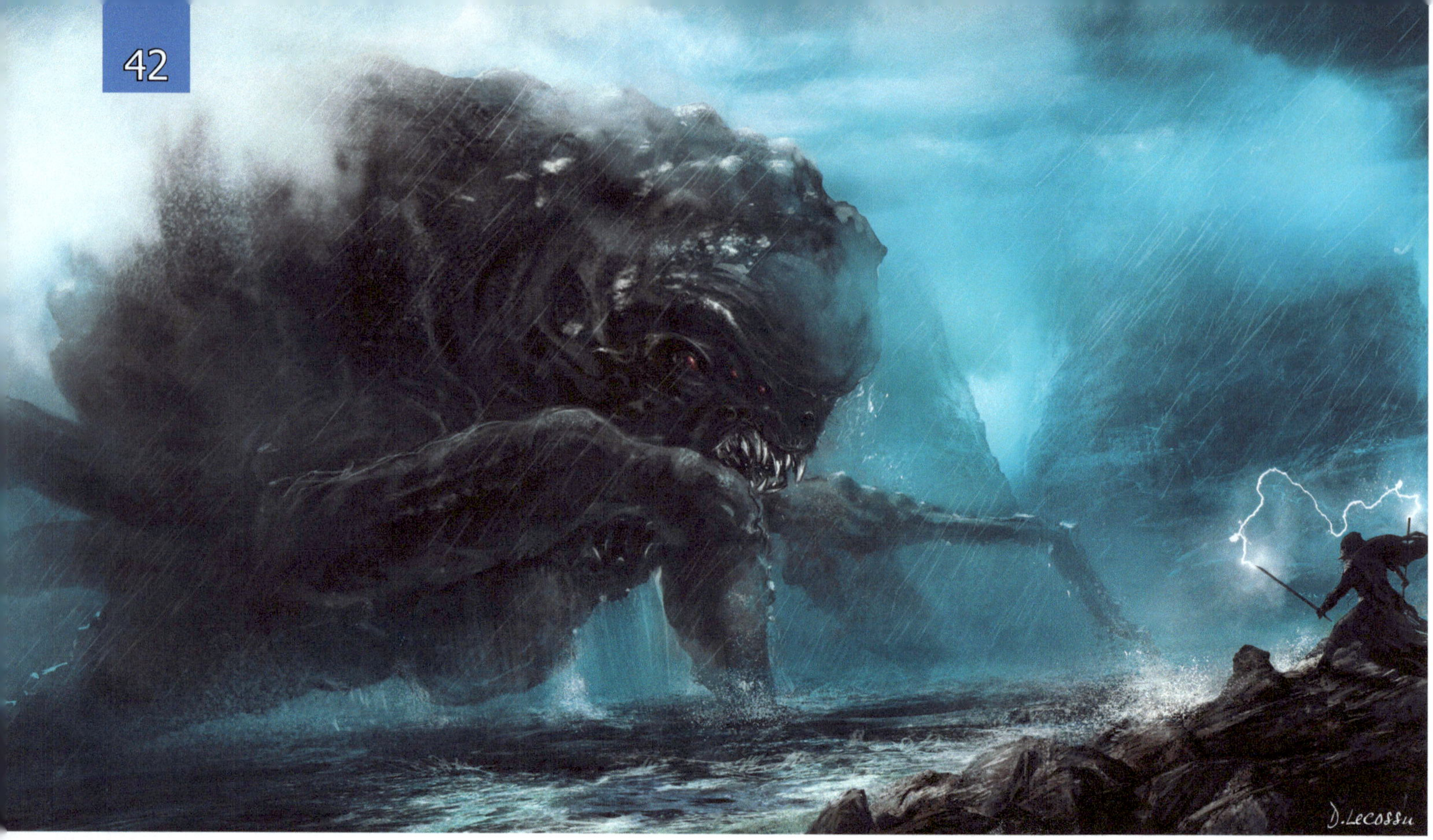

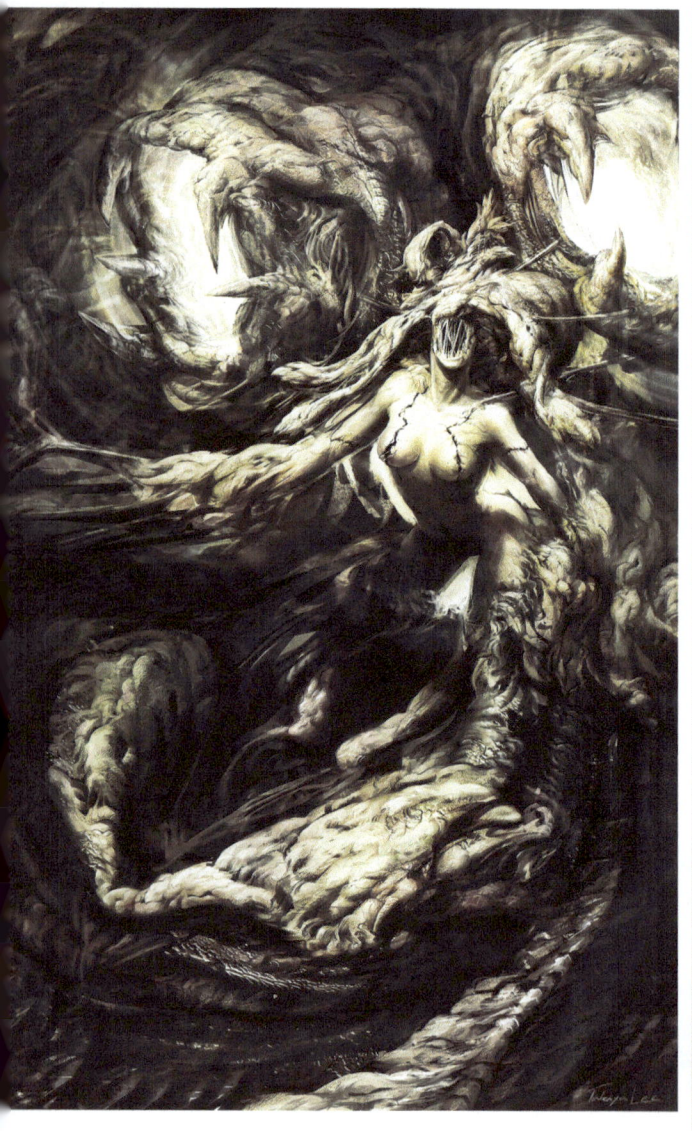

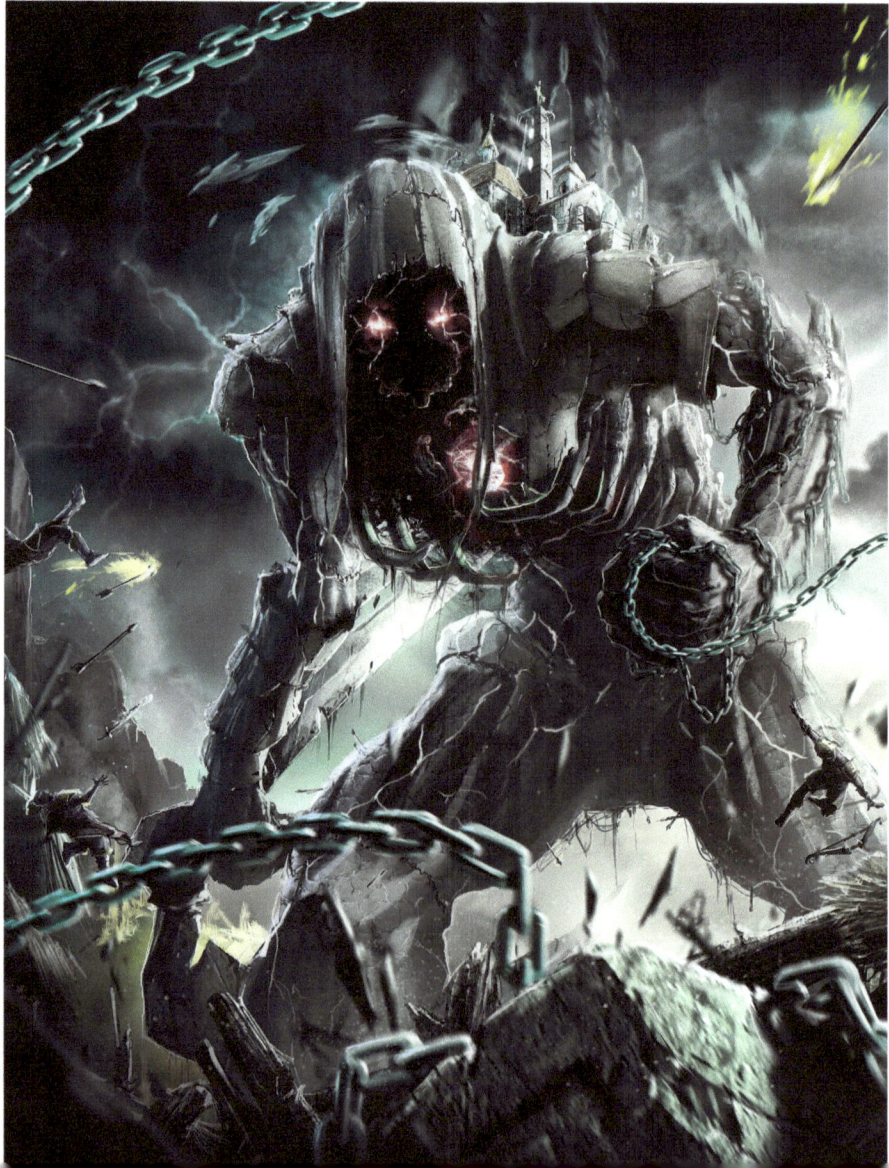

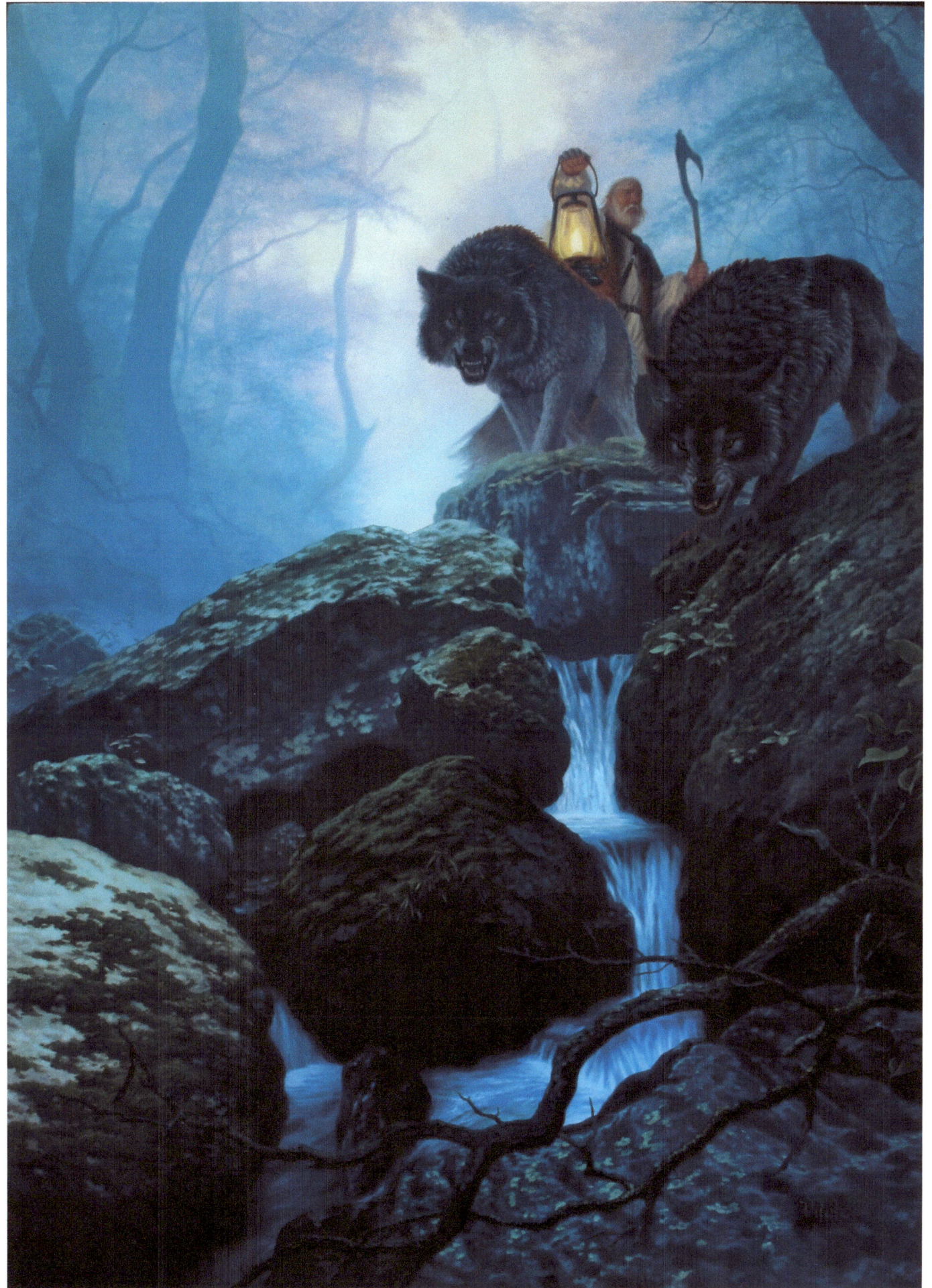

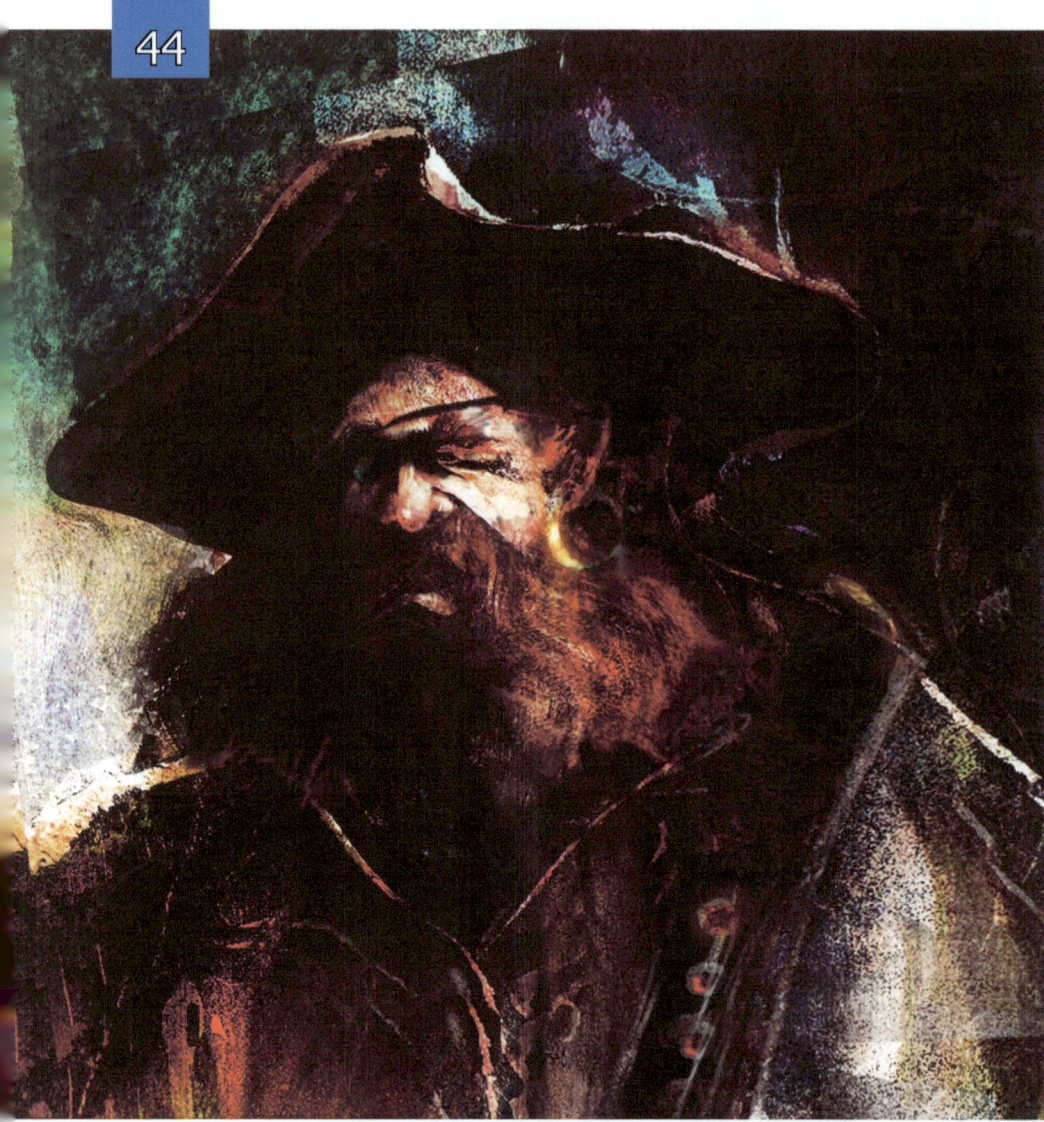

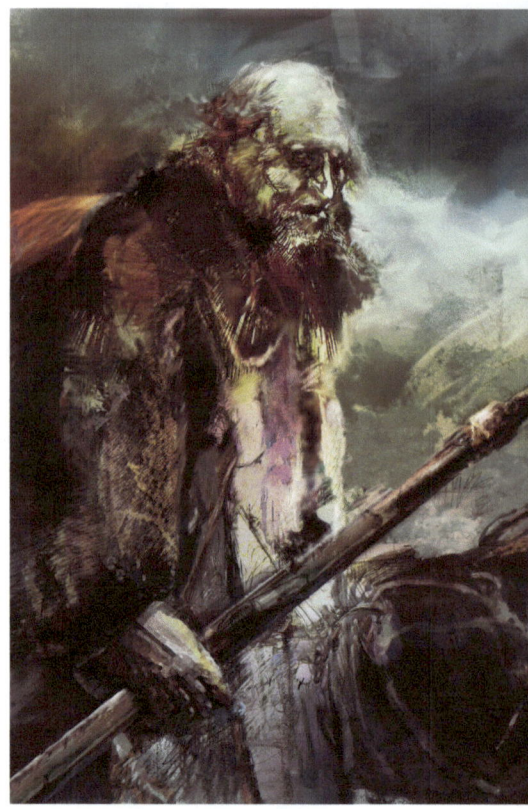

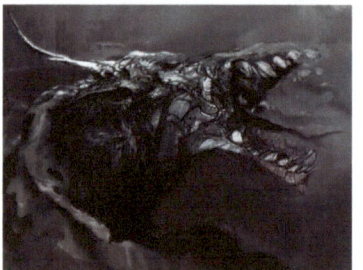

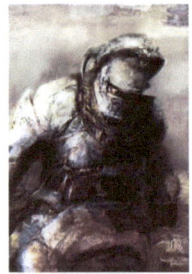

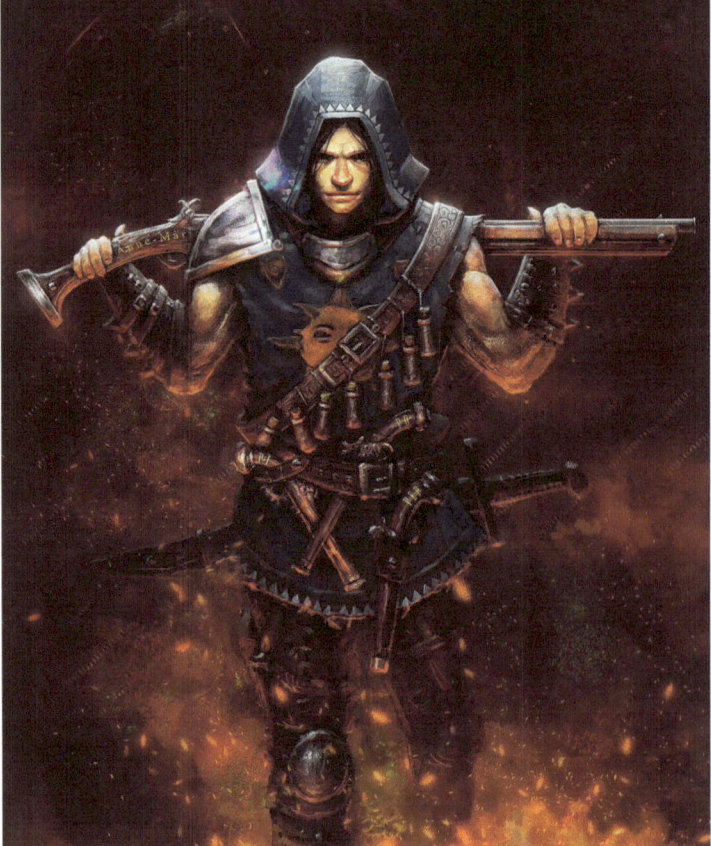

ABOVE TOP RIGHT

WIL OBERDIER
Pencil/Digital (USA)
Obsessed with a White Whale

ABOVE FAR LEFT

WIL OBERDIER
Pencil/Digital (USA)
The Pirate

ABOVE BOTTOM RIGHT

WIL OBERDIER
Pencil/Digital (USA)
Dregen

FAR LEFT

WIL OBERDIER
Pencil/Digital (USA)
Sir

RIGHT

GABRIEL VERDON
Photoshop(Canada)
Musketeer

(Previous Spread)

LEFT PAGE TOP
DAVID LECOSSU
Photoshop (France)
Sea Beast

LEFT PAGE BOTTOM LEFT
TAKAYA LEE
Photoshop (Thailand)
World Negator

LEFT PAGE BOTTOM RIGHT
VINCENT LEFEVRE
Photoshop (France)
Colosse of the Dead

RIGHT PAGE
RAOUL VITALE
Oil on masonite (USA)
Twilight Tracker

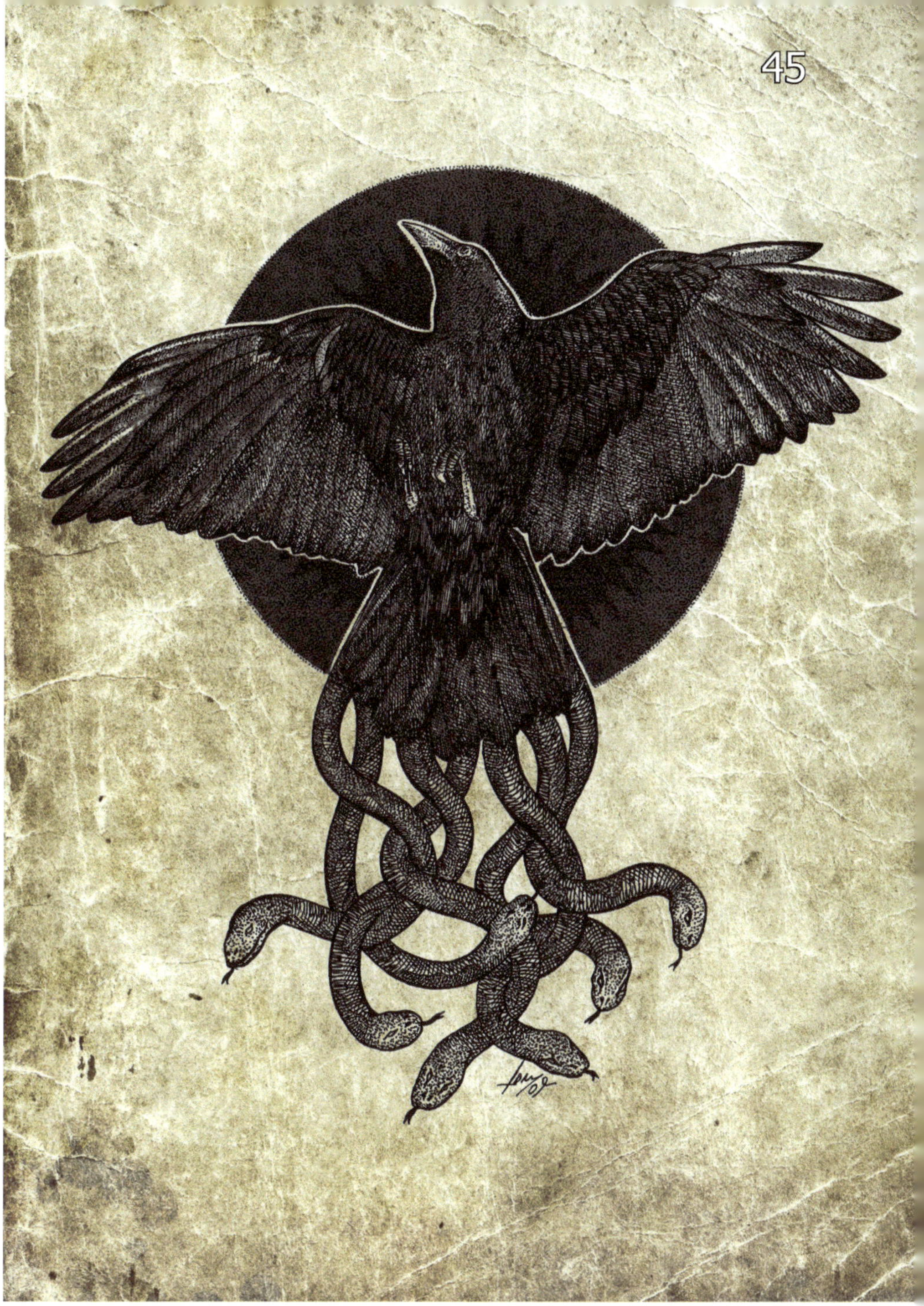

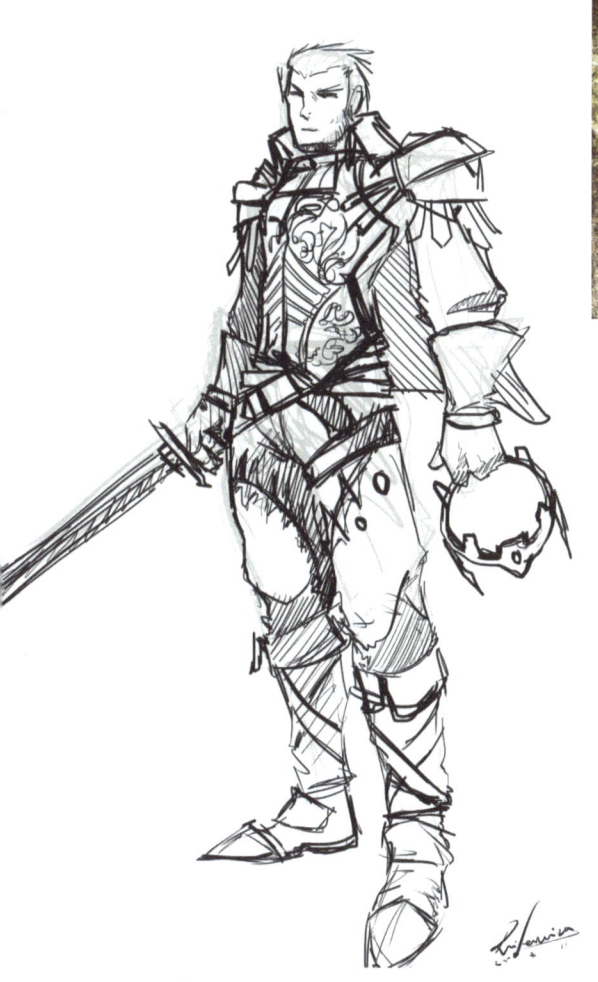

(Overleaf)

ABOVE
IRENE DM AKA
NAMTARU
Ink and Digital (Spain)
Plagues Bringer

RIGHT PAGE
ANGELA TYGERSON ROSS
Photoshop Painting (USA)
Jared

LEFT
RUI FERREIRA
Painter XII (Portugal)
Ahsante

LEFT PAGE
AHMED ALDOORI
Photoshop (USA)
Ballroom

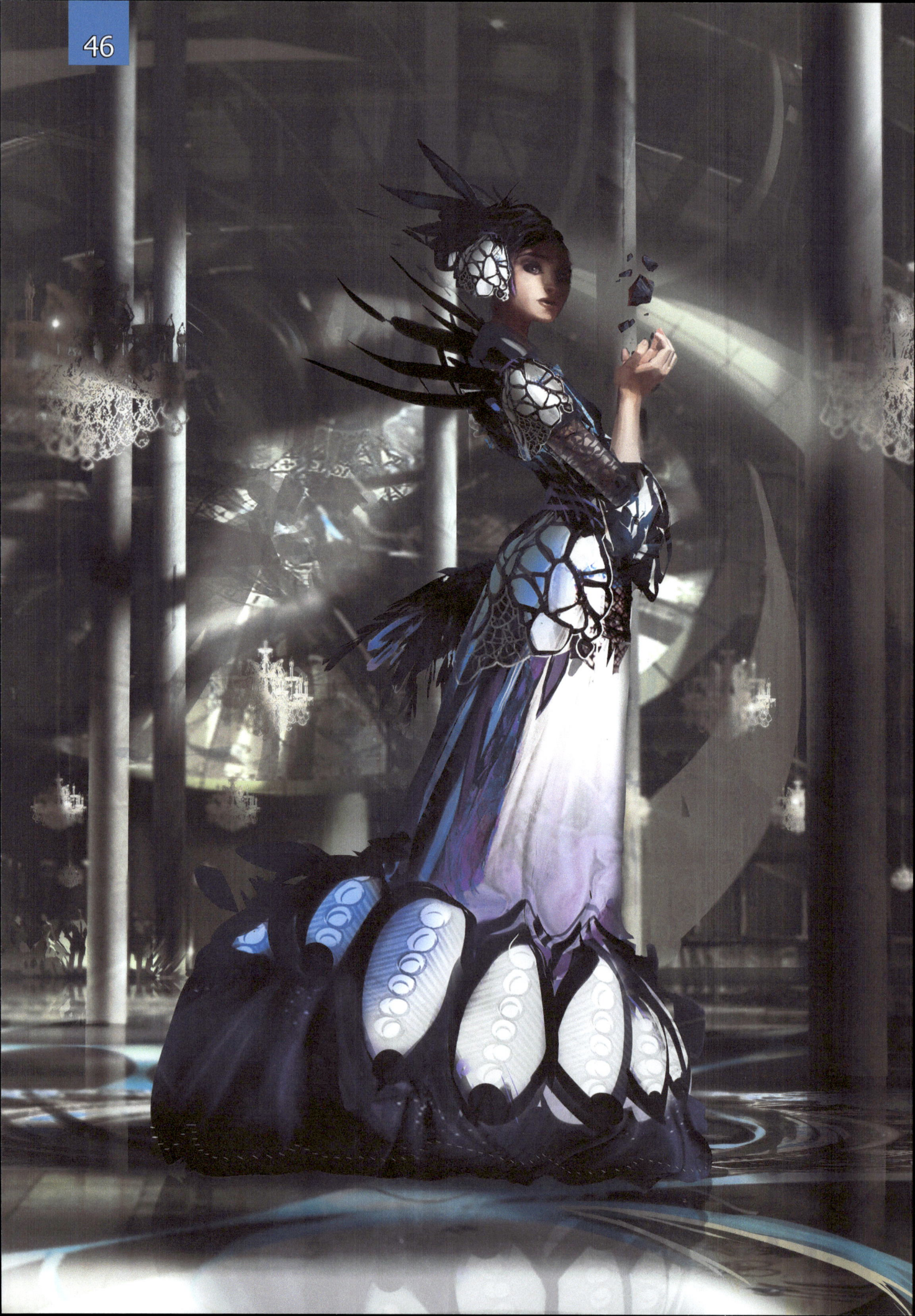

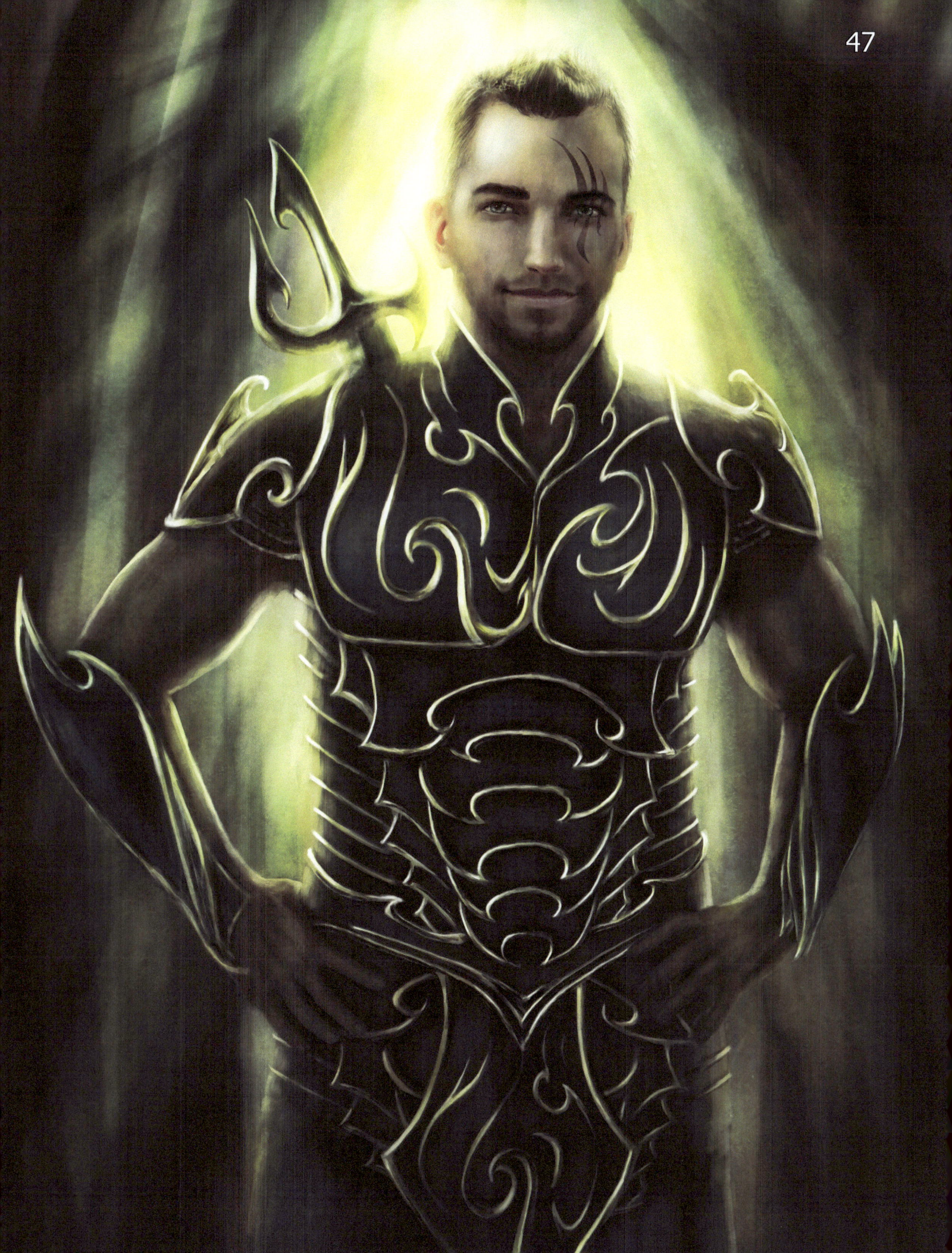

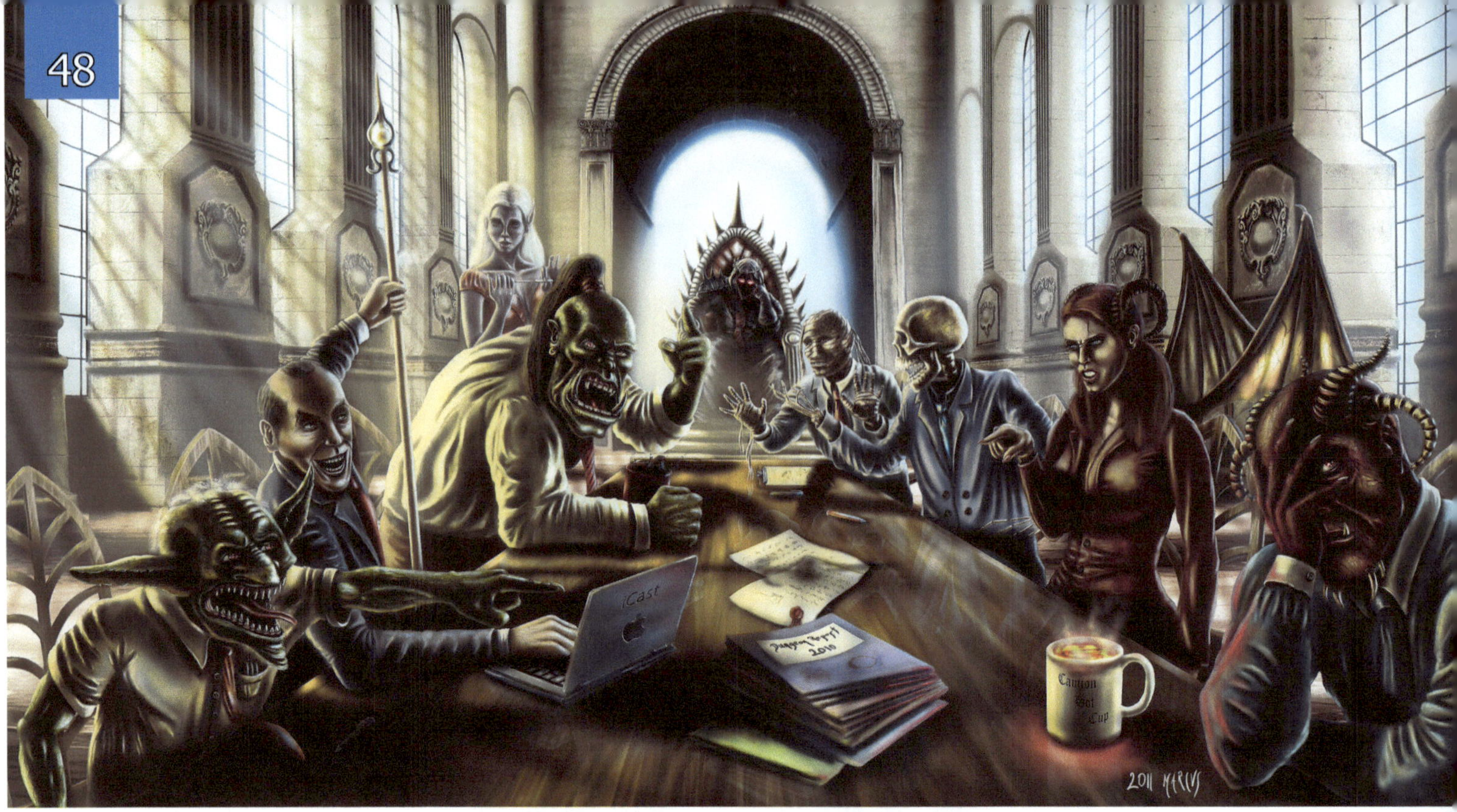

TOP

MARKUS STADLOBER
Photoshop and Painter (Austria)
Evil Empire Inc.

BELOW

RYAN ARMS
Graphite & GIMP (USA)
Yakuza Apology

RIGHT

IMMAR PALOMERA
Photoshop (USA)
RED

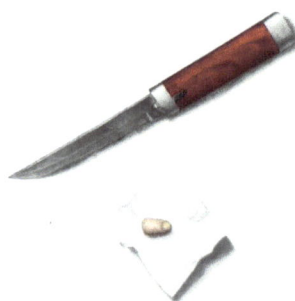

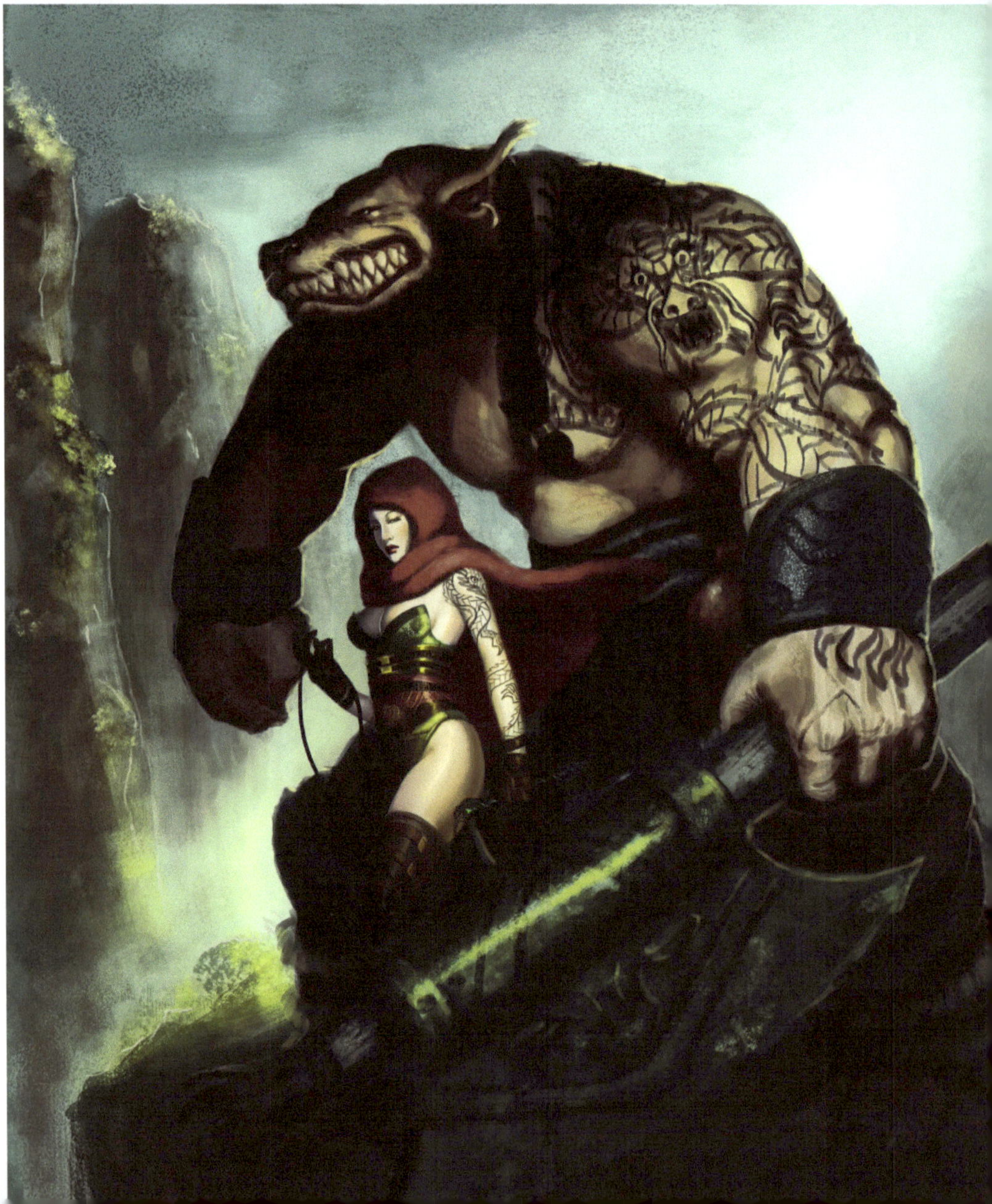

OPPOSITE TOP

RICARDO CARBAJAL
Acrylic on Cardboard (Mexico)
Battle to the Death

OPPOSITE BOTTOM

MARKUS STADLOBER
Photoshop and Painter (Austria)
Mooing Down the Enemy

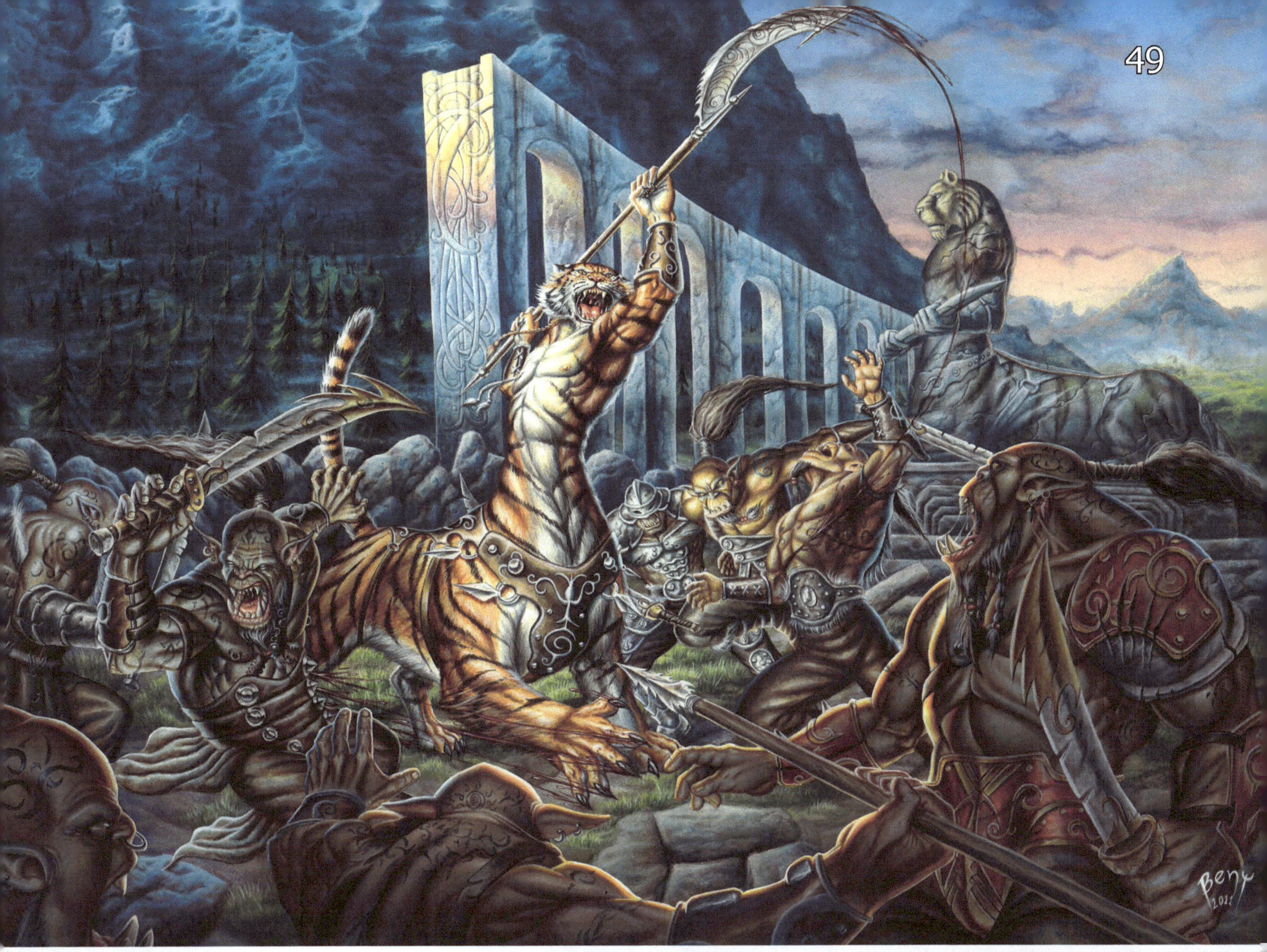

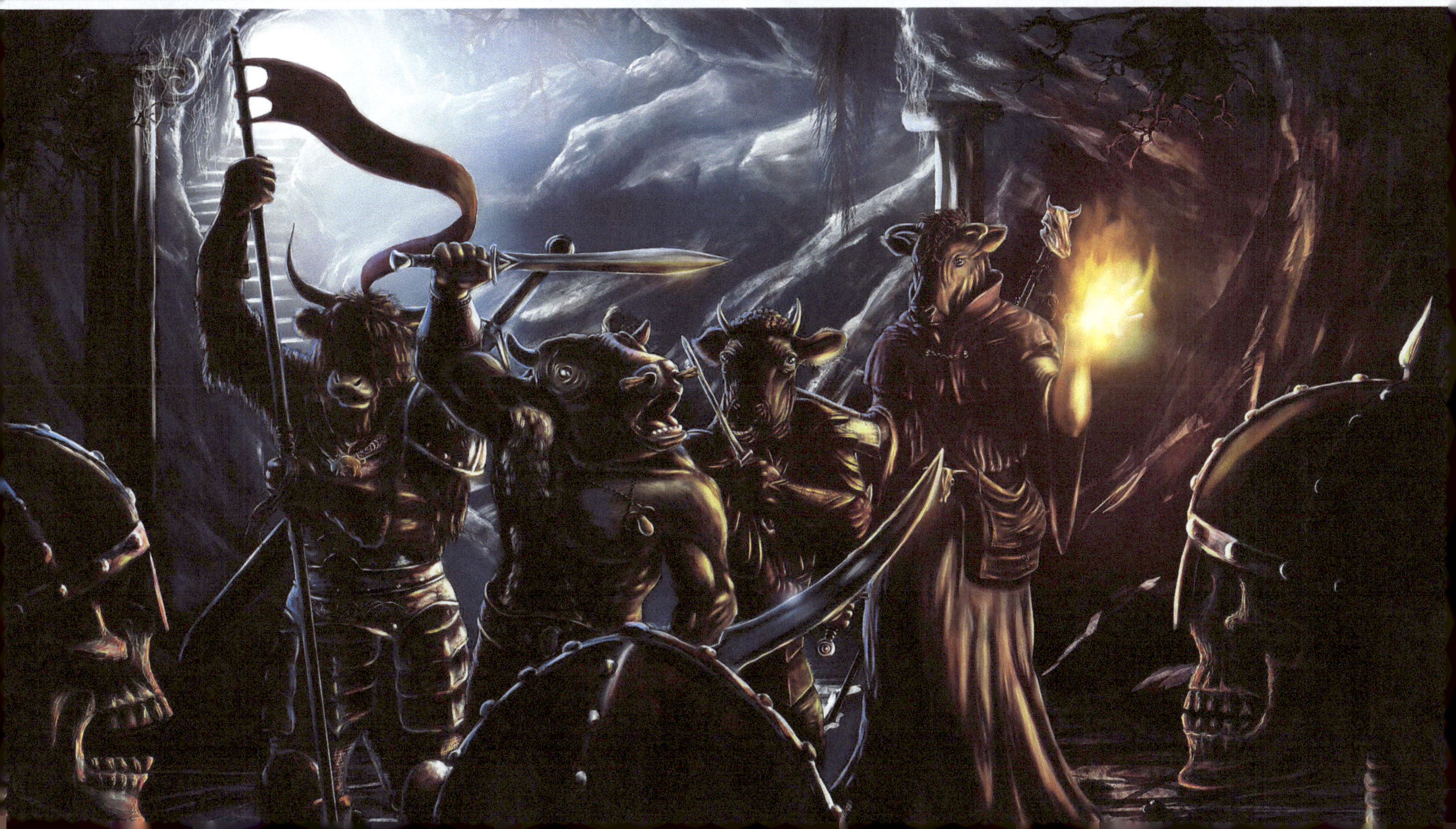

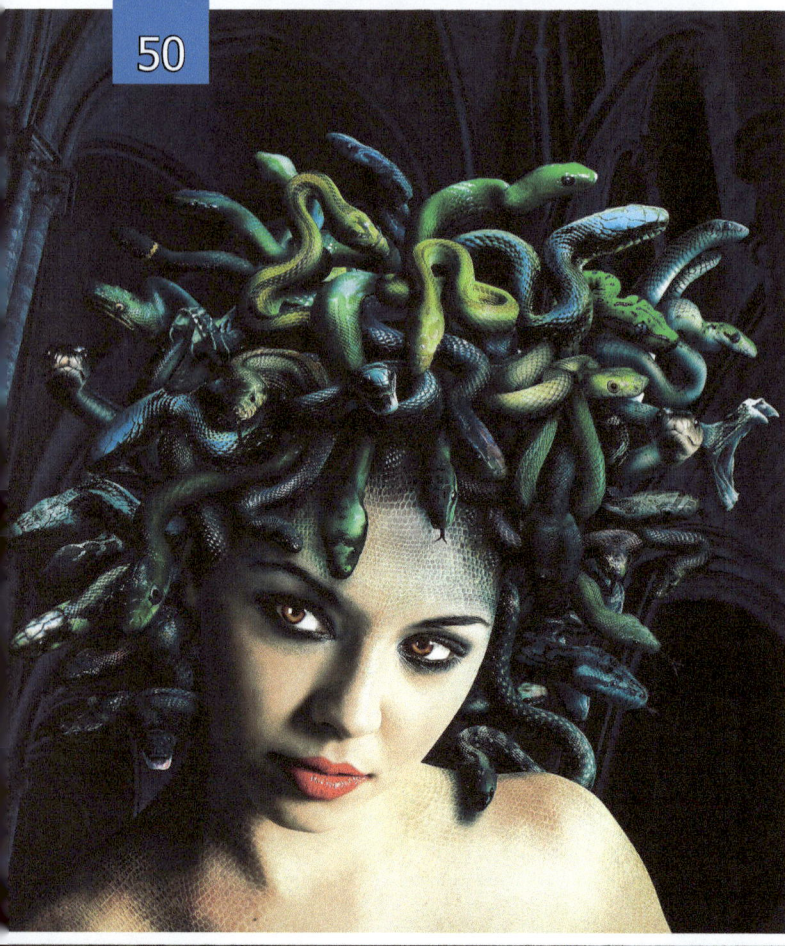

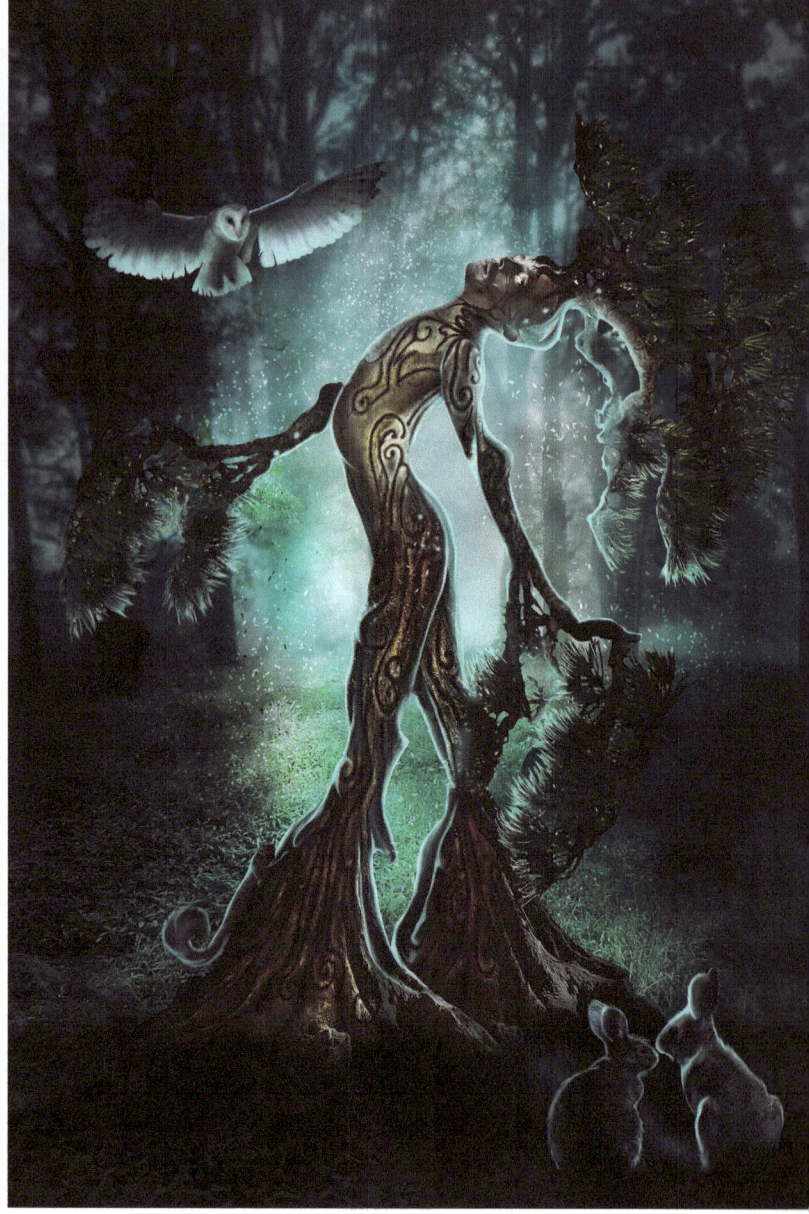

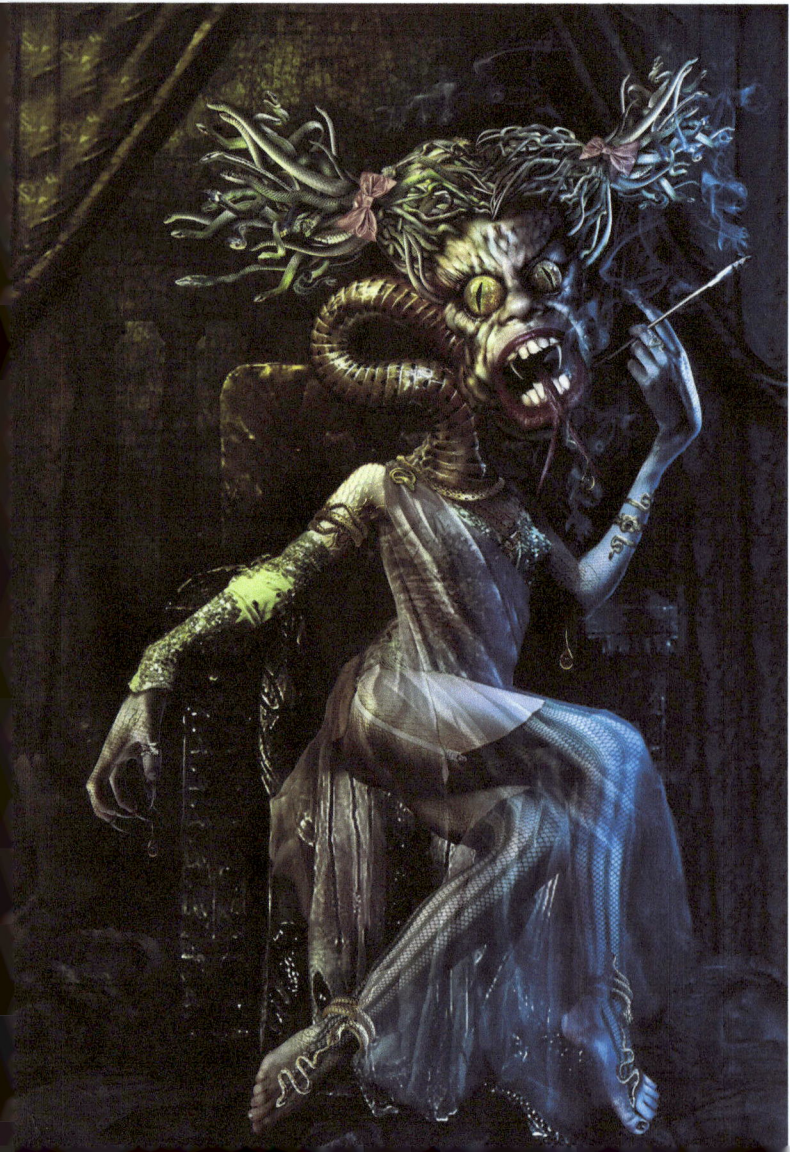

ABOVE LEFT
ONA LOOTS
Photomanipulation (South Africa)
Credit: sxc.hu, iStockphoto
Medusa

ABOVE
MADAMETHENADIER
Photoshop (The Netherlands)
Awakening

LEFT
HOWARD VAUSE
Photoshop (England)
Gorgon

OPPOSITE

VINCENT LEFEVRE
Photoshop (France)
baby dino

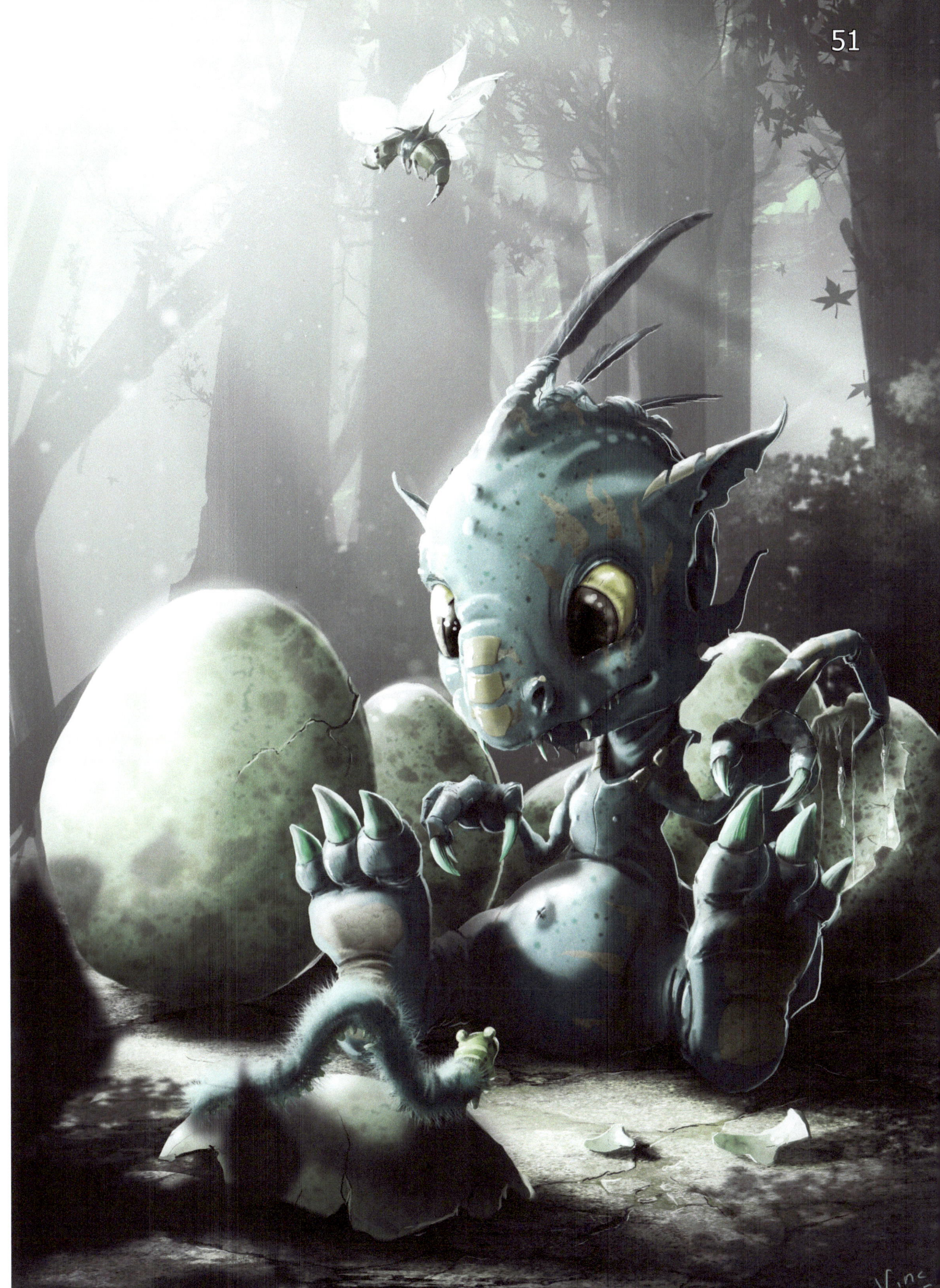

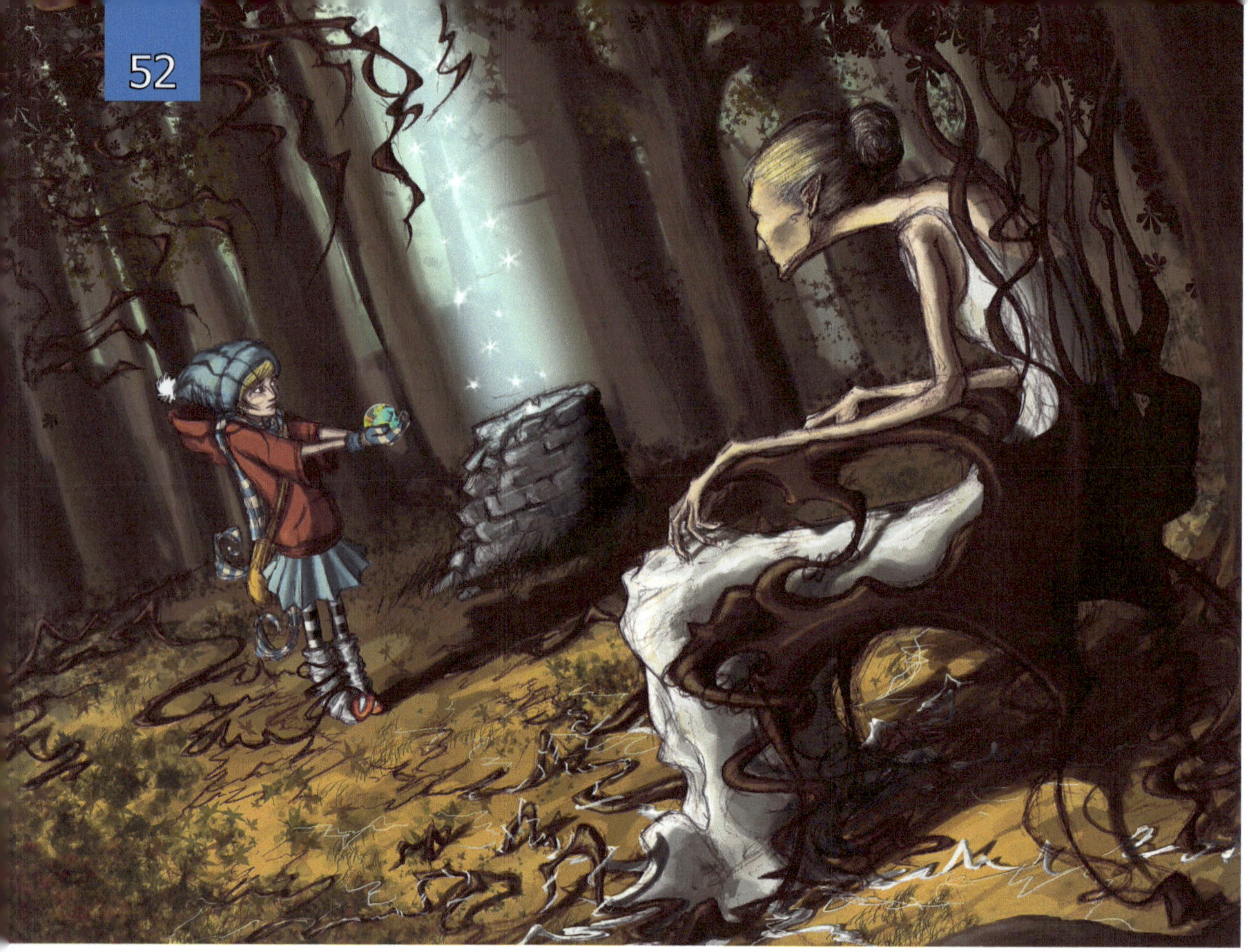

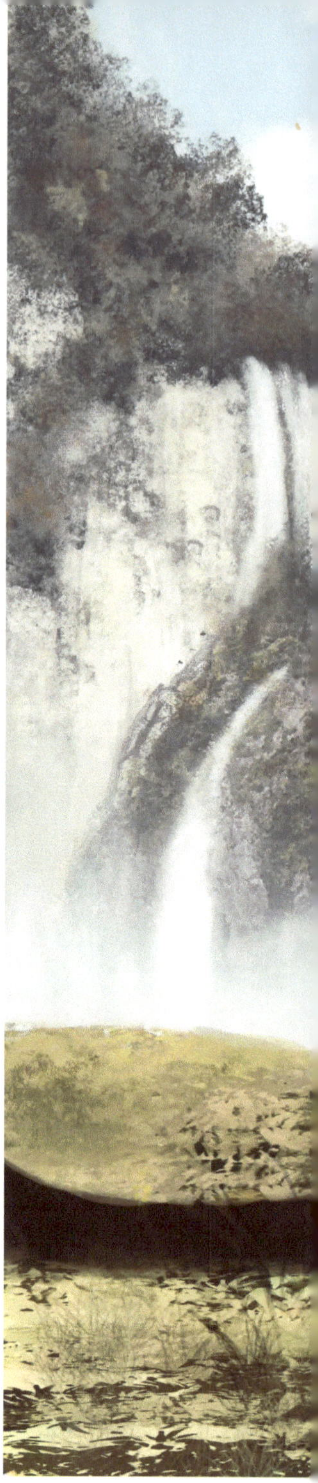

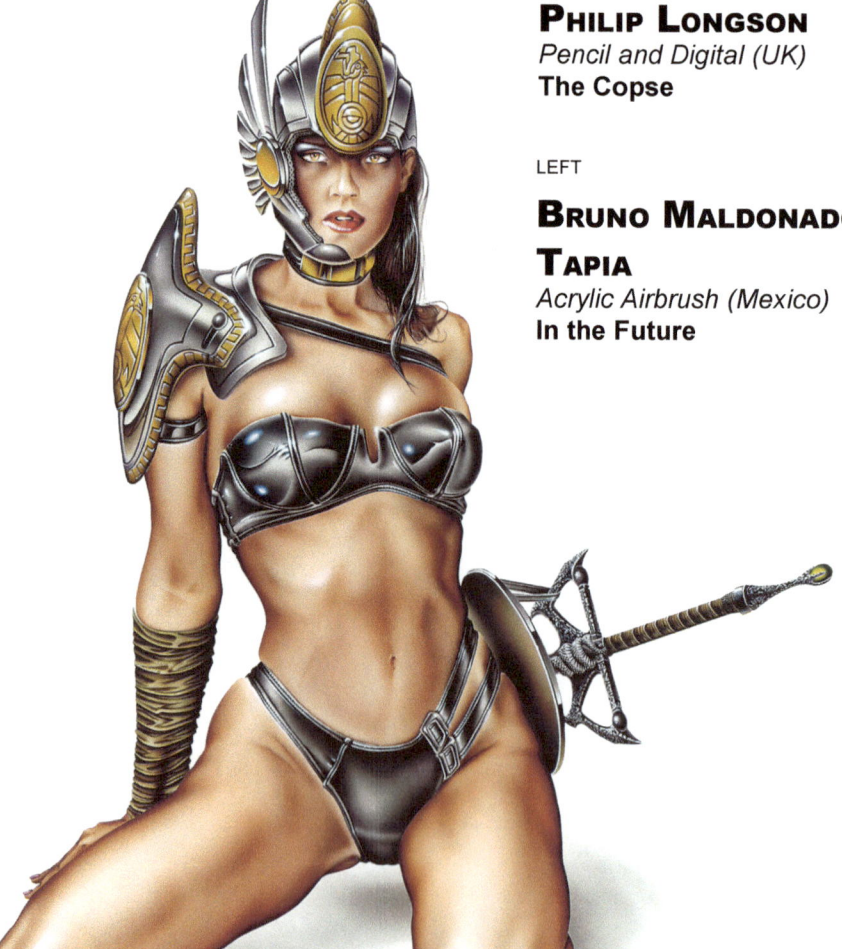

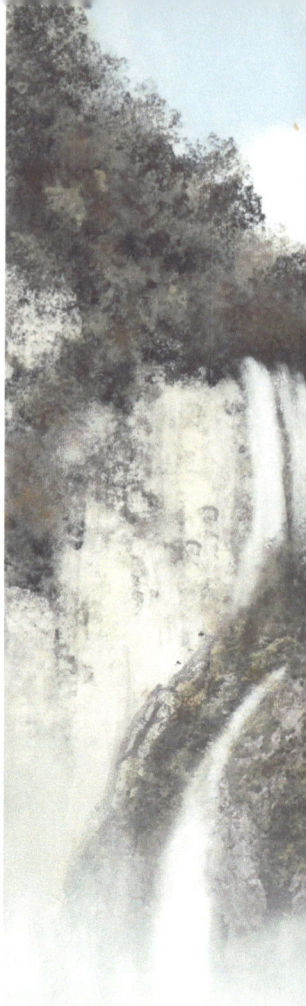

ABOVE

PHILIP LONGSON
Pencil and Digital (UK)
The Copse

LEFT

BRUNO MALDONADO TAPIA
Acrylic Airbrush (Mexico)
In the Future

OPPOSITE TOP

IMMAR PALOMERA
Photoshop (USA)
Beauty and Beast

OPPOSITE RIGHT

ANDREA GATTI
Photoshop (Italy)
InTheClouds

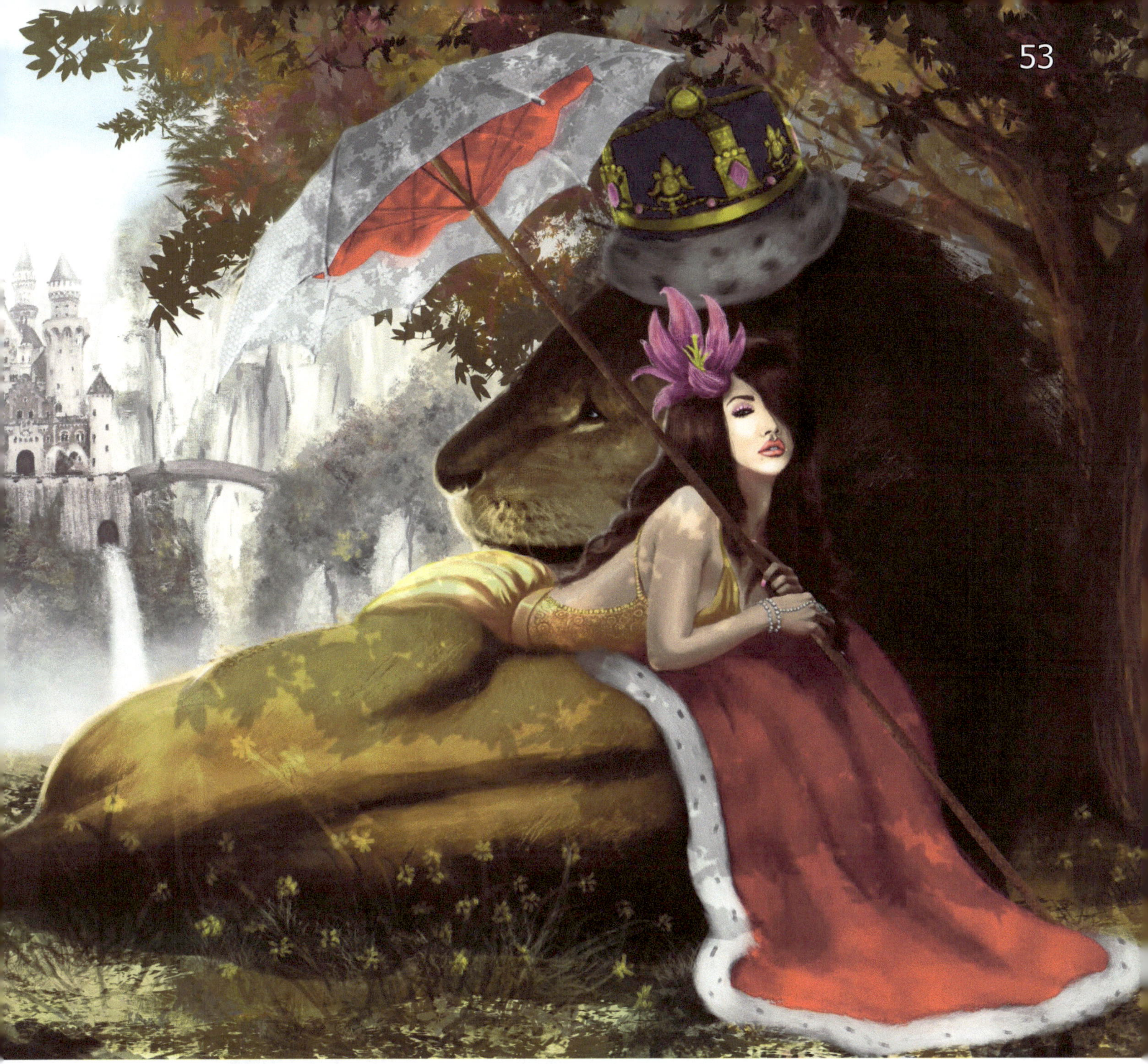

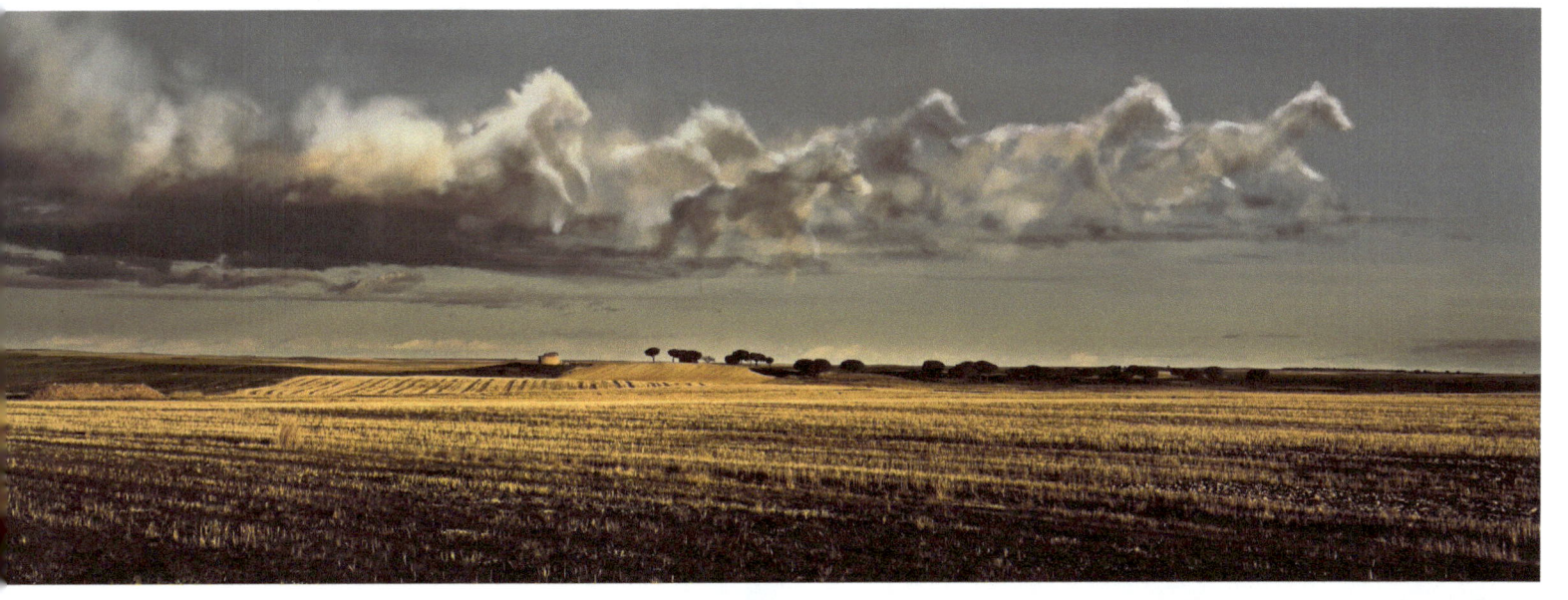

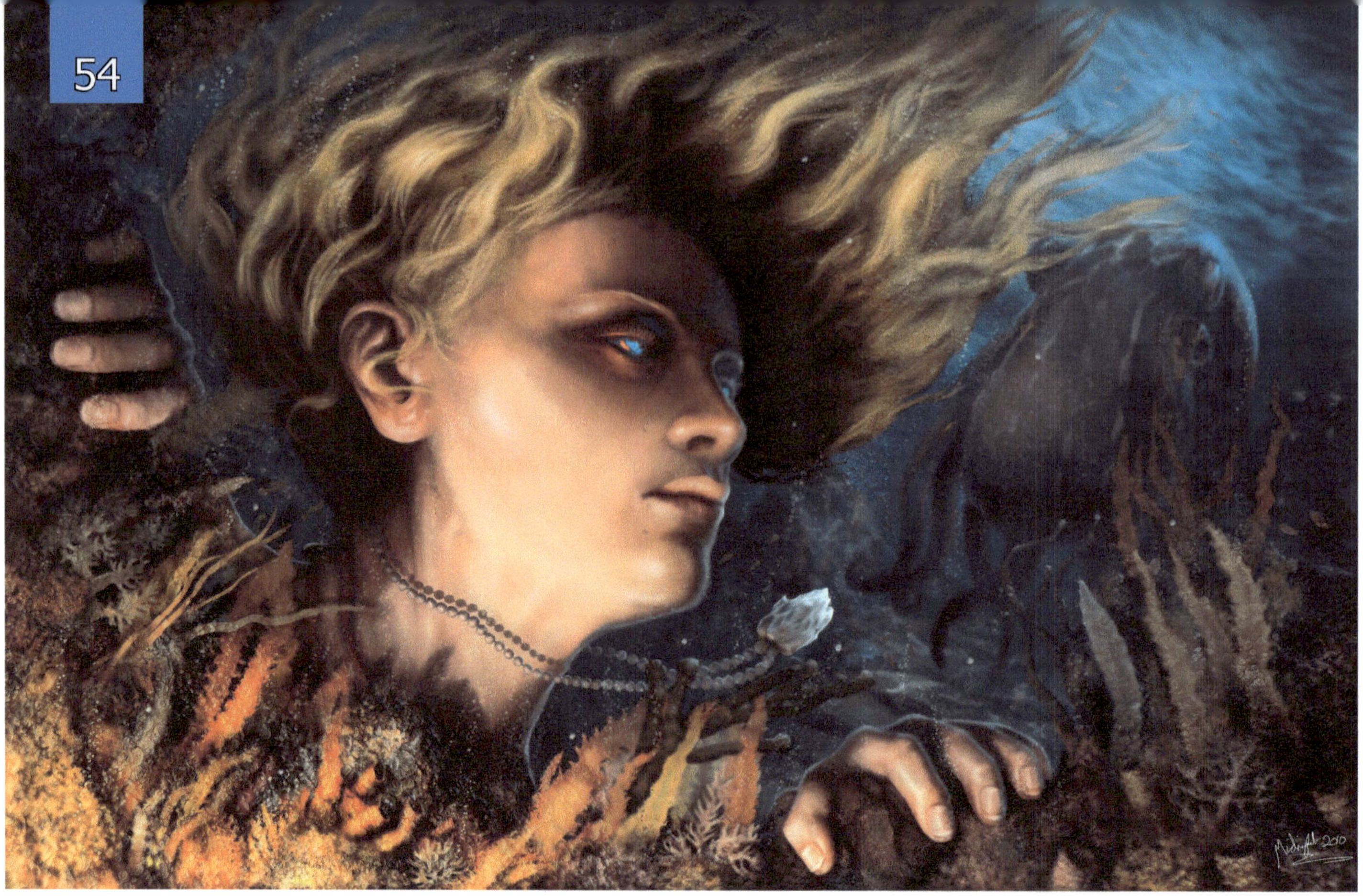

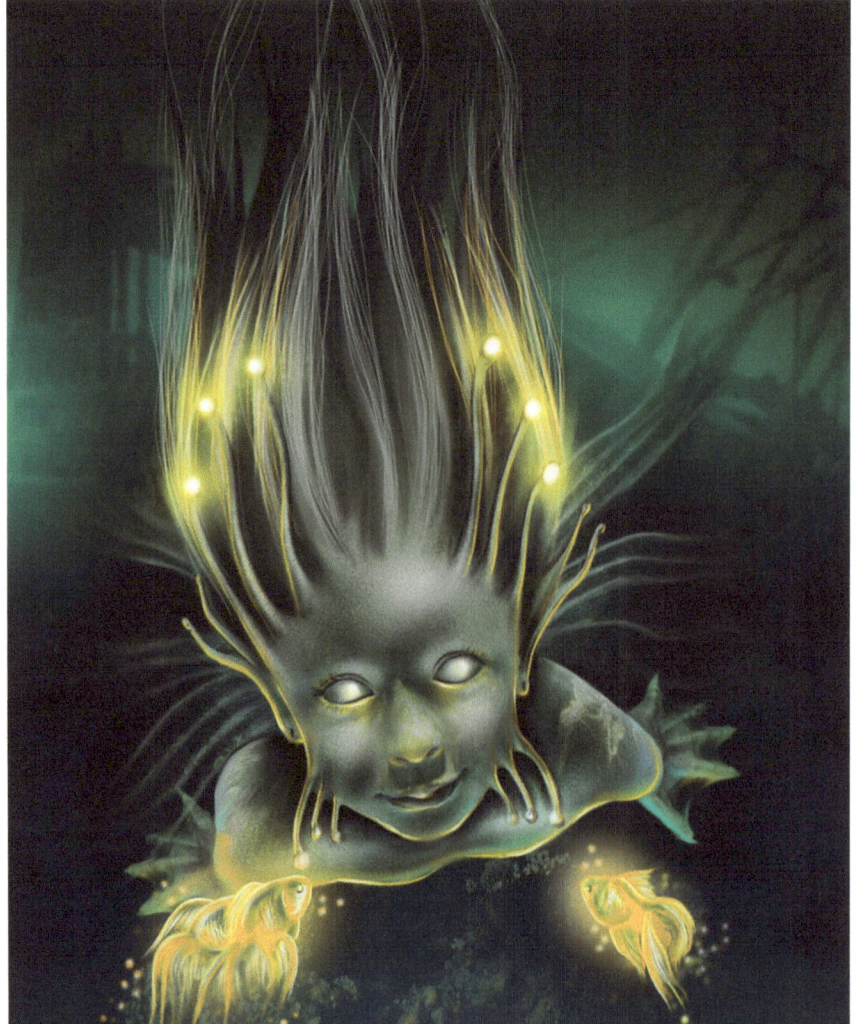

ABOVE

SAM MANLEY
Photoshop (England)
Glow

LEFT

MADAME THENADIER
Photoshop (The Netherlands)
Water Creature

OPPOSITE TOP

KURT WILLIAMS
Digital (USA)
The Devil's Mermaid

OPPOSITE NEAR RIGHT

YANGTIAN LI
Photoshop (Australia)
Water Dragon Drojin

OPPOSITE BOTTOM RIGHT

EKO PUTEH HANDRIYANTO
Photoshop (Indonesia)
Treasure Keeper

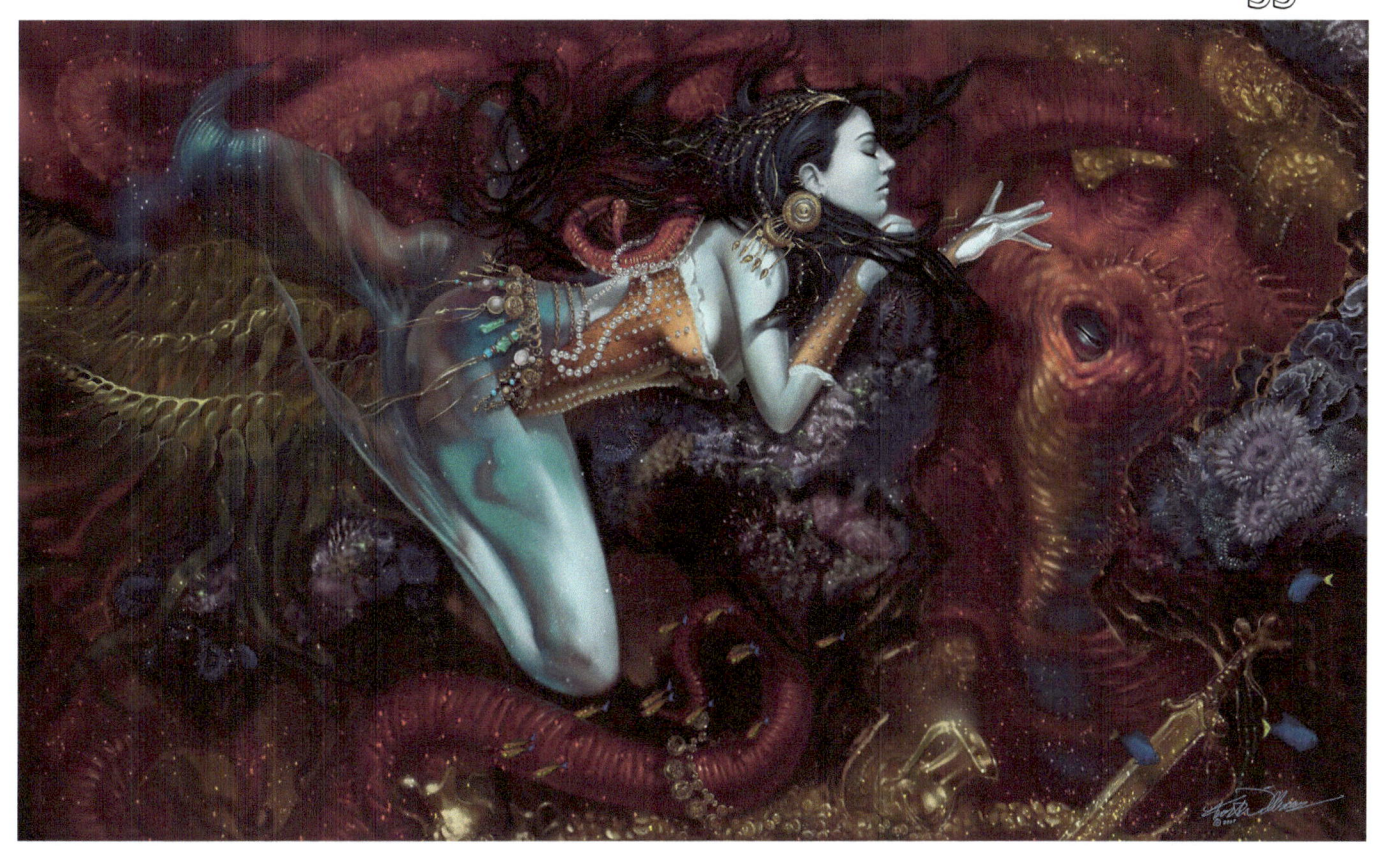

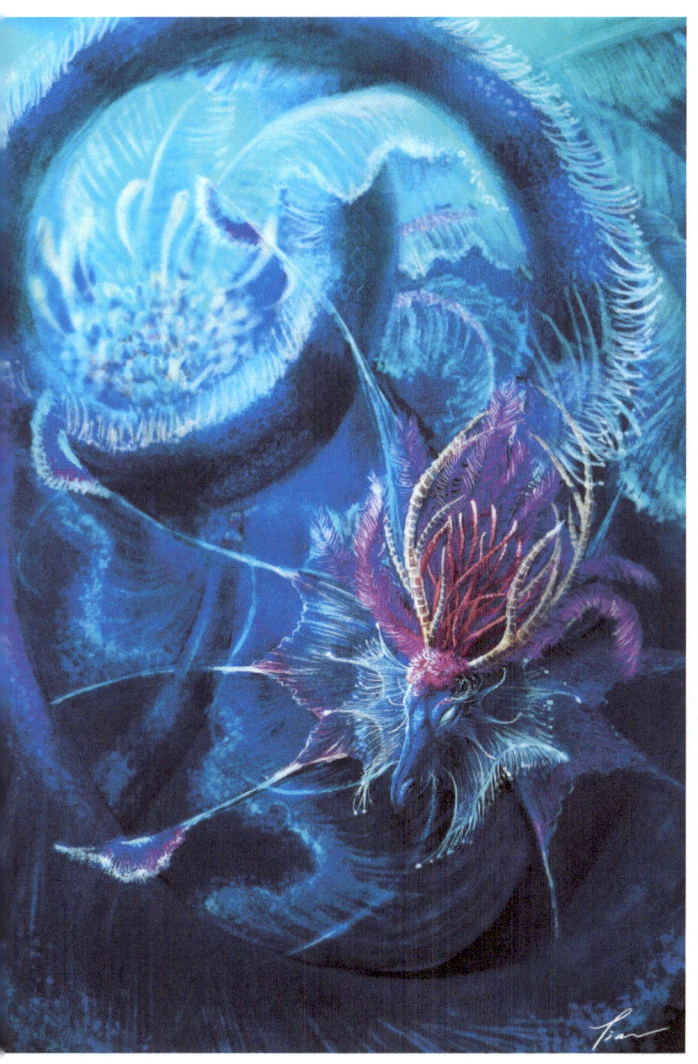

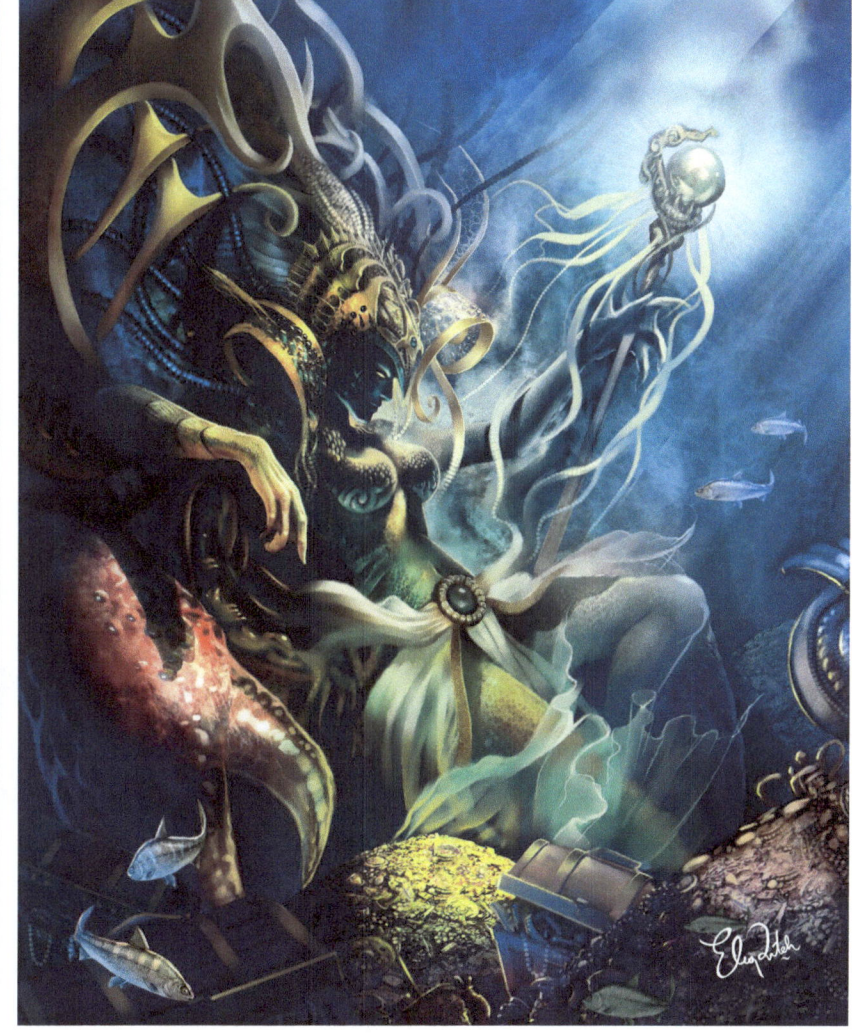

RIGHT
MALCOLM BROWN
Acrylic (England)
On Guard

BELOW LEFT
MALCOLM BROWN
Acrylic (England)
Nobody Told the Dodo

BELOW RIGHT
MALCOLM BROWN
Acrylic (England)
Winter

OPPOSITE
MALCOLM BROWN
Acrylic (England)
Mouse and Musician

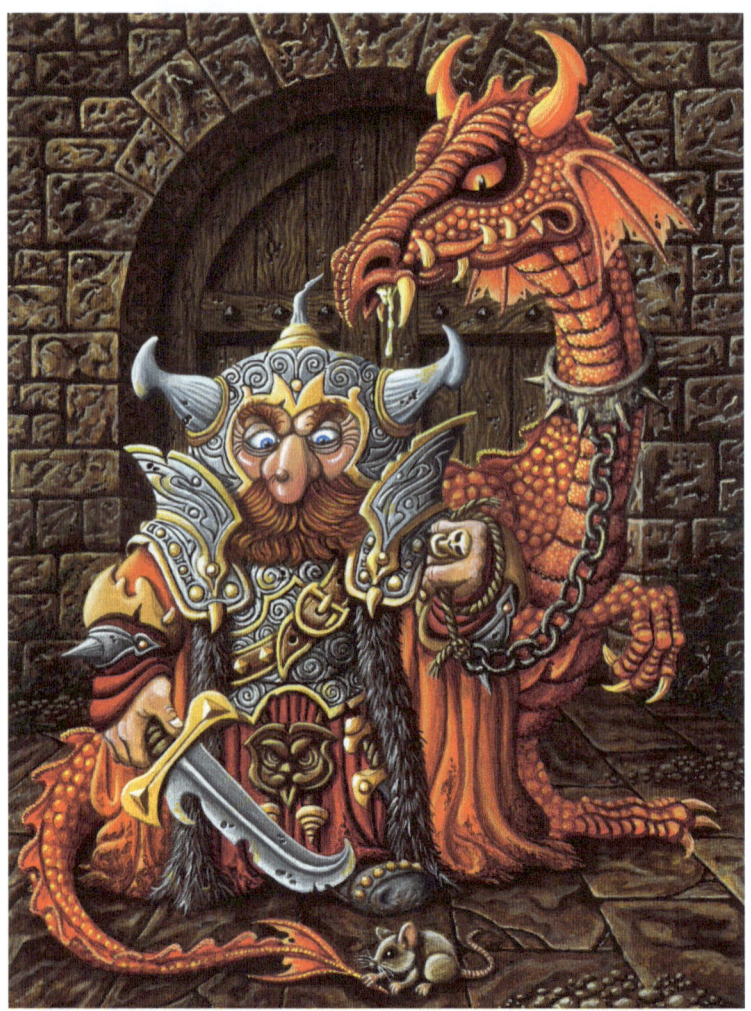

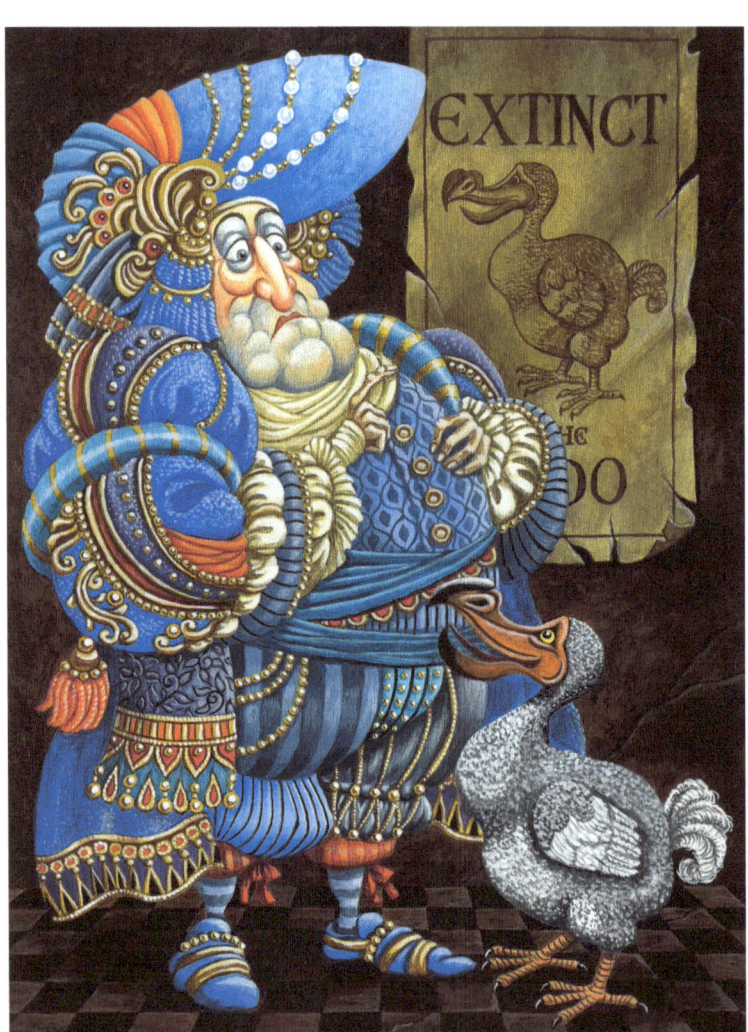

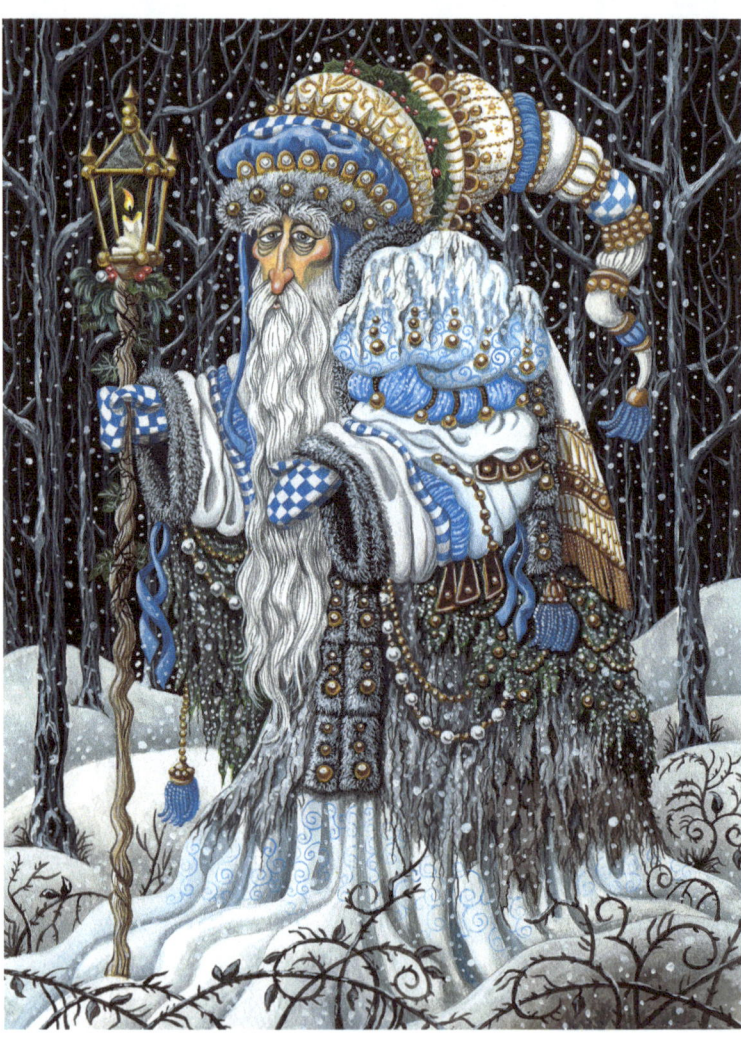

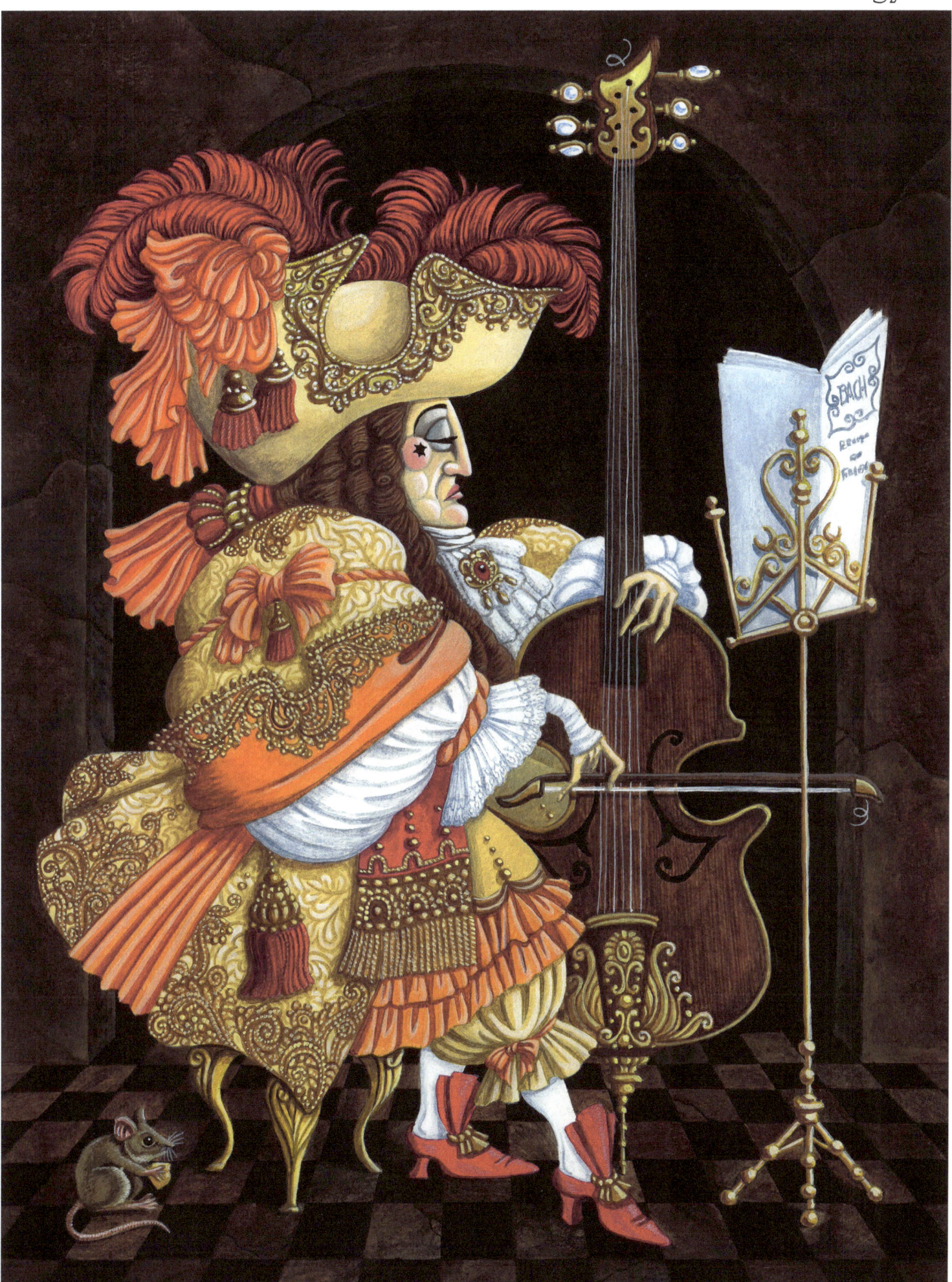

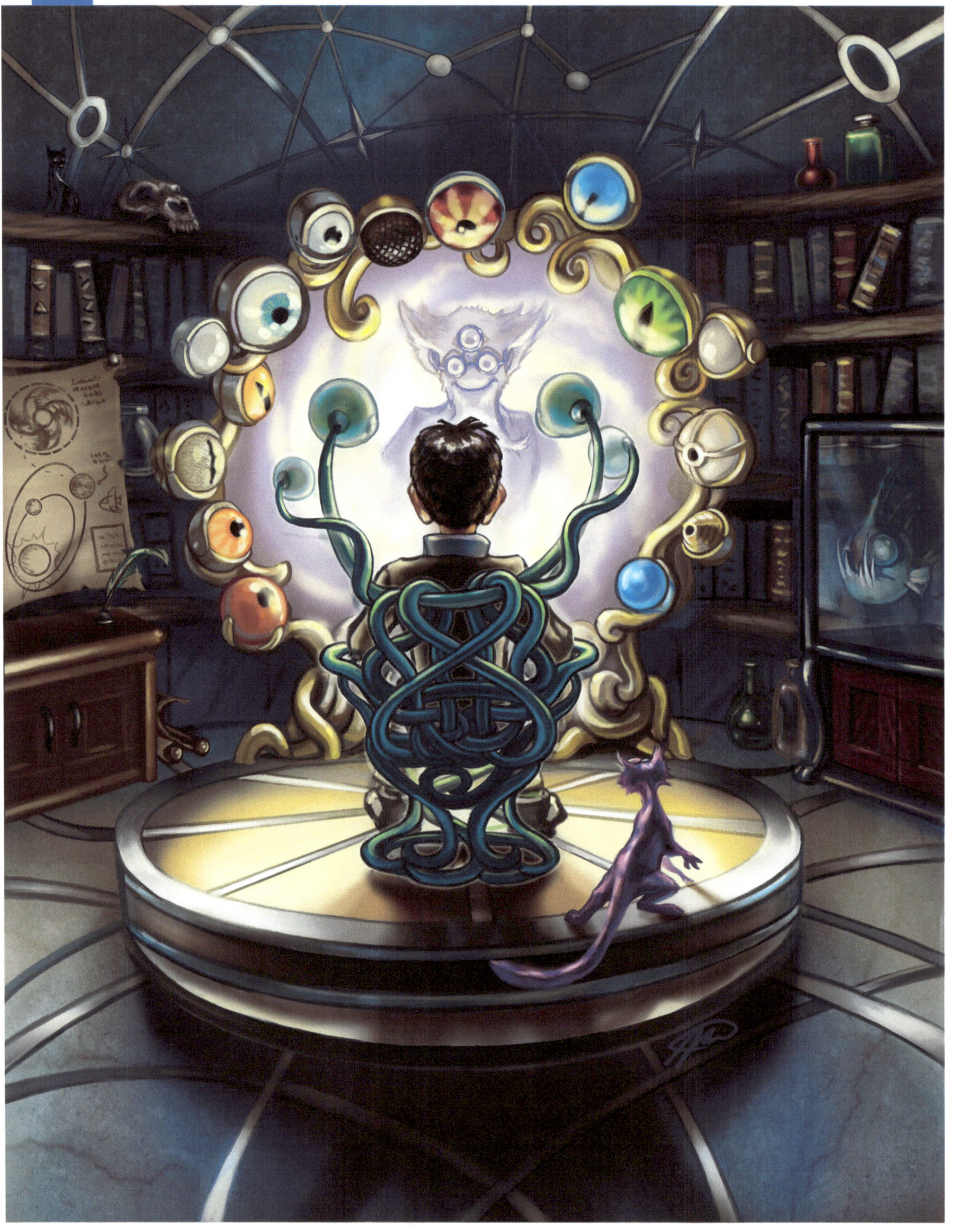

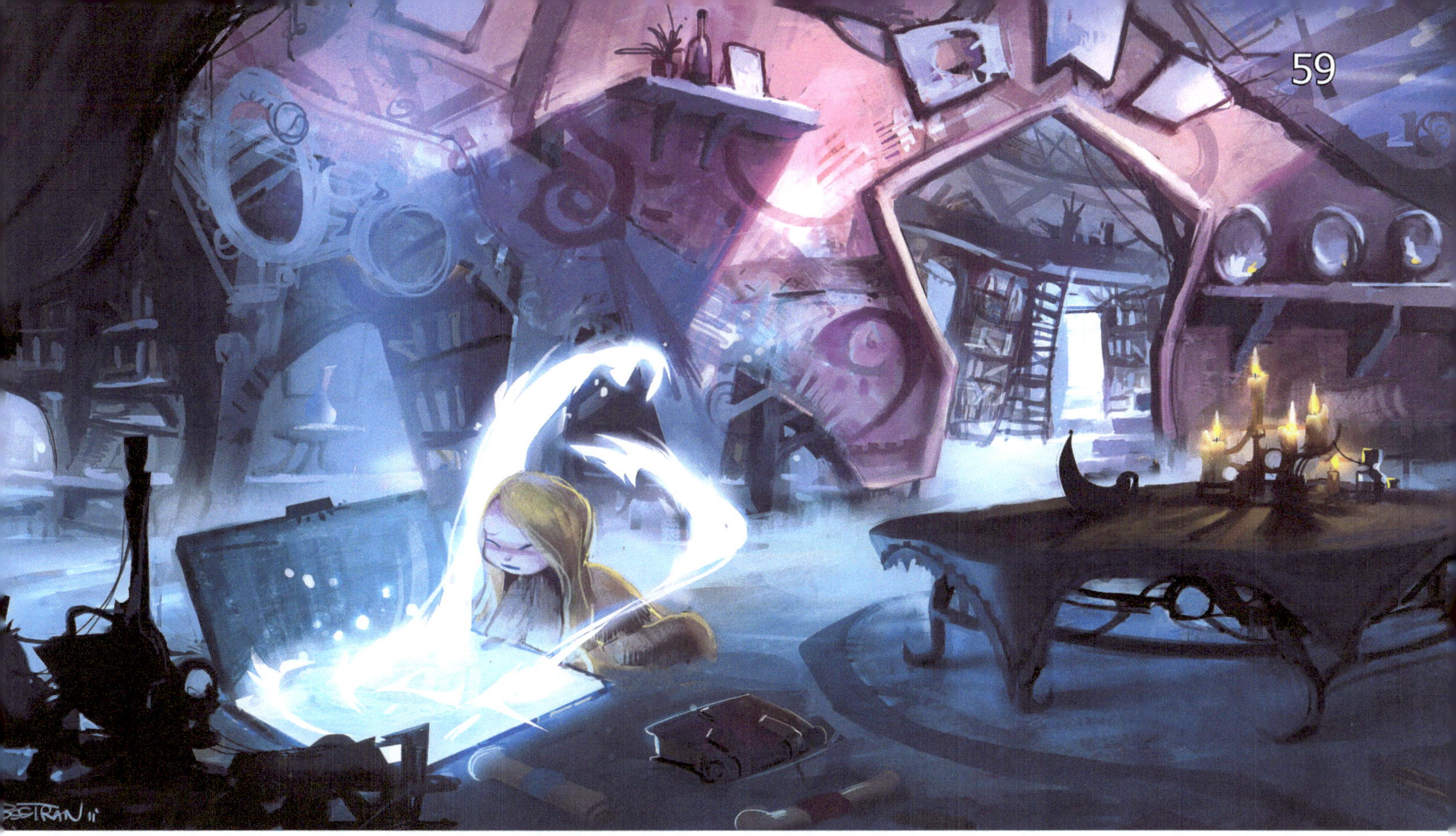

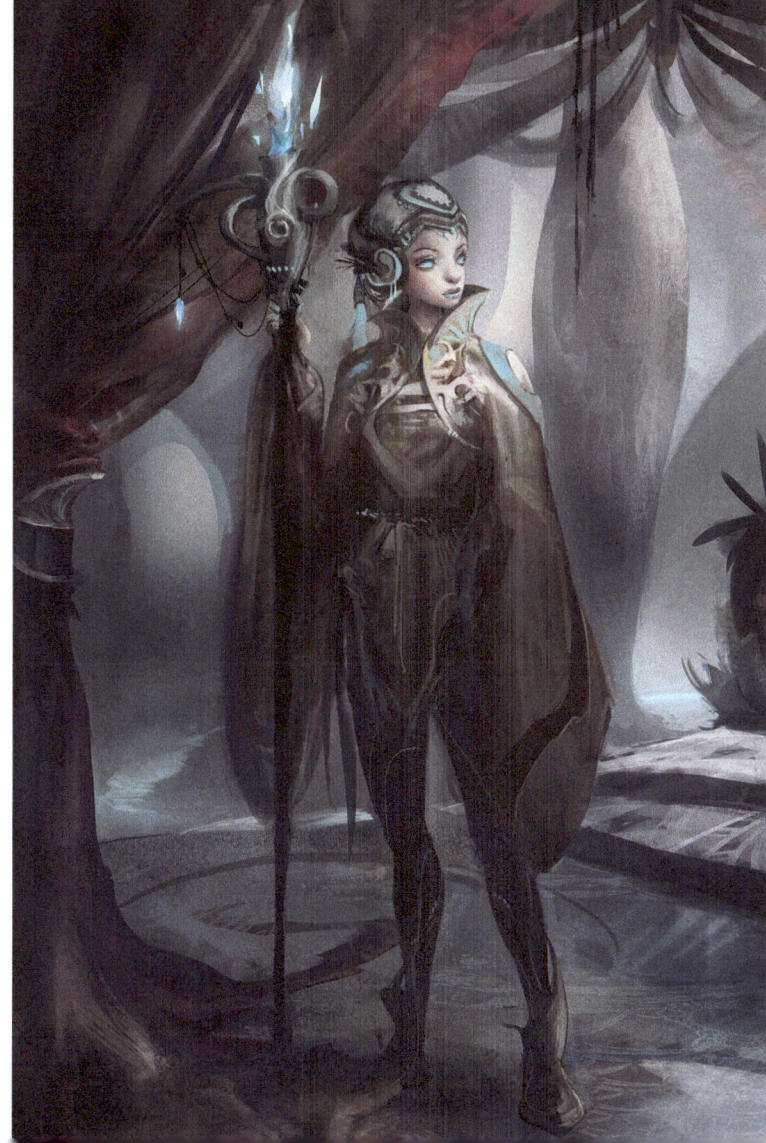

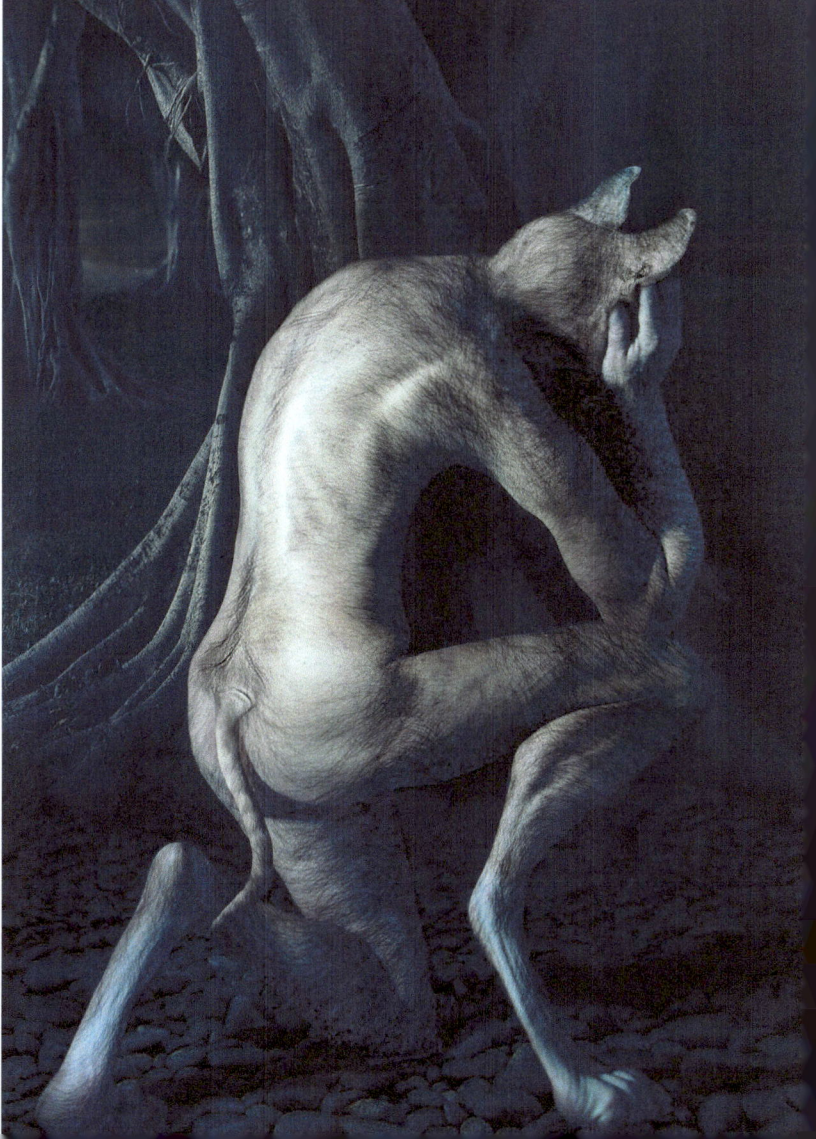

RIGHT

ROB REY
Oil (USA)
Close Call

BELOW

RAOUL VITALE
Oil on masonite (USA)
Treebeard

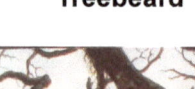

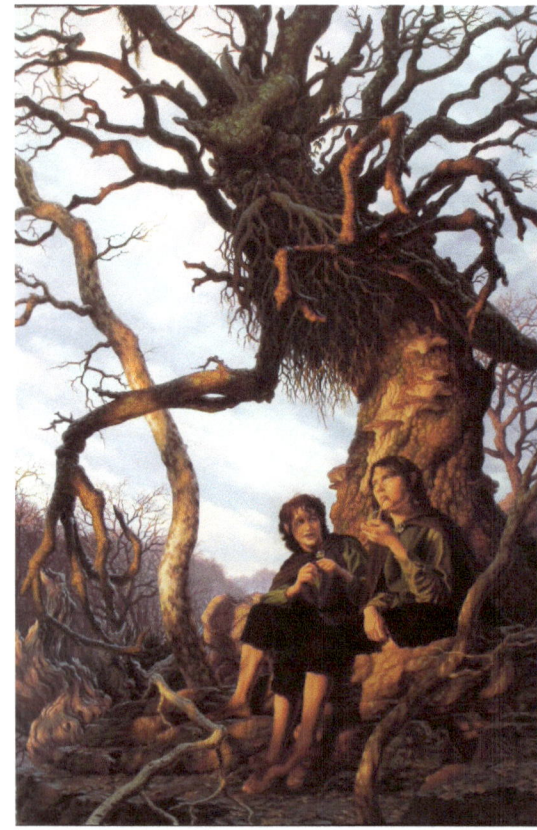

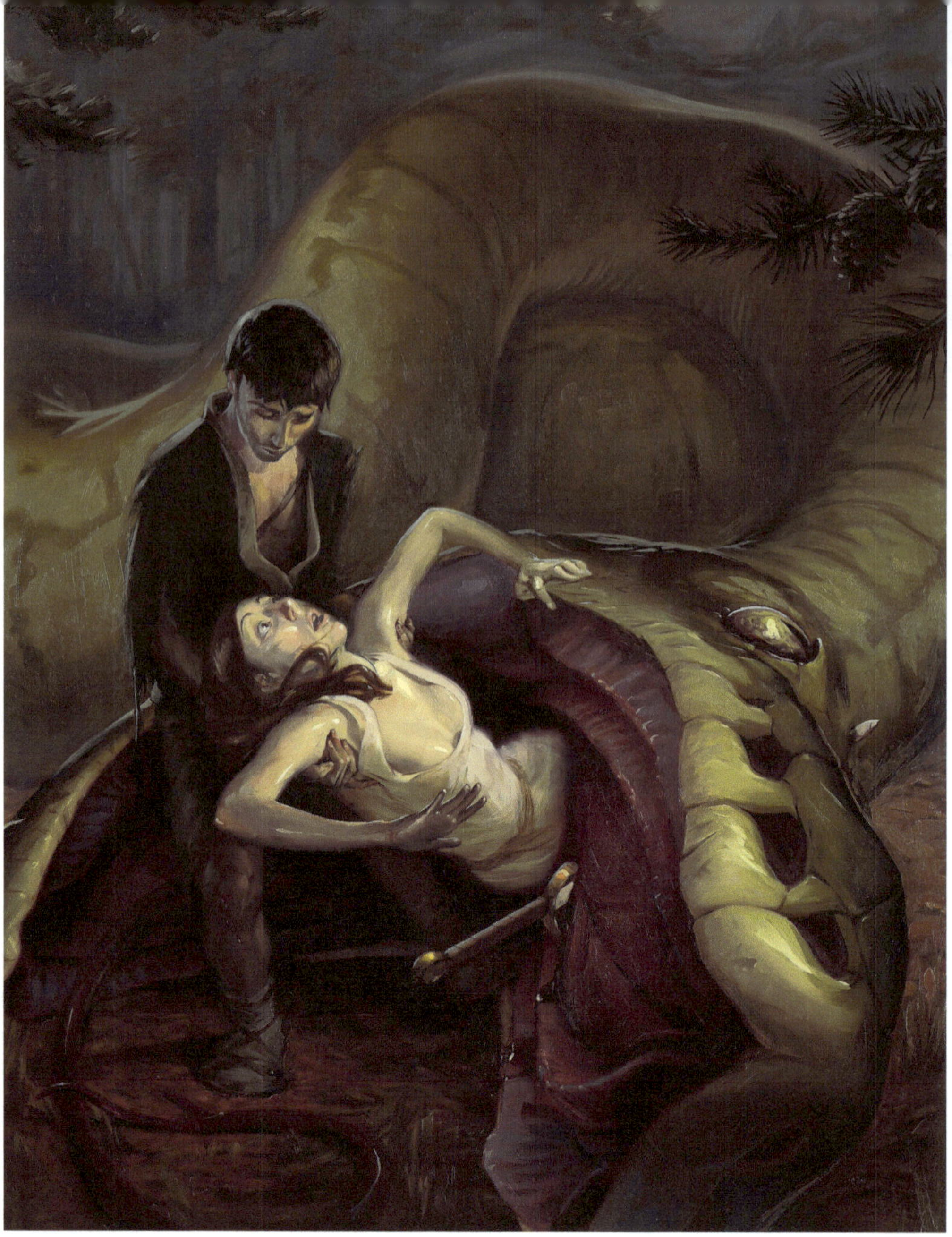

(Previous)

LEFT PAGE

JASON MARTIN
Digital (USA)
Seer's Glass

RIGHT PAGE TOP

ROSS TRAN
Digital (USA)
Mystery Door

RIGHT PAGE BOTTOM LEFT

ROSS TRAN
Digital (USA)
Looking Important

RIGHT PAGE BOTTOM RIGHT

ONA LOOTS
Photomanipulation (South Africa)
Credit: Lee Penrod, sxc.hu
Transformation

(Overleaf)

LEFT PAGE TOP LEFT

CHANTELLE BASSON
Photoshop (South Africa)
Emimaf

LEFT PAGE TOP RIGHT

CHANTELLE BASSON
Photoshop (South Africa)
Adomant

LEFT PAGE BOTTOM

DARION LEIGH
Photoshop (UK)
Underwater Attack

RIGHT PAGE

LIIGA SMILSHKALNE
Corel Painter (Latvia)
Centaur

(Opposite)

OPPOSITE TOP LEFT

RUI FERREIRA
Photoshop (Portugal)
Summoning

OPPOSITE TOP RIGHT

MALCOLM BROWN
Photoshop (England)
Gryphon

OPPOSITE BOTTOM

IMMAR PALOMERA
Painter XI (USA)
Ye Rustic Inn

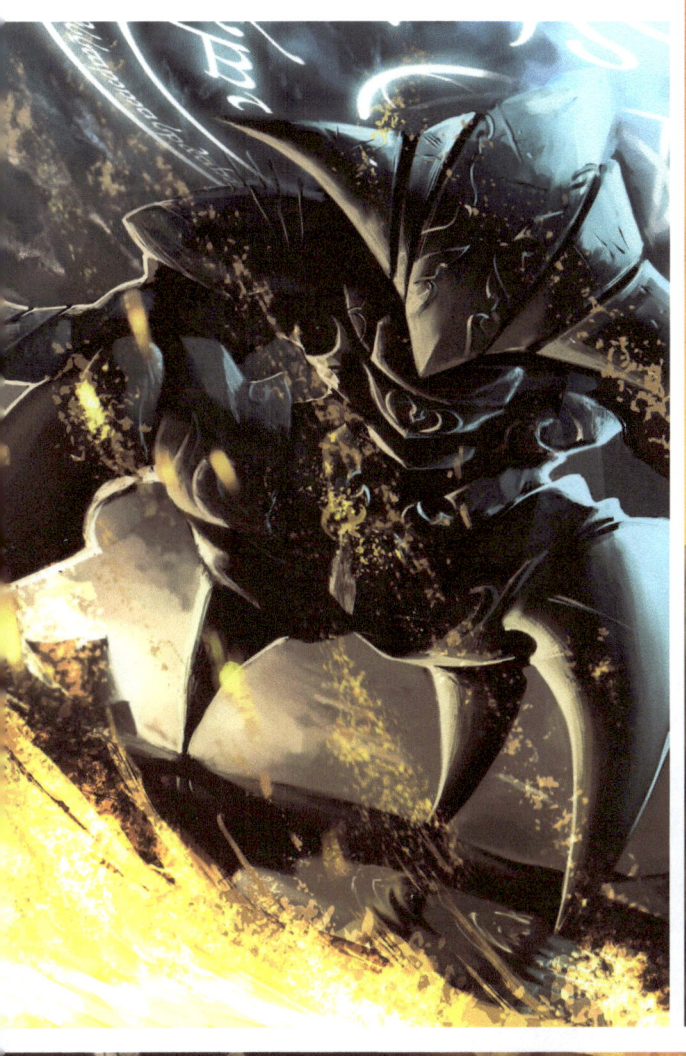

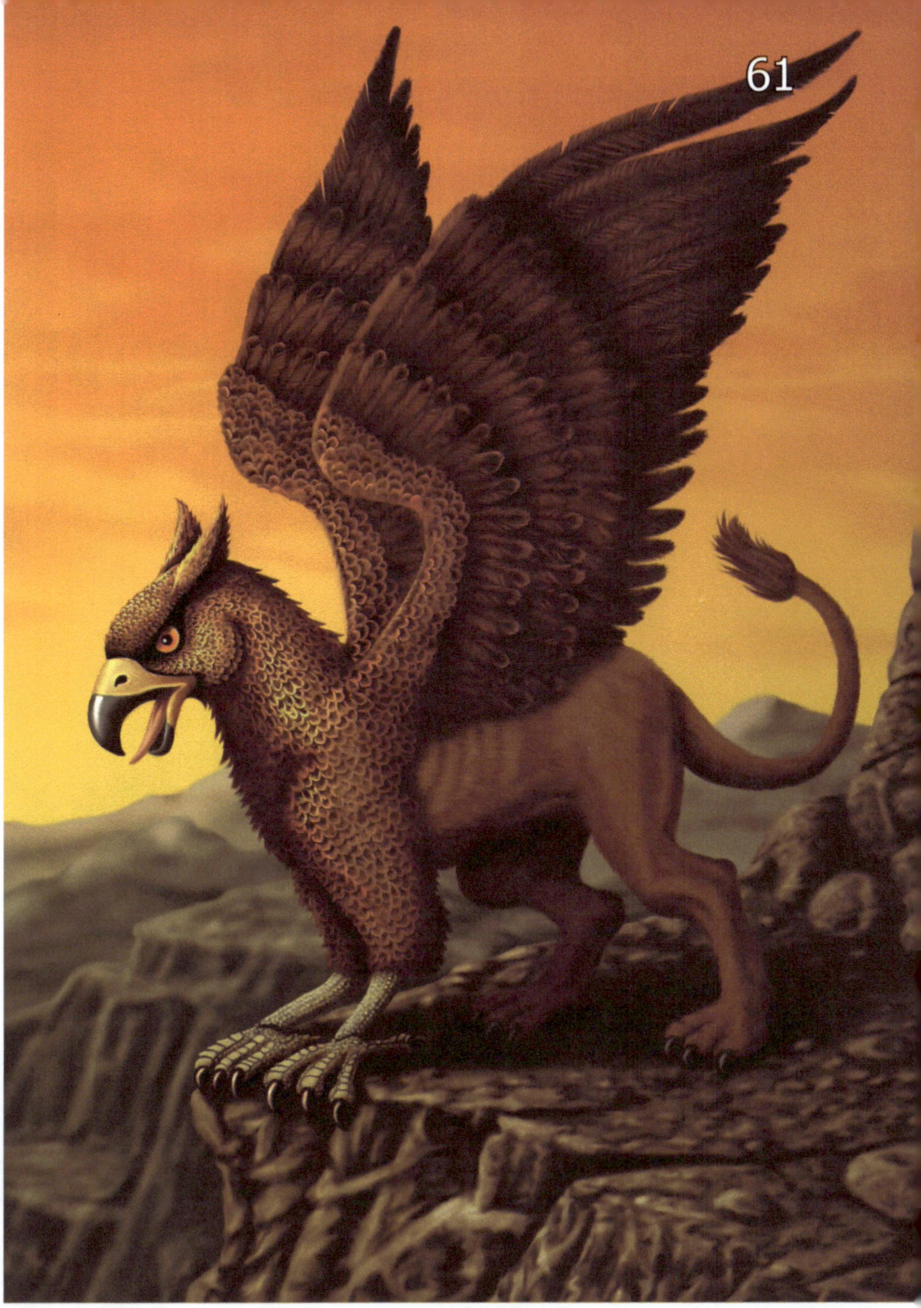

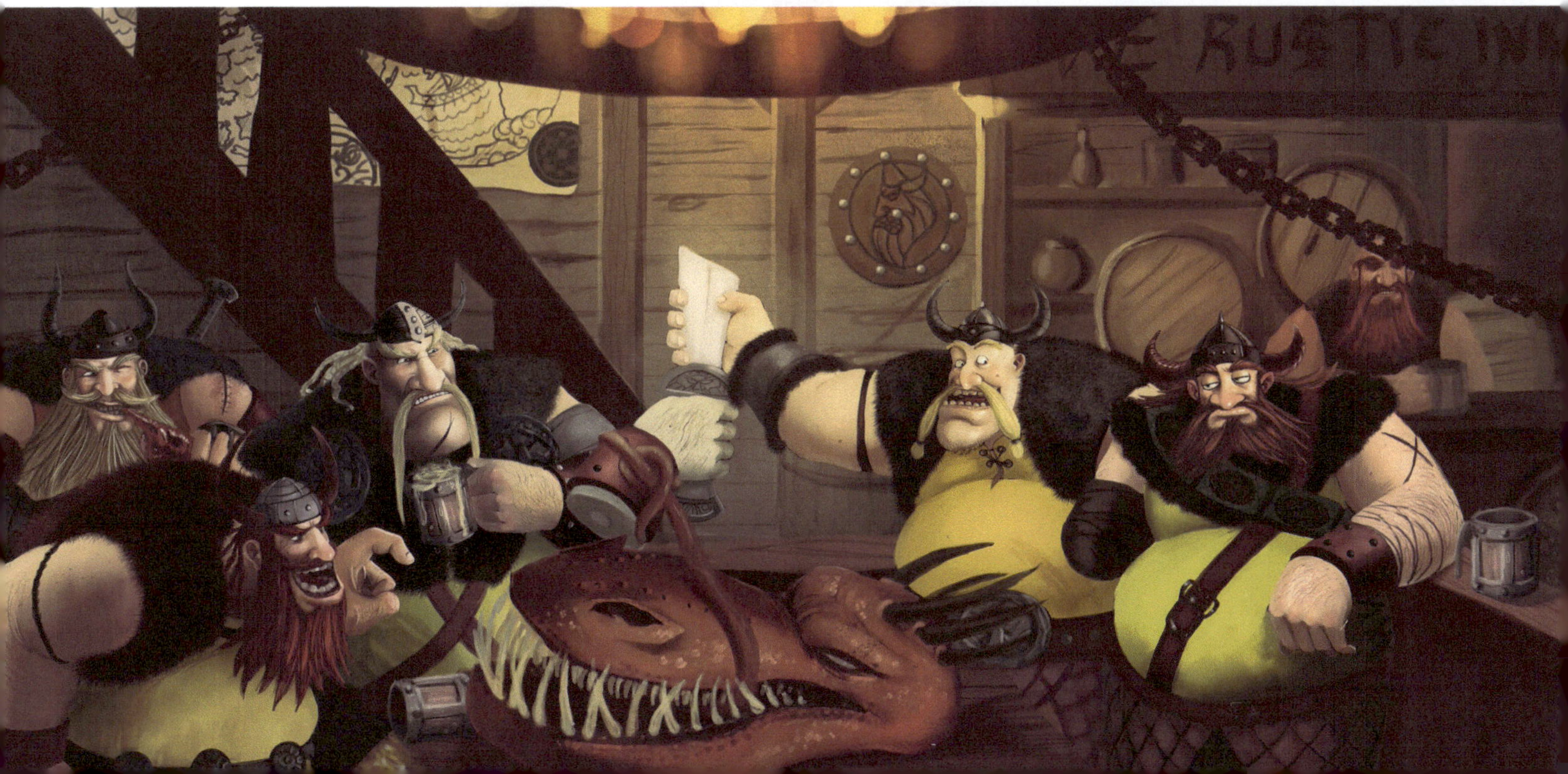

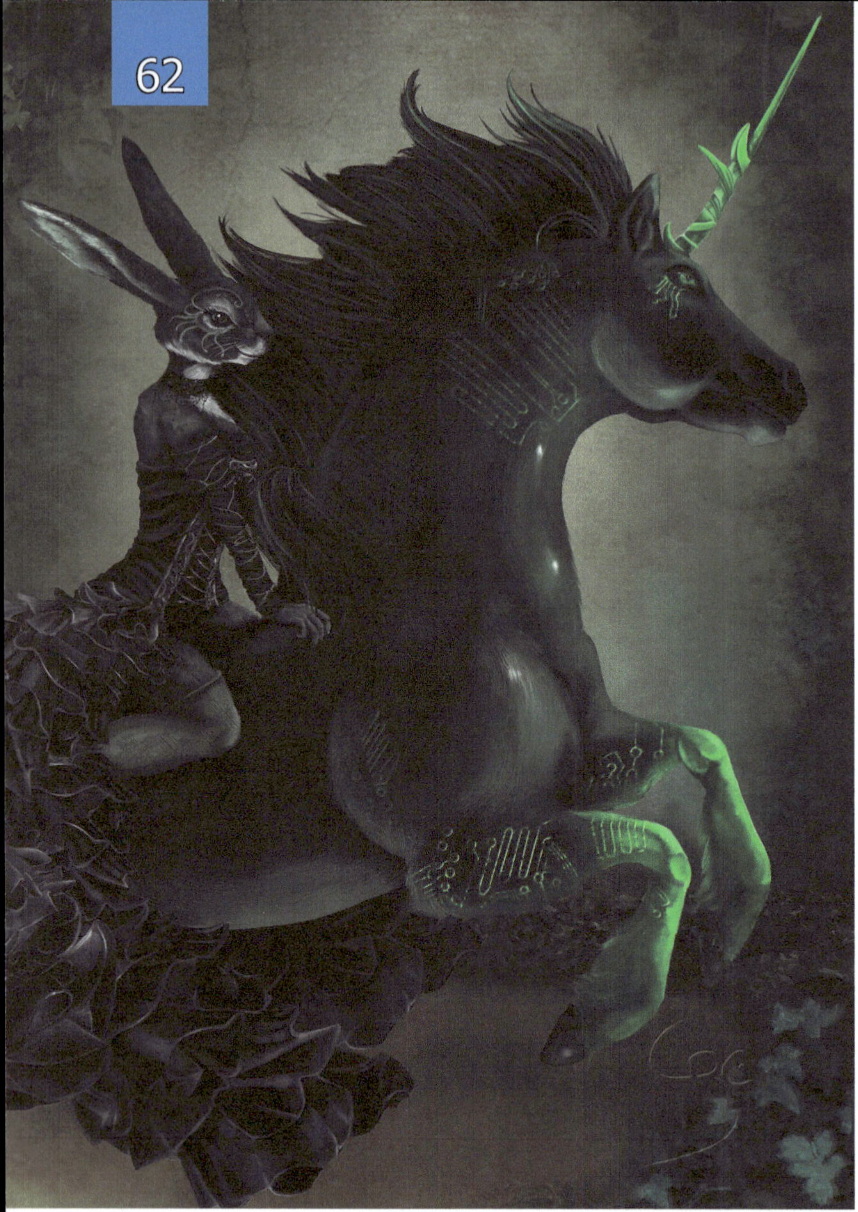

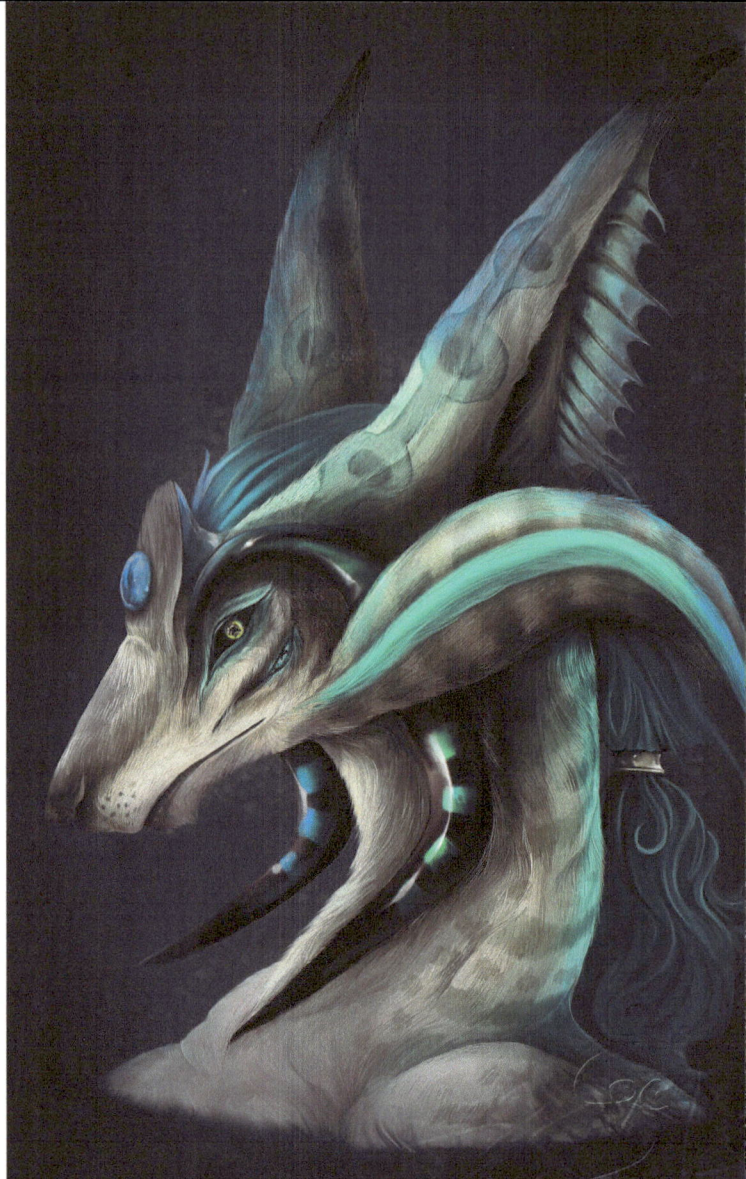

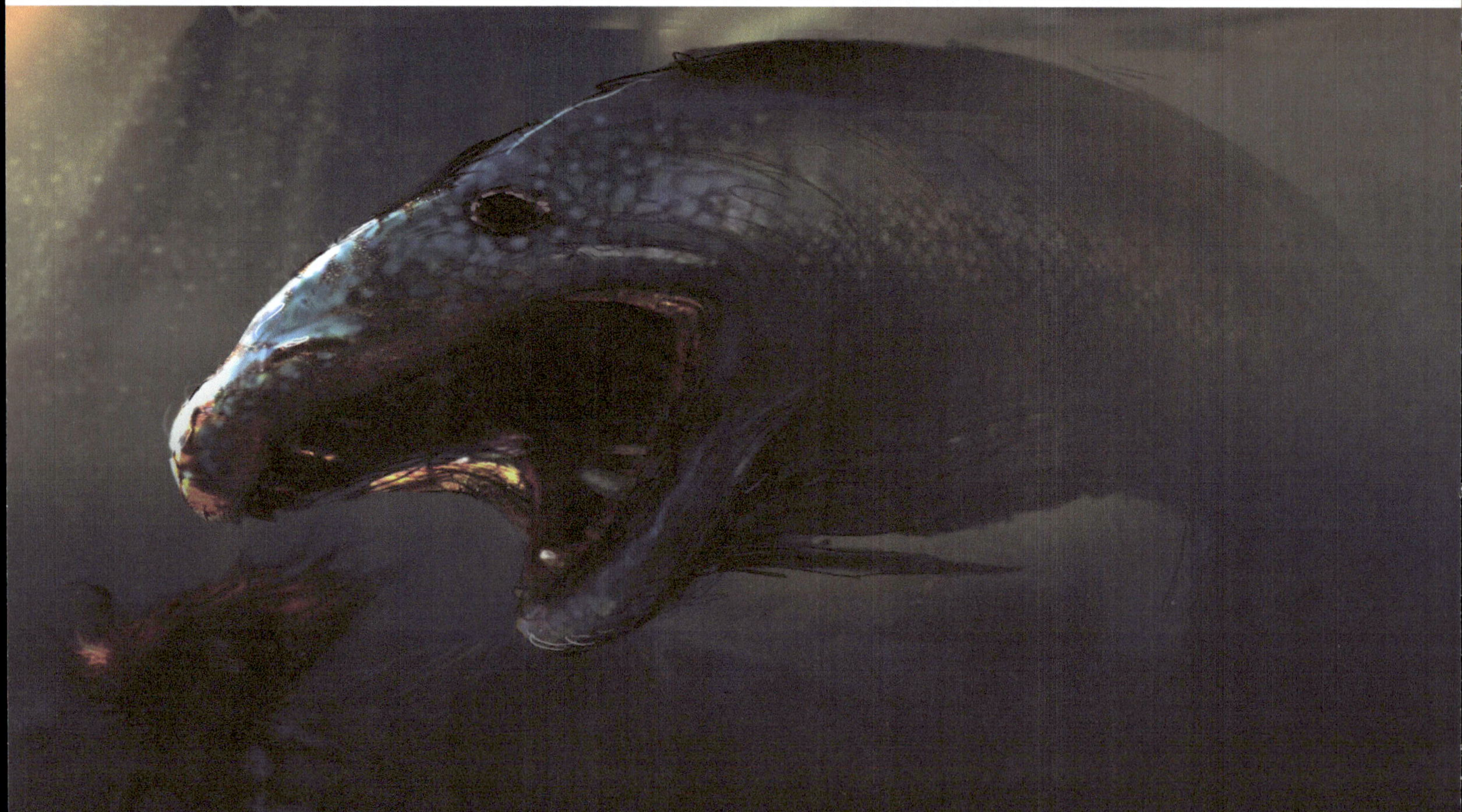

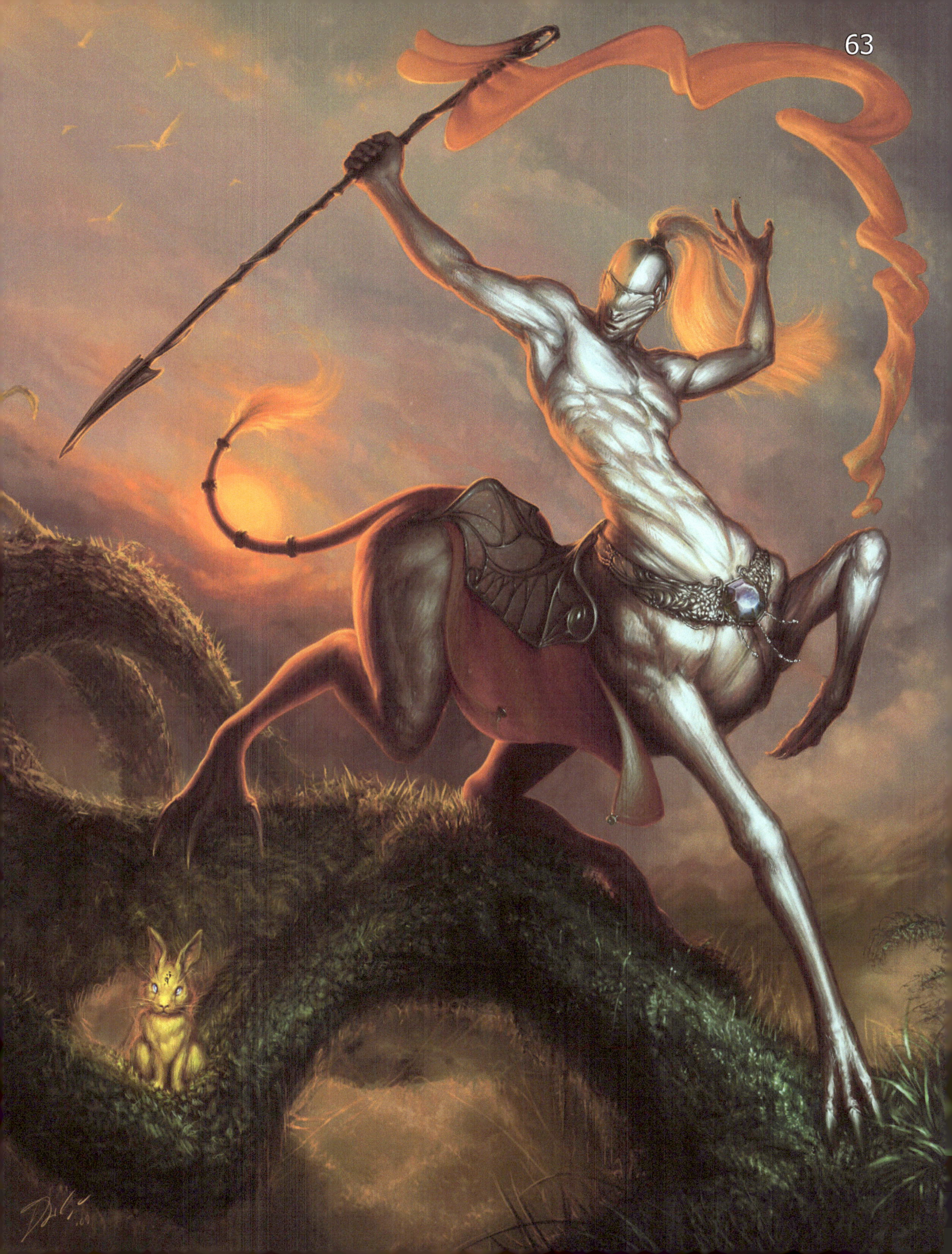

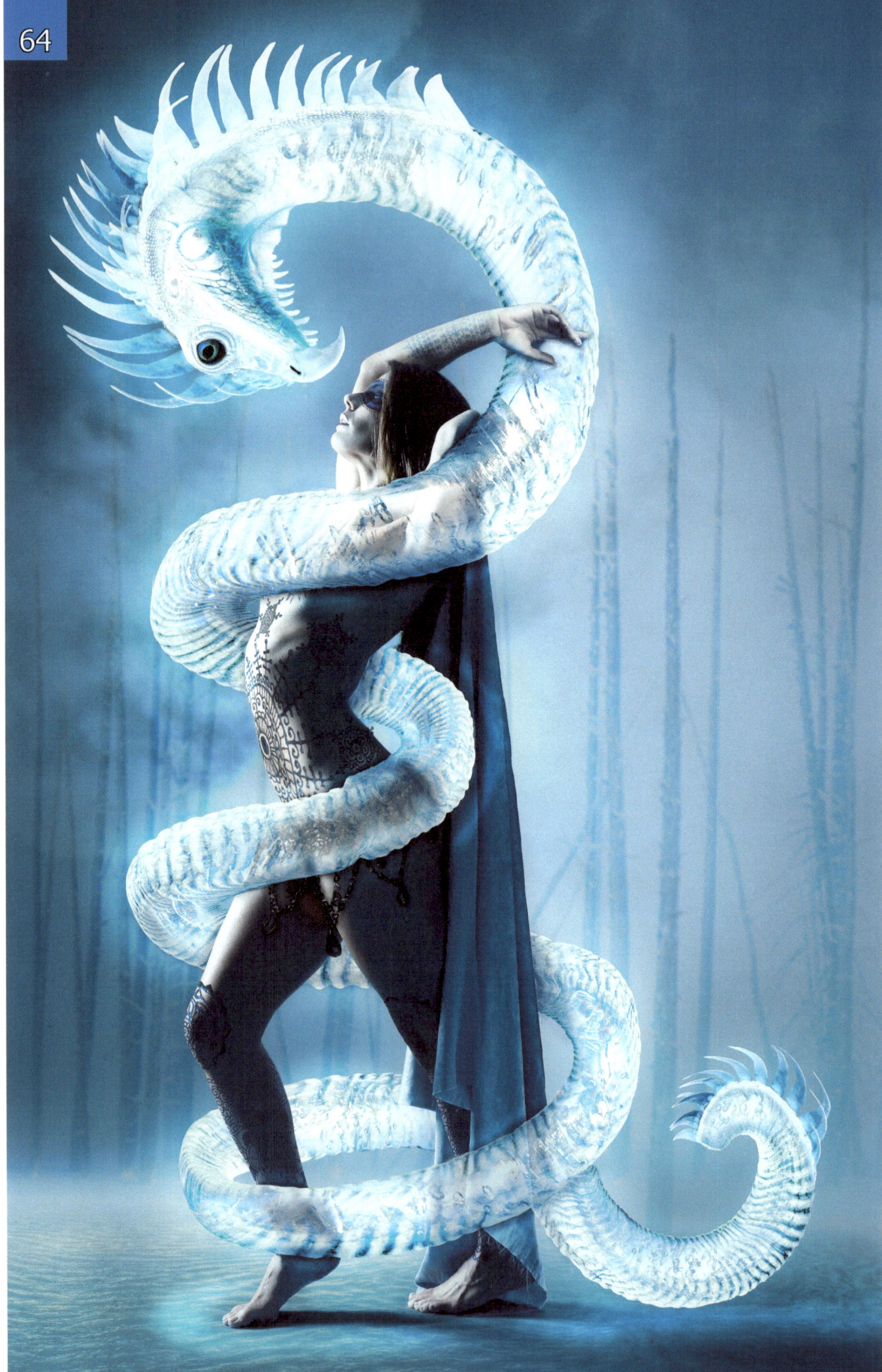

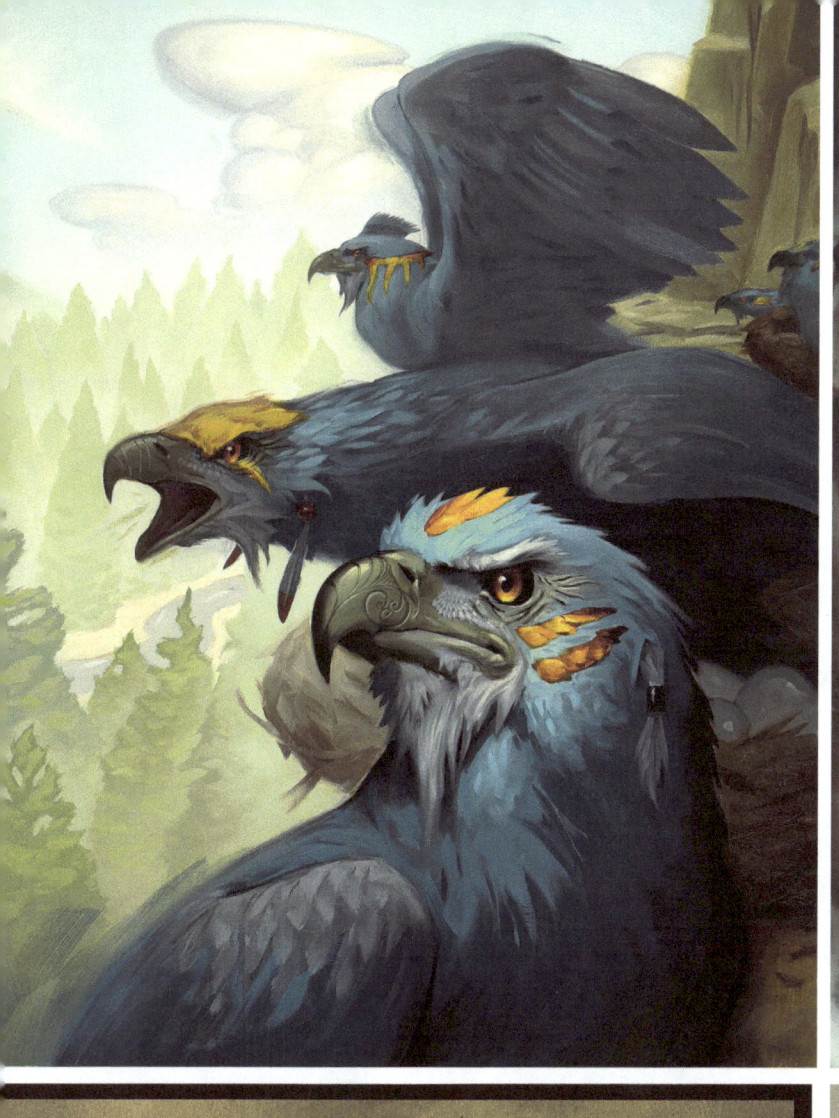

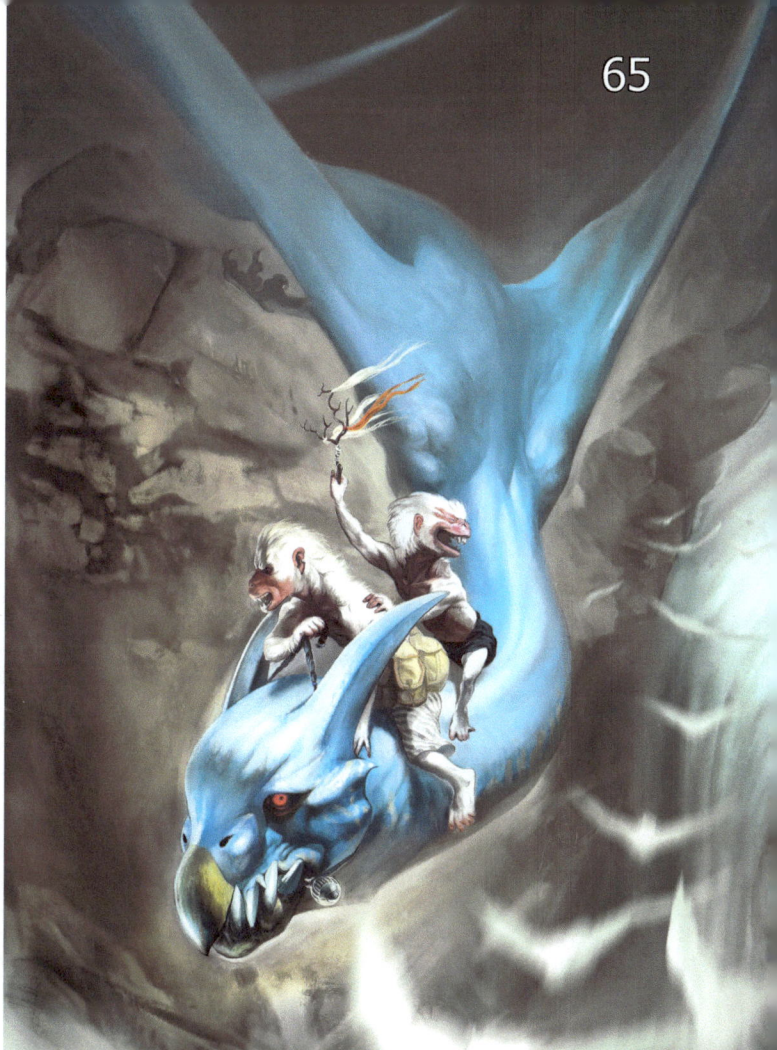

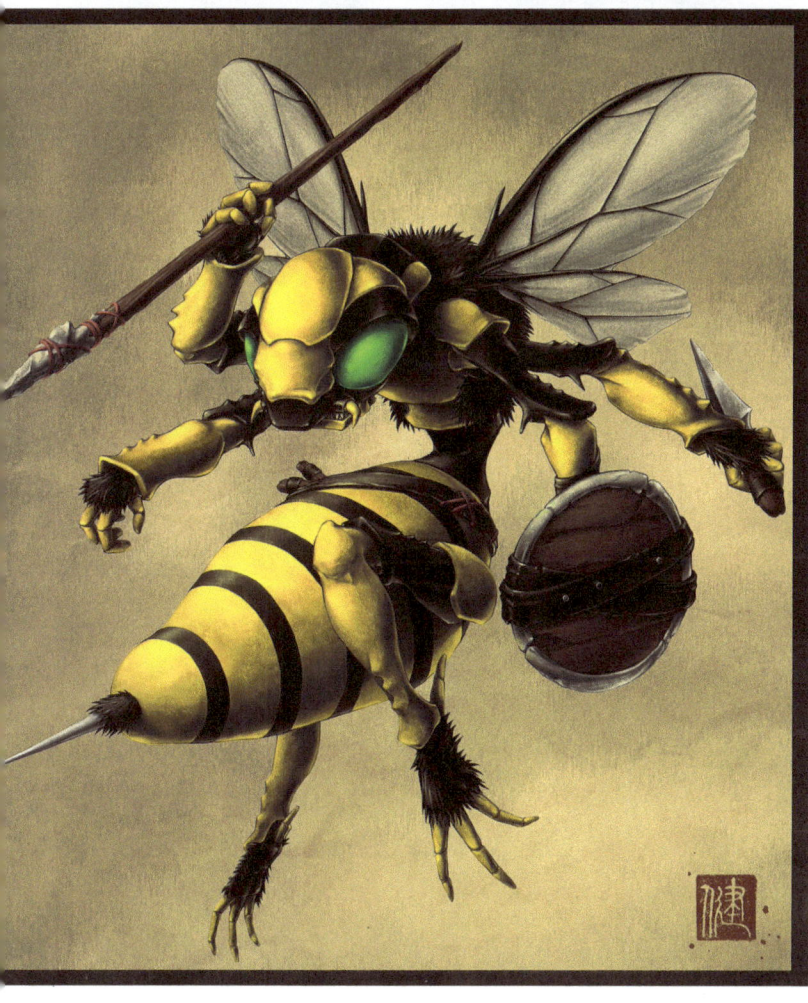

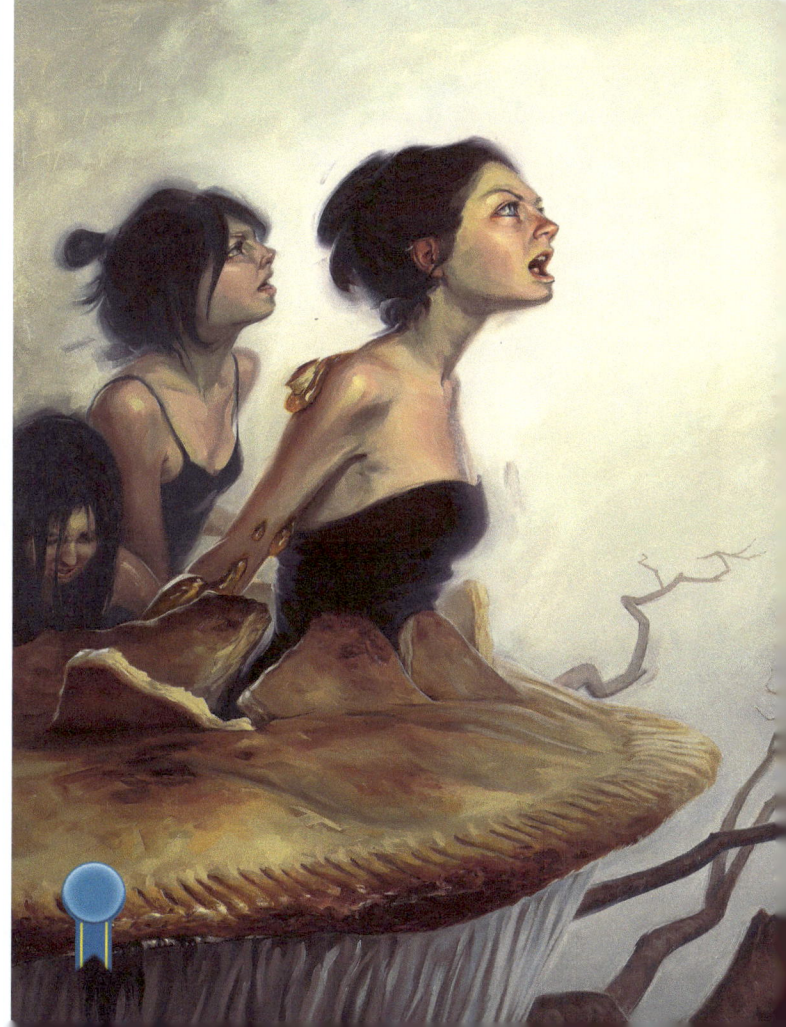

(Previous)

LEFT PAGE

ONA LOOTS
Photomanipulation (South Africa)
Credit: Marcus Ranum, sxc.hu
Elemental Magic

RIGHT PAGE TOP LEFT

ROB REY
Oil (USA)
Eagle Tribe

RIGHT PAGE BOTTOM LEFT

JAMES NG
Pencil, Charcoal Photoshop
(Hong Kong/ Canada)
Angry Beee

RIGHT PAGE TOP RIGHT

YUKARI MASUIKE
Photoshop (Japan)
Dragonrider

RIGHT PAGE BOTTOM RIGHT

ROB REY
Oil (USA)
Four and Twenty

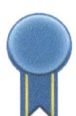

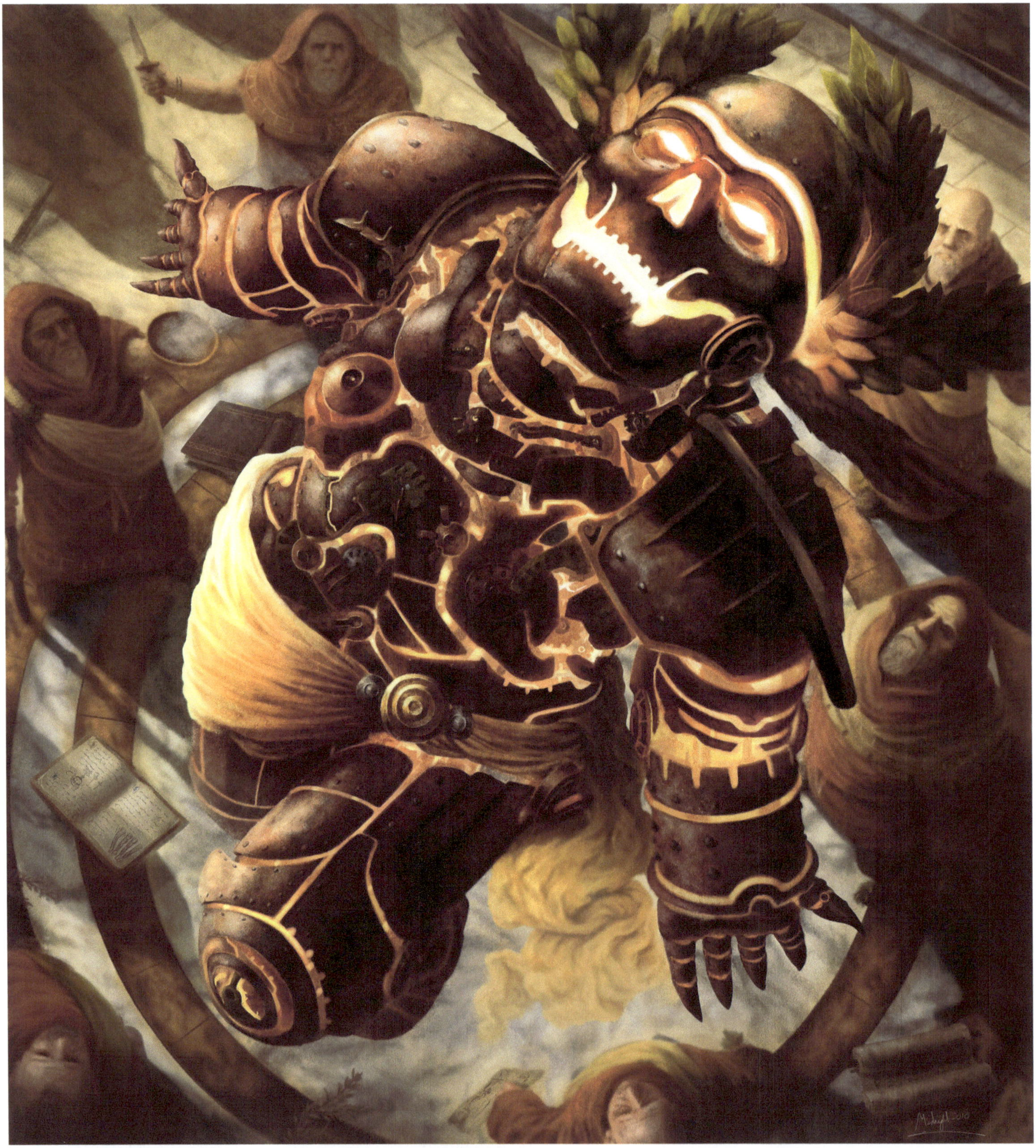

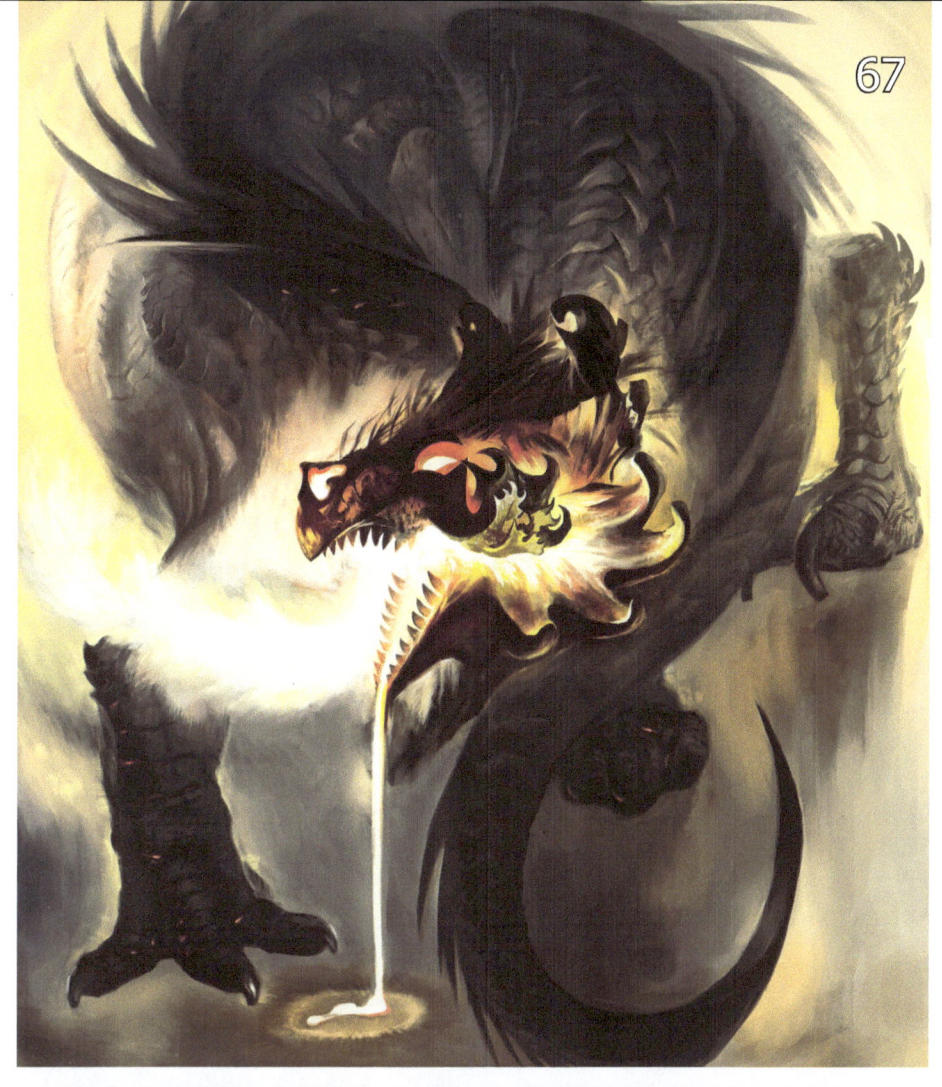

OPPOSITE

SAM MANLEY
Photoshop (England)
Ritual

RIGHT

YUKARI MASUIKE
Photoshop (Japan)
Blackdragon

BELOW

JAMES NG
*Pencil, Charcoal, Painter, Photoshop
(Hong Kong/ Canada)*
Bridal Carriage

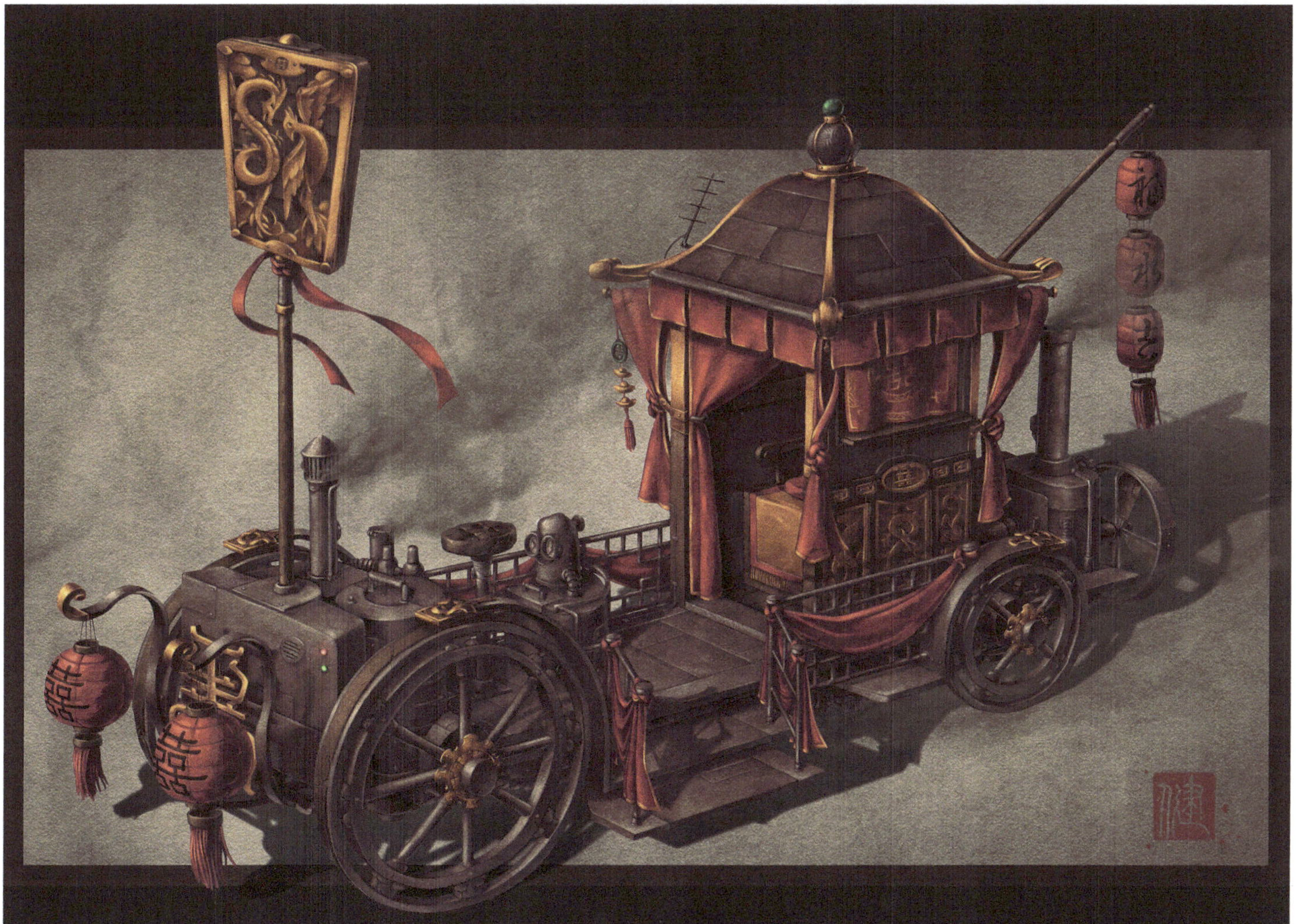

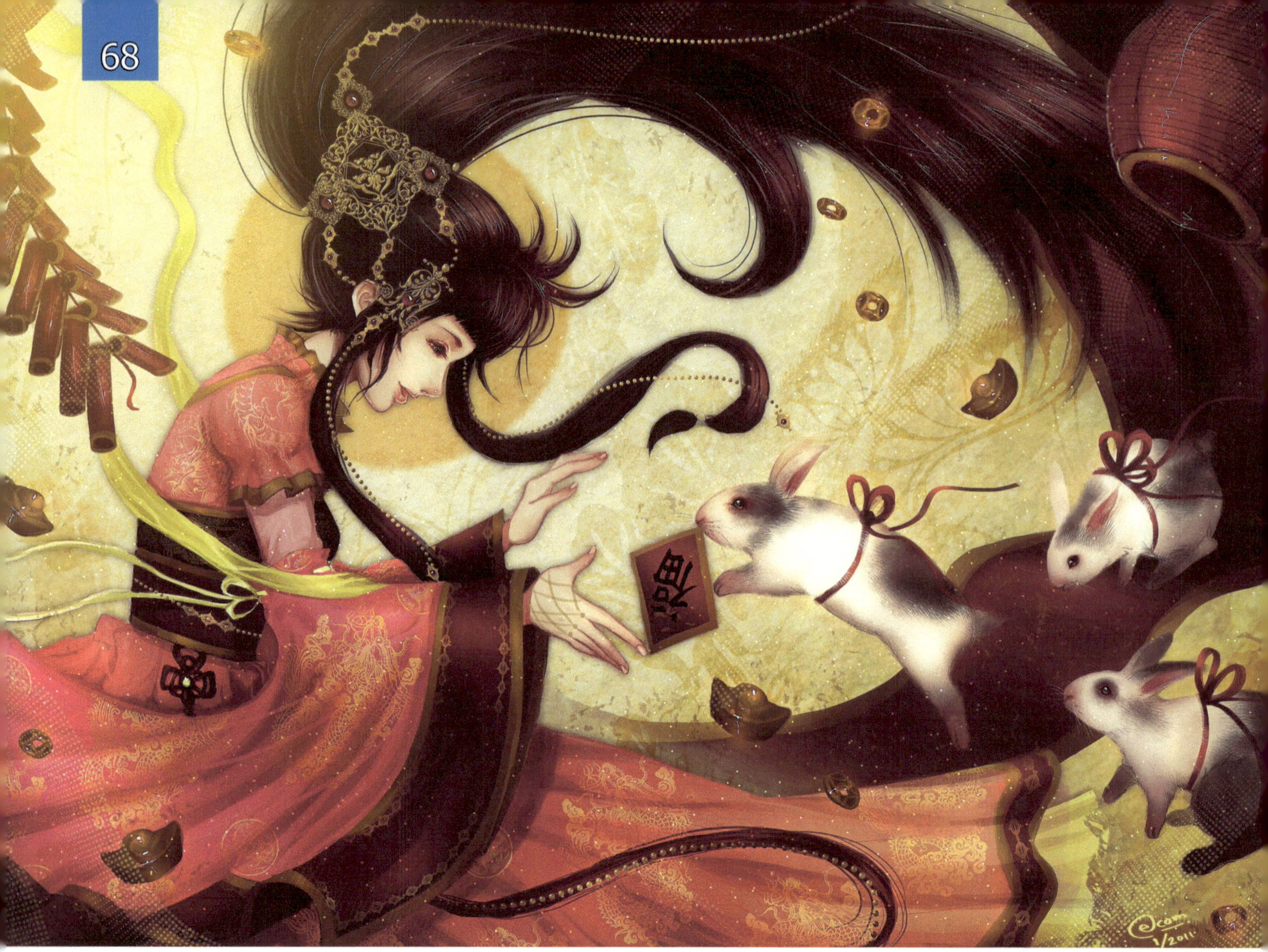

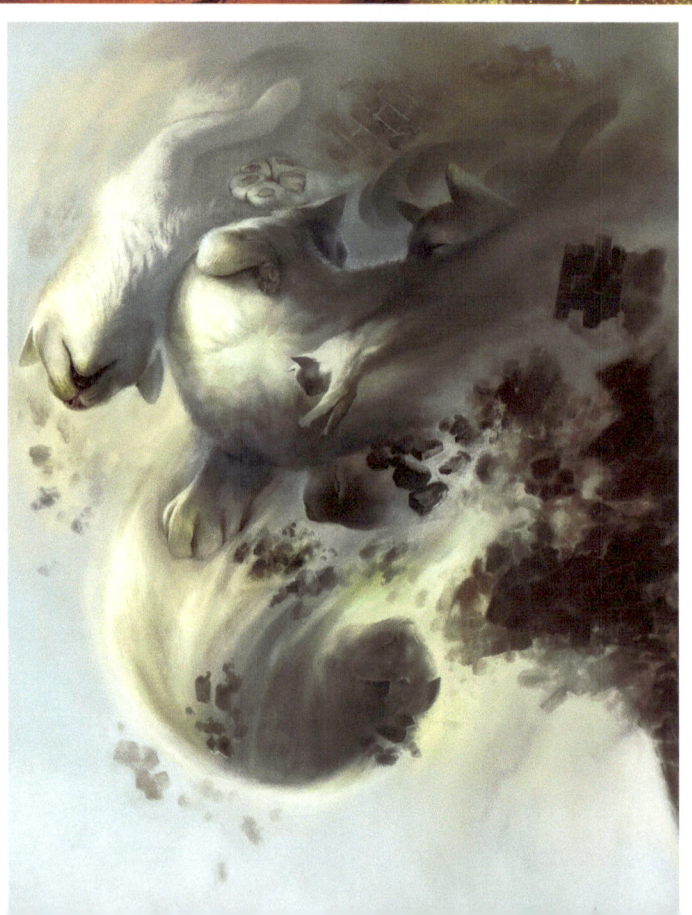

ABOVE

YEE-LING CHUNG
Digital (Malaysia)
Happy Bunny Year

RIGHT

YUKARI MASUIKE
Photoshop (Japan)
Sleep Down

OPPOSITE BOTTOM LEFT

PHILIP LONGSON
Photoshop (UK)
This is Our Playground

OPPOSITE BOTTOM RIGHT

YUKARI MASUIKE
Photoshop (Japan)
Little Black Demonr

OPPOSITE TOP

PHILIP LONGSON
Photoshop (UK)
Murder on the Rooftops

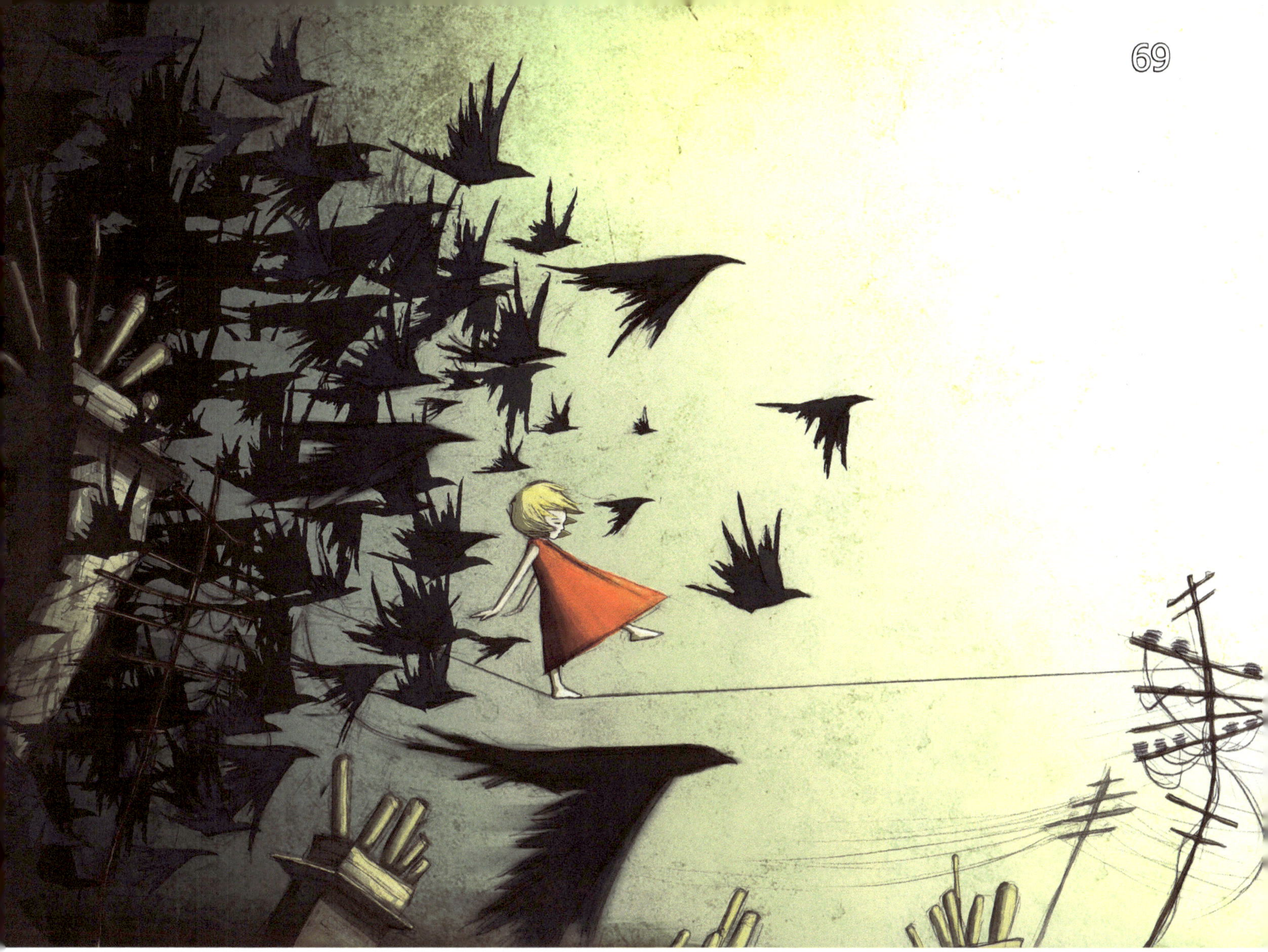

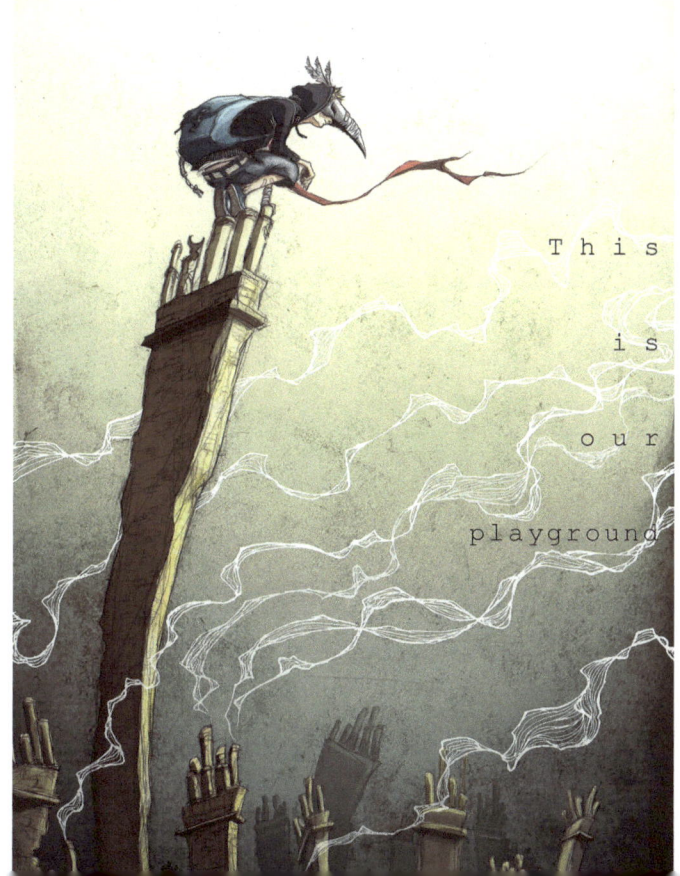

This is our playground

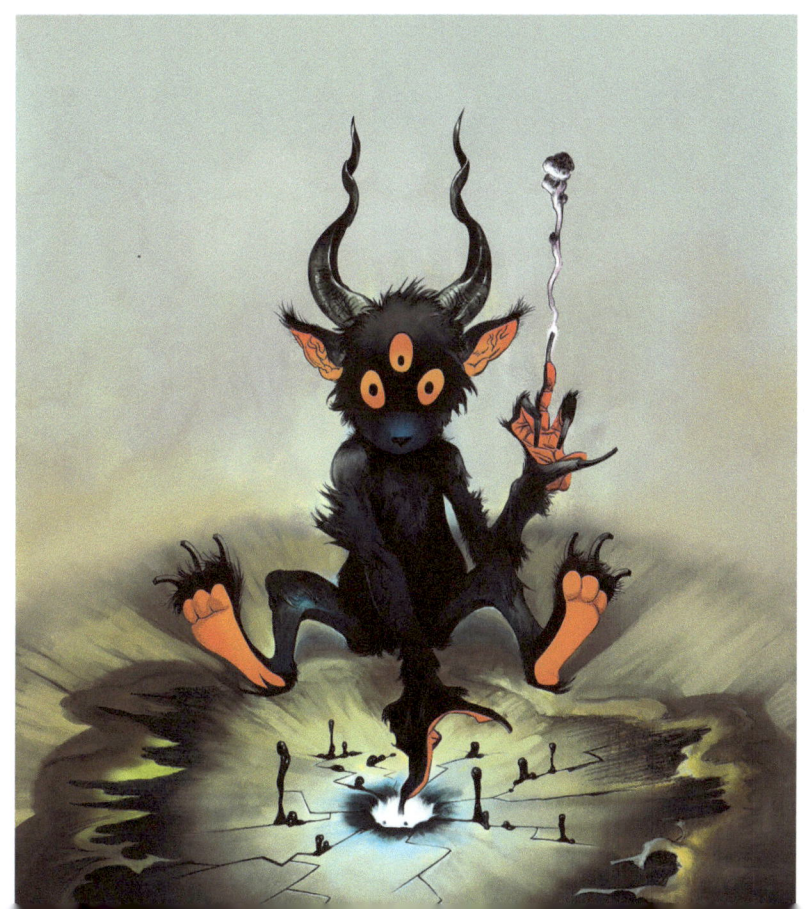

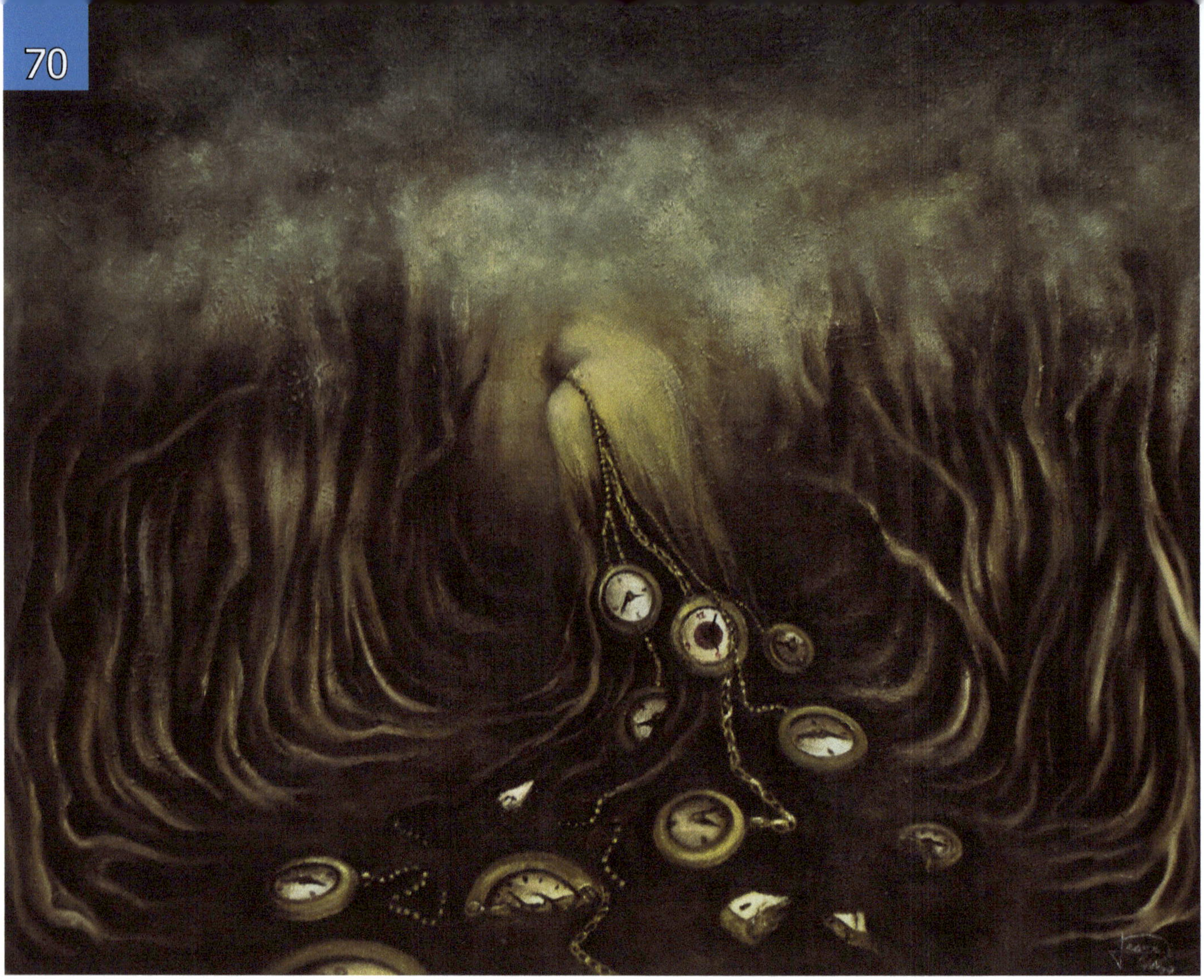

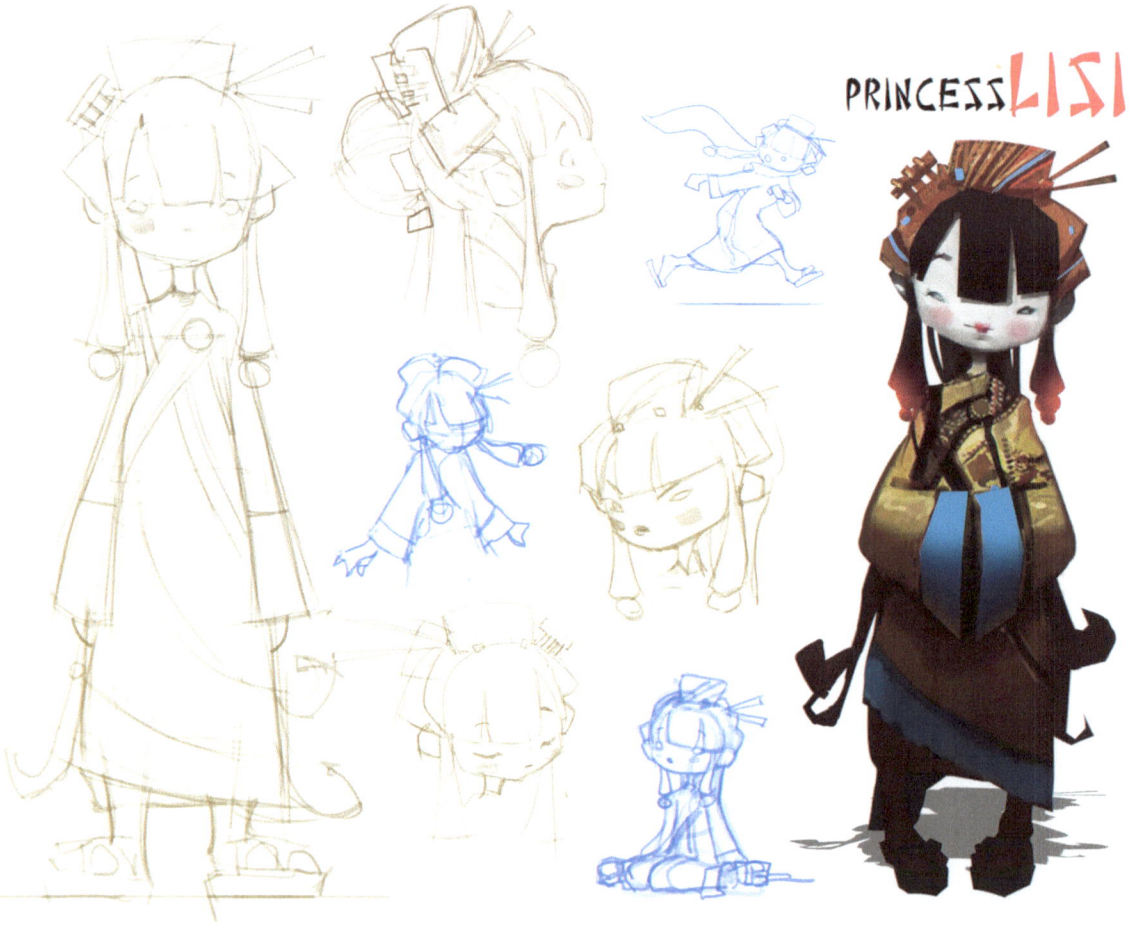

PRINCESS LISI

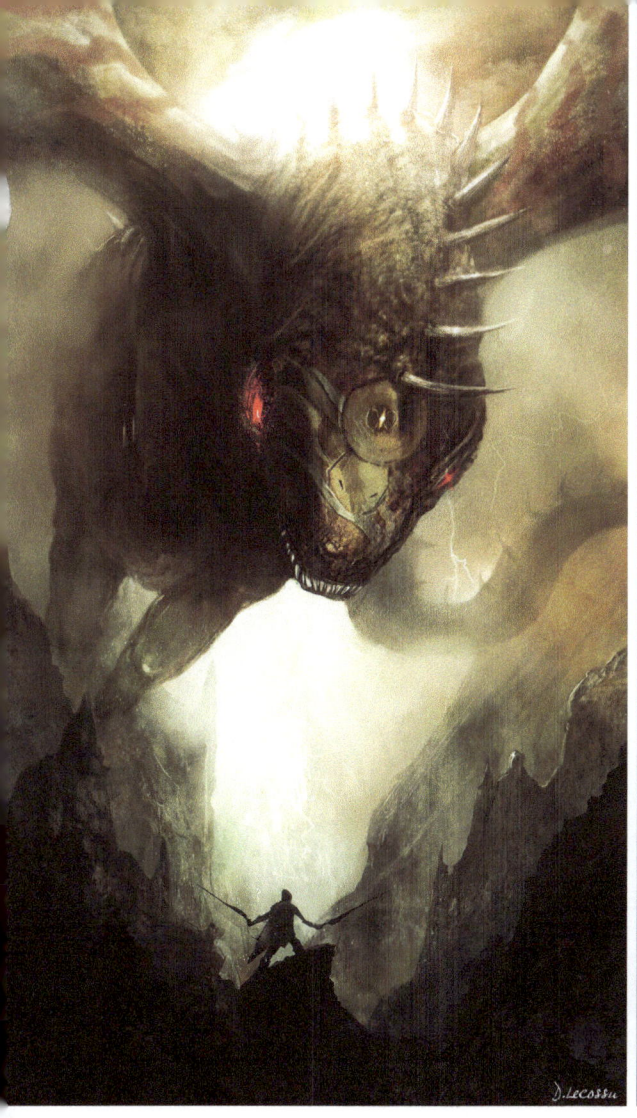

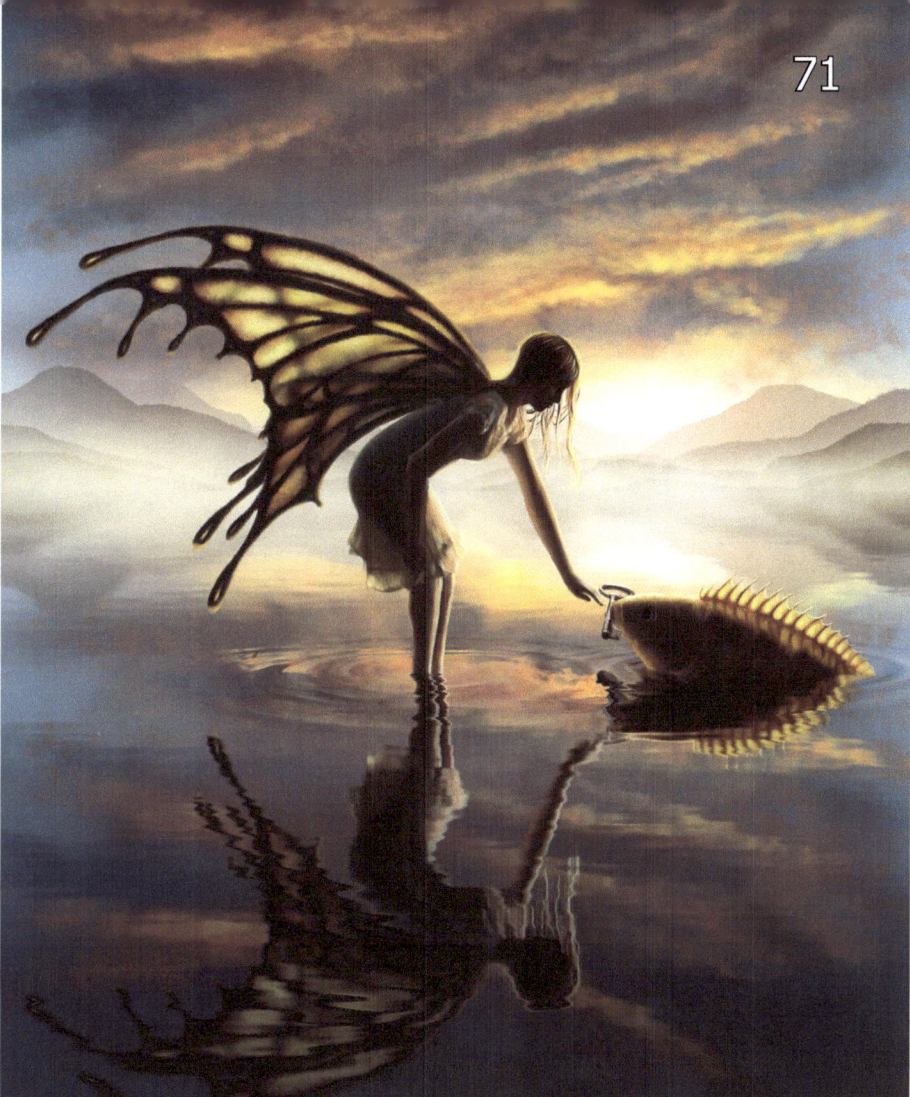

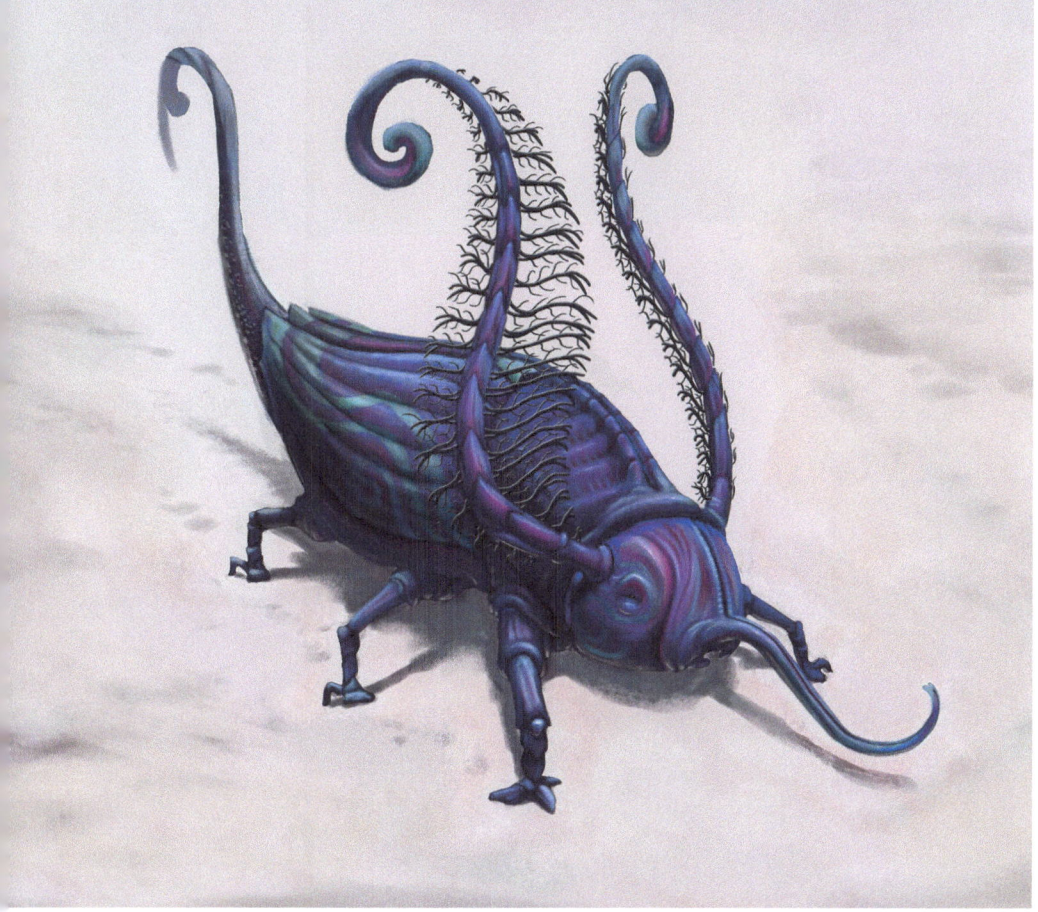

OPPOSITE TOP

IRENE DM AKA NAMTARU
Oil on Canvas (Spain)
Cronos Losing the Time

OPPOSITE BOTTOM

AHMED ALDOORI
Photoshop (USA)
Princess Lisi

ABOVE LEFT

DAVID LECOSSU
Photoshop (France)
The Dragon

ABOVE RIGHT

ANGELA TYGERSON ROSS
Photoshop Painting (USA)
*Credit: deviantart.com: Eirian-stock,
flickr.com: VangieAdH, sxc.hu: verzerk*
Lost and Found

LEFT

DANIEL OGUIN
Pencil and Photoshop (USA)
Purple Listener

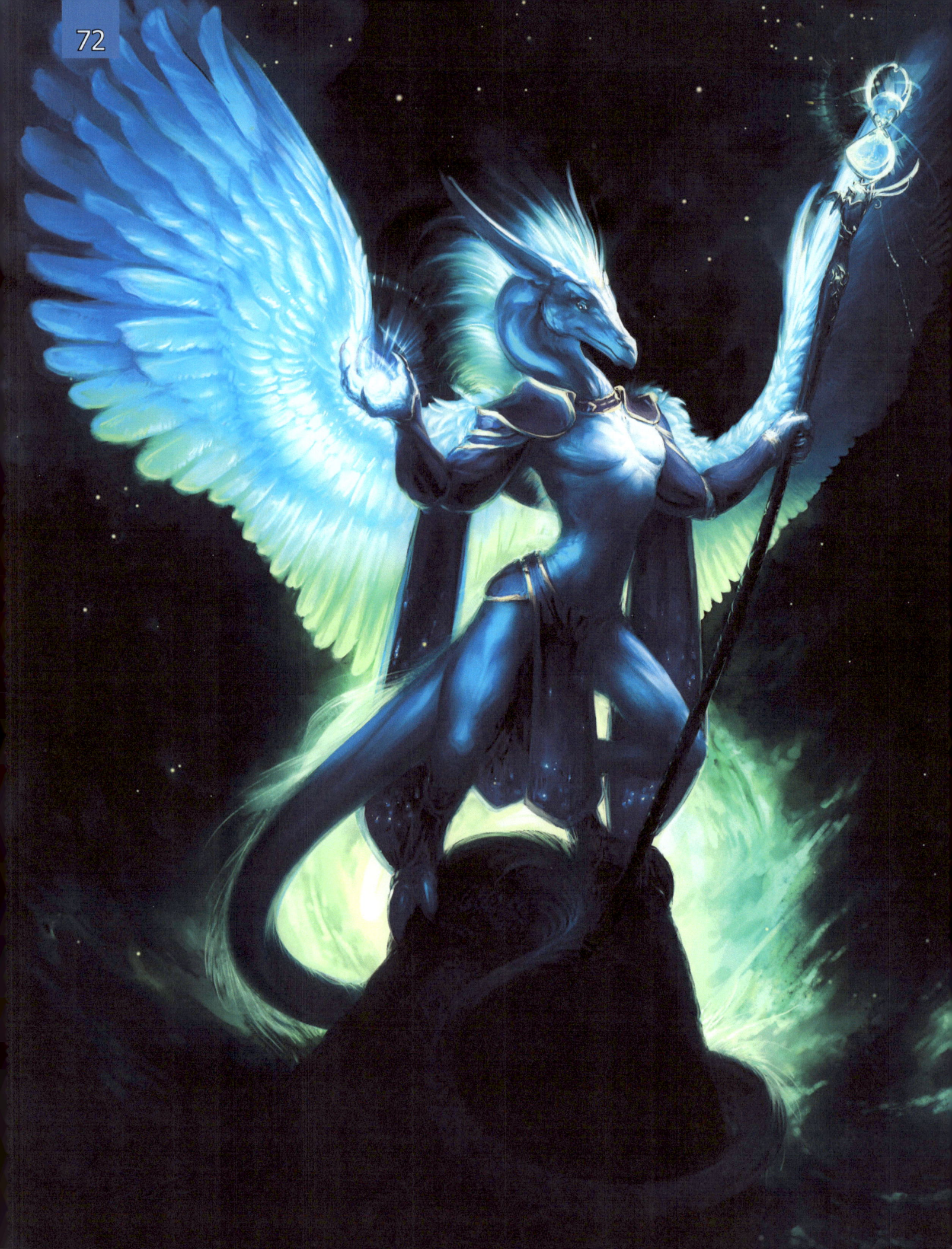

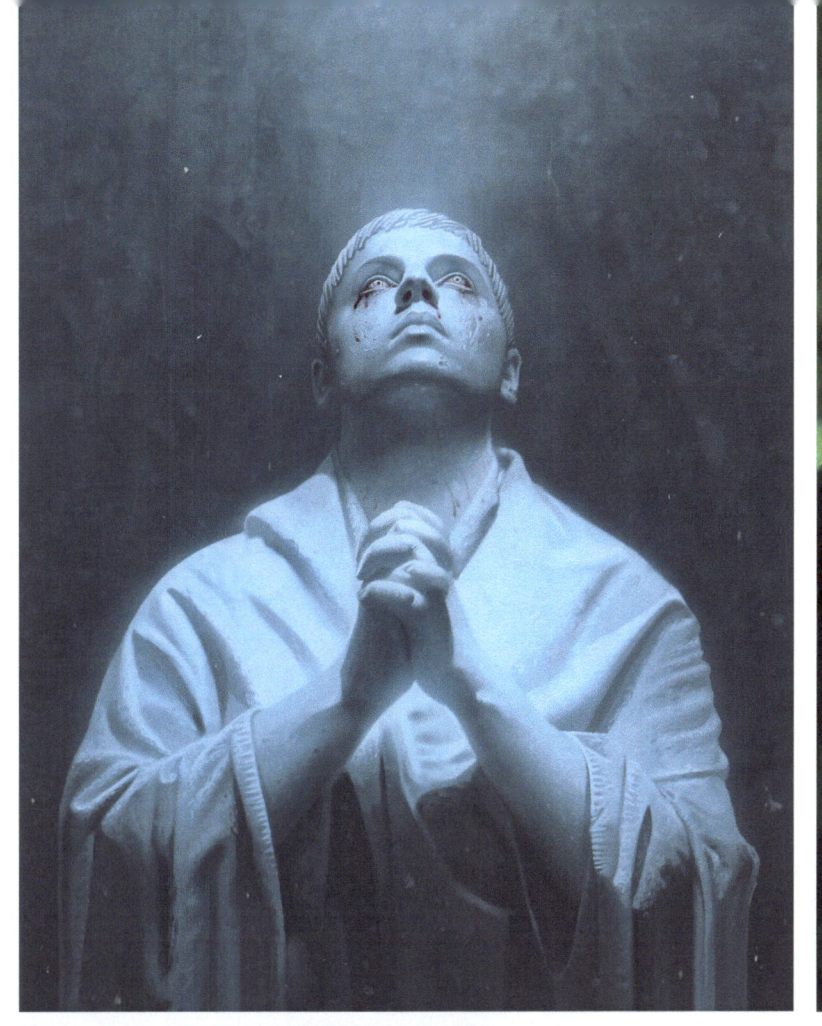

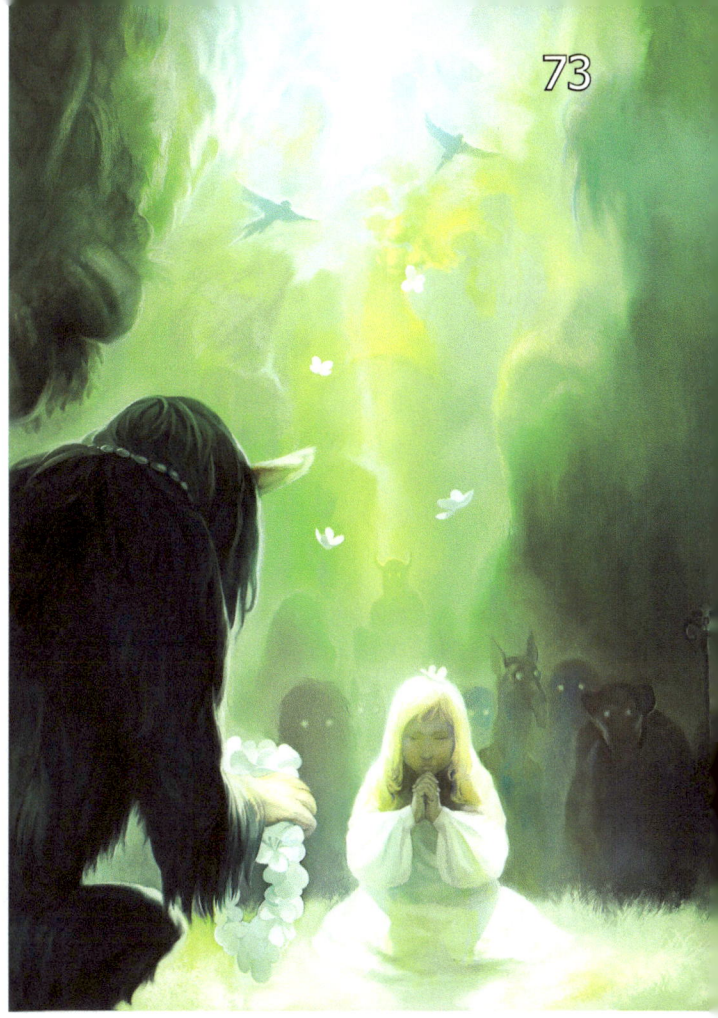

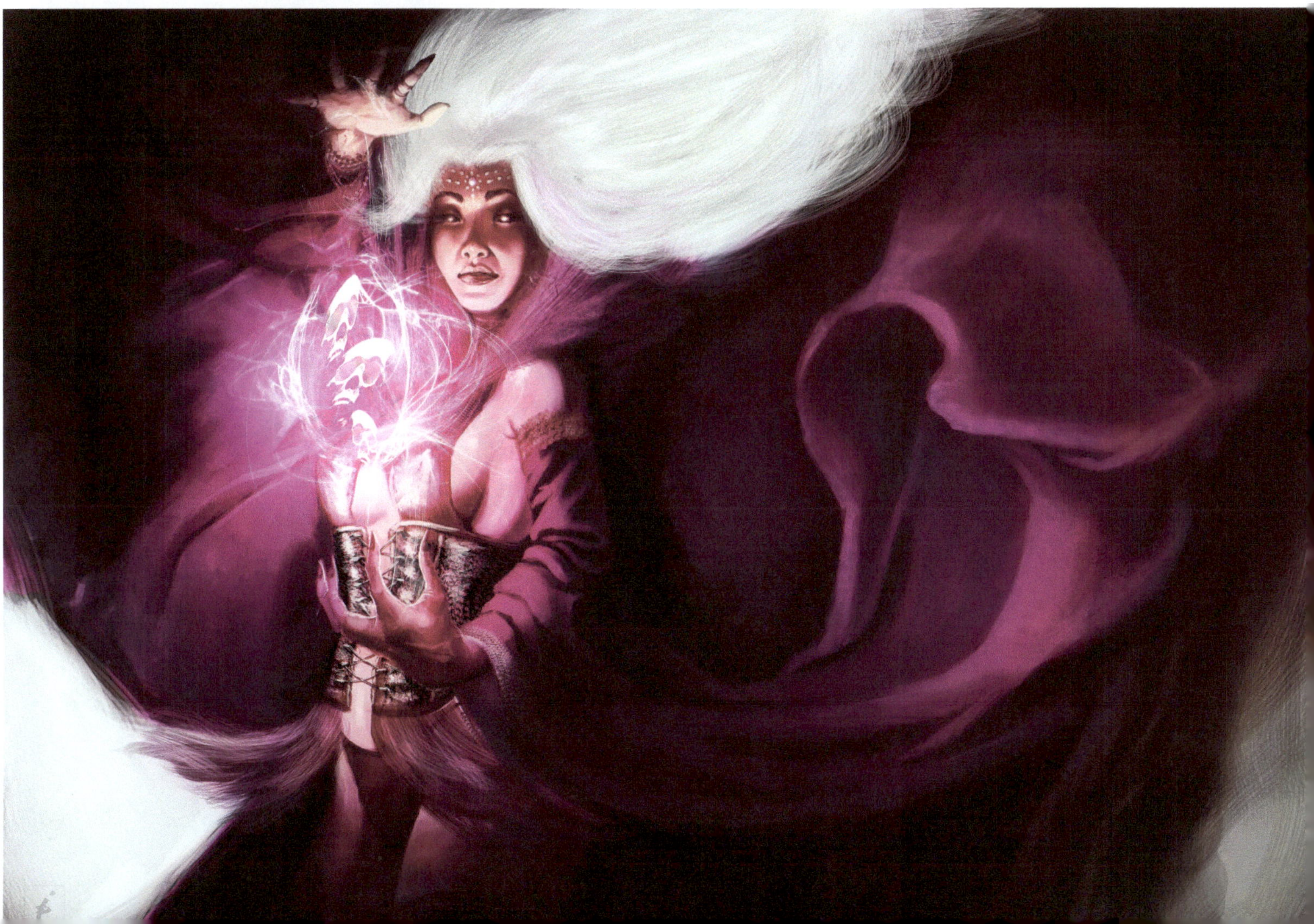

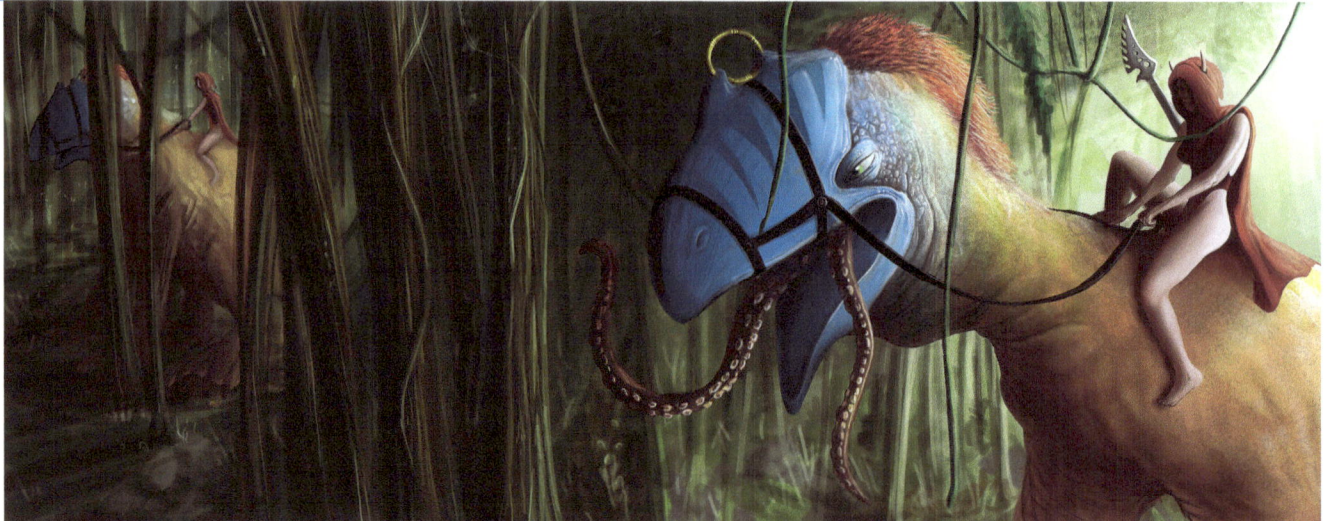

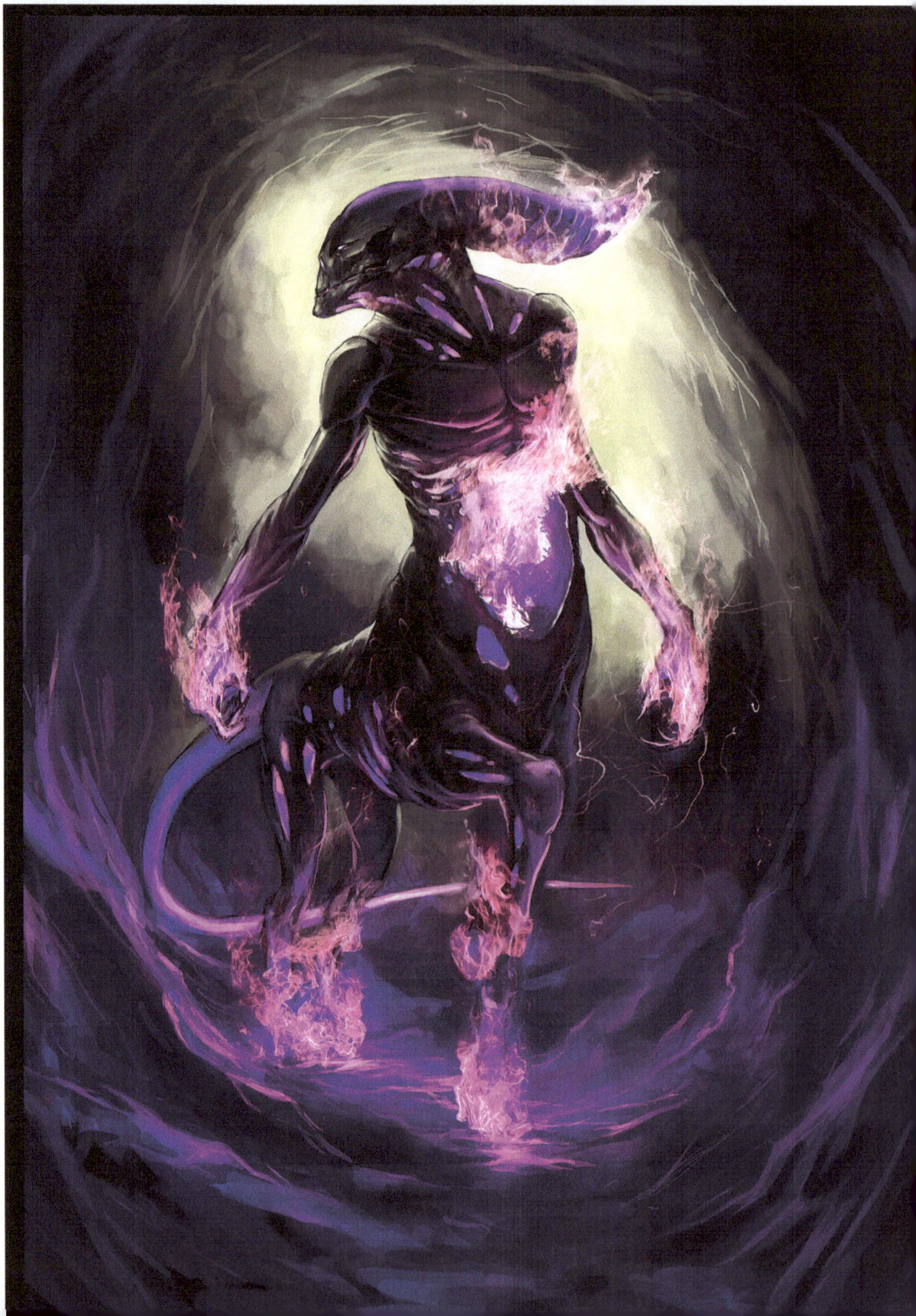

(*Previous*)

LEFT PAGE
Liiga Smilshkalne
Corel Painter (Latvia)
Client: K.T. Pape
Brenell

RIGHT PAGE BOTTOM
Immar Palomera
Photoshop (USA)
Soul collector

RIGHT PAGE TOP RIGHT
Yukari Masuike
Photoshop (Japan)
Departure

RIGHT PAGE TOP LEFT
George Patsouras
Photoshop Painting (USA)
Save Us

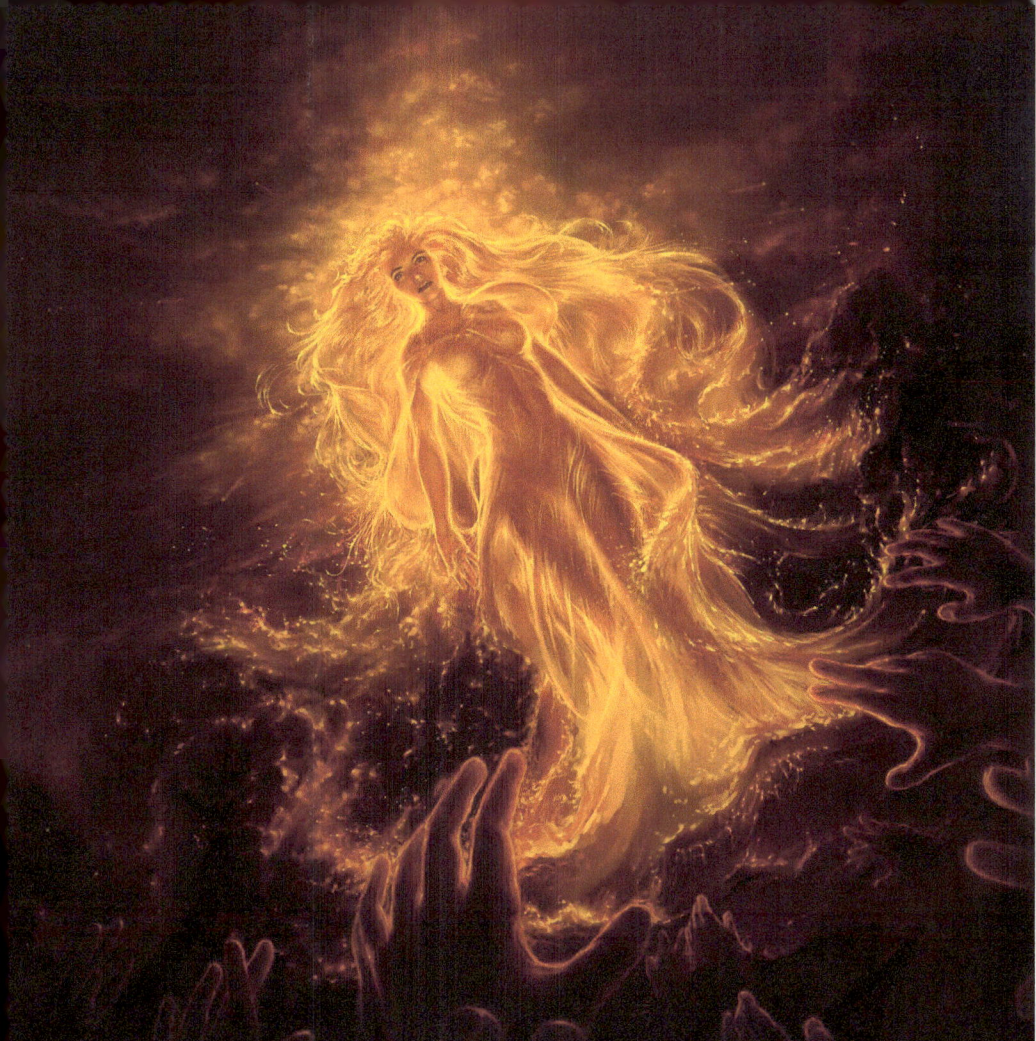

OPPOSITE TOP

SIMON VARISTO
Photoshop Painting (Finland)
Roamers

OPPOSITE BOTTOM

DIMITRI SIRENKO
Photoshop (Canada)
Shadow And Flame

LEFT

LIIGA SMILSHKALNE
Corel Painter (Latvia)
Client: Aventale
Catalyst

BELOW

LIIGA SMILSHKALNE
Corel Painter (Latvia)
Drama Llama

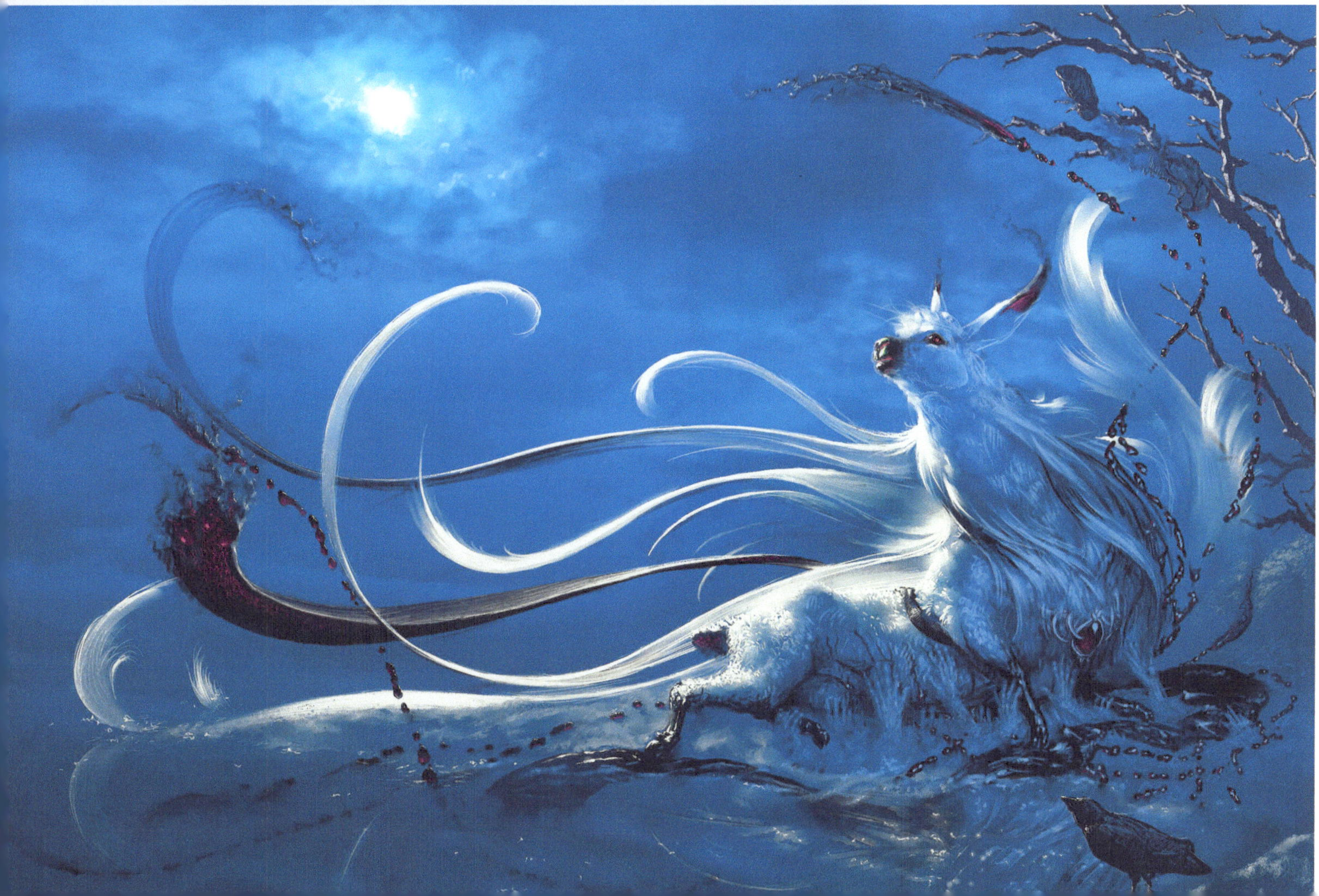

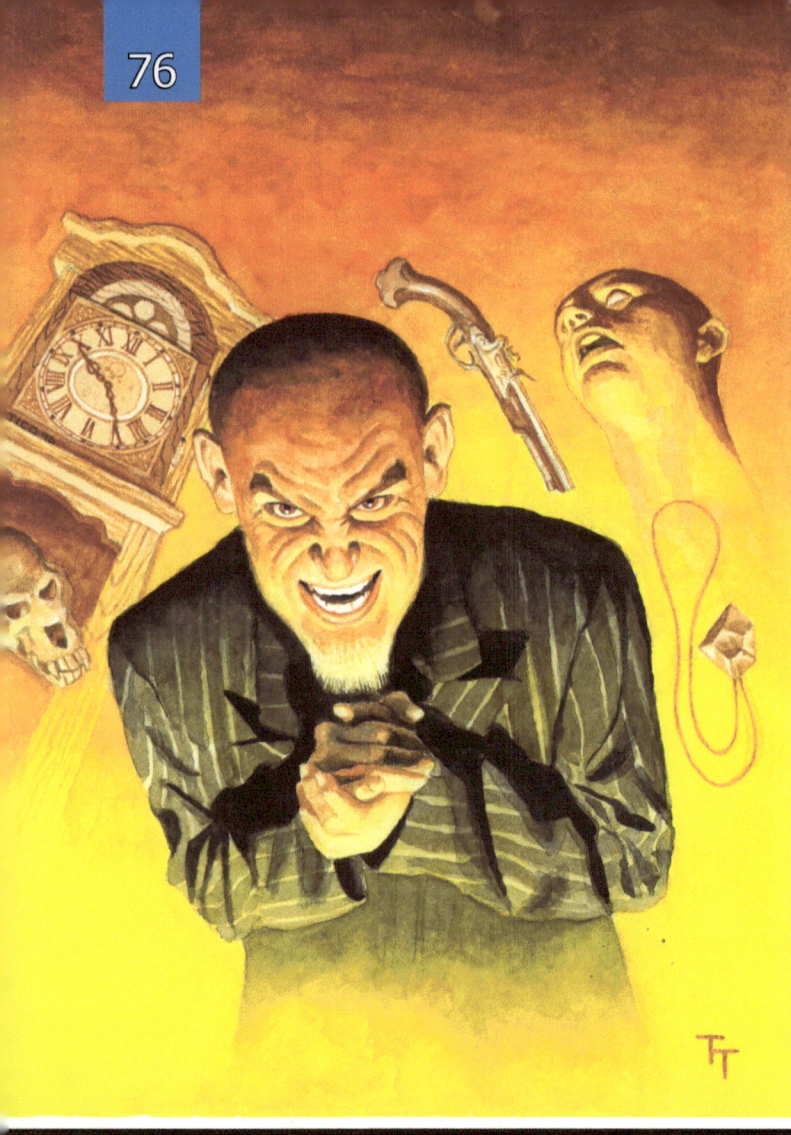

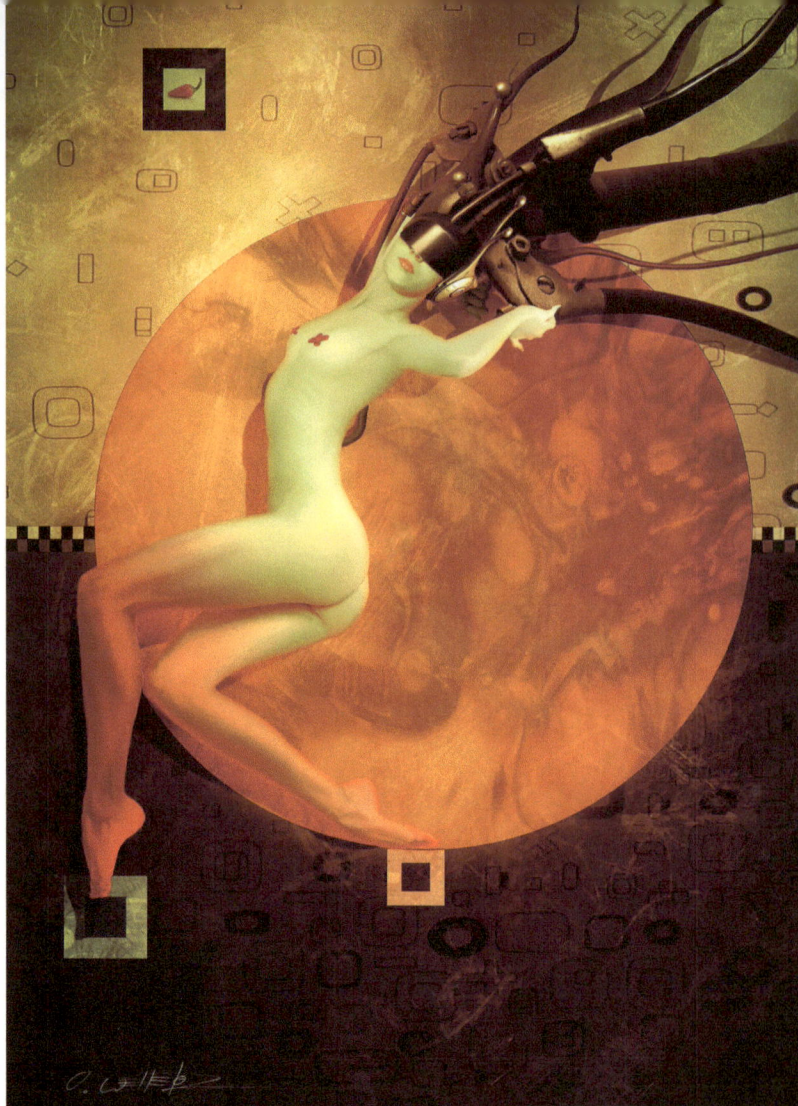

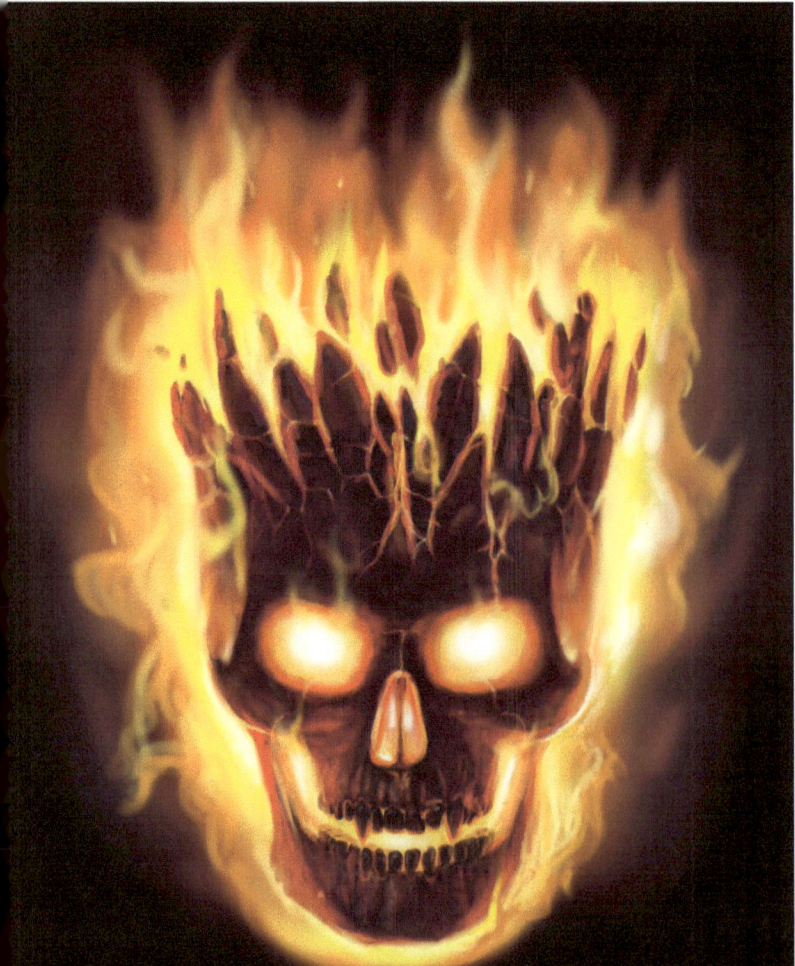

ABOVE LEFT

TIHOMIR TIKULIN
Watercolour (Croatia)
Client: Sarah 93 Publisher for
Stephen King - Croatian Ed.
Needful Things

ABOVE

OLIVER WETTER
Photoshop (Germany)
Cyberpepper

LEFT

GORDON NAPIER
Digital(UK)
Volcanic Skull

OPPOSITE

OLIVER WETTER
Photoshop (Germany)
Spirit of the Crow

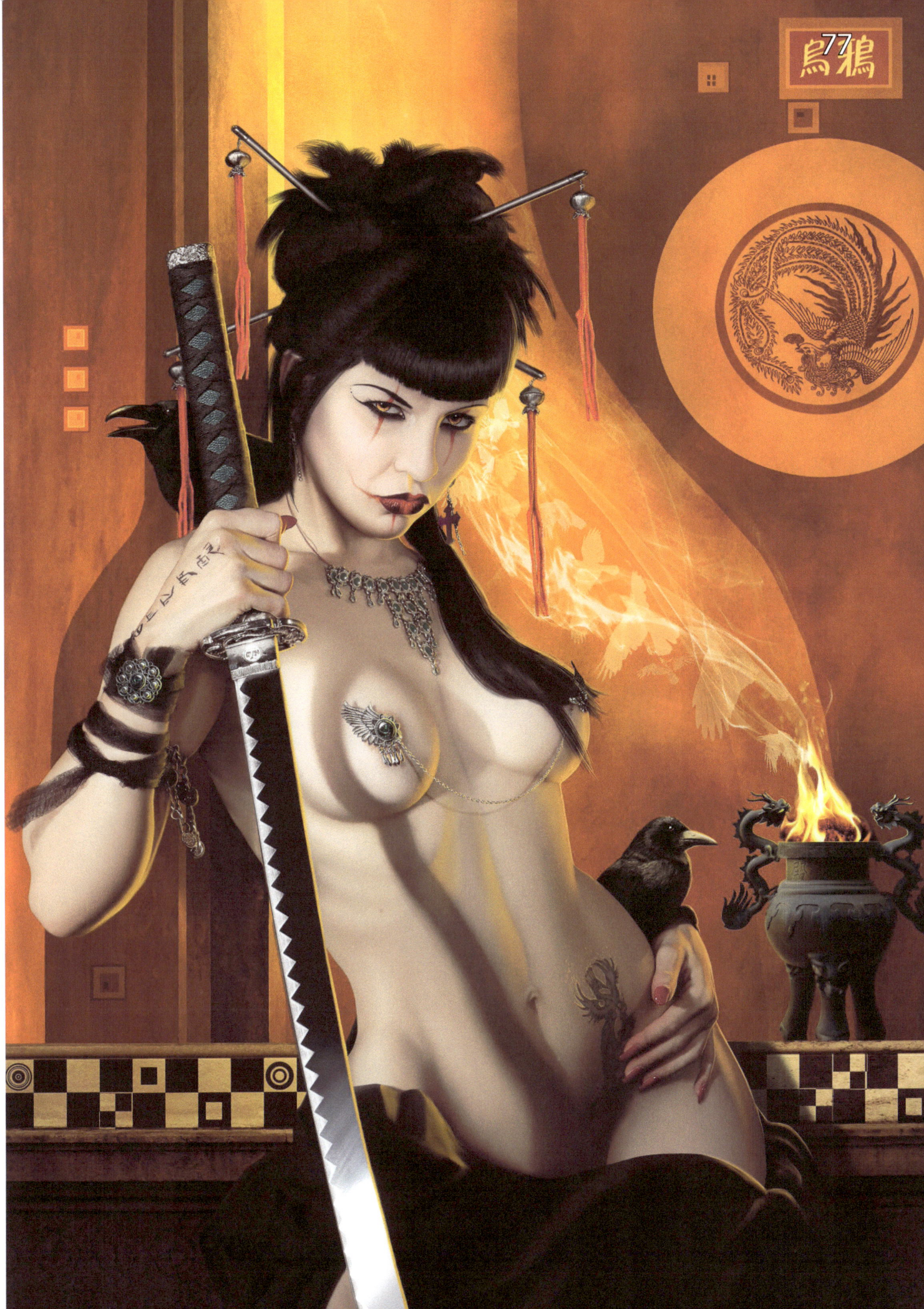

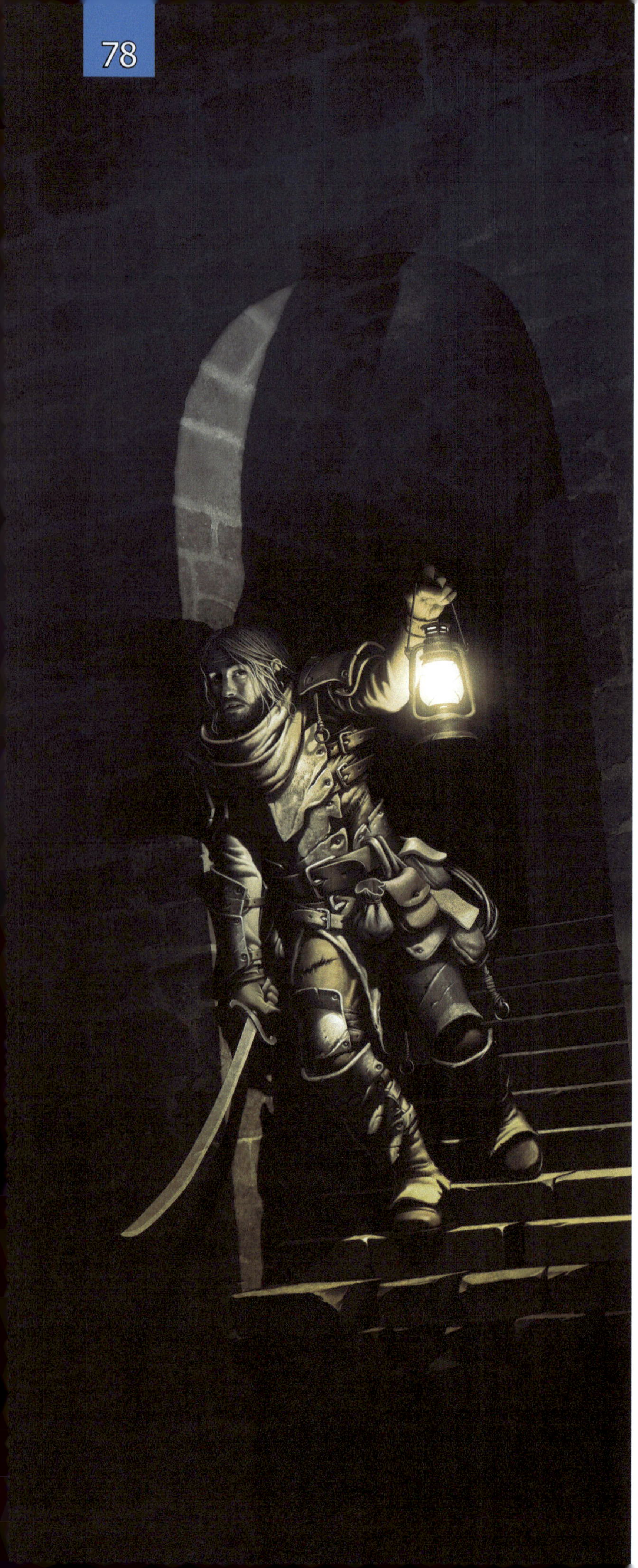

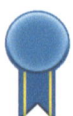

LEFT

KRISZTIAN BALLA
Pencil and Digital (Hungary)
Dungeon Delve

BELOW

DANIEL OGUIN
Pencil and Photoshop (USA)
Stitch

OPPOSITE

BRIAN KELSEY
Photomanipulation (USA)
At the Watchtower

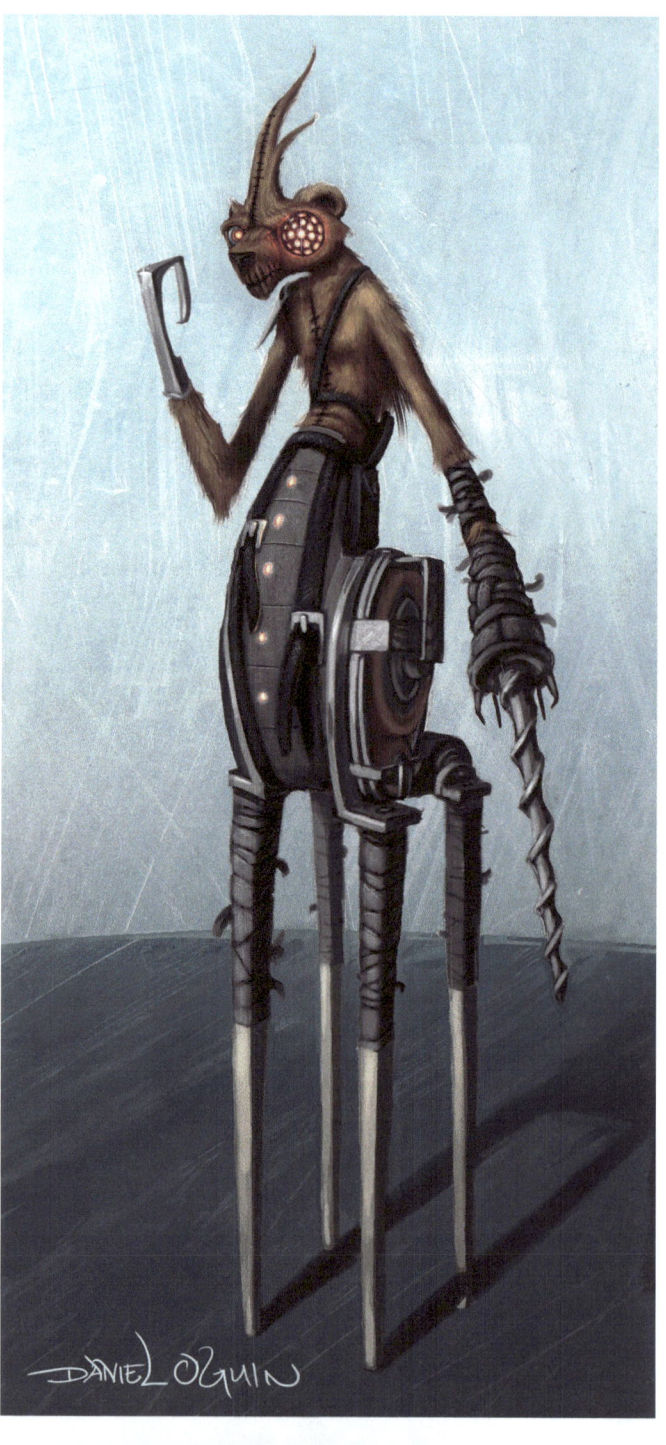

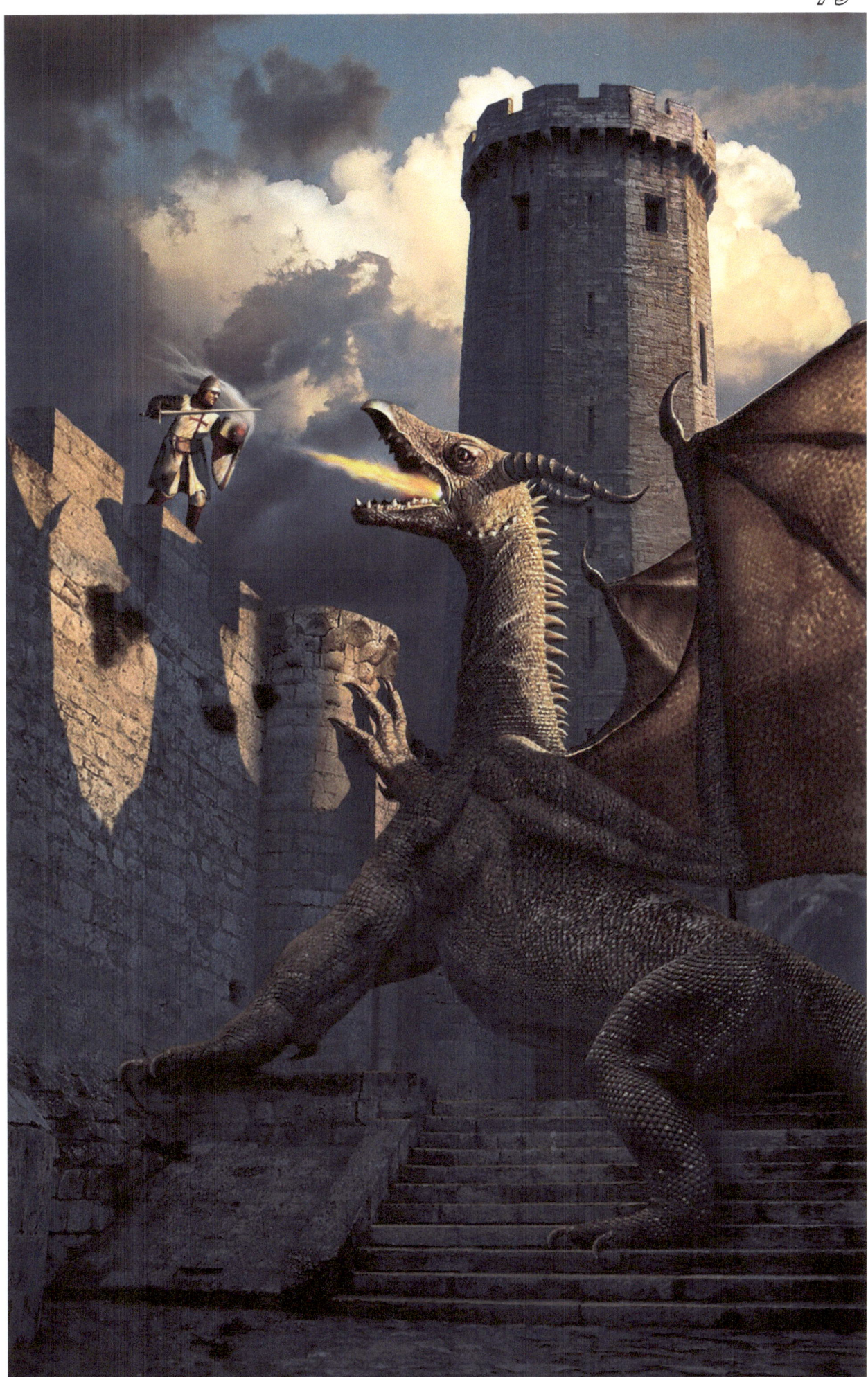

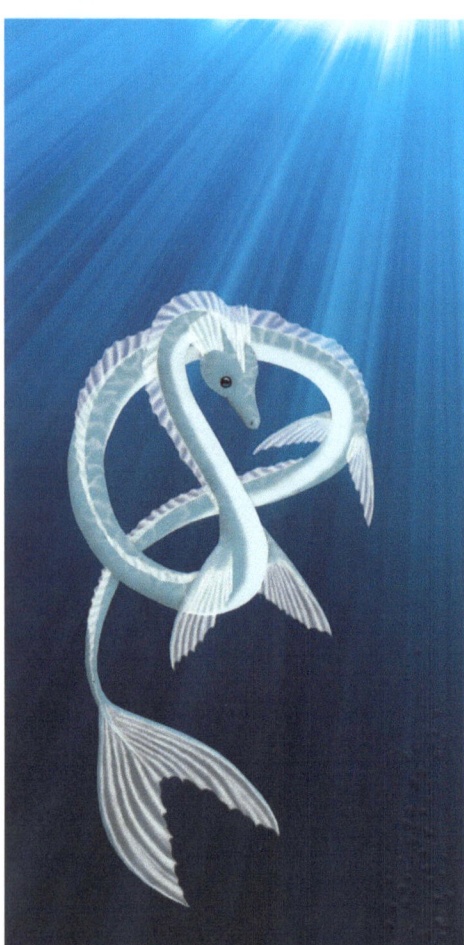

LEFT
CLAIRE NORTH
Photoshop (England)
Elemental Dragon of the Sea

BELOW LEFT
CLAIRE NORTH
Photoshop (England)
Elemental Dragon of the Air

OPPOSITE
DANIEL OGUIN
Pencil and Photoshop (USA)
Atlantis Guardian

BELOW
JASON MARTIN
Digital (USA)
Running With Your Imagination

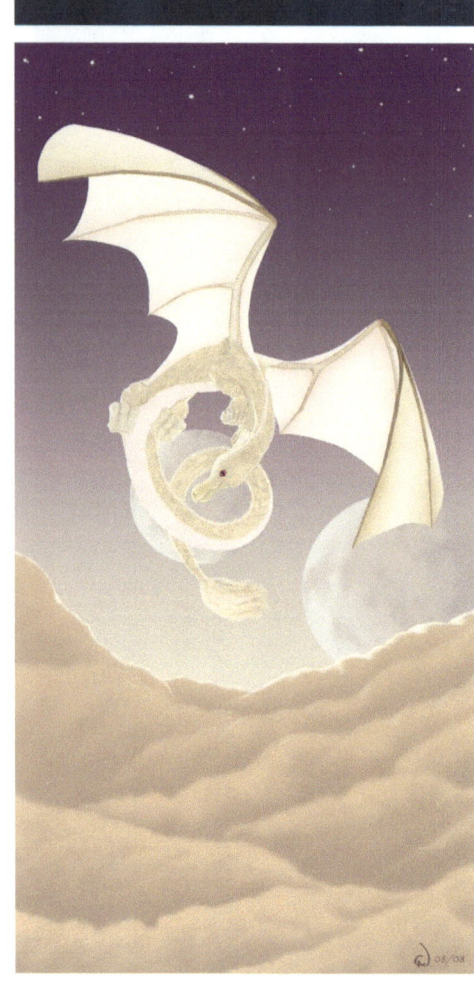

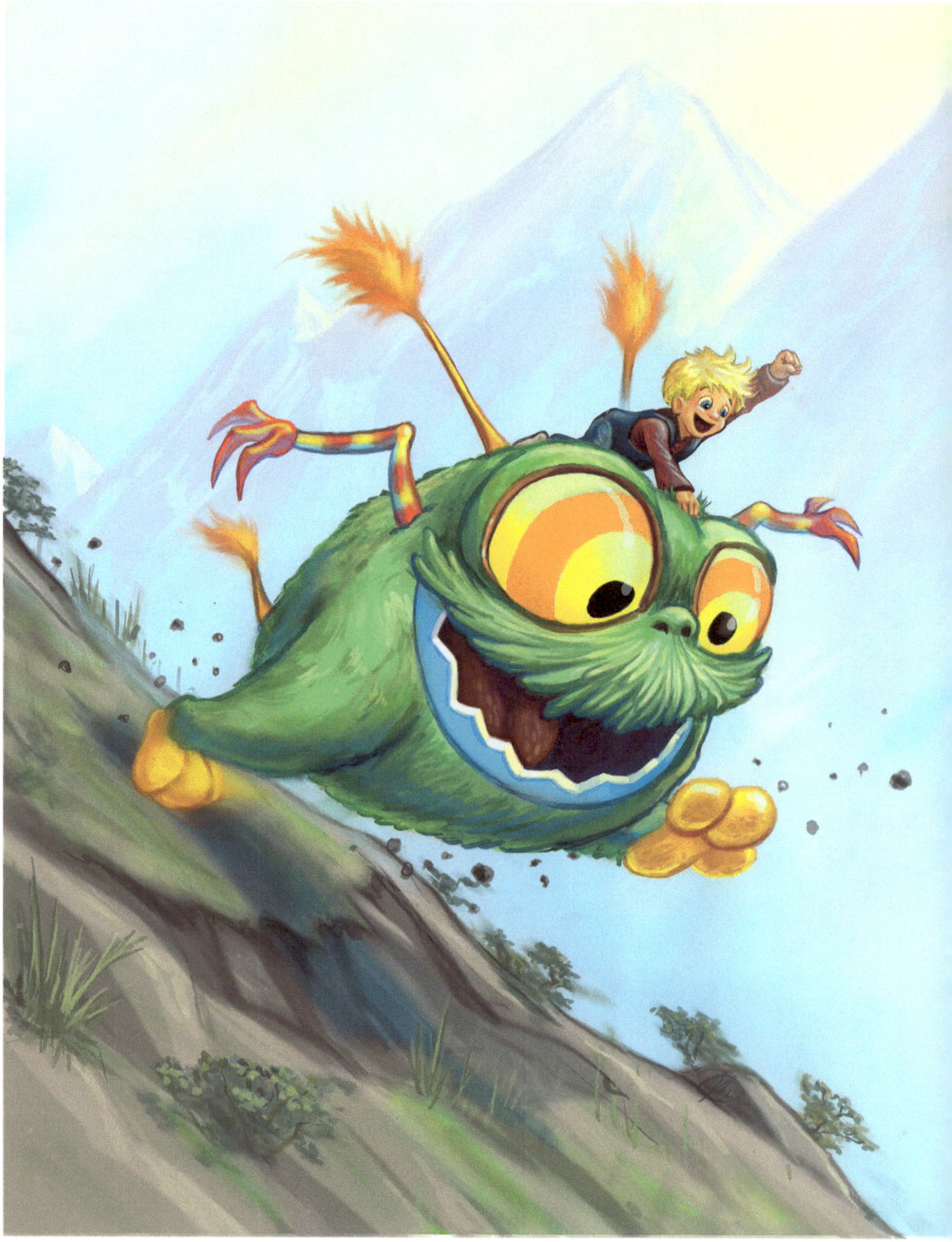

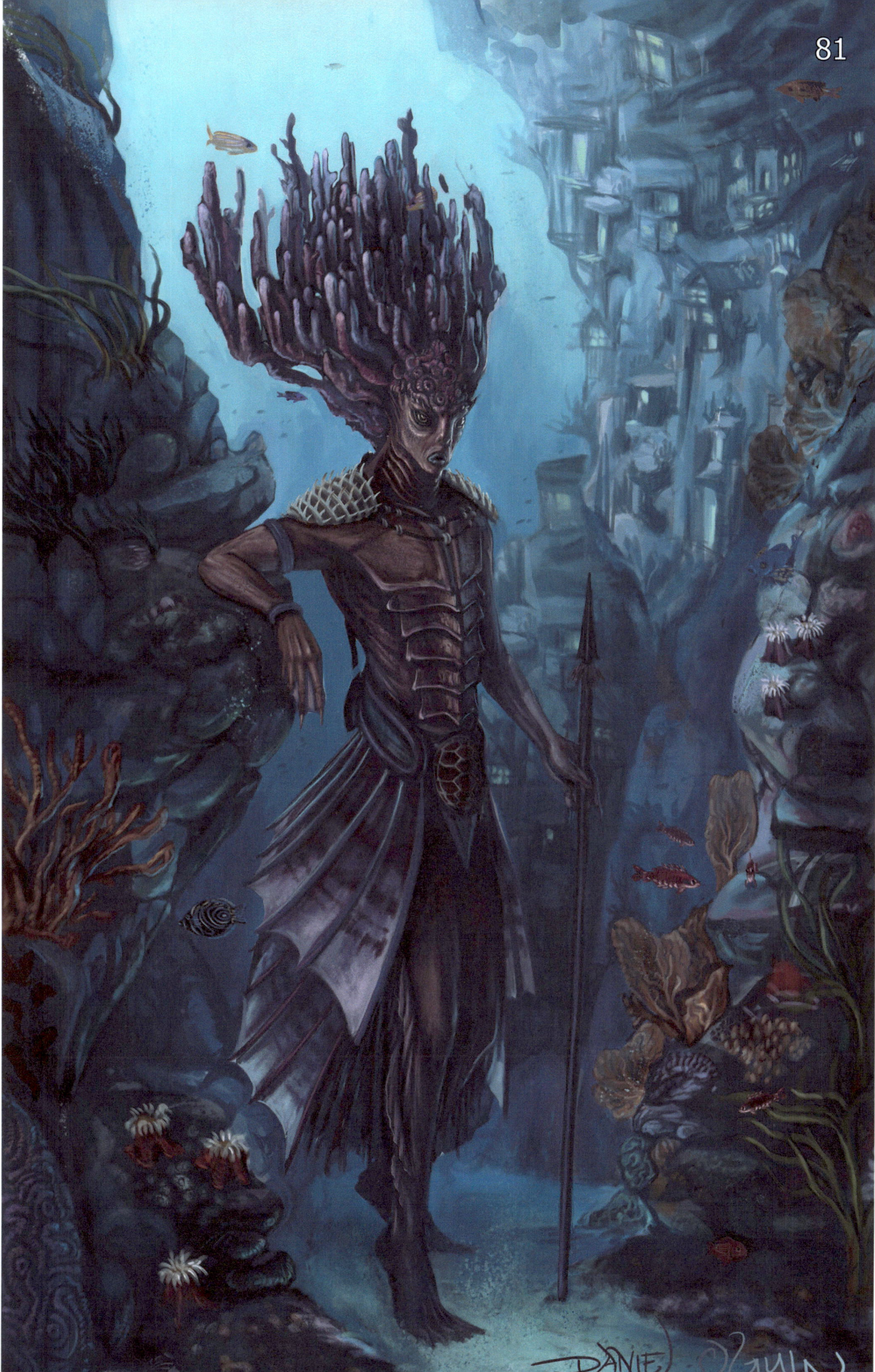

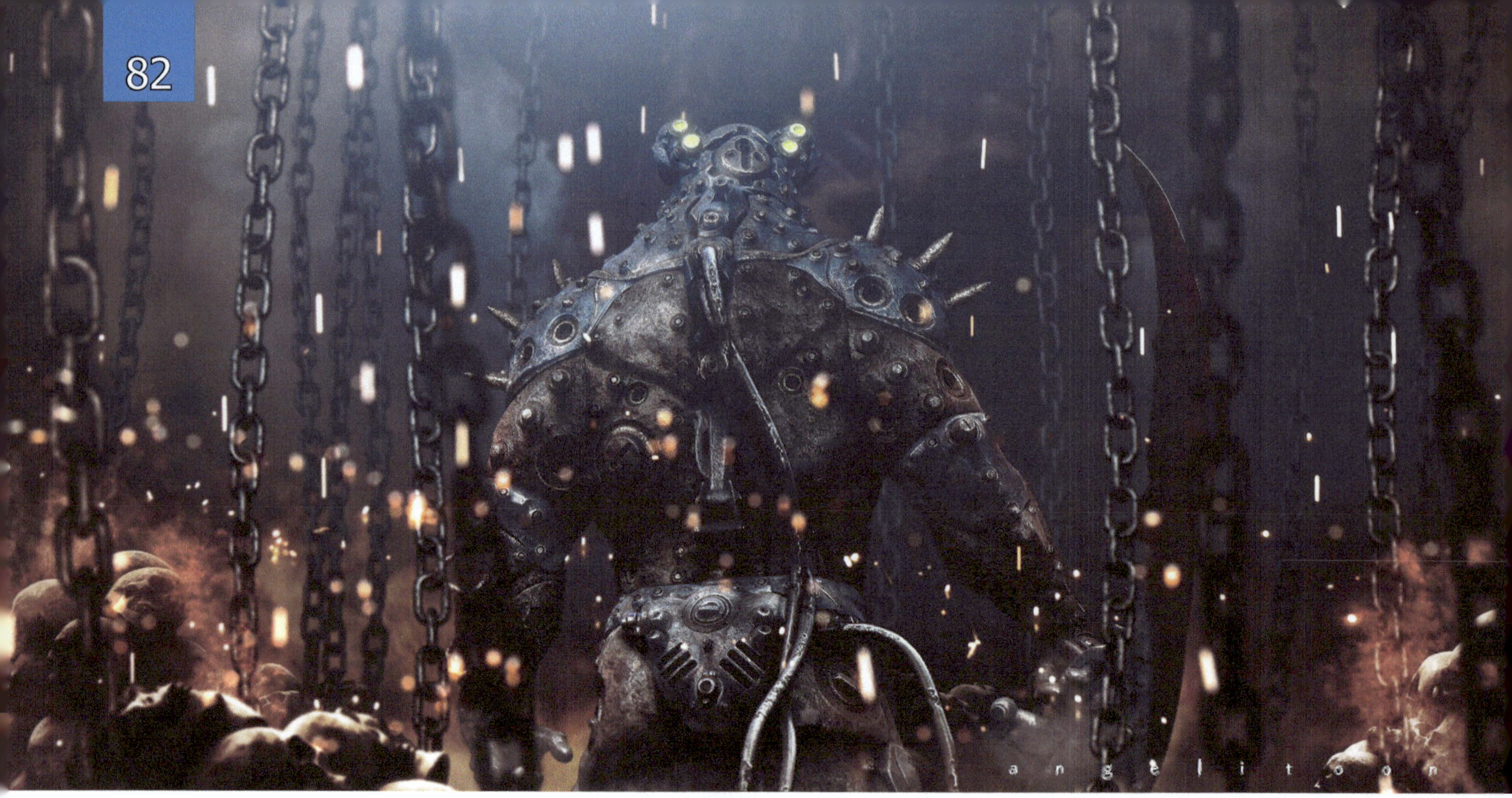

ABOVE
ANGEL ALONSO
Digital 3D (Spain)
The Reaper

RIGHT
HOWARD VAUSE
Photoshop (England)
Jacque and Murk the Giant

OPPOSITE
HOWARD VAUSE
Photoshop (England)
Box of Tricks

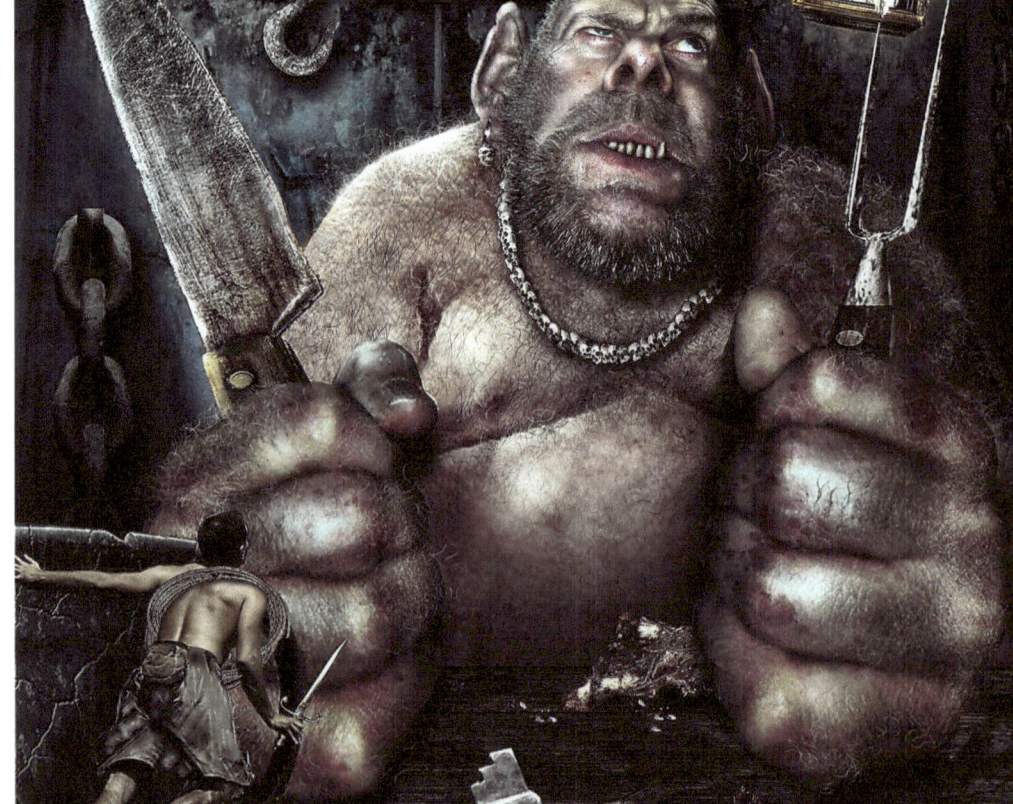

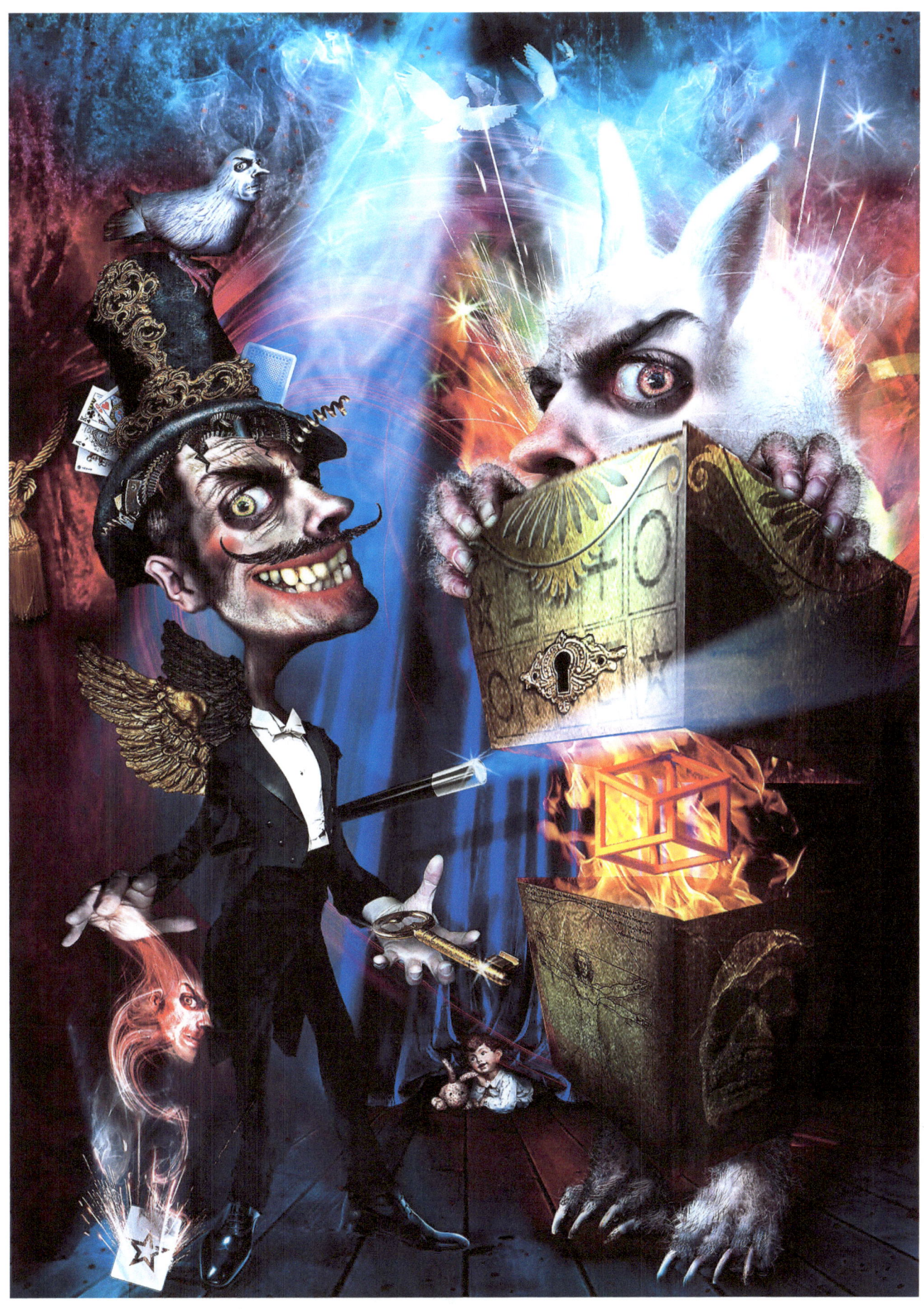

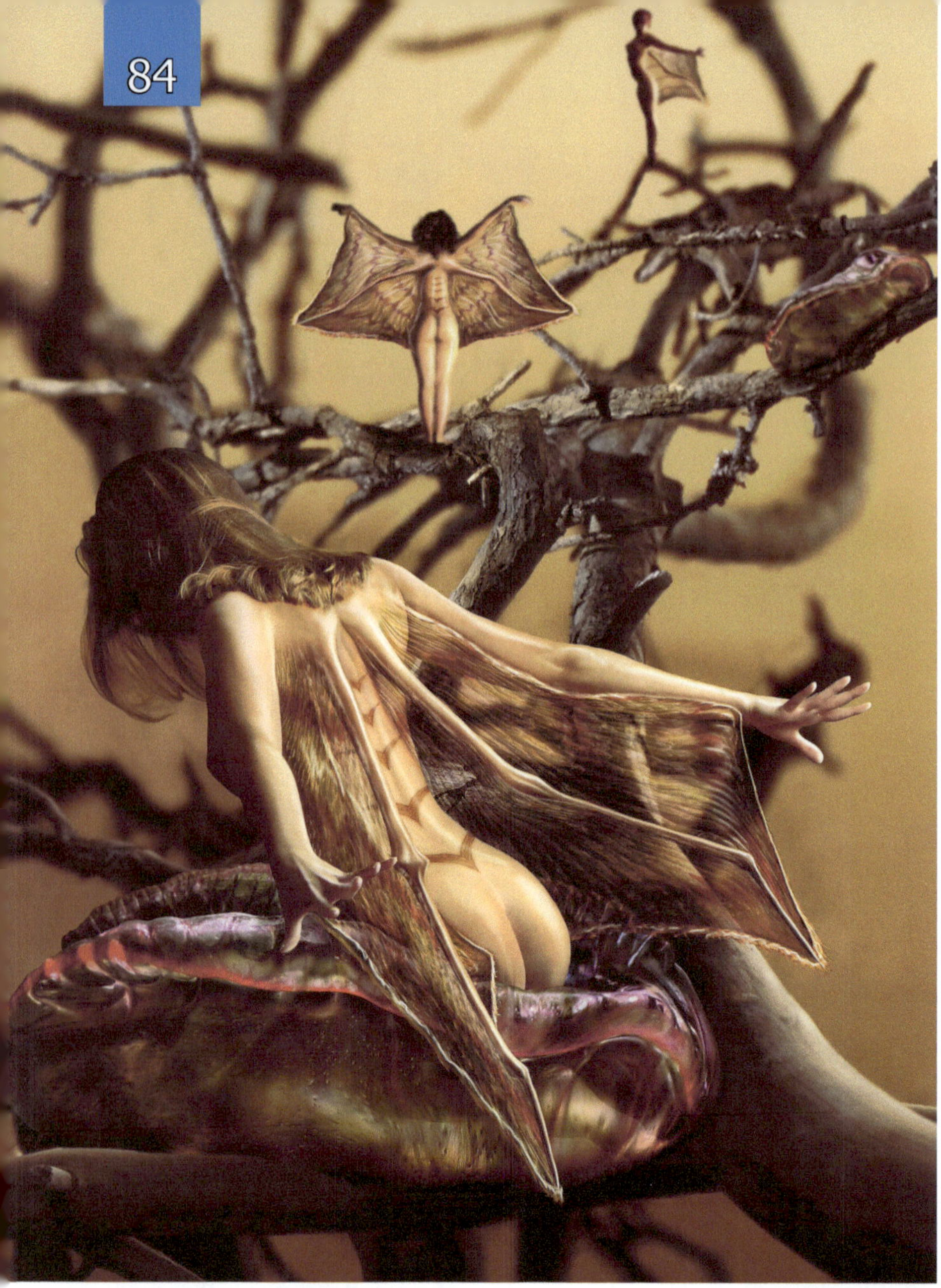

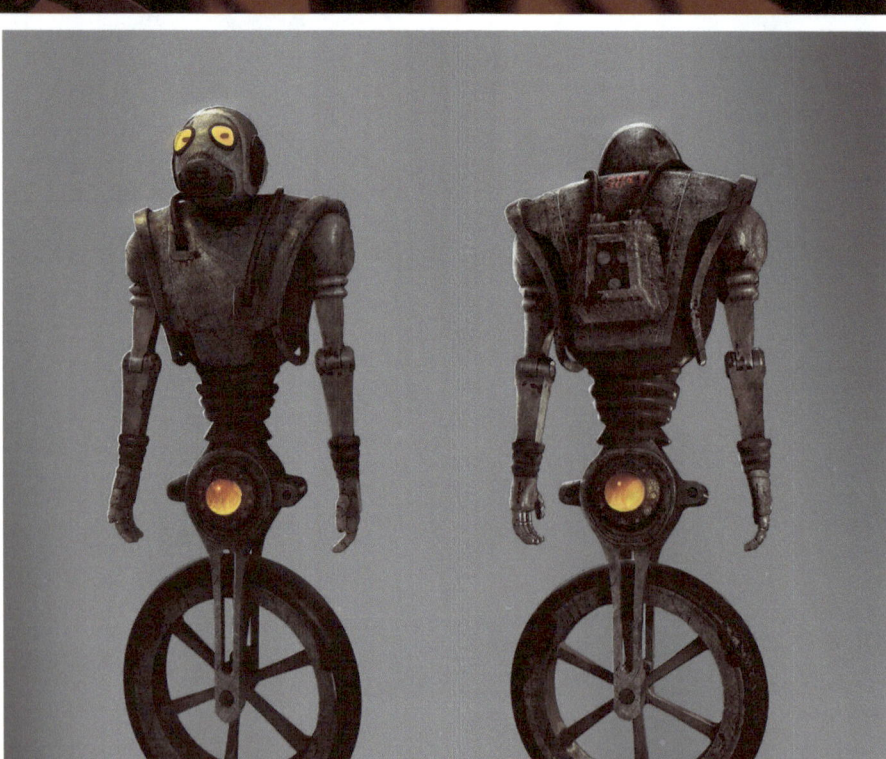

TOP LEFT

TOP LEFT
ONA LOOTS
Photomanipulation (South Africa)
Credit: Marcus Ranum, sxc.hu
Wind Sprites

BOTTOM LEFT
IRENE ZELESKOU
3D (Greece)
Robo Q Character Sheet

OPPOSITE TOP LEFT
NHUNG THAI
Photomanipulation (USA)
Prayers 3

OPPOSITE TOP RIGHT
ROB REY
Oil (USA)
Last Stand

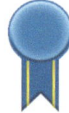

OPPOSITE BOTTOM
MICHAEL C. TURNER
Acrylic and Digital (USA)
SpaceHenge

(Overleaf)

LEFT PAGE
CRAIG MUSSELMAN
Photomanipulation (Canada)
Credit: Marcus Ranum, sxc.hu
The Celtic Machine

RIGHT PAGE TOP
CRAIG MUSSELMAN
Photomanipulation (Canada)
Credit: Marcus Ranum, sxc.hu
Autumn Legerdemain

RIGHT PAGE BOTTOM
SAM MANLEY
Photoshop (England)
Where Giants Once Roamed

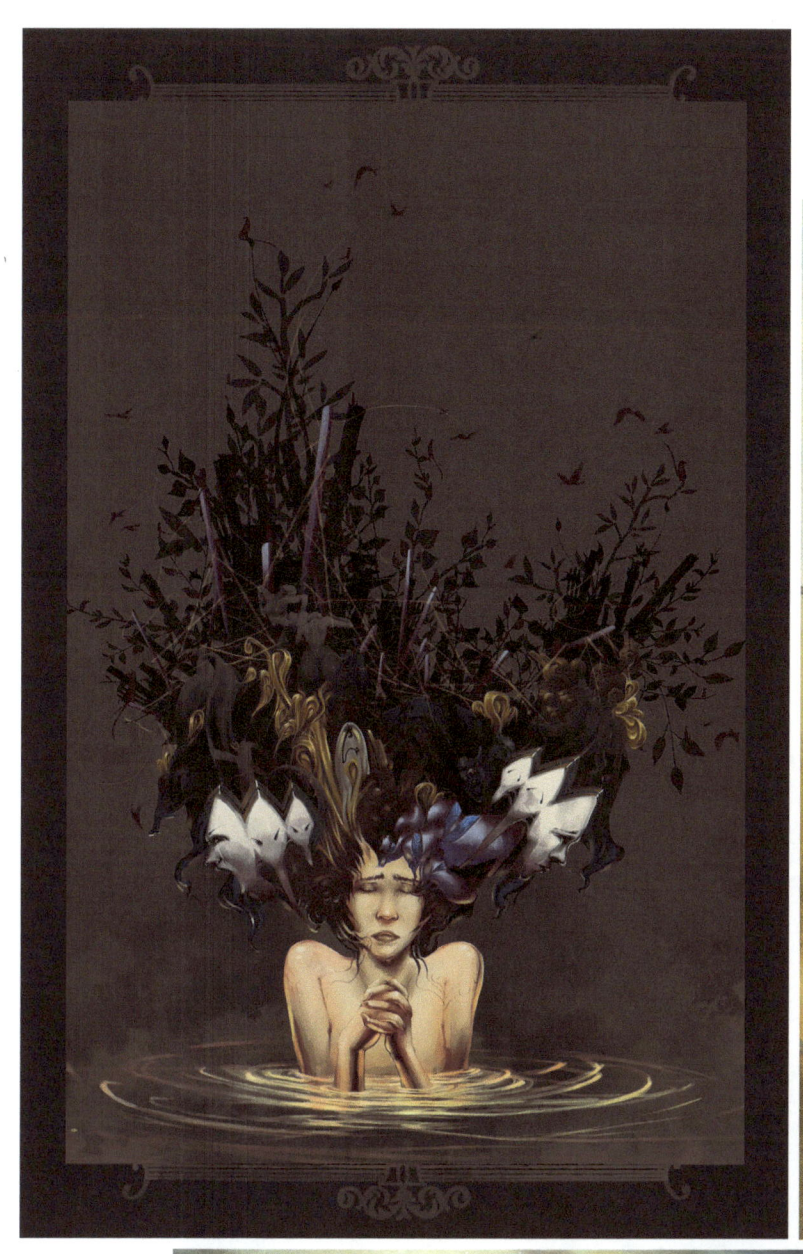

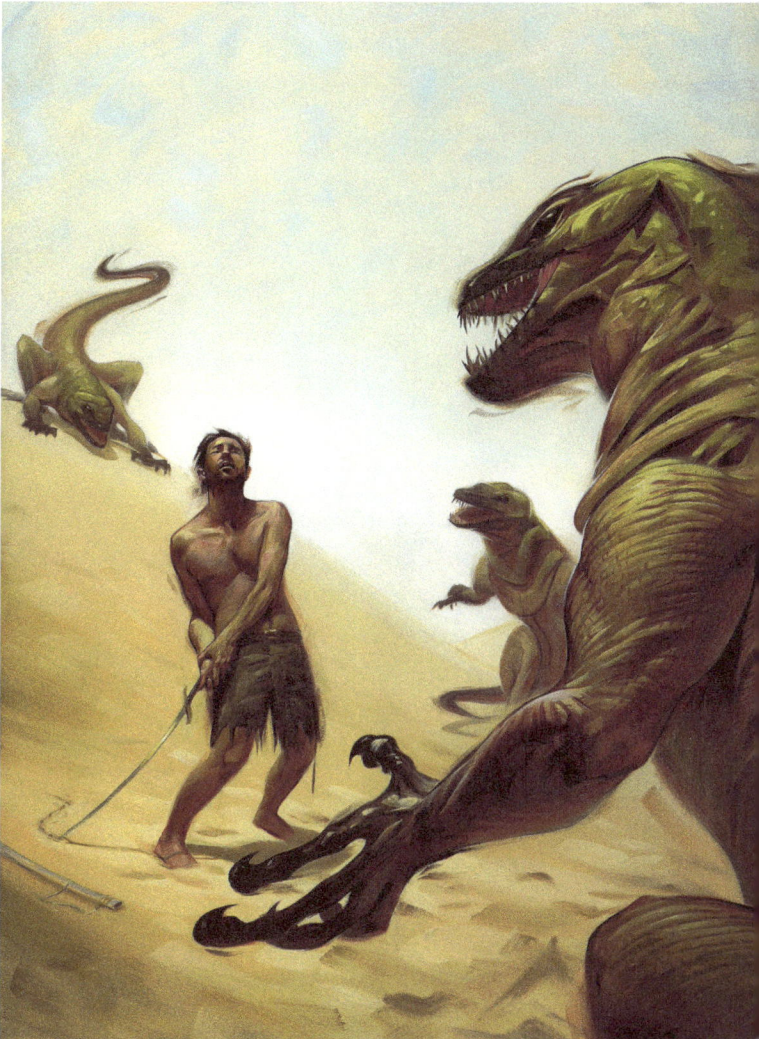

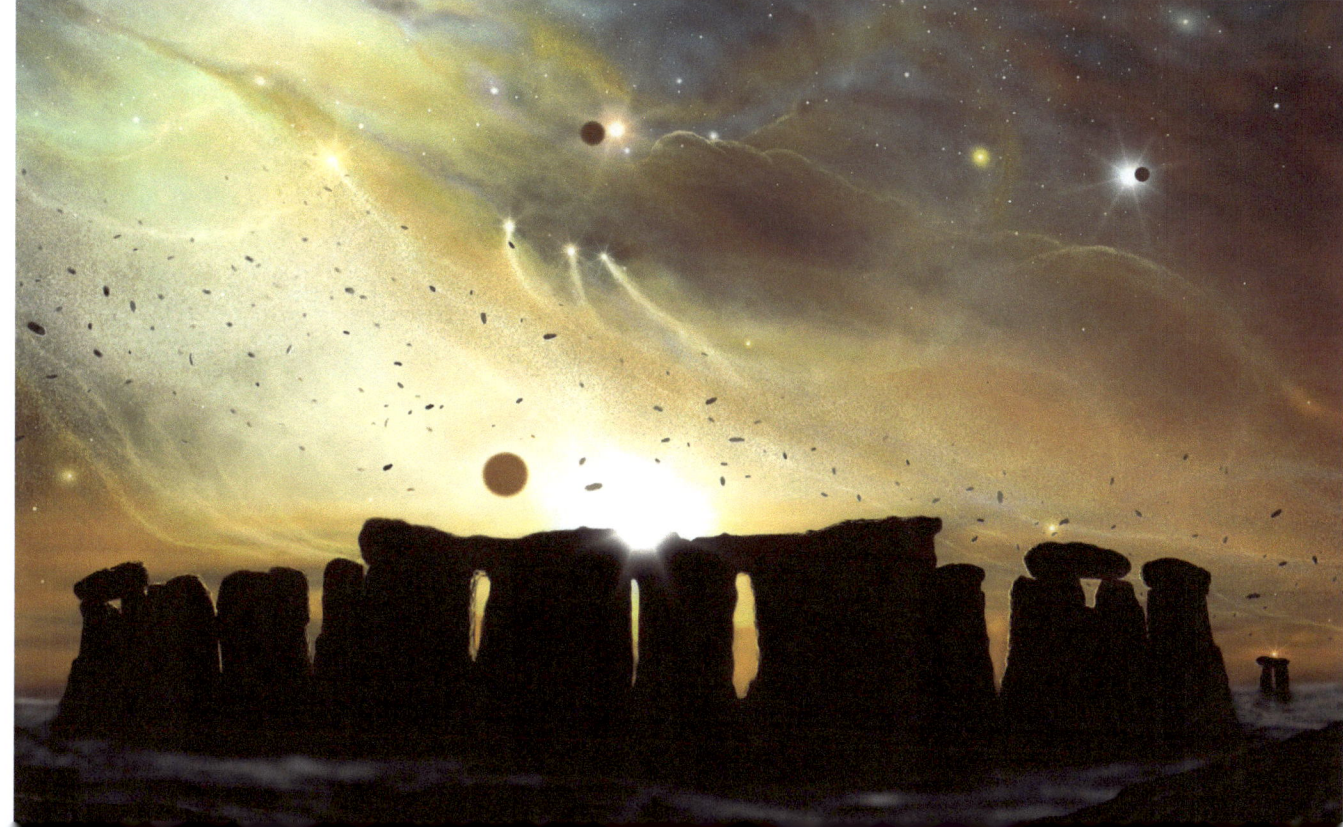

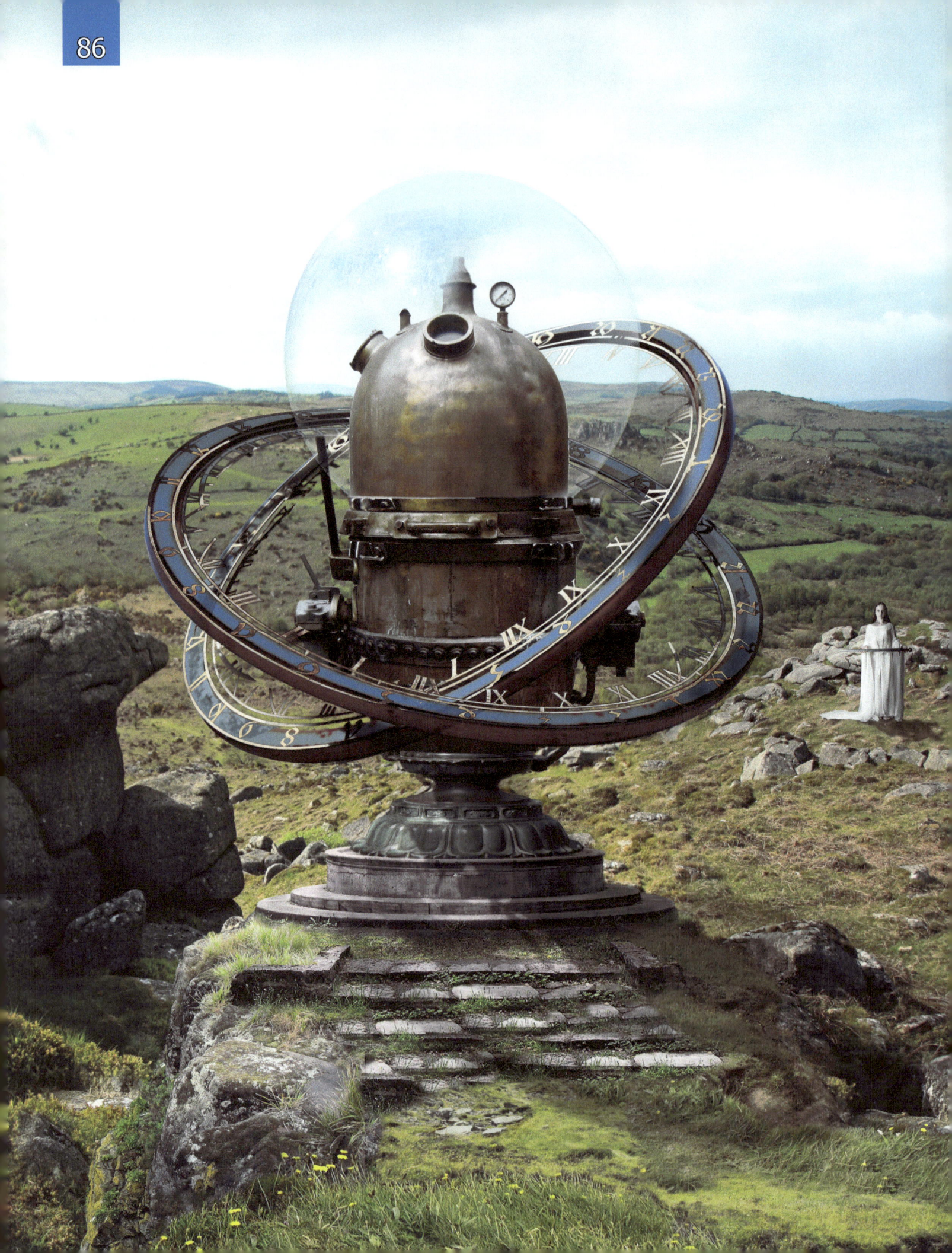

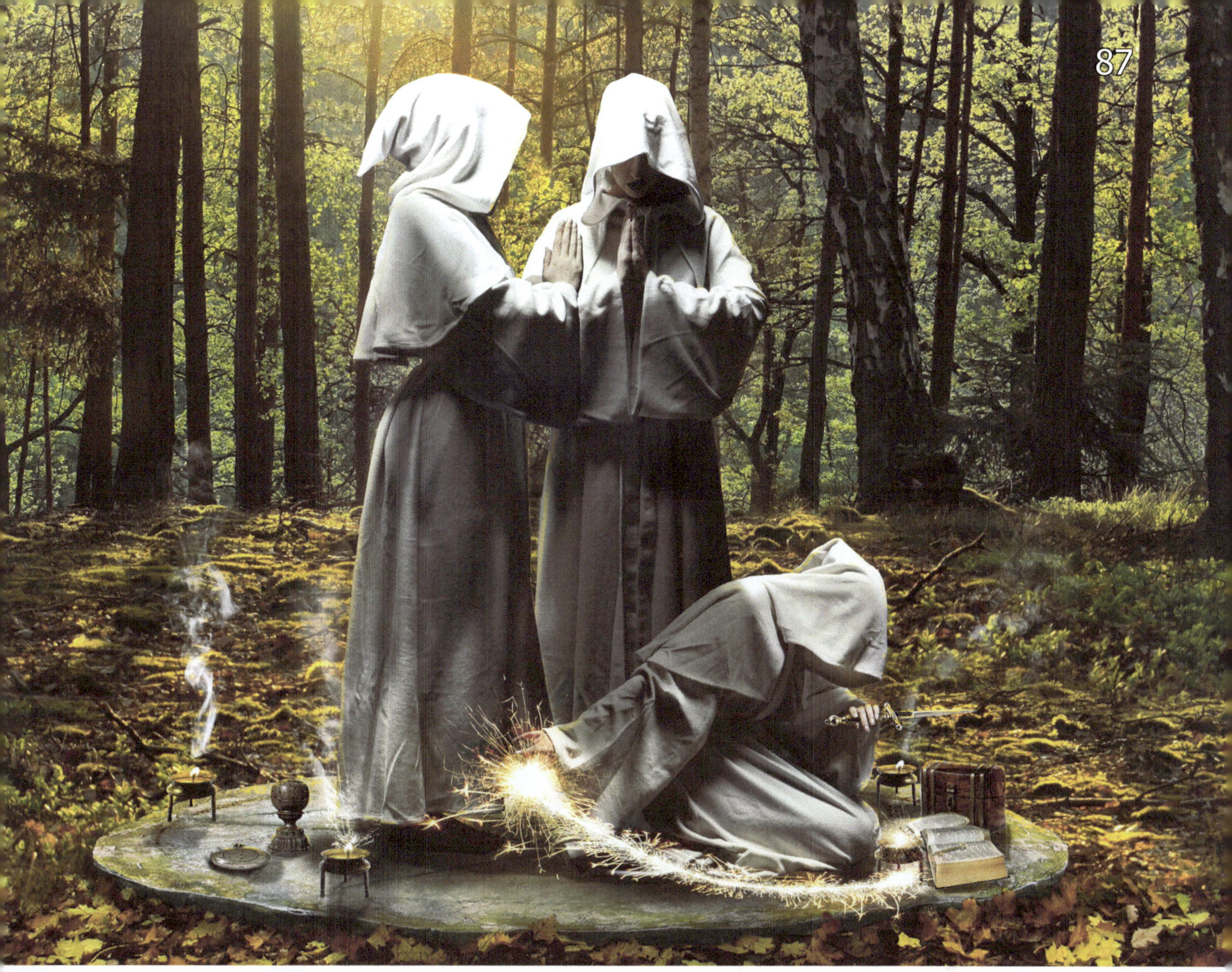

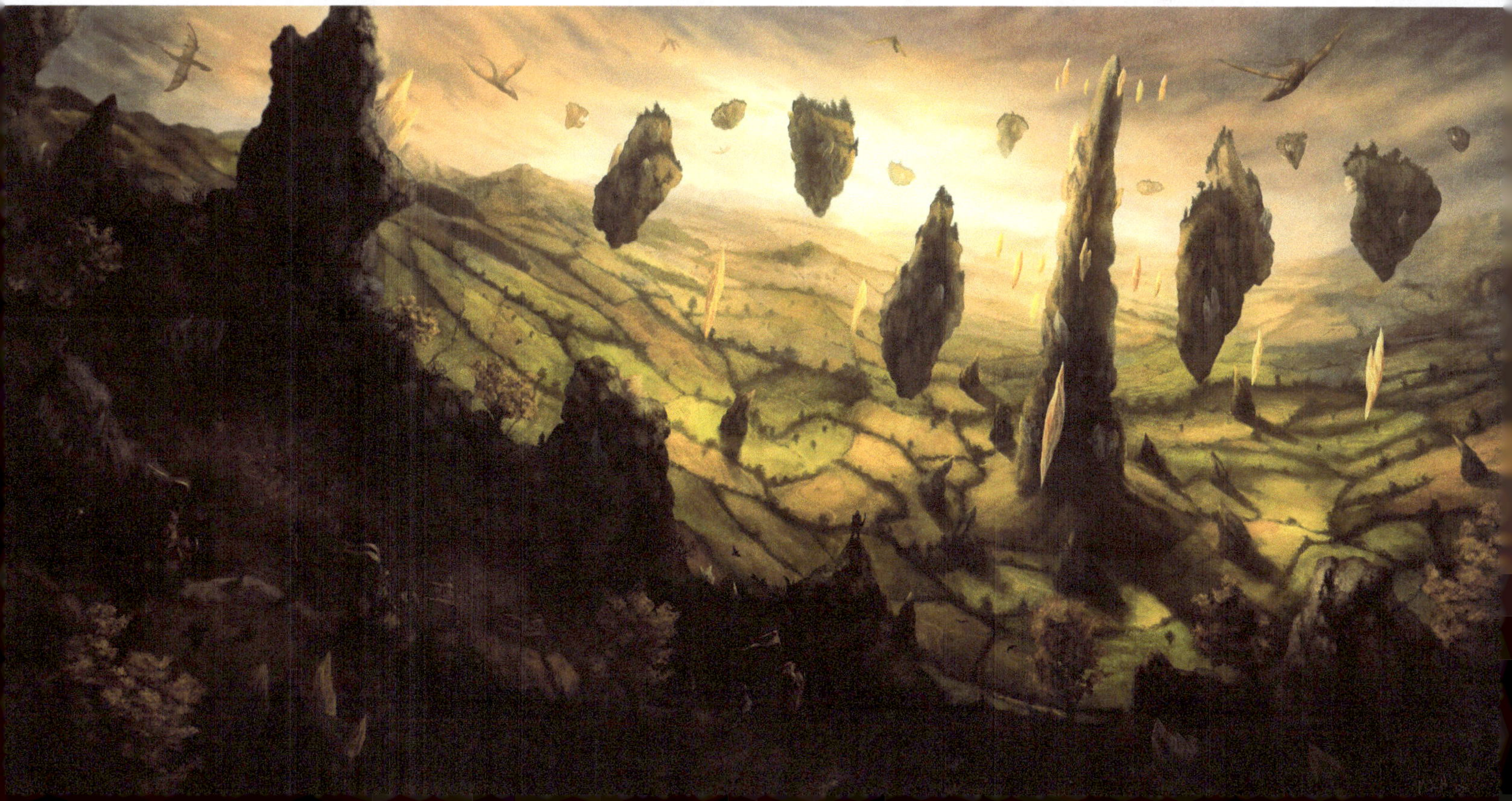

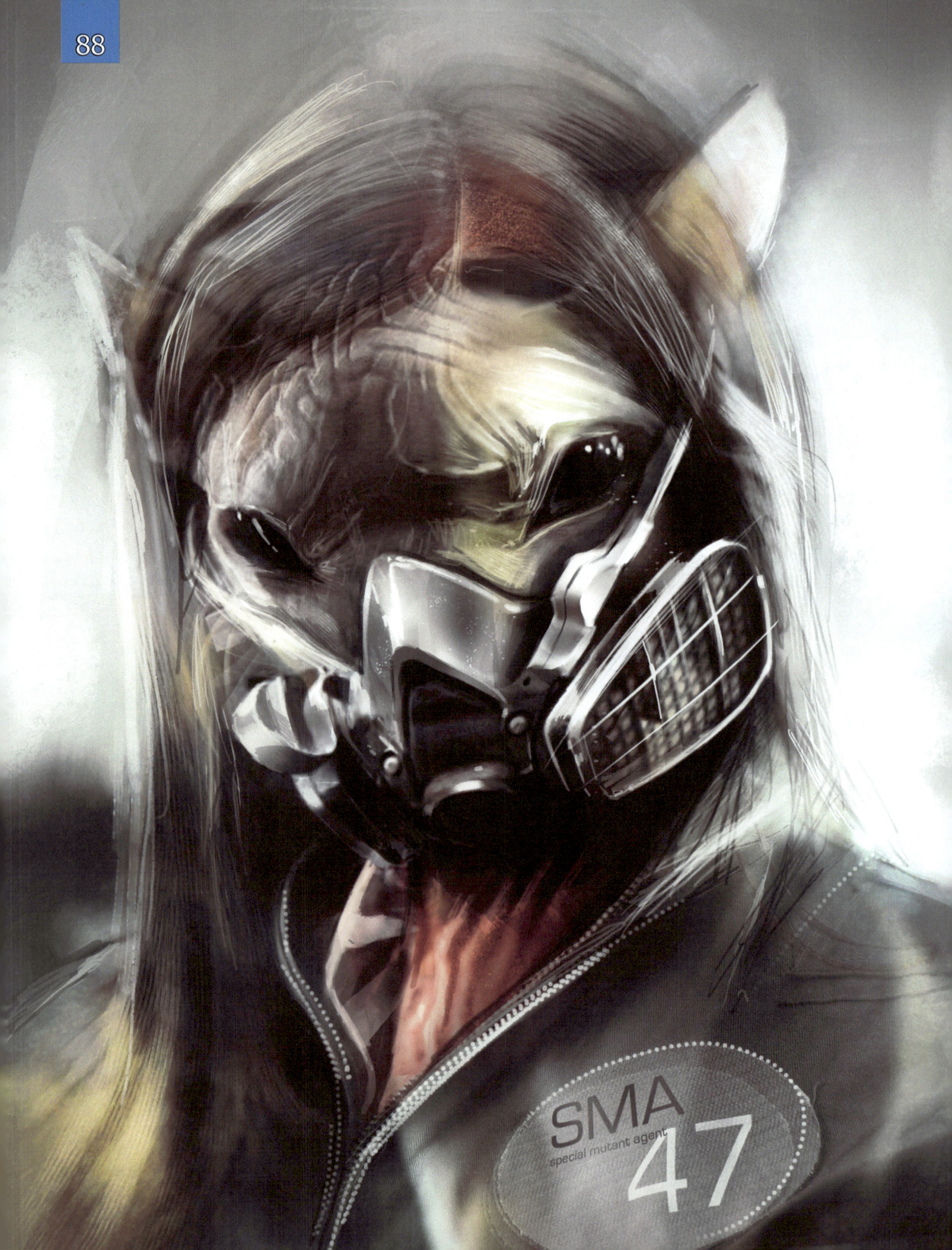

SMA
special mutant agent
47

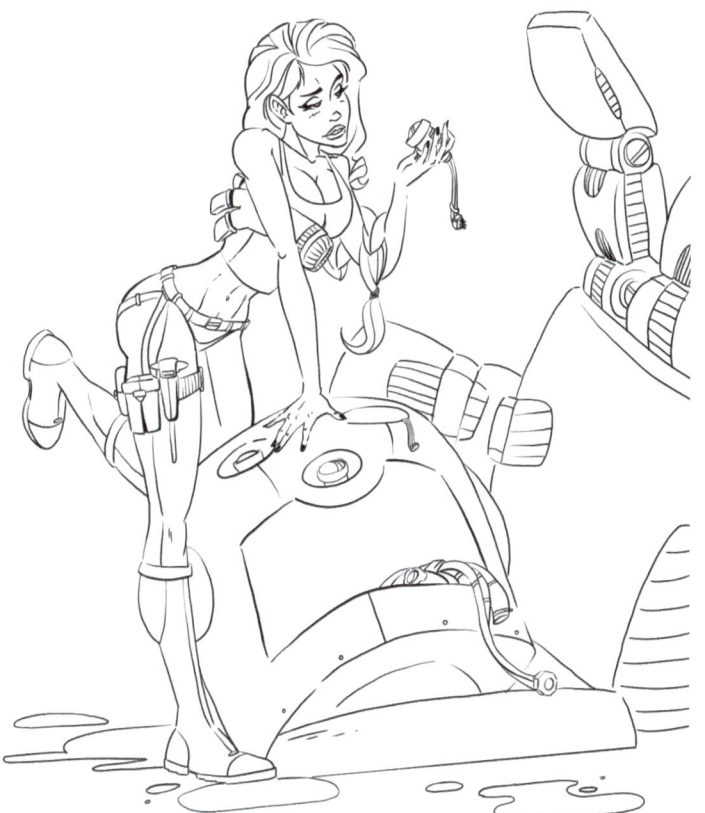

OPPOSITE
LIVIU TUDORAN
Photoshop (Italy)
Special Mutant Agent

LEFT
EDWARD ROCHA
Photoshop (Australia)
Robot Repair Chic

BOTTOM LEFT
AL SEROV
Photoshop, Painter, Cinema 4D (Canada)
Roman Fantasy

BELOW
LINCOLN RENALL
Photoshop (New Zealand)
Breeze

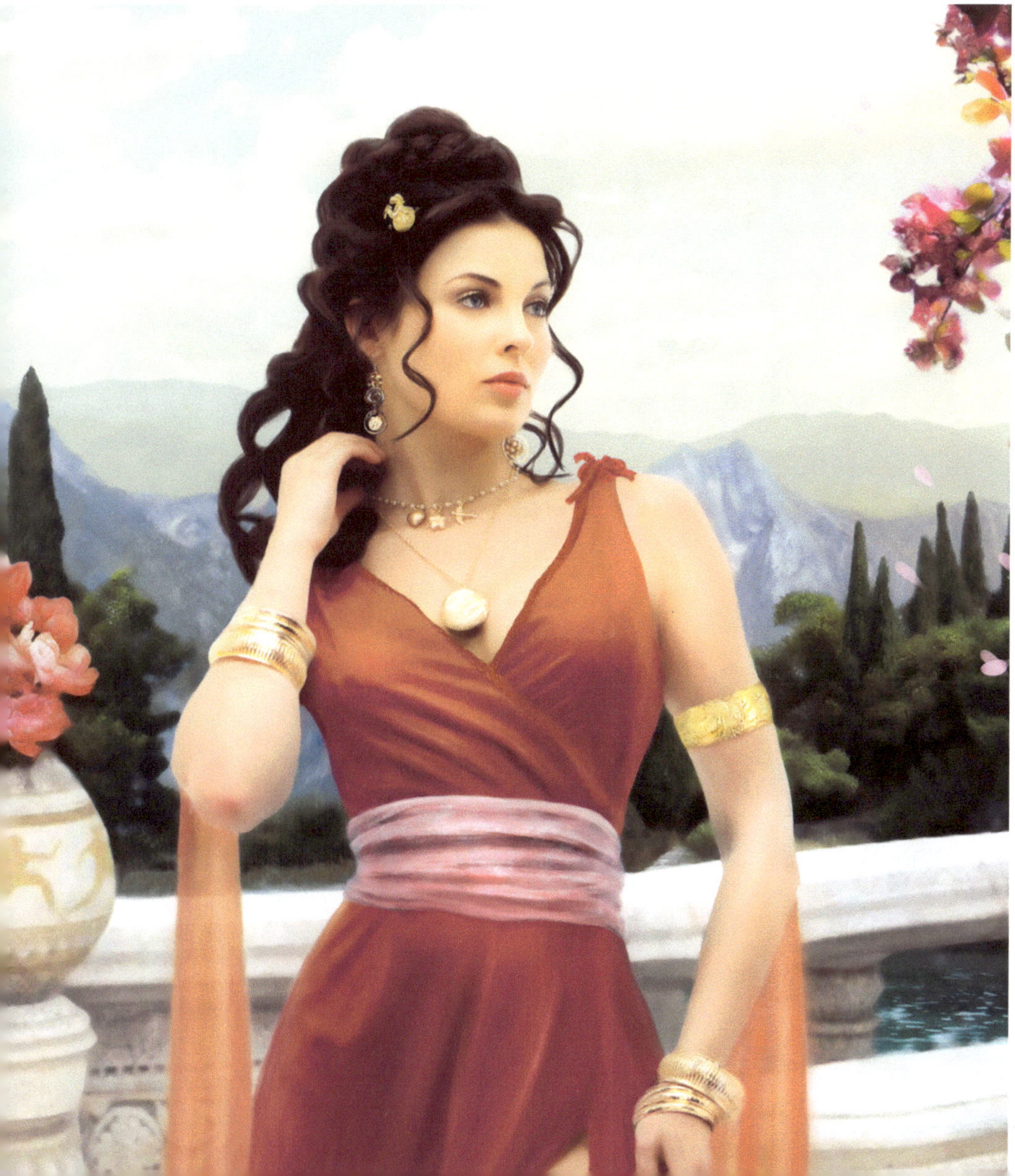

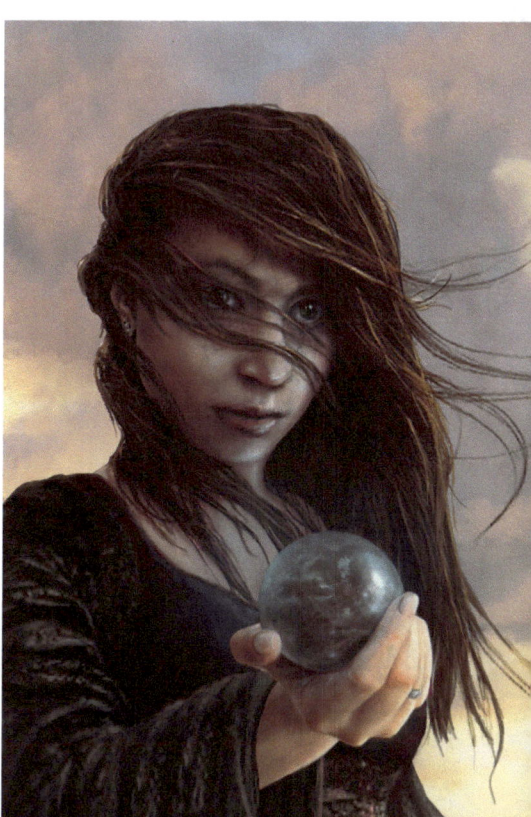

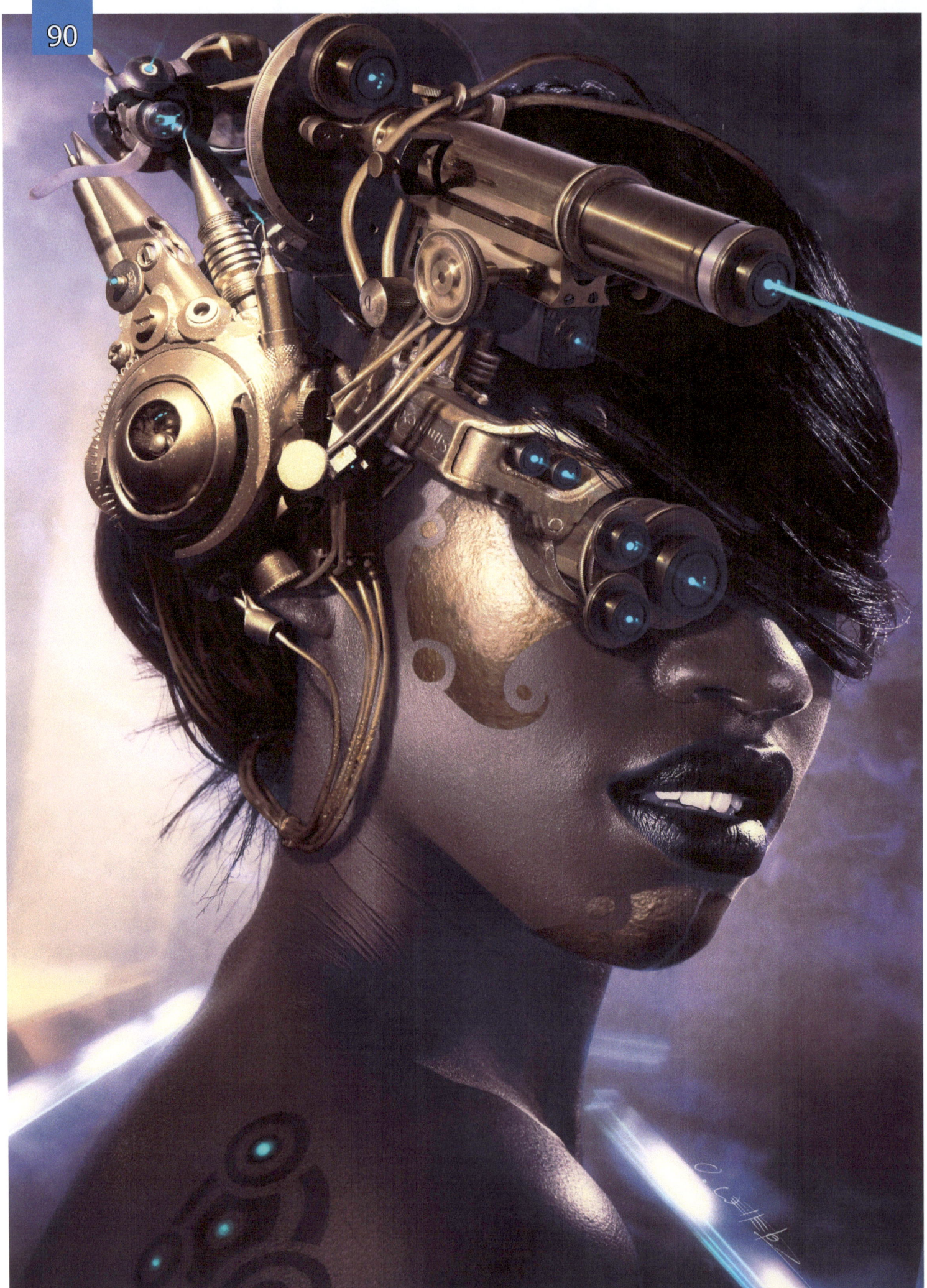

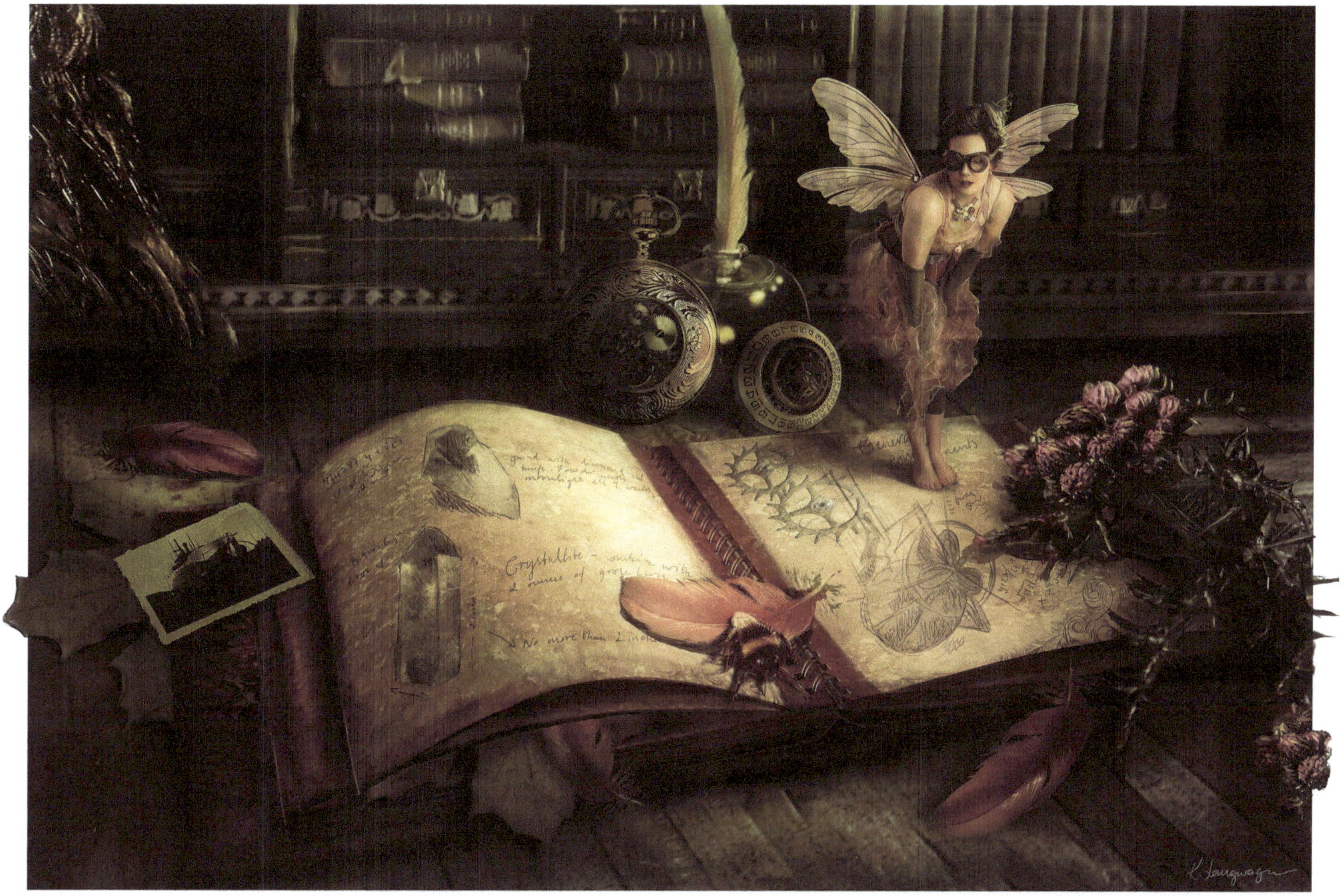

OPPOSITE
Oliver Wetter
Sculpture and Photoshop (Germany)
Bladerunner

ABOVE
Cathrine Langwagen
Photoshop (UK)
Credit: Deviantart.com (magikstock, goblin-stock)
The Journal

LEFT
Wil Oberdier
Pencil/Digital (USA)
More than a Survivor

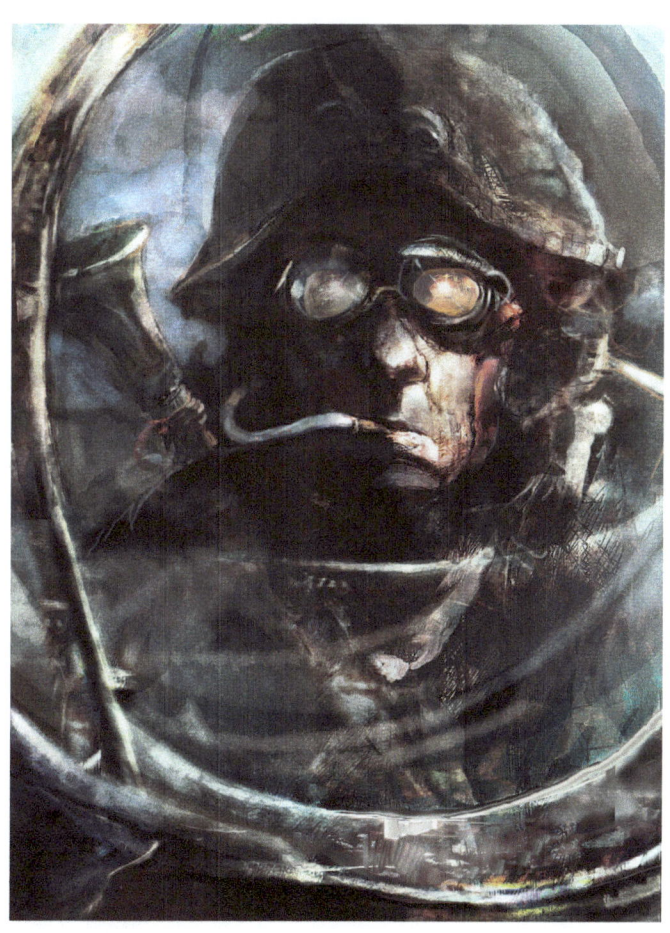

RIGHT

KATHERINE ELLIS
Photoshop (England)
Reflections

BELOW LEFT

KATHERINE ELLIS
Photoshop (England)
Joey and Jack

BELOW RIGHT

KATHERINE ELLIS
Photoshop (England)
The Rider

OPPOSITE

KATHERINE ELLIS
Photoshop (England)
The Mechanic

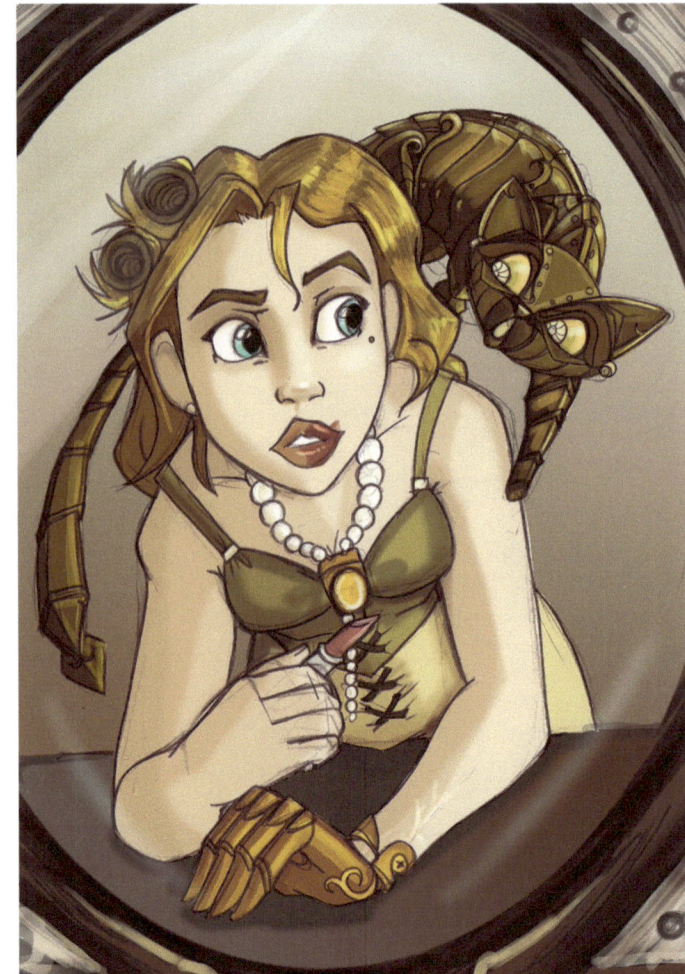

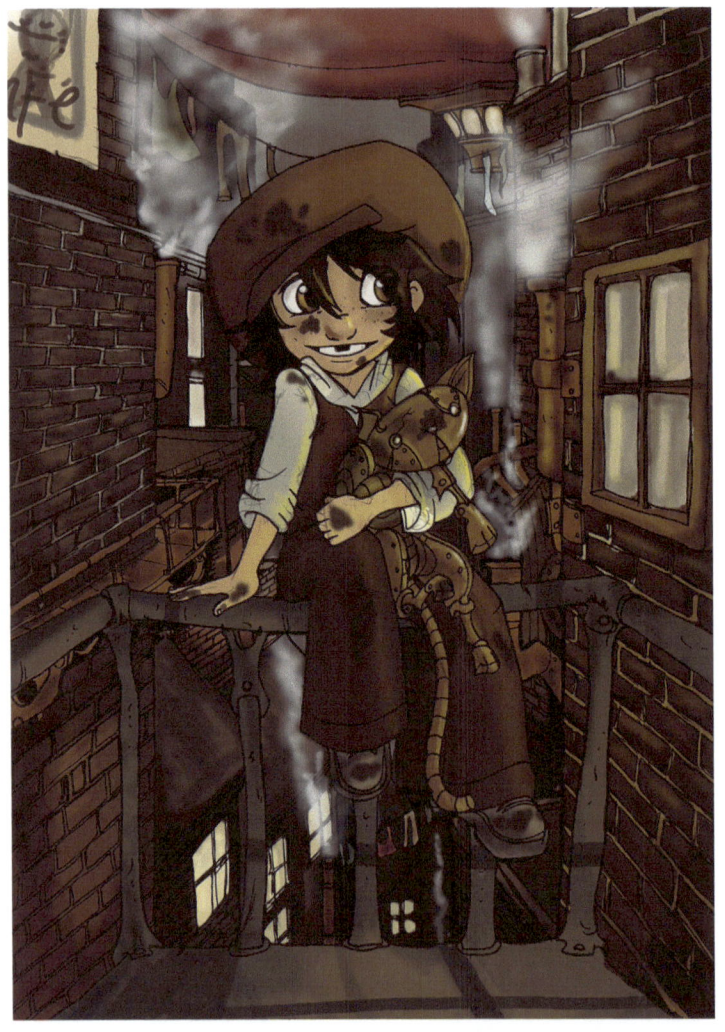

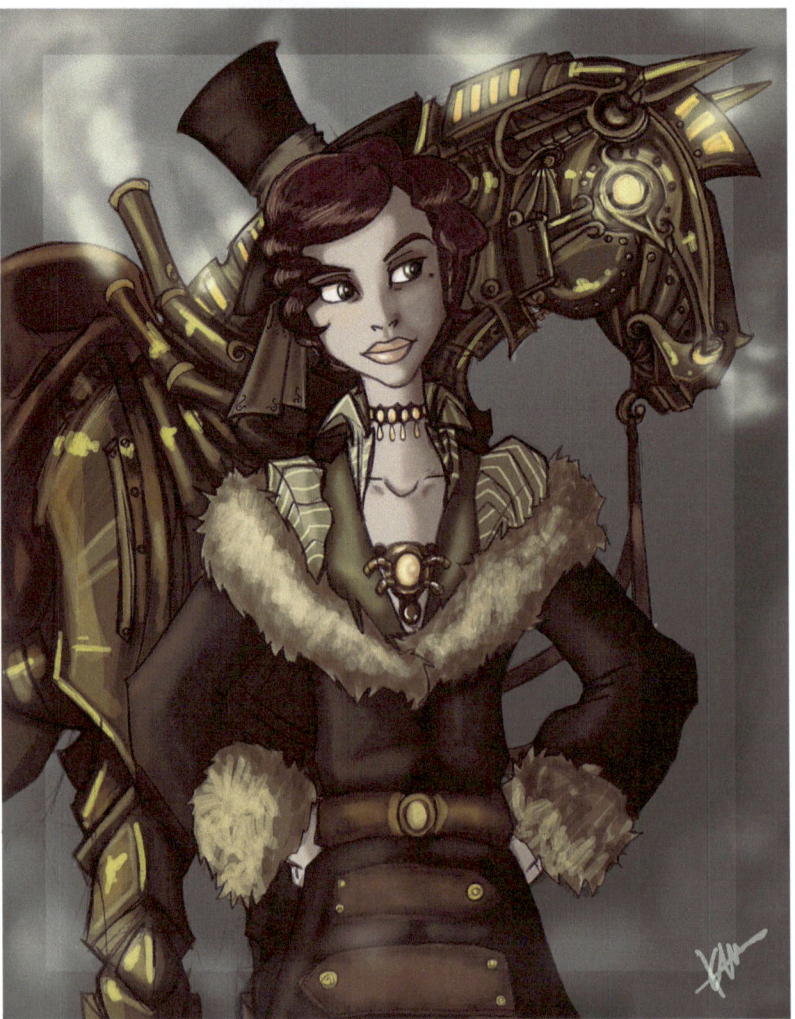

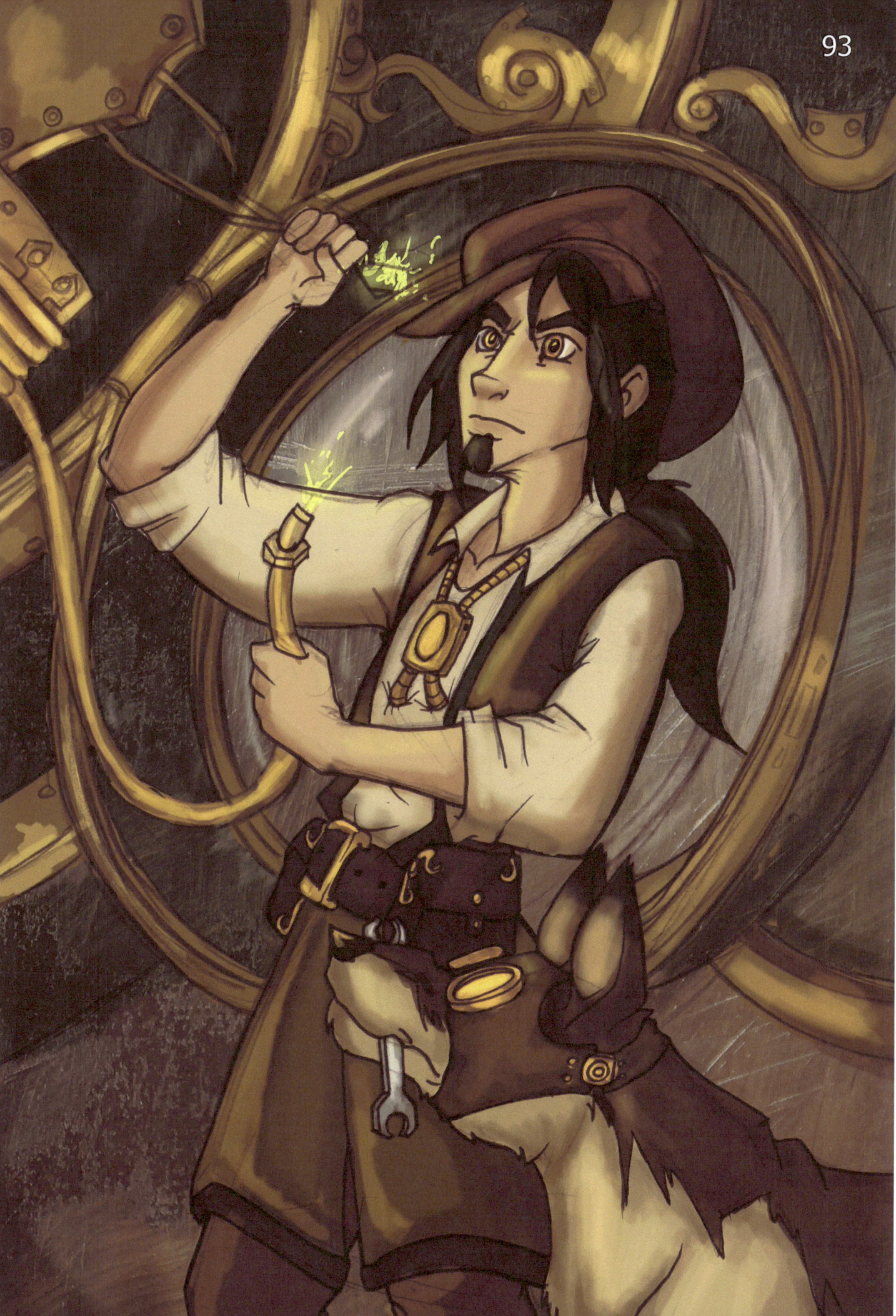

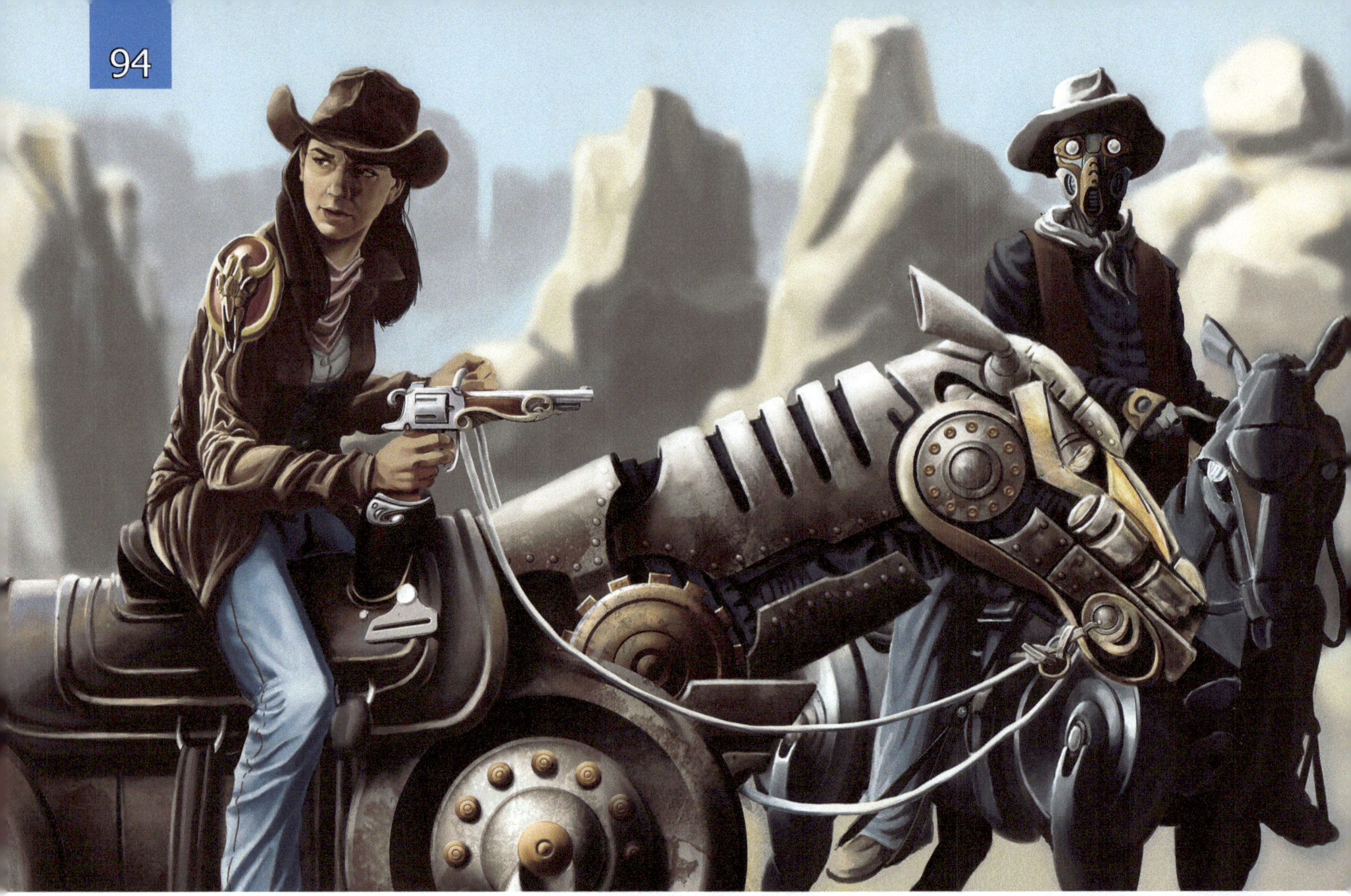

ABOVE
LUCAS DURHAM
Photoshop and Illustrator (USA)
Steam, Steal, and True Grit

RIGHT
LINCOLN RENALL
Photoshop (New Zealand)
Dreamscape

OPPOSITE
PETER WHITE
Pencil and Photoshop (USA)
Escape Through Maintenance 3

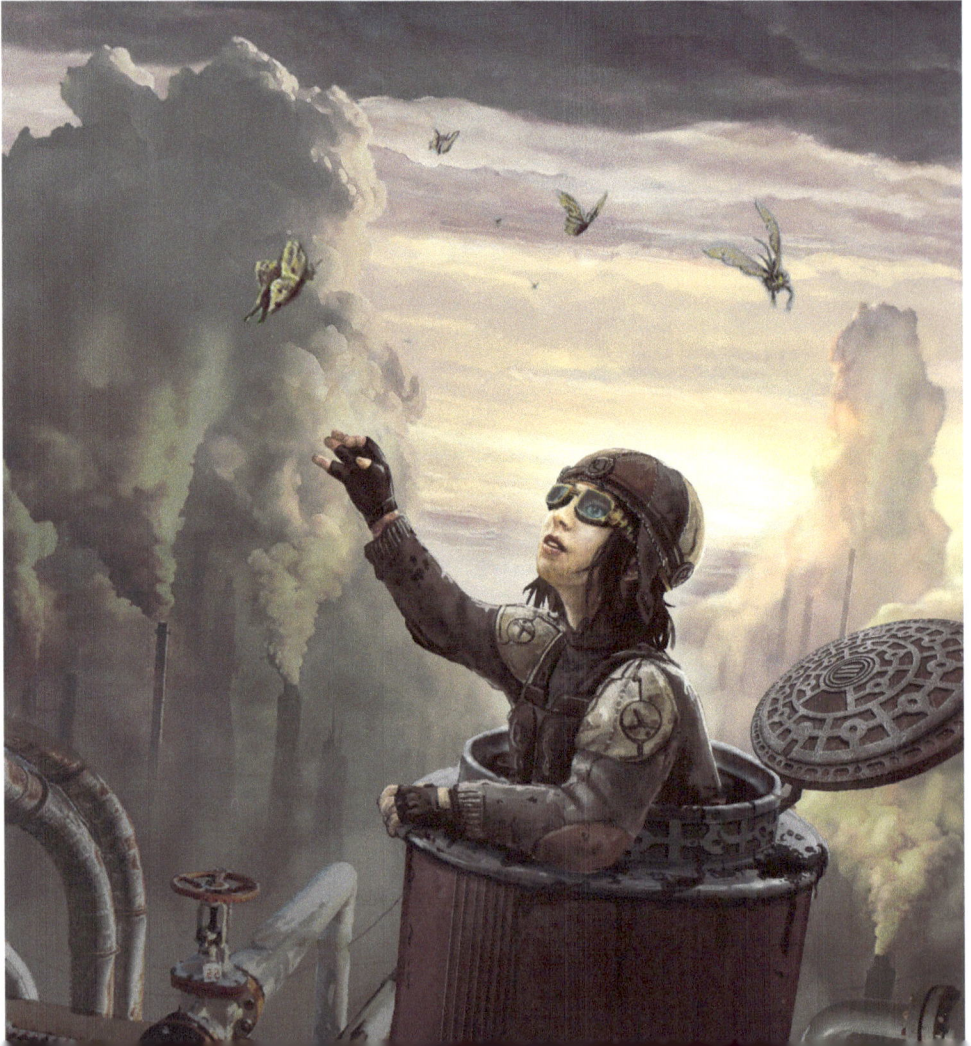

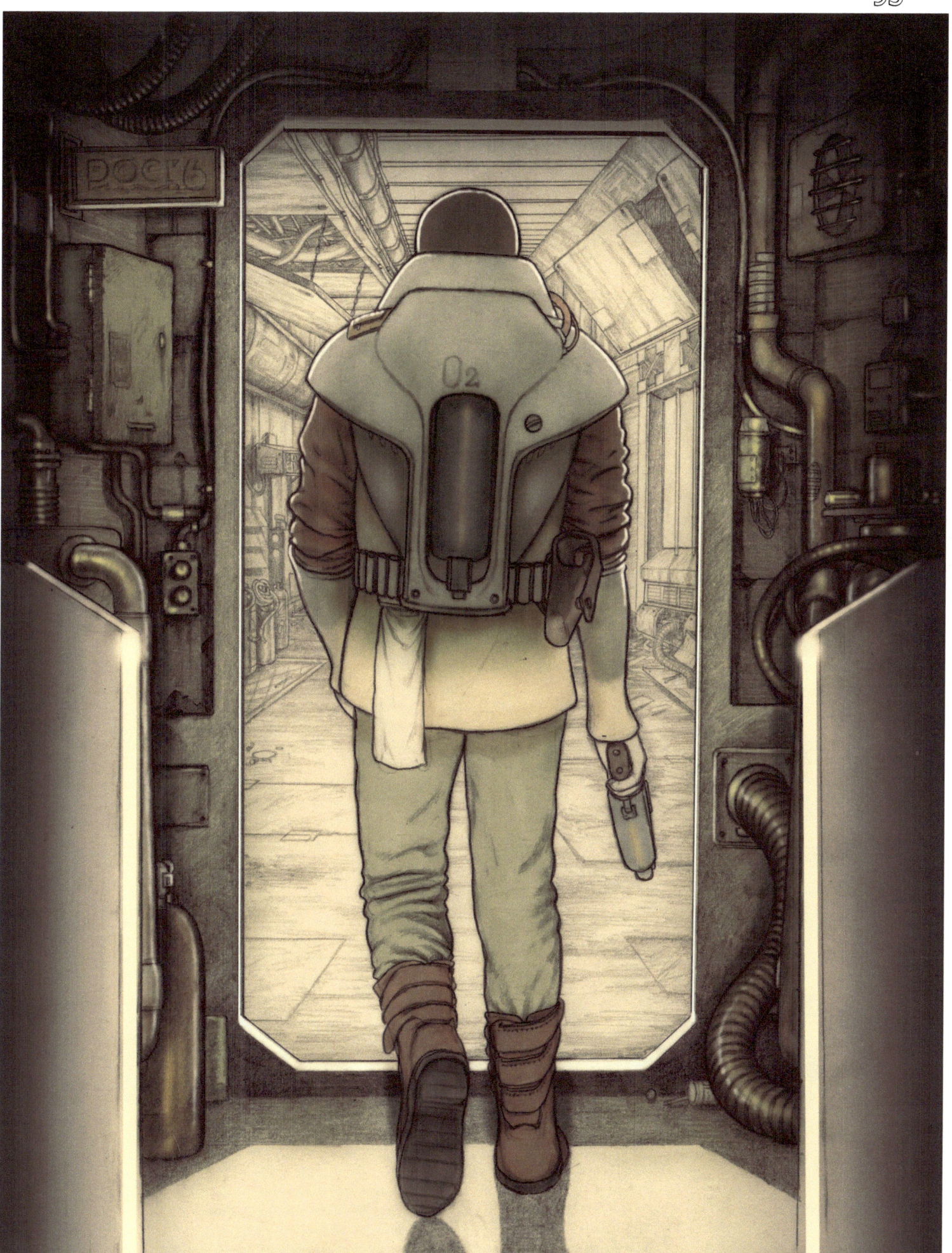

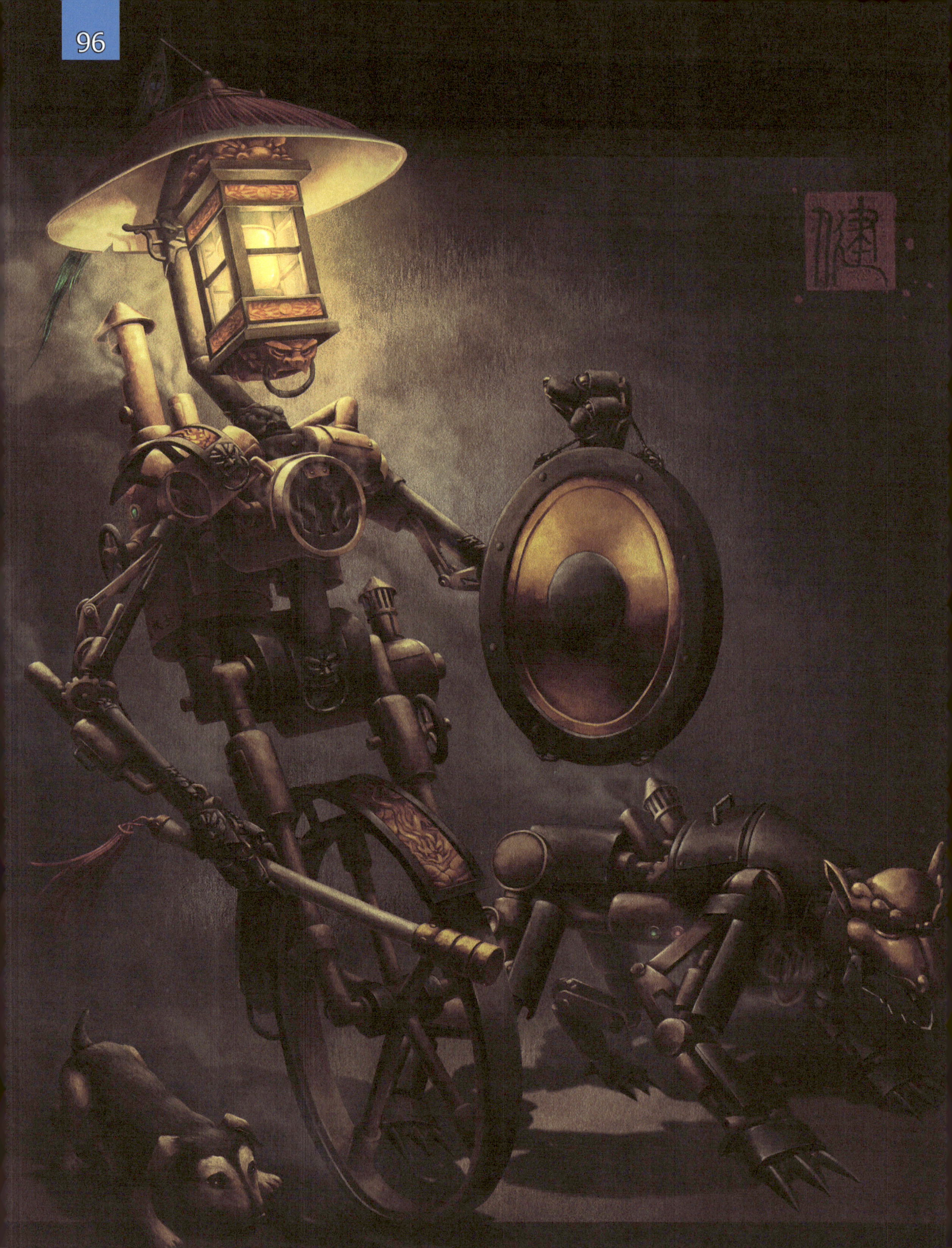

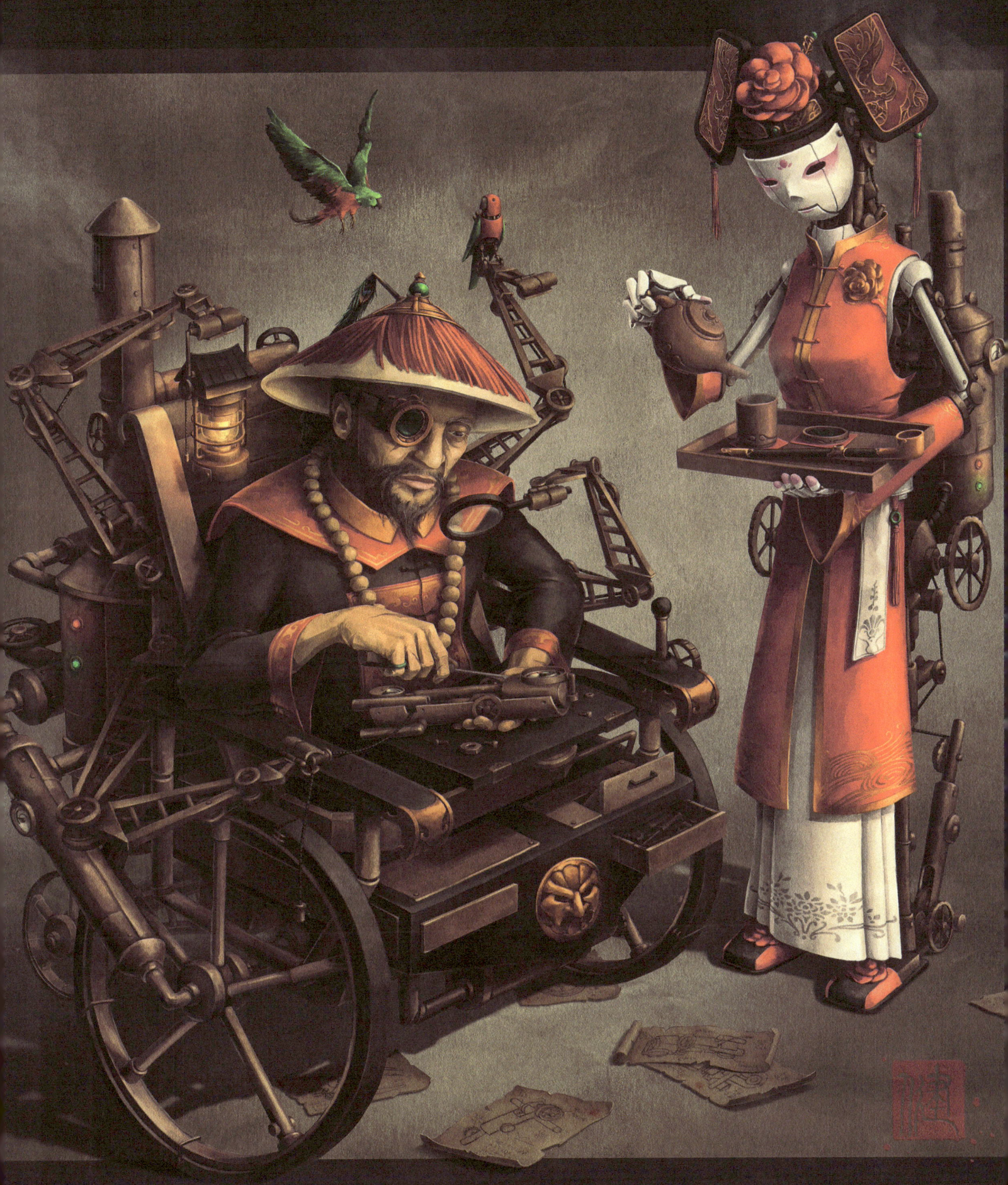

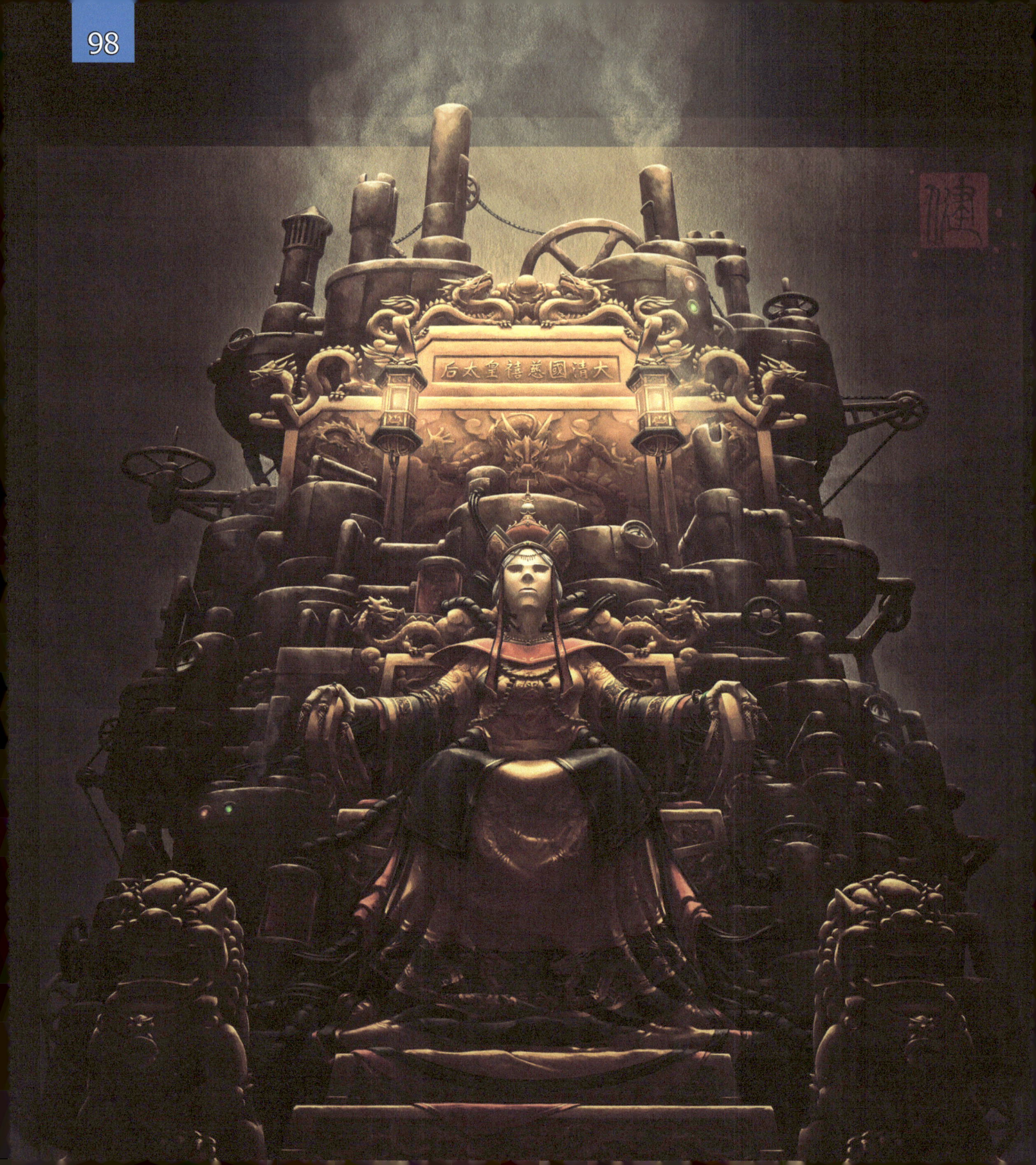

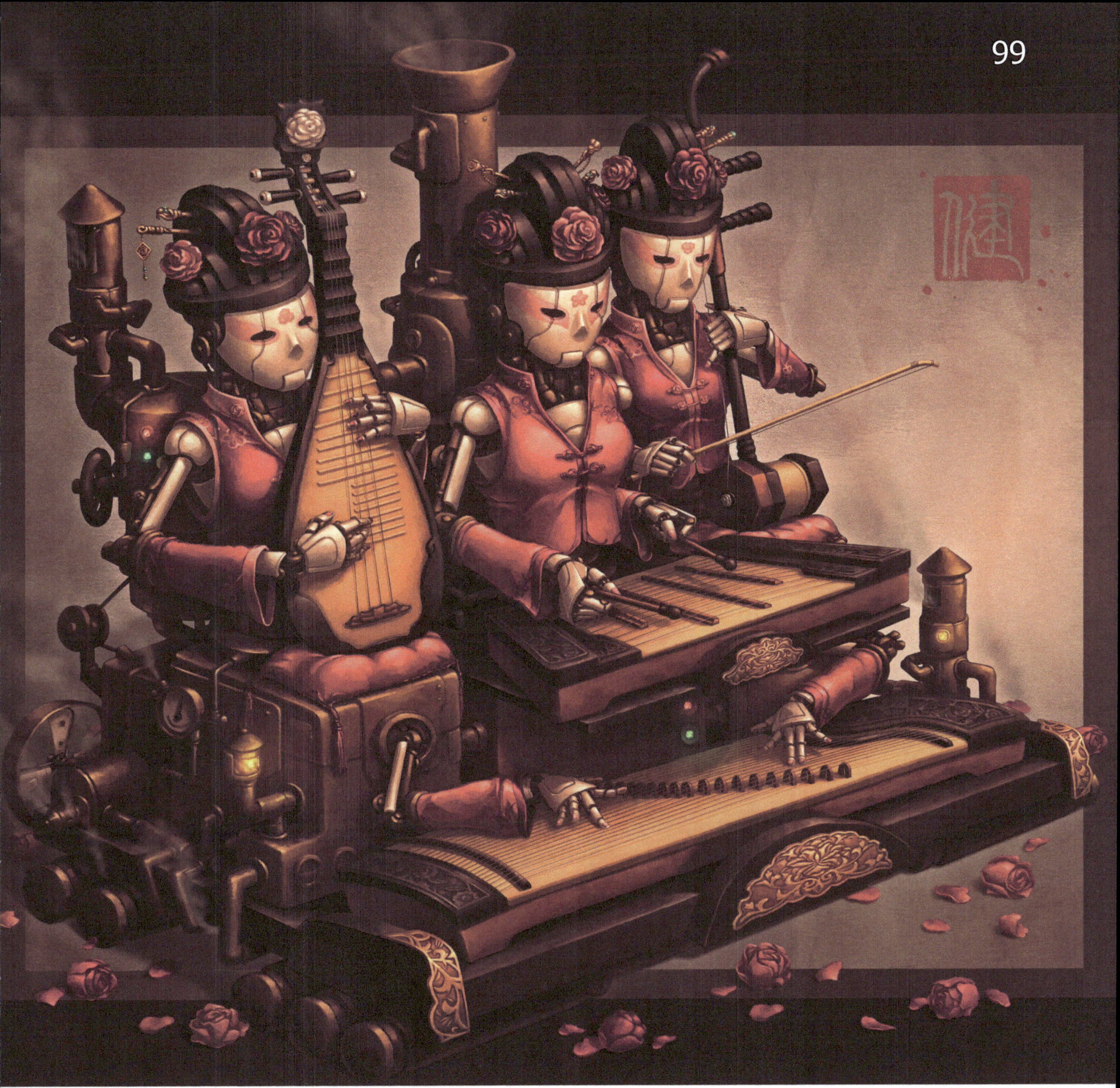

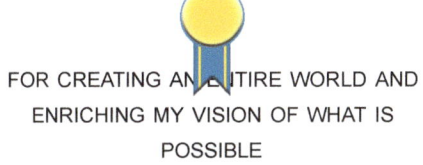

(Previous)

LEFT PAGE

JAMES NG
Pencil, Charcoal, Painter, Photoshop (Hong Kong/ Canada)
Night Patrol

RIGHT PAGE

JAMES NG
Pencil, Charcoal, Painter, Photoshop (Hong Kong/ Canada)
Imperial Inventor

(Current Page)

ABOVE

JAMES NG
Pencil, Charcoal, Painter, Photoshop (Hong Kong/ Canada)
Court Band

OPPOSITE

JAMES NG
Pencil, Charcoal, Painter, Photoshop (Hong Kong/ Canada)
Immortal Empress

EDITOR'S CHOICE AWARD 2011

JAMES NG

FOR CREATING AN ENTIRE WORLD AND ENRICHING MY VISION OF WHAT IS POSSIBLE

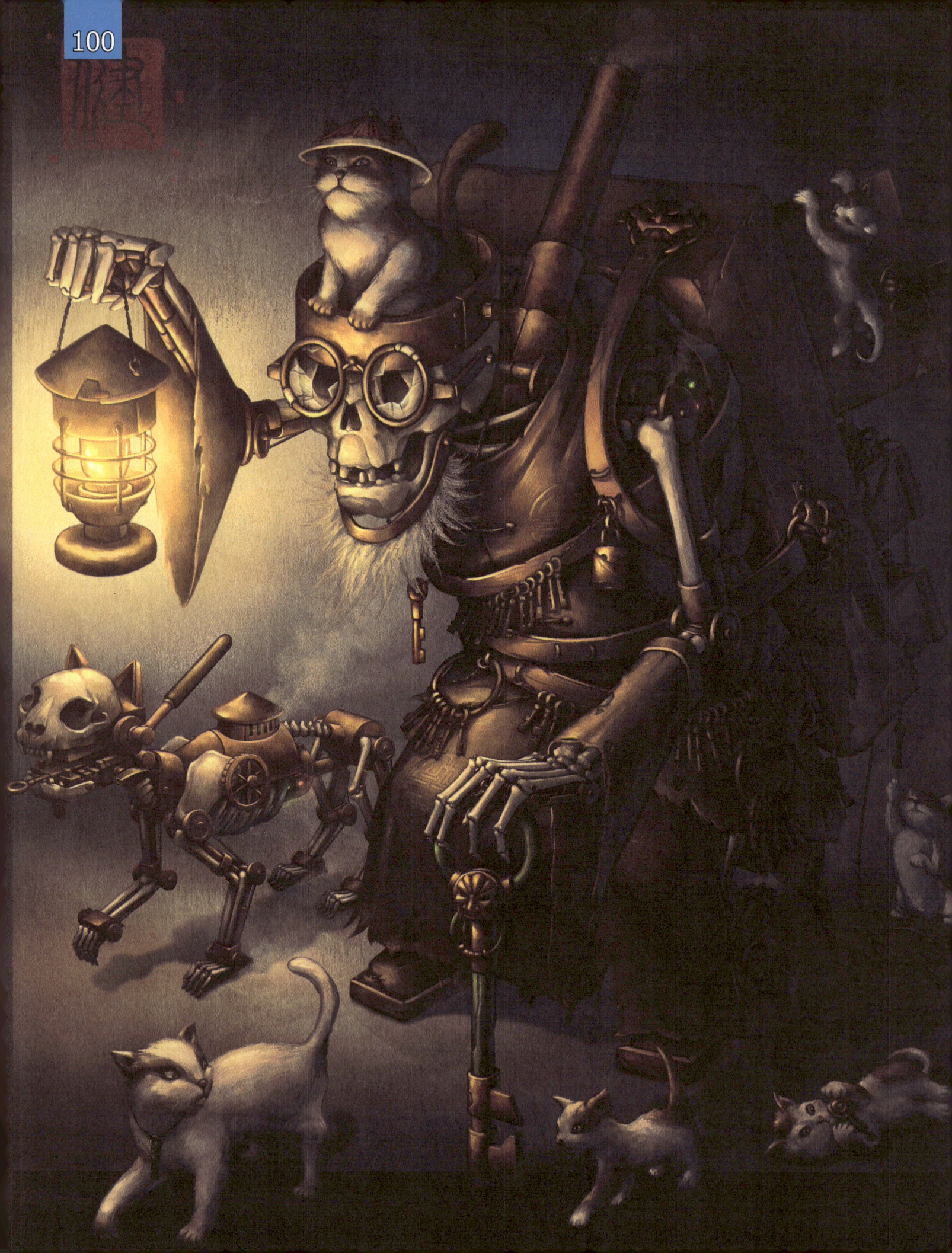

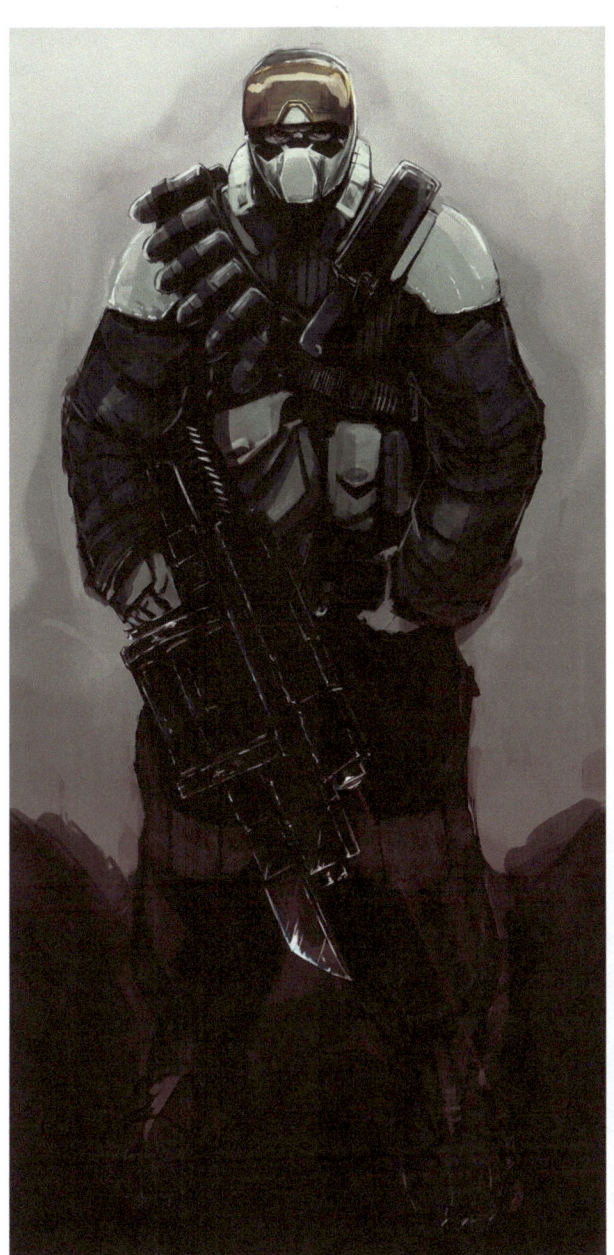

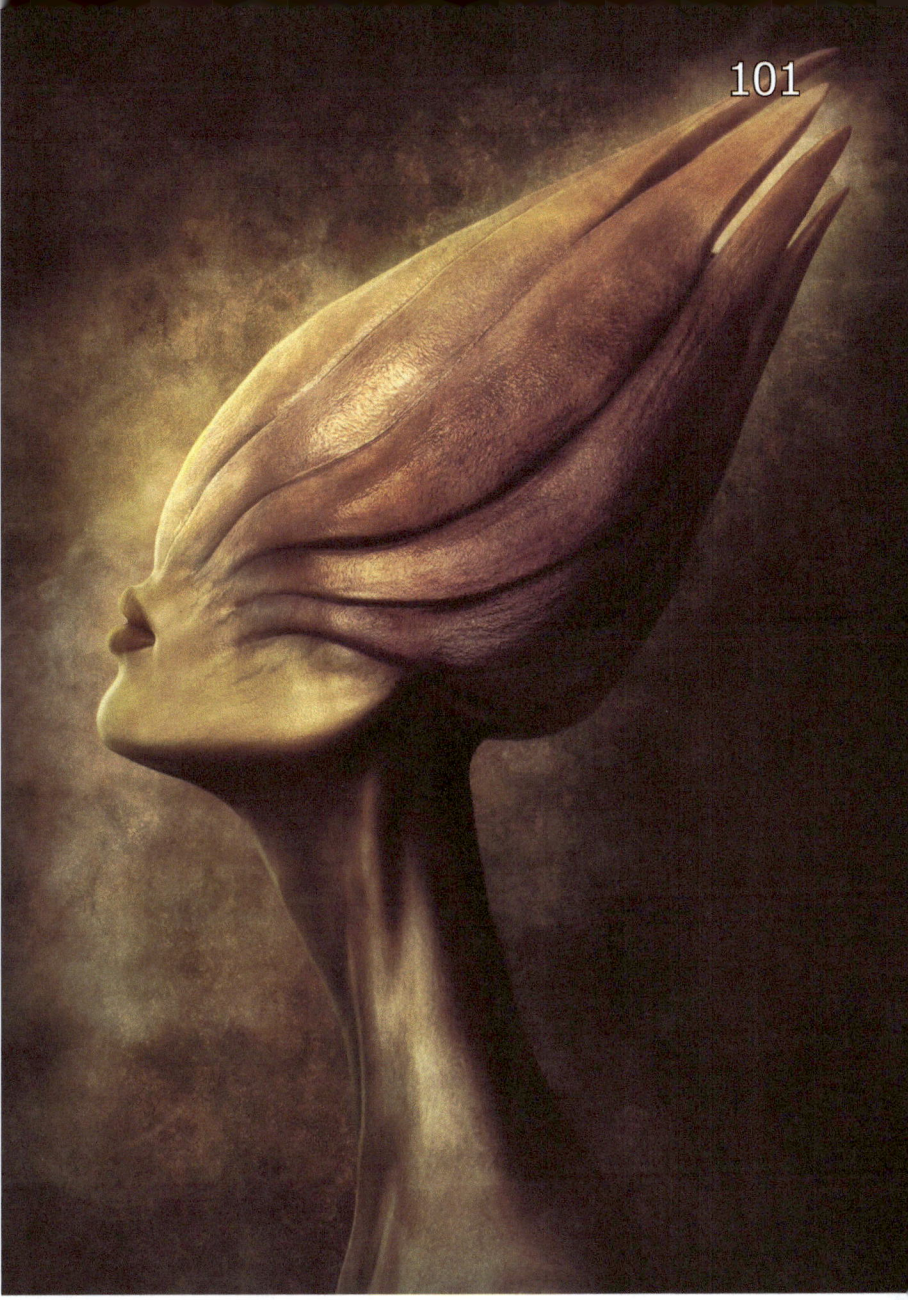

OPPOSITE

JAMES NG
Pencil, Charcoal, Painter,
Photoshop (Hong Kong/ Canada)
Key Keeper

ABOVE LEFT

JULIAN LANCASTER
Photoshop (Canada)
Grenadier

ABOVE RIGHT

RIYAHD CASSIEM
Zbrush and Photoshop (South Africa)
Dahlia

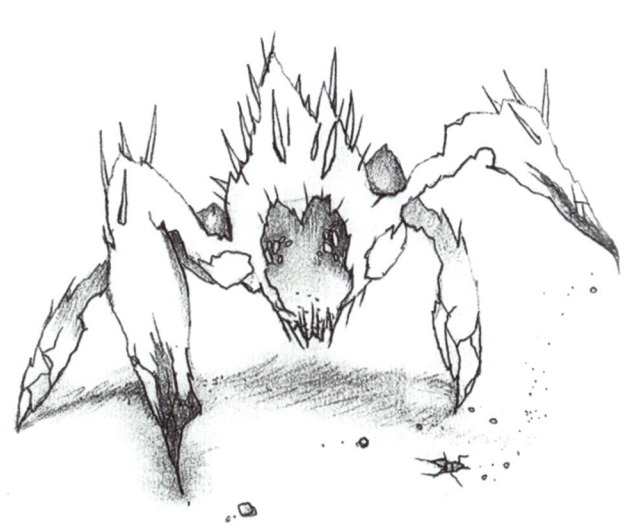

BOTTOM

FRANCIS-LEE PIMENTEL
Pencil (England)
Demon II

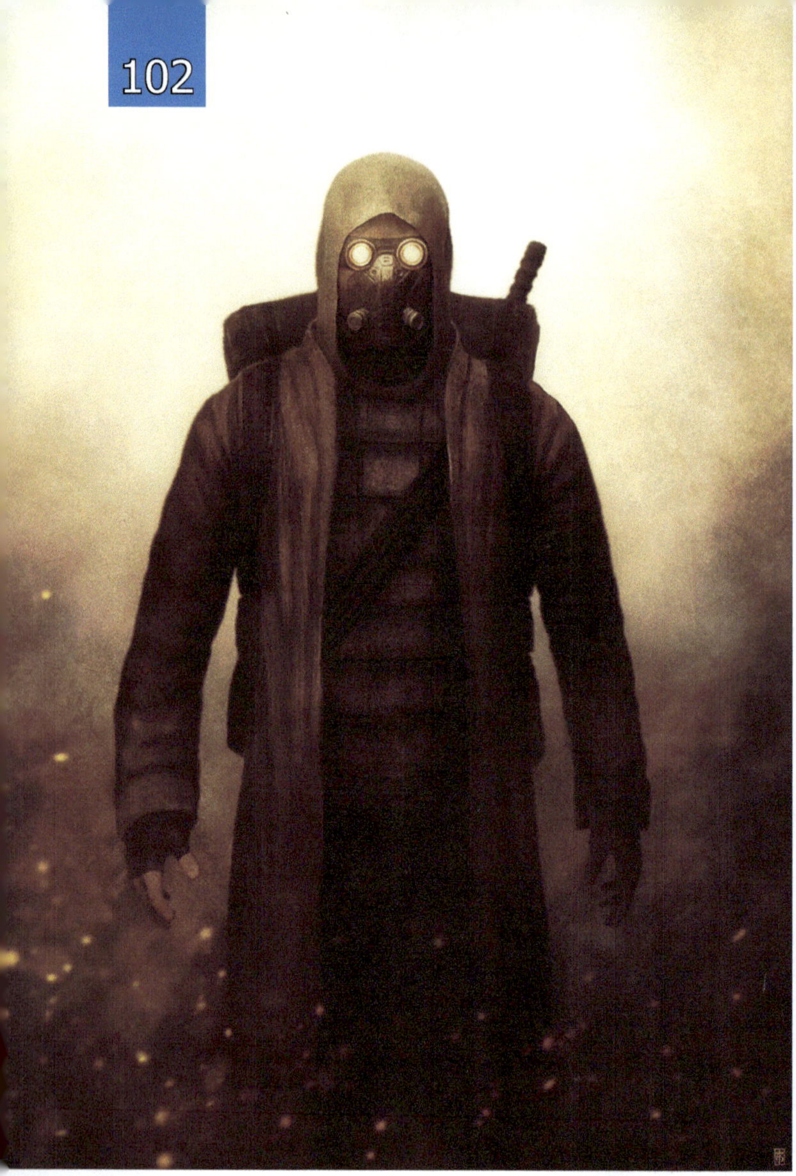

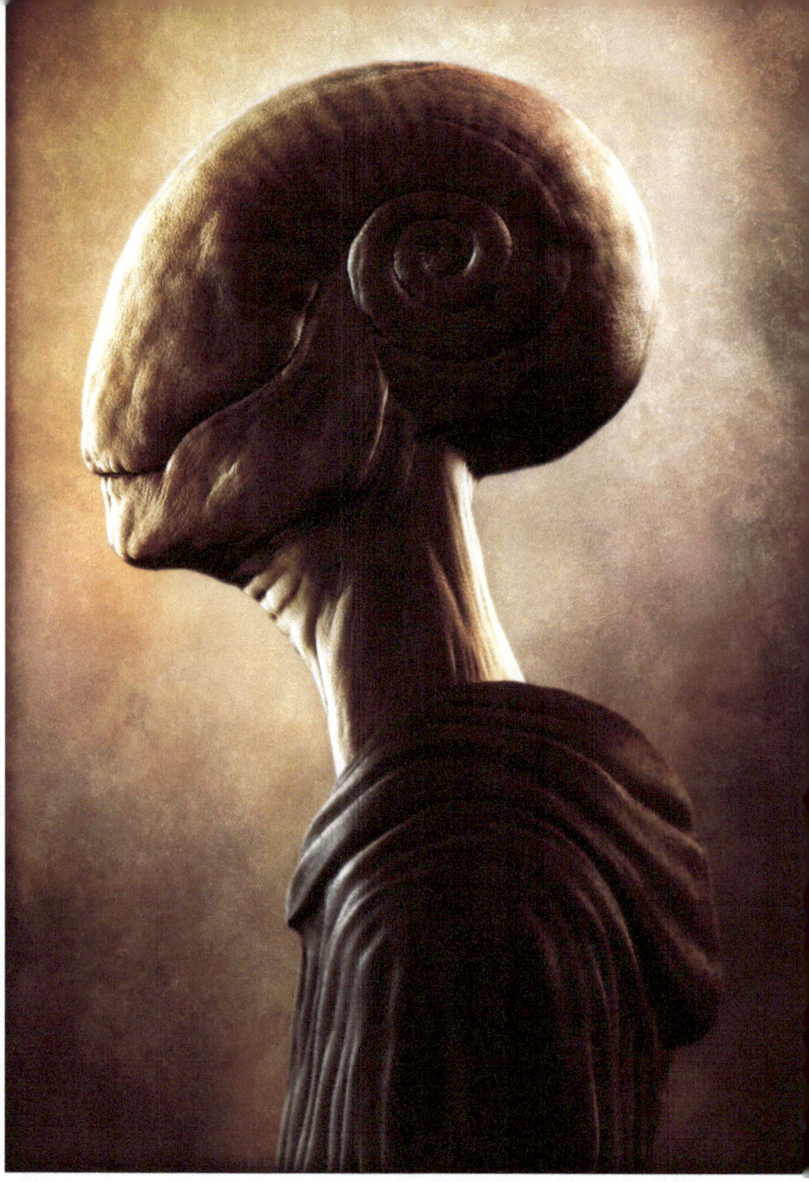

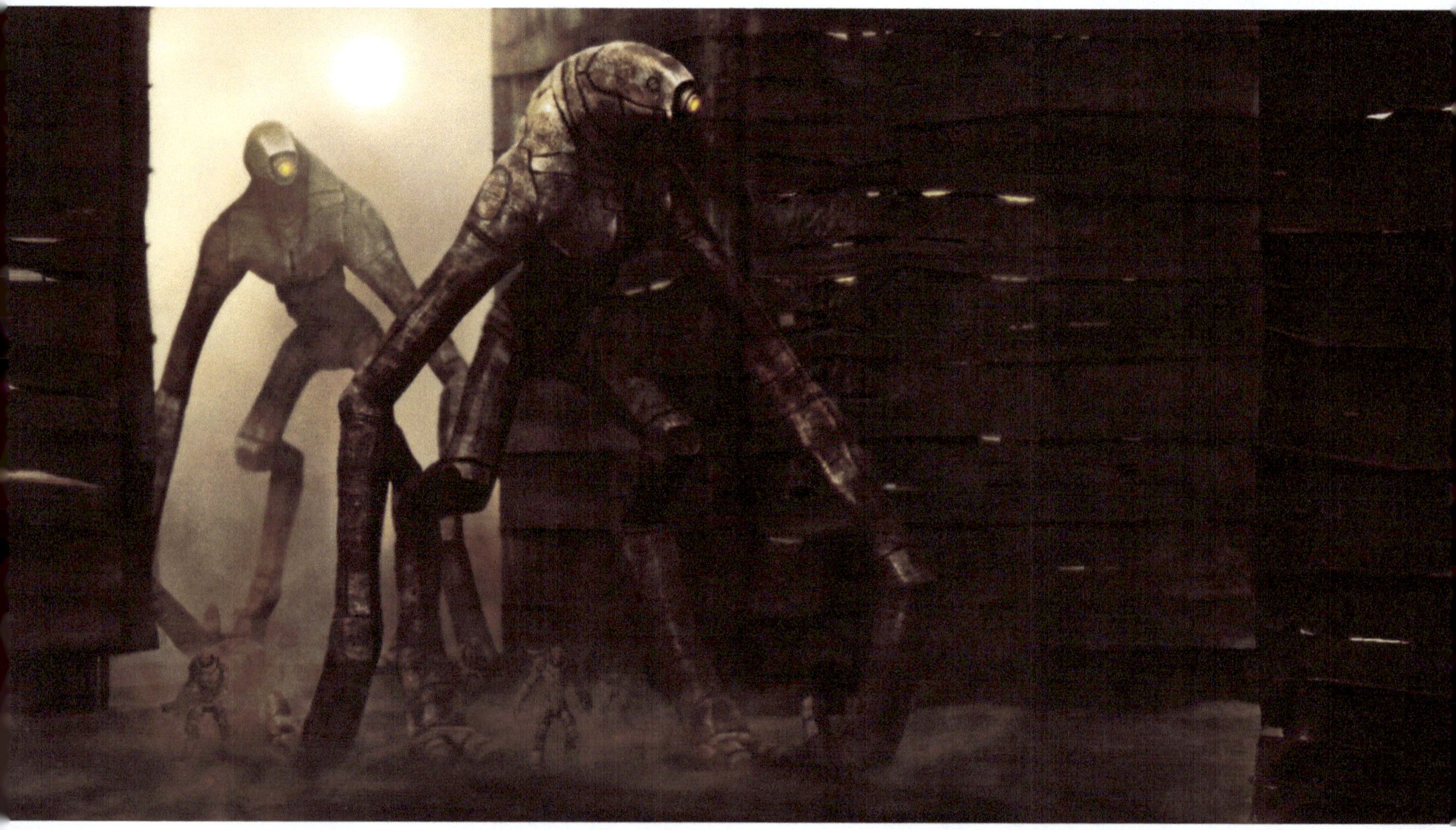

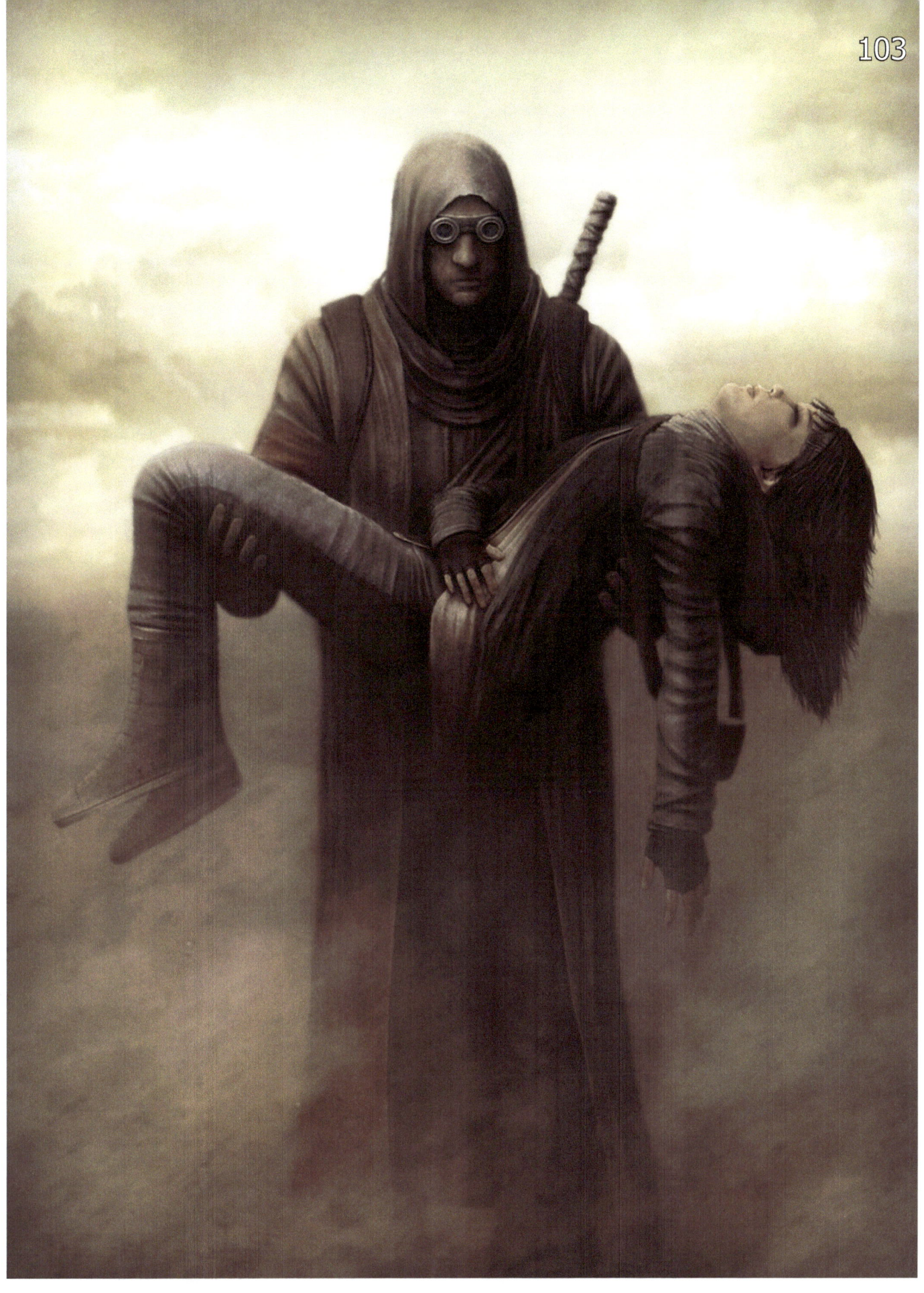

RIYAHD CASSIEM
Zbrush and Photoshop (South Africa)

OPPOSITE TOP LEFT
Apac

OPPOSITE TOP RIGHT
Sheleb

OPPOSITE BOTTOM
Drone

ABOVE
Salvation

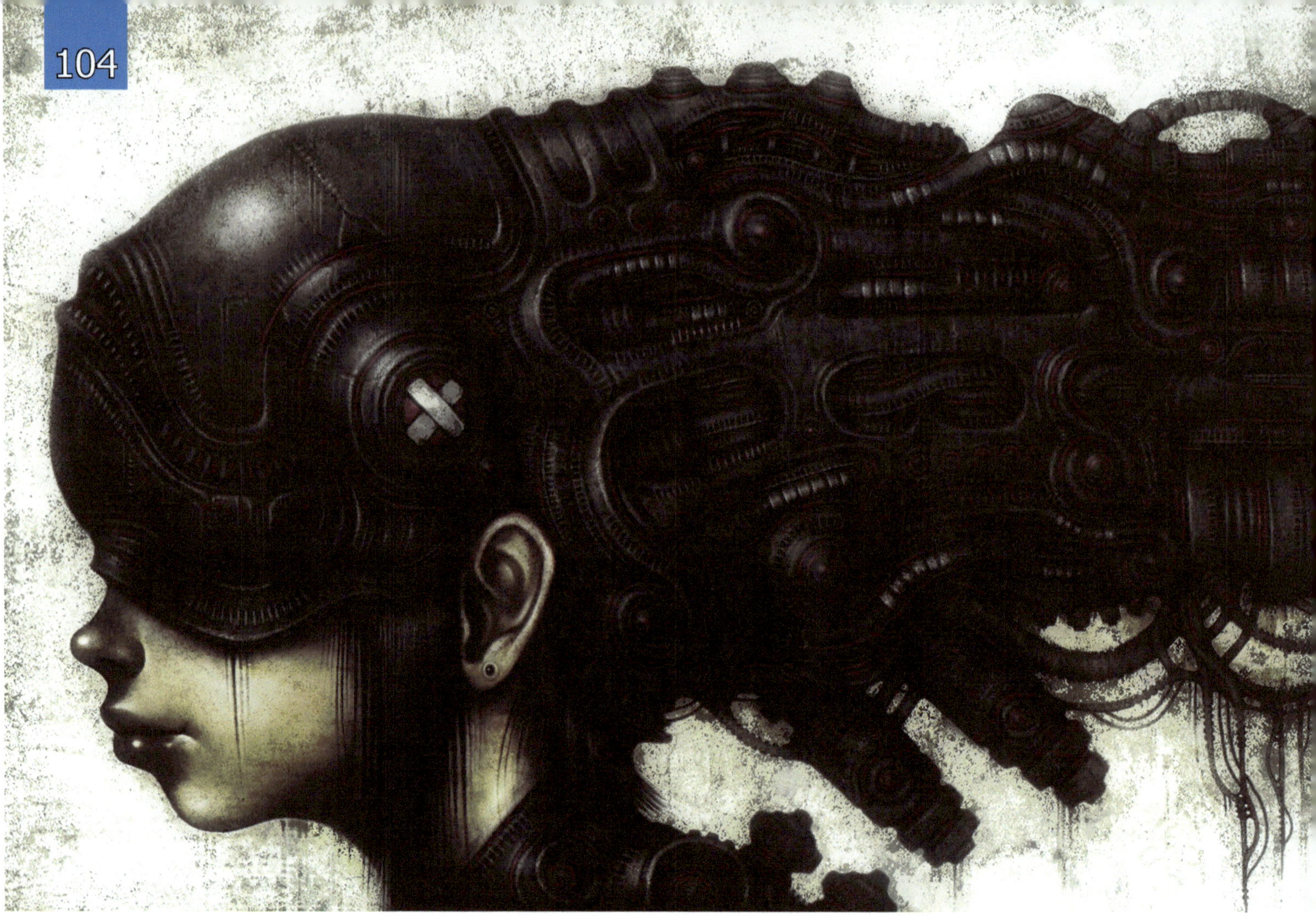

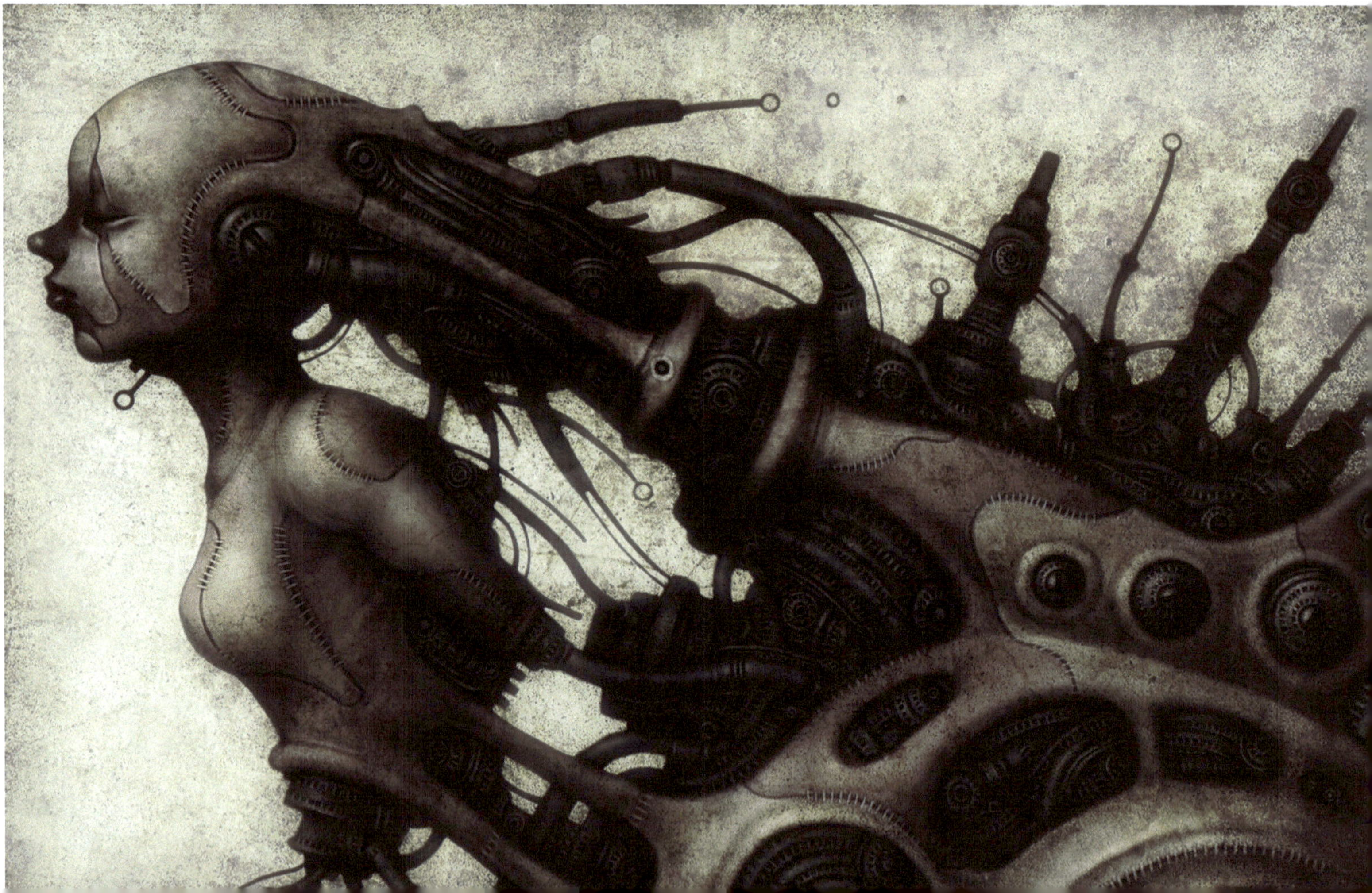

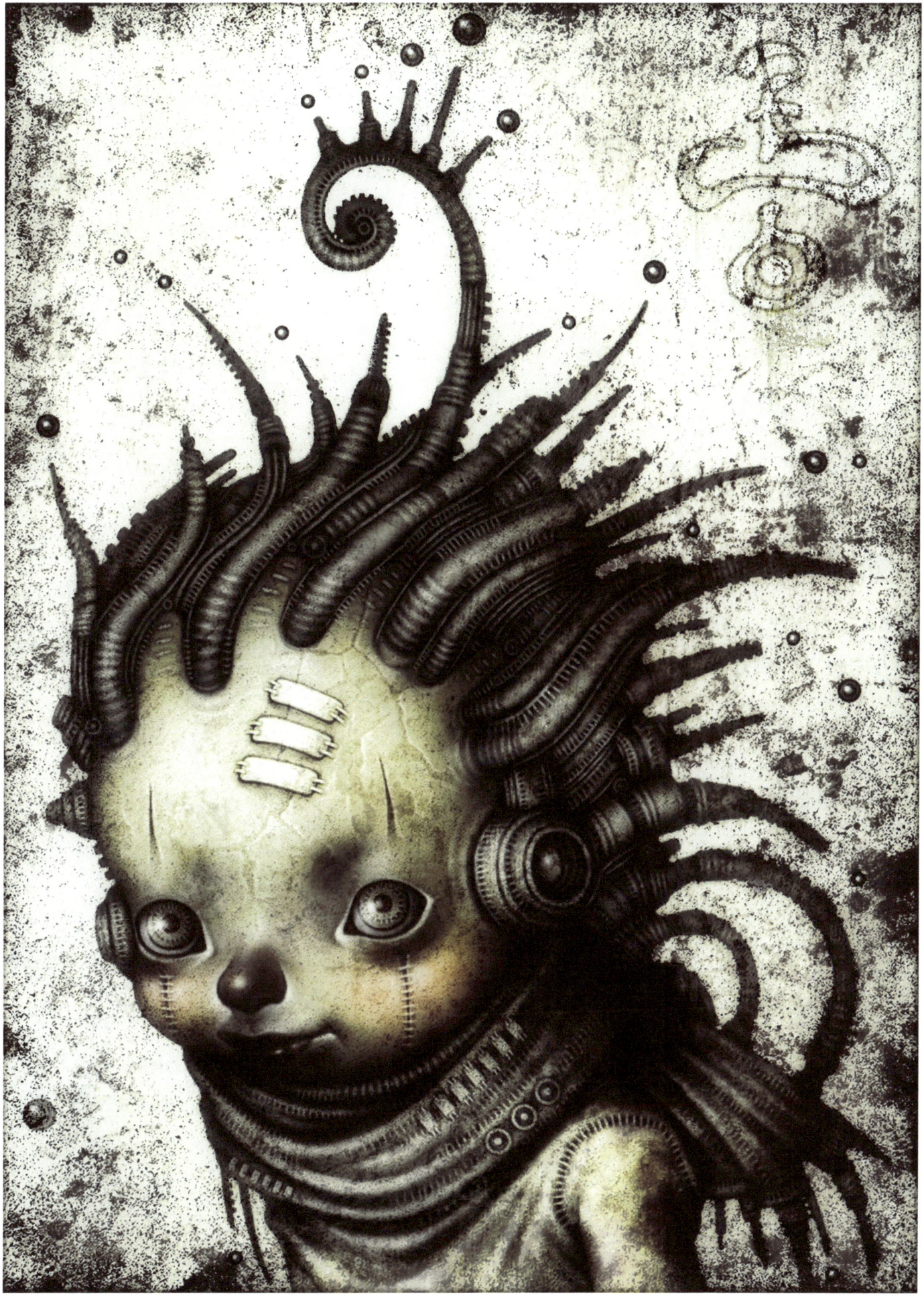

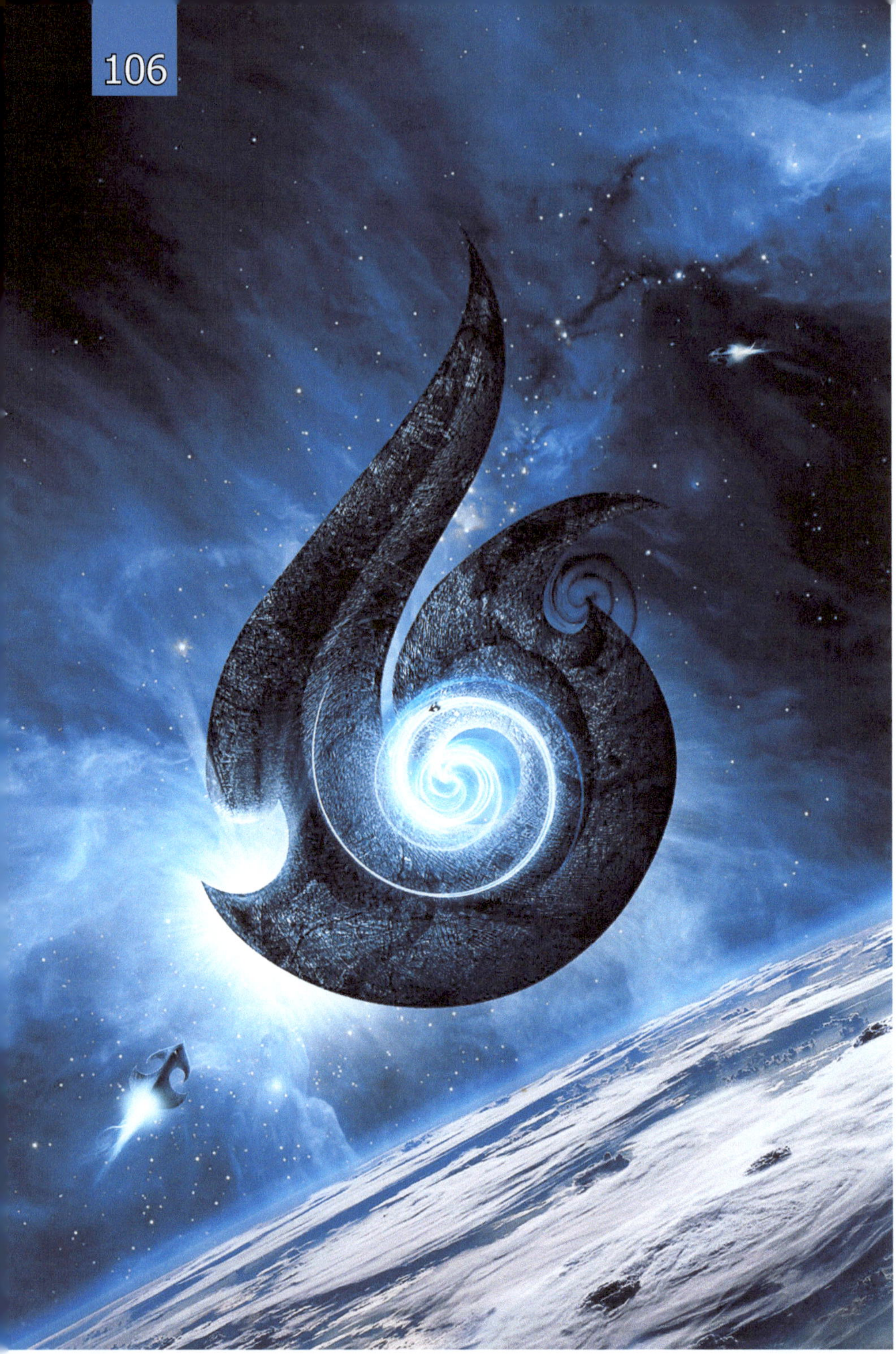

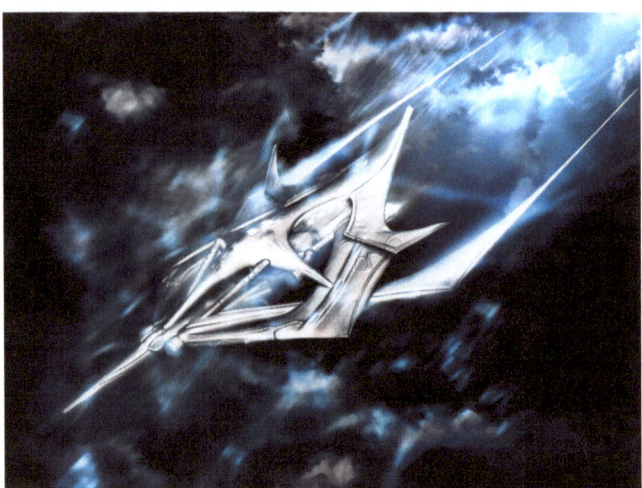

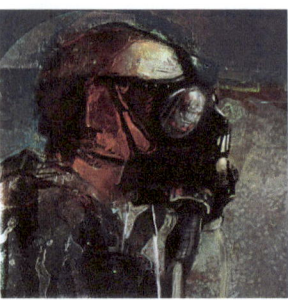

(Previous)

LEFT PAGE TOP

SHICHIGORO-SHINGO
Photoshop (Japan)
Red Line

LEFT PAGE BOTTOM

SHICHIGORO-SHINGO
Photoshop (Japan)
Hito-kikai 3

LEFT PAGE BOTTOM

SHICHIGORO-SHINGO
Photoshop (Japan)
9

LEFT

ANGELA TYGERSON ROSS
Photoshop (USA)
New Zealand, 3047 A.D.

BOTTOM LEFT

WIL OBERDIER
Pencil/Digital (USA)
Left Behind

BOTTOM RIGHT

ANTON CHEREVAN
Zbrush and Photoshop(Ukraine)
Shining

OPPOSITE TOP

ANGEL ALONSO
Digital 3D (Spain)
Witch of Thought

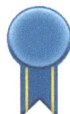

OPPOSITE BOTTOM

DAVID DEMARET
Digital (France)
The Breach

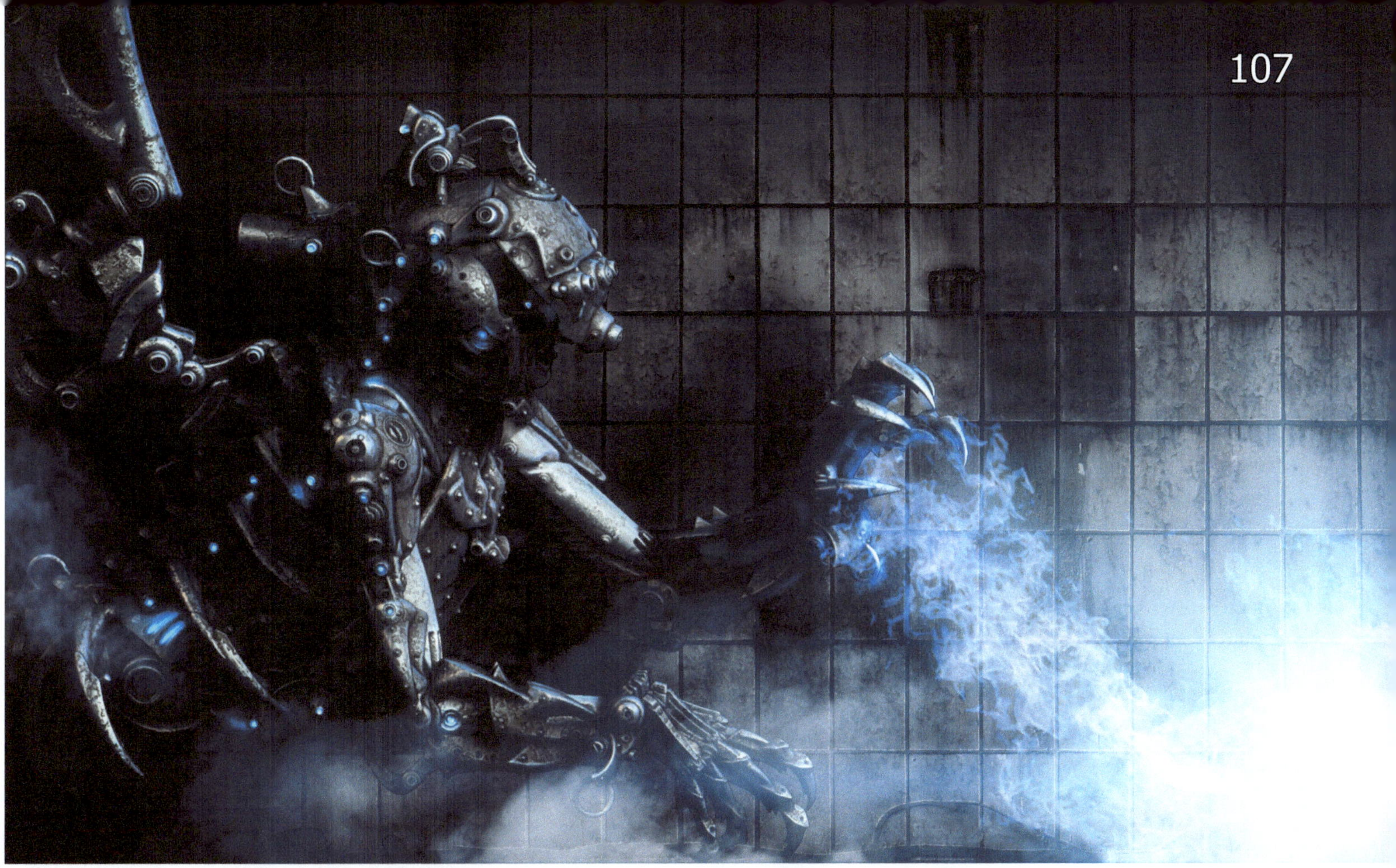

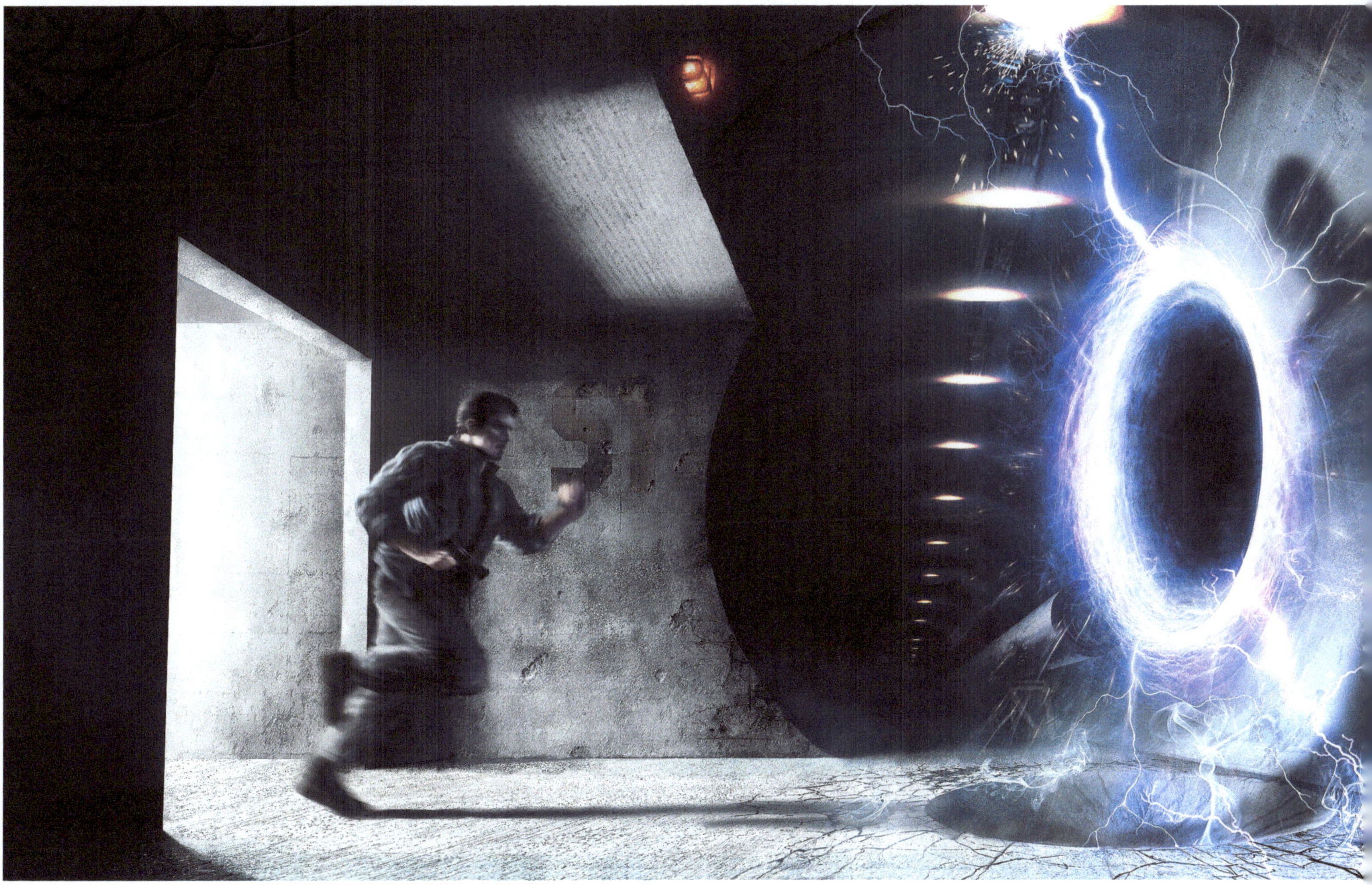

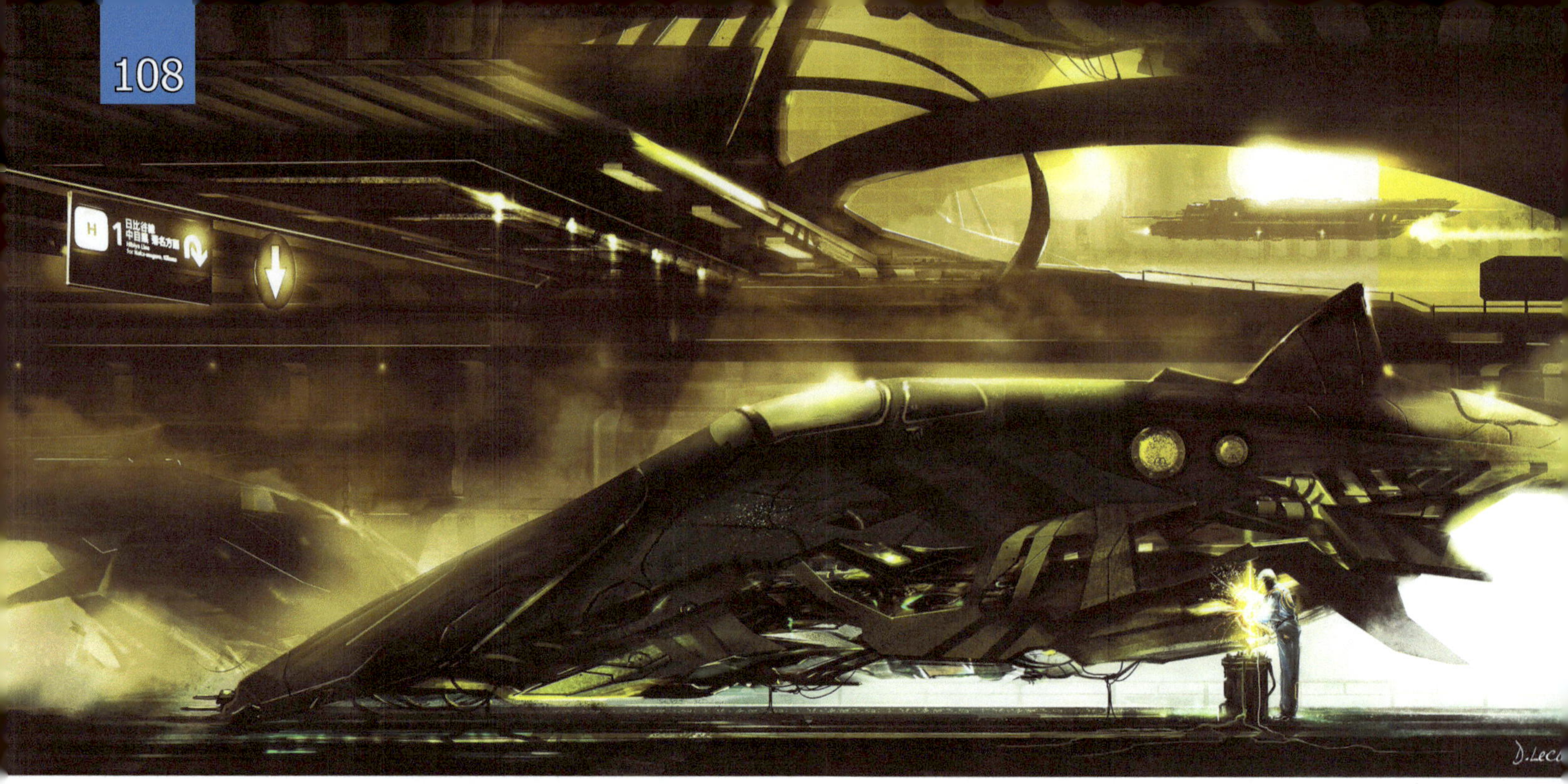

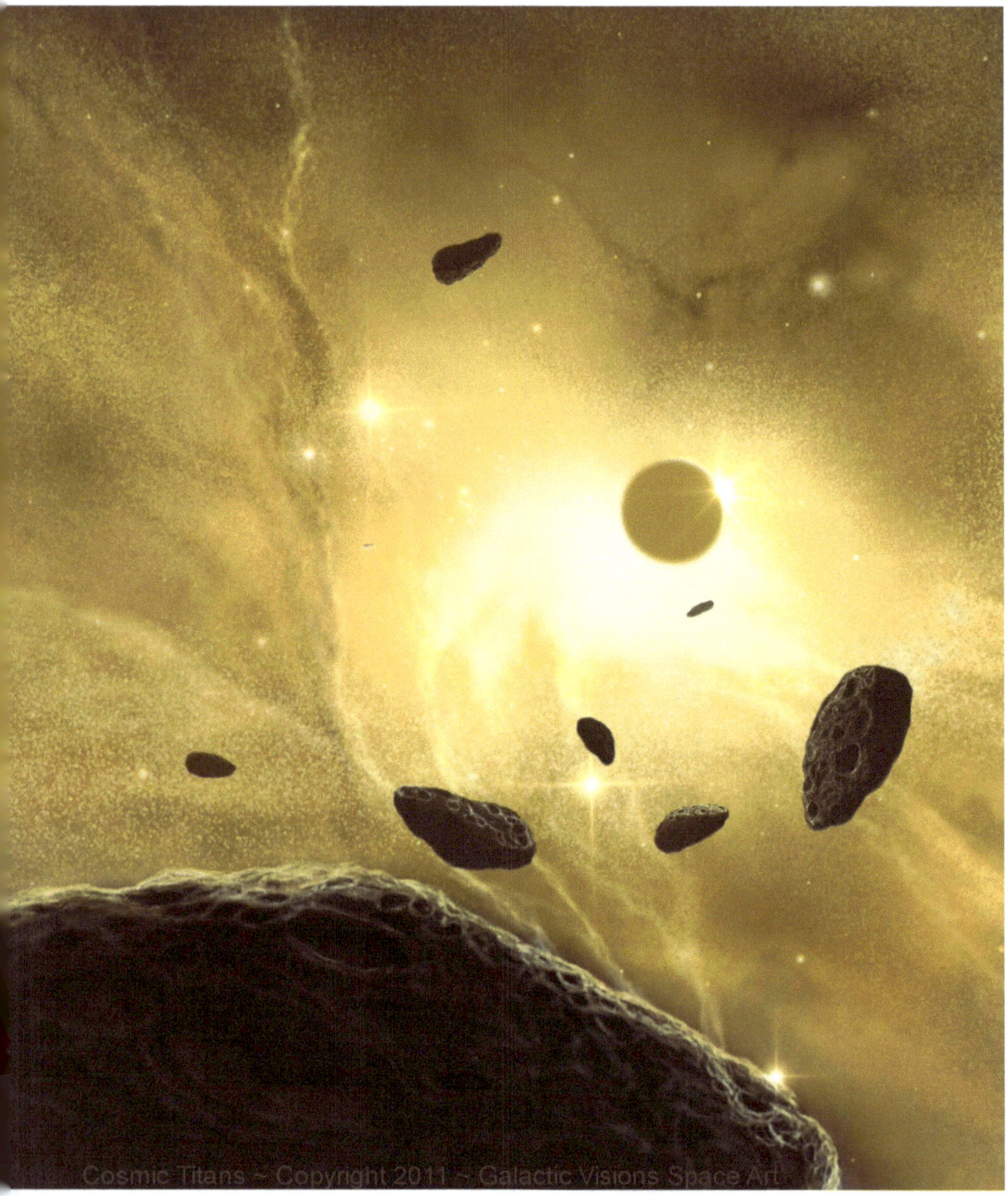

ABOVE
DAVID LECOSSU
Photoshop (France)
The Repair

LEFT
MICHAEL C. TURNER
Acrylic (USA)
Cosmic Titans

OPPOSITE TOP
GIA NGUYEN HOANG
Photoshop (VietNam)
Industry Zone

OPPOSITE BOTTOM LEFT
DAVID LECOSSU
Photoshop (France)
Find

OPPOSITE BOTTOM RIGHT
VINCENT LEFEVRE
Photoshop (France)
Angel Révanche

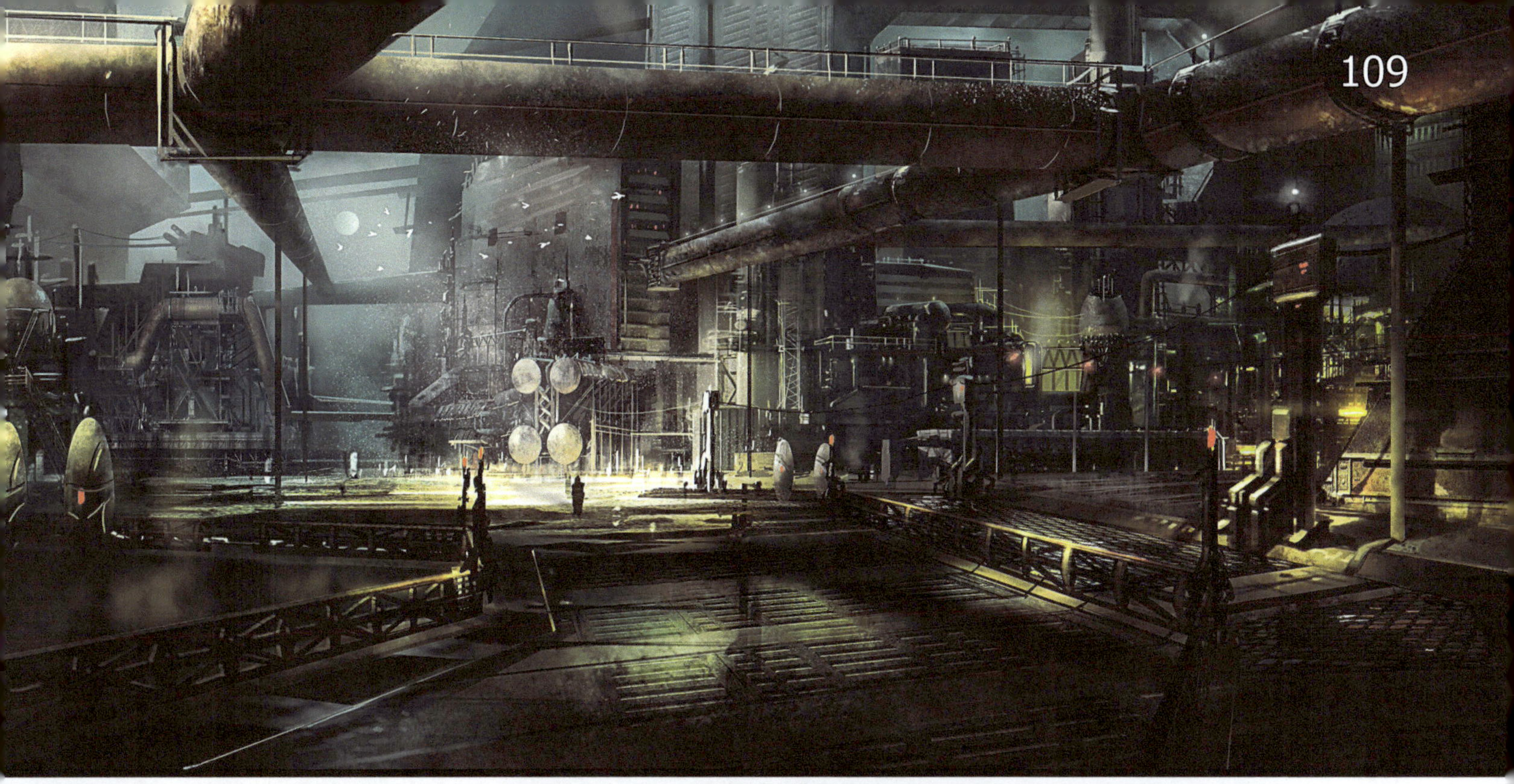

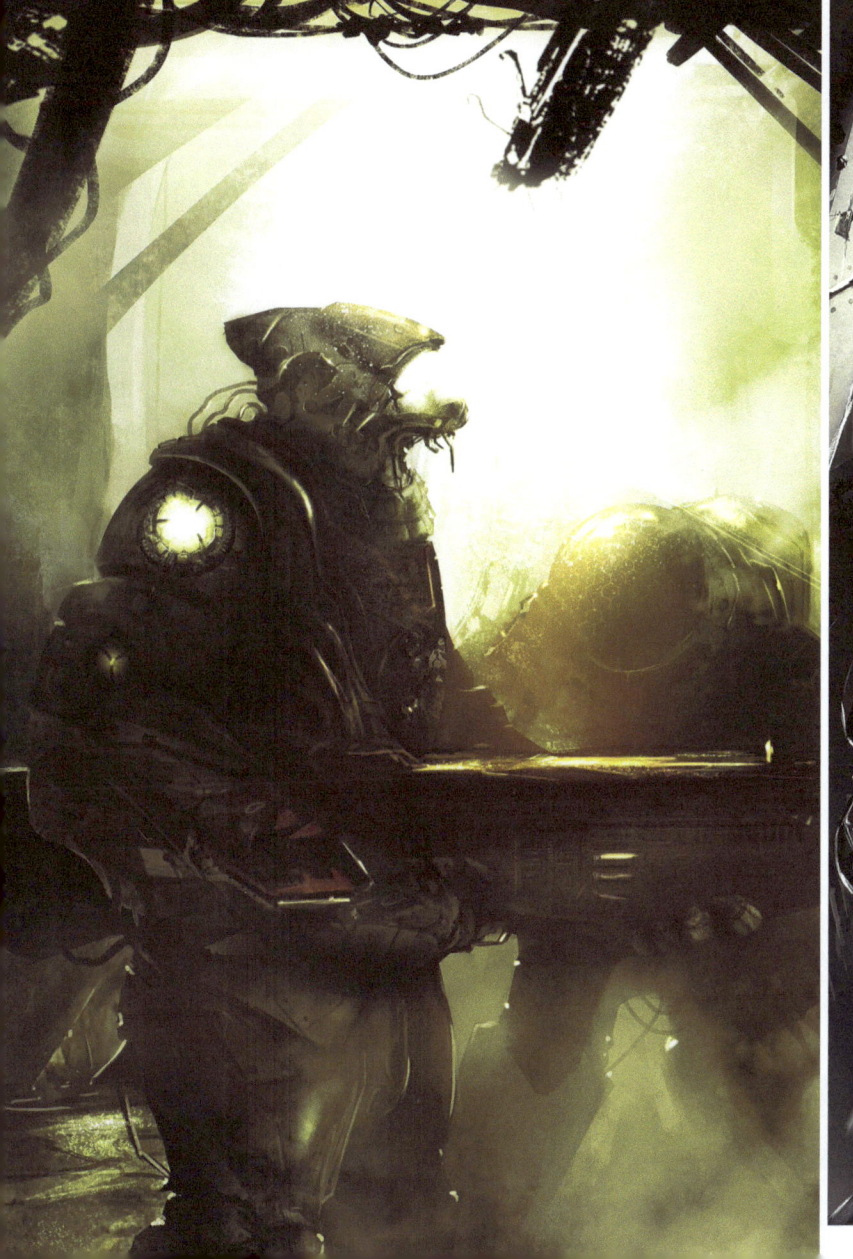

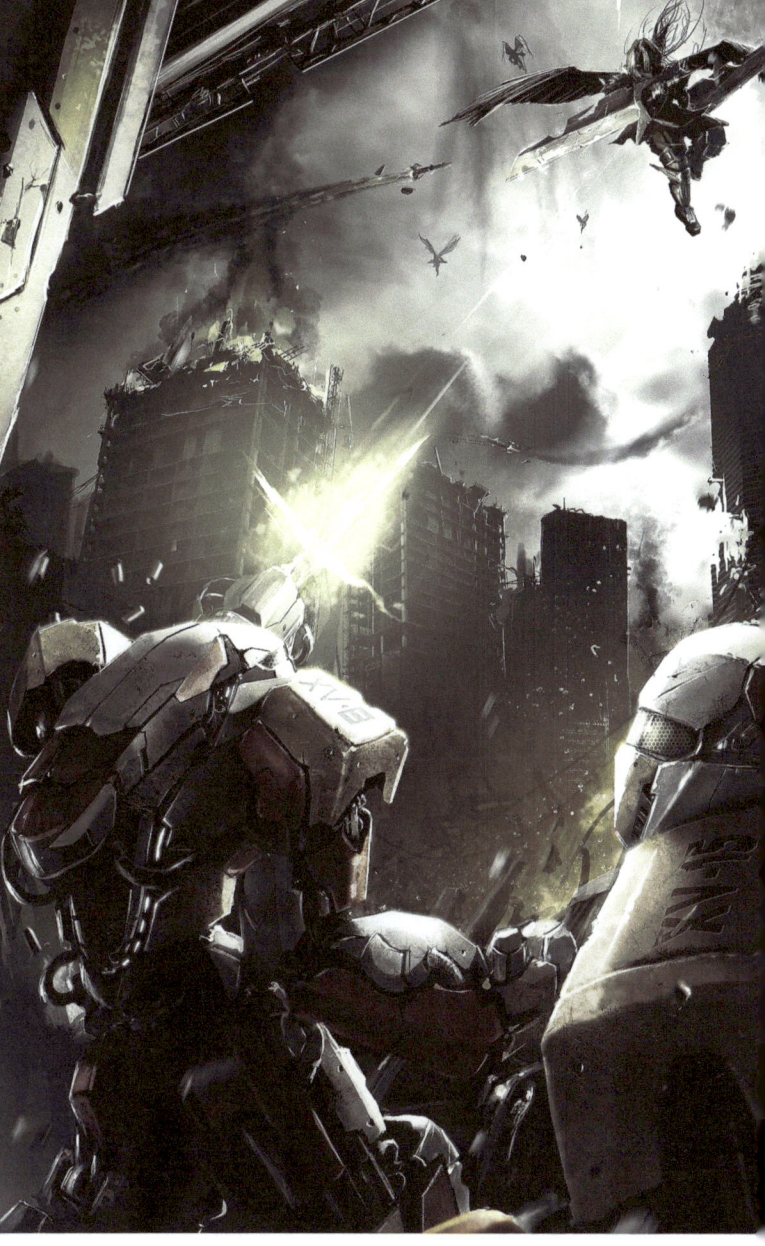

RIGHT

LORENZ HIDEYOSHI RU-WWE
Digital Photoshop (Germany)
City of Magicians

BELOW

ANGEL ALONSO
Digital 3D (Spain)
Searchers

OPPOSITE TOP LEFT

LIIGA SMILSHKALNE
Corel Painter (Latvia)
Eternal Winter

OPPOSITE TOP RIGHT

ANGELA TYGERSON ROSS
Photoshop (USA)
Destroyer.

OPPOSITE BOTTOM LEFT

ZLATKA SUBOTIČANEC
Photoshop (Croatia)
Death Colossus

OPPOSITE BOTTOM RIGHT

ODETTE CORTÉS
Photoshop (México)
Hang On

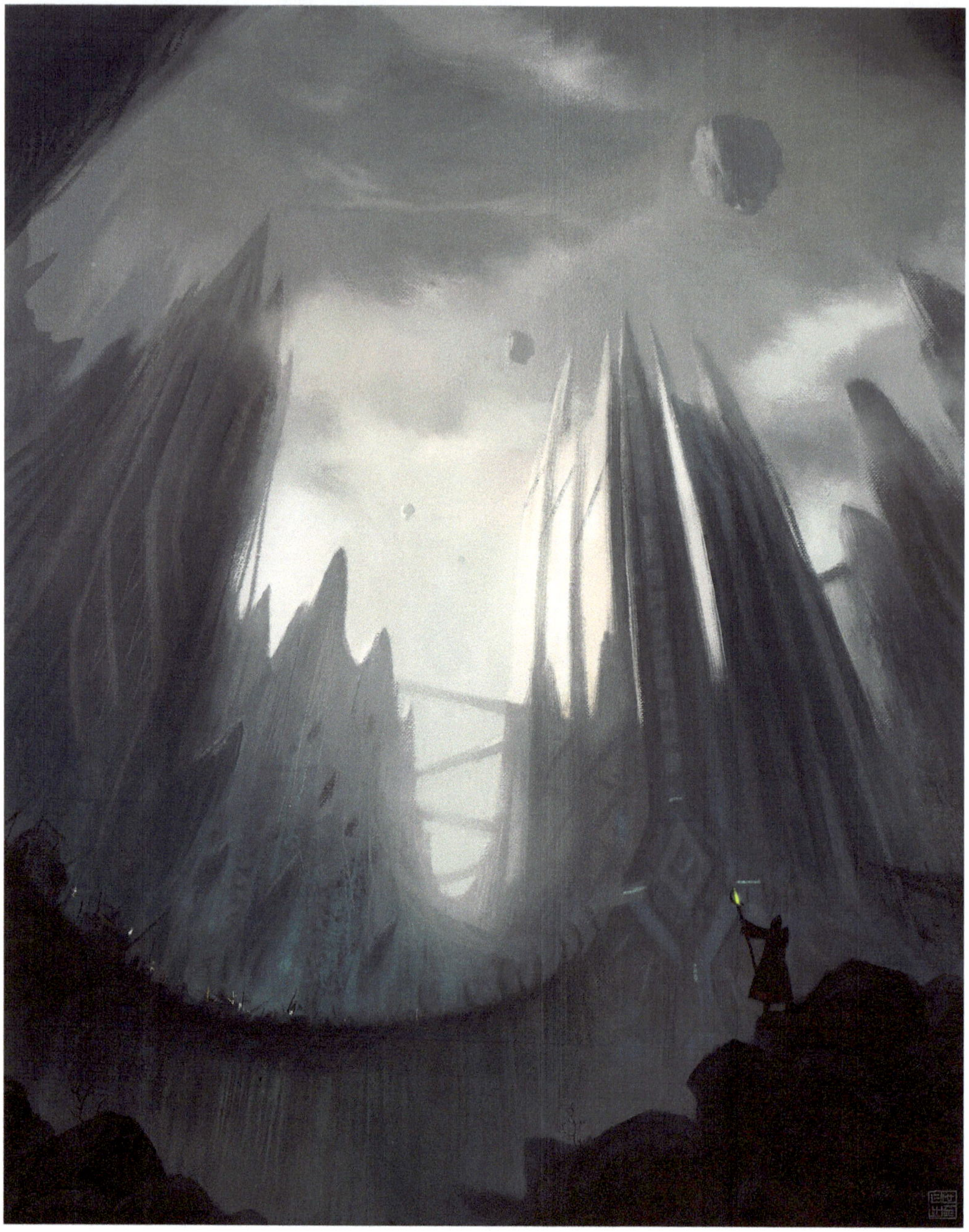

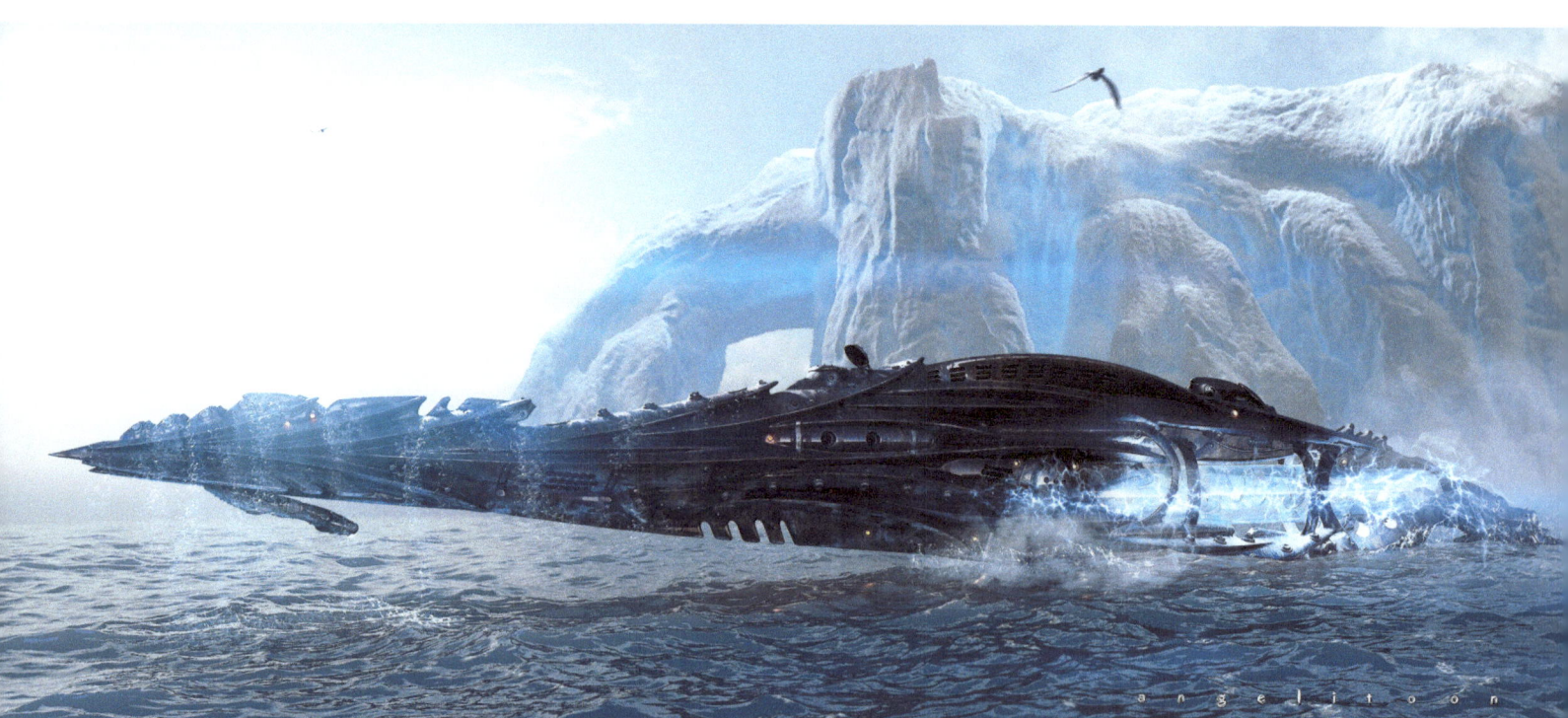

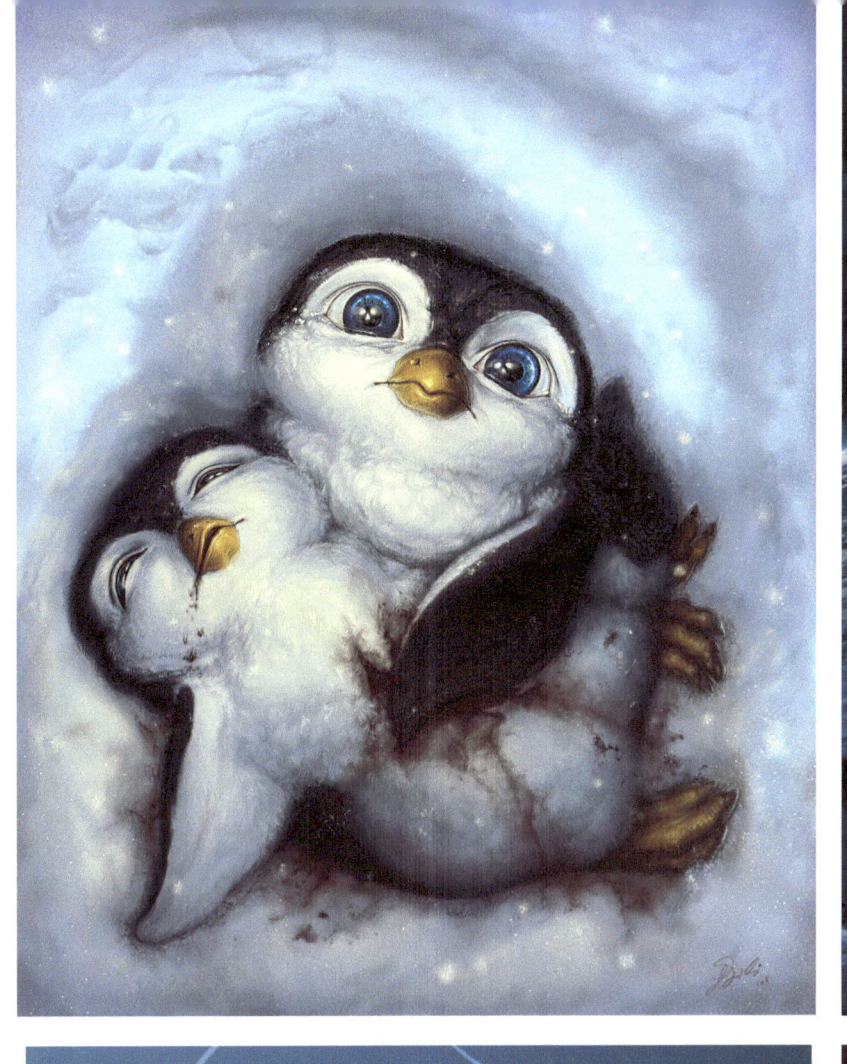

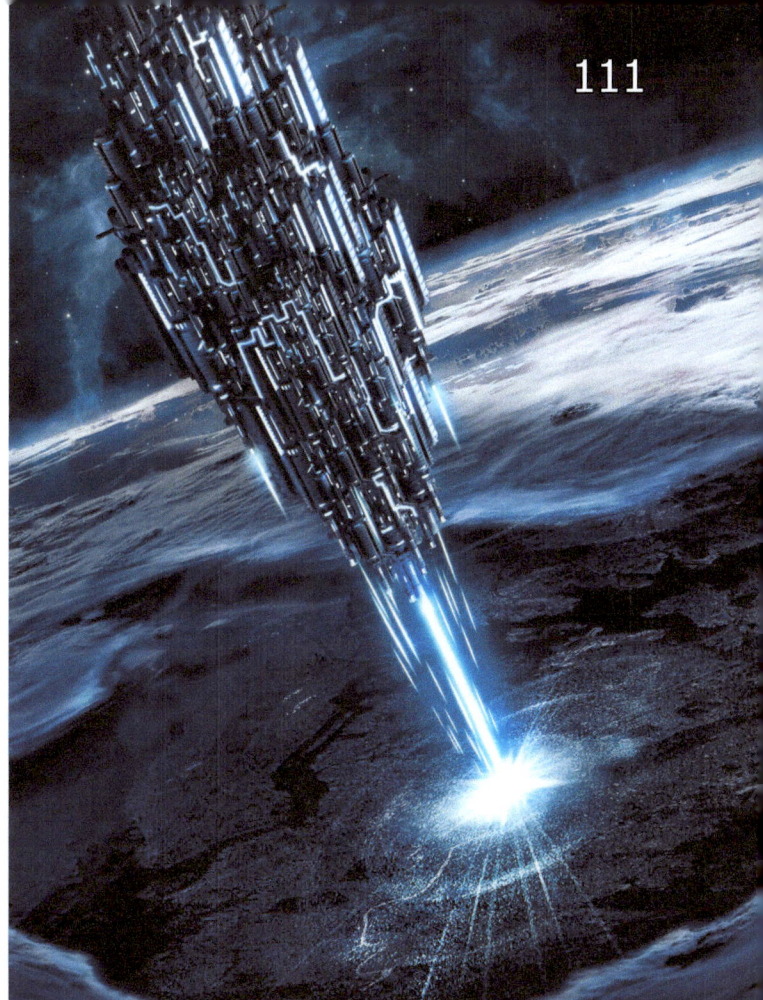

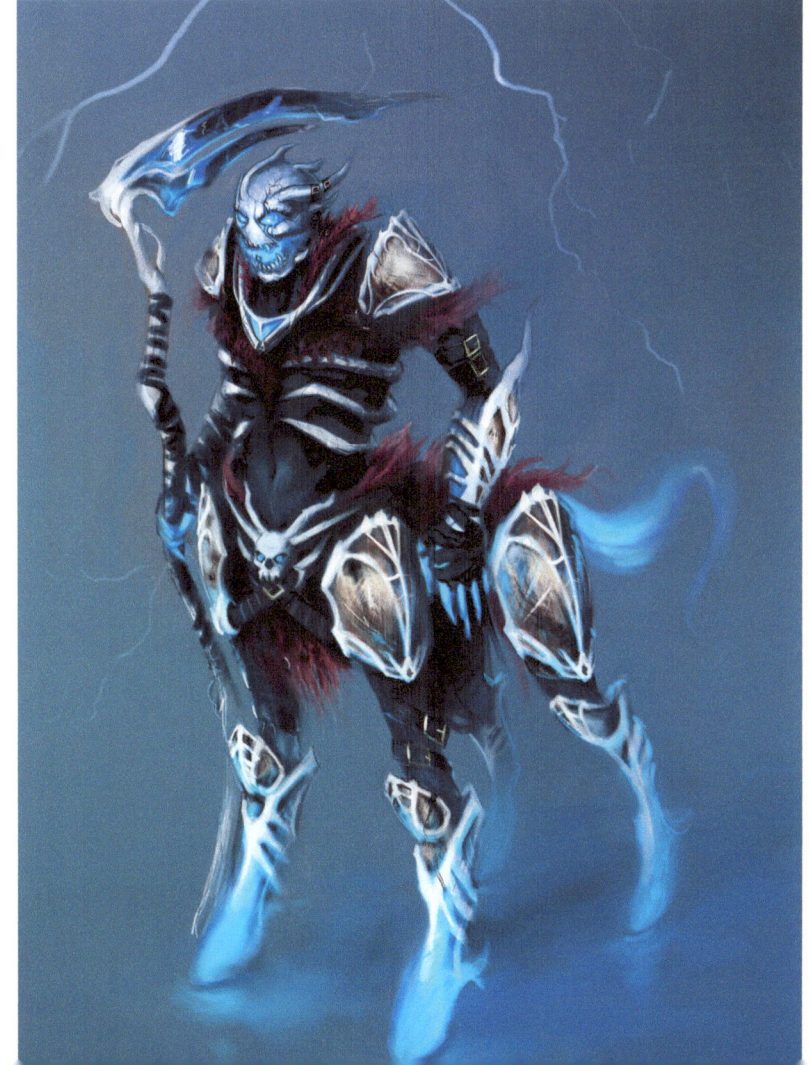

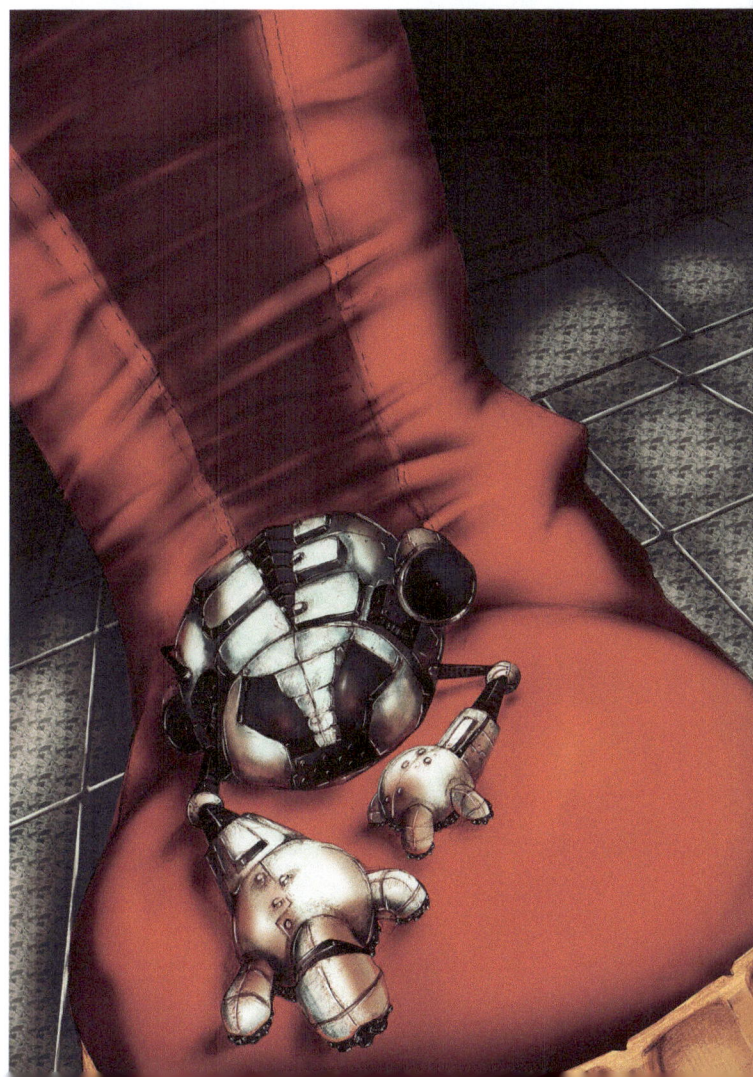

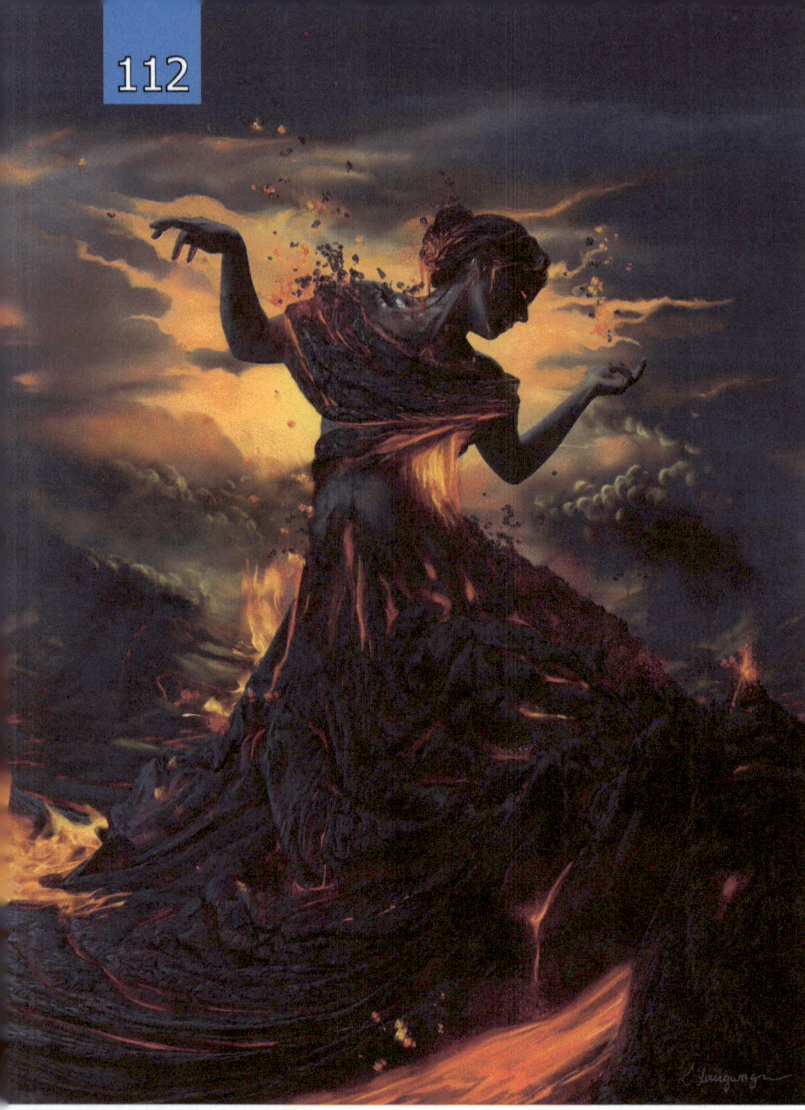

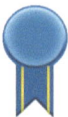

LEFT

CATHRINE LANGWAGEN
Photoshop(UK)
Credit: Eva Langwagen
Elements – Fire

BELOW

GAÉTAN WELTZER
Photoshop (France)
The Last World

OPPOSITE TOP

YVAN FEUSI
GAÉTAN WELTZER
Photoshop & Cinema4D (Switzerland & France)
Zone Zero

OPPOSITE BOTTOM LEFT

LUCAS DURHAM
Photoshop and Illustrator (USA)
Firstborn

OPPOSITE BOTTOM RIGHT

RIYAHD CASSIEM
Zbrush and Photoshop (South Africa)
Mec Ranger

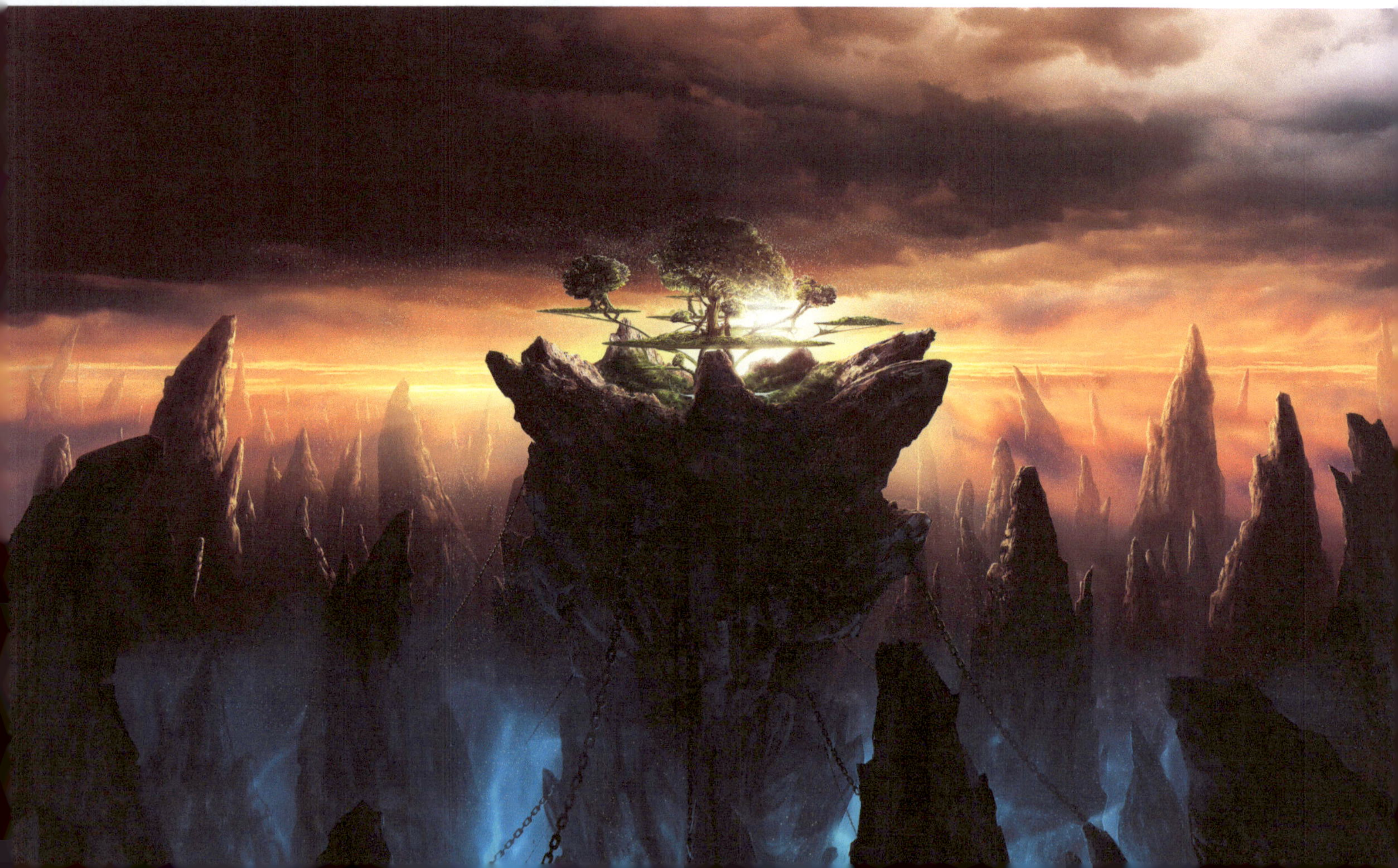

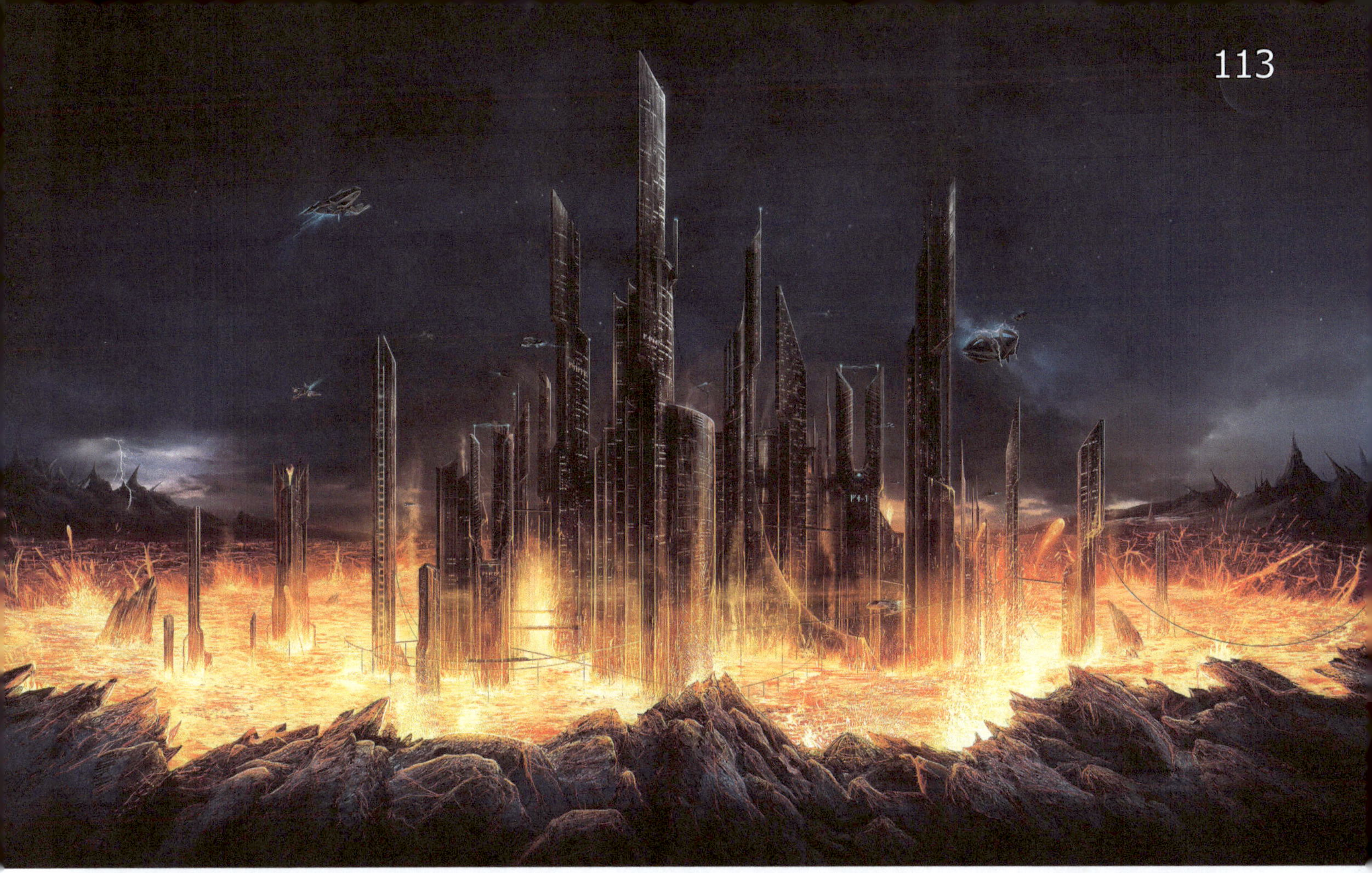

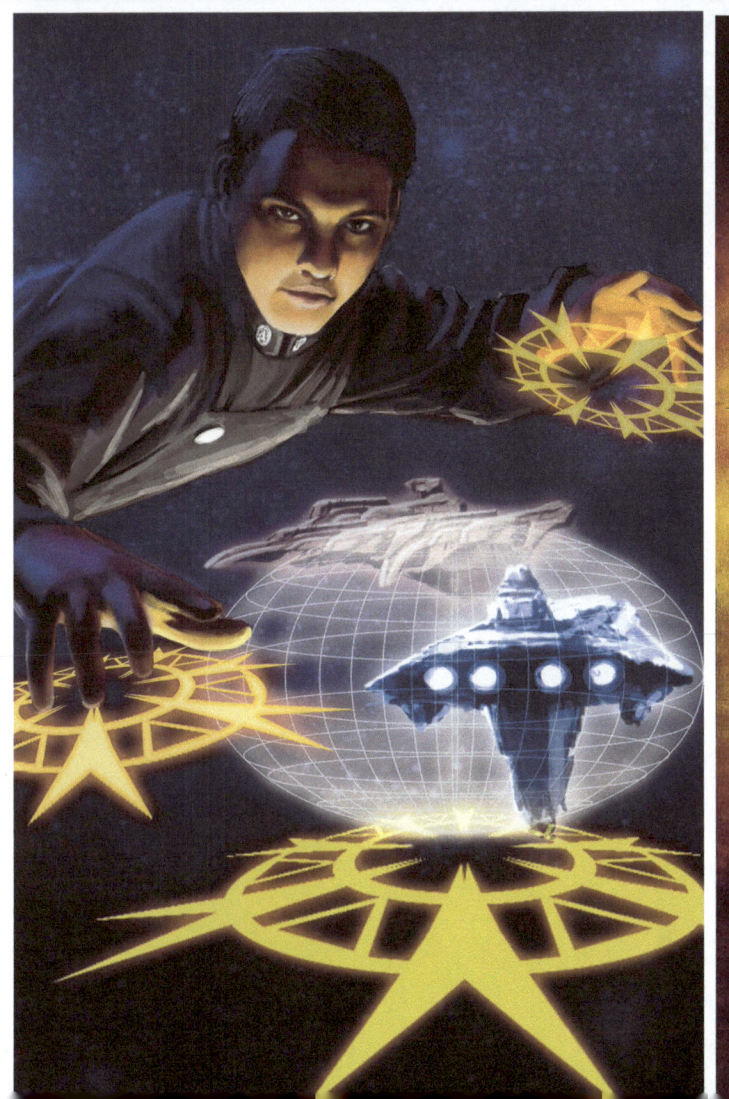

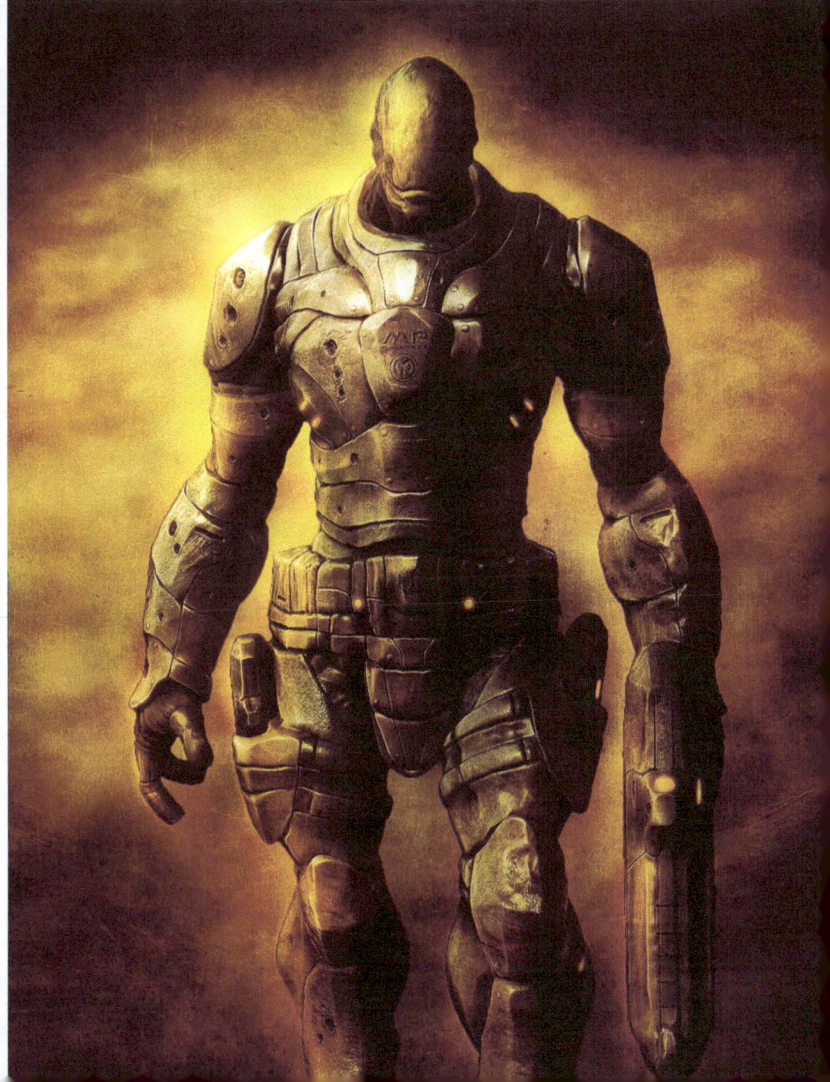

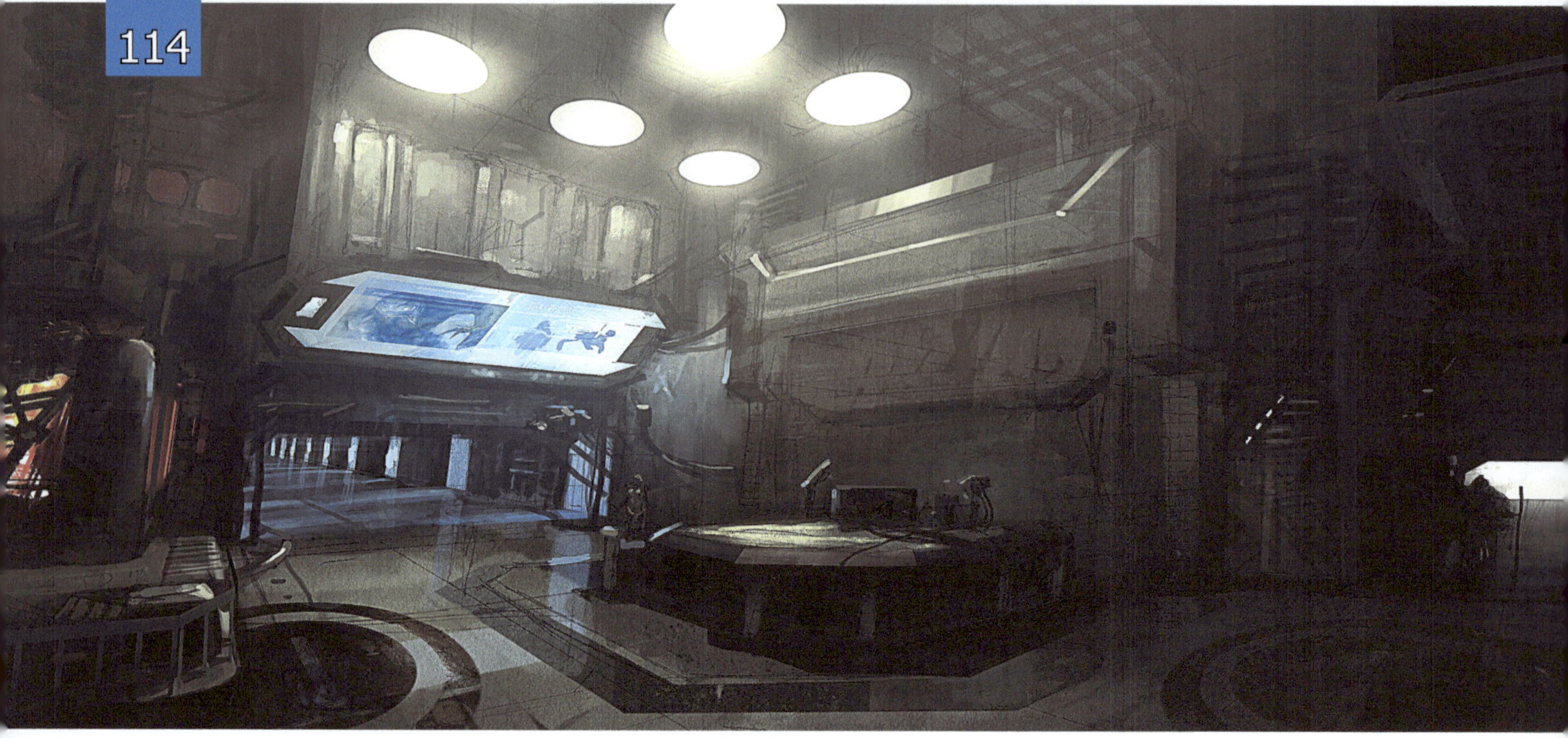

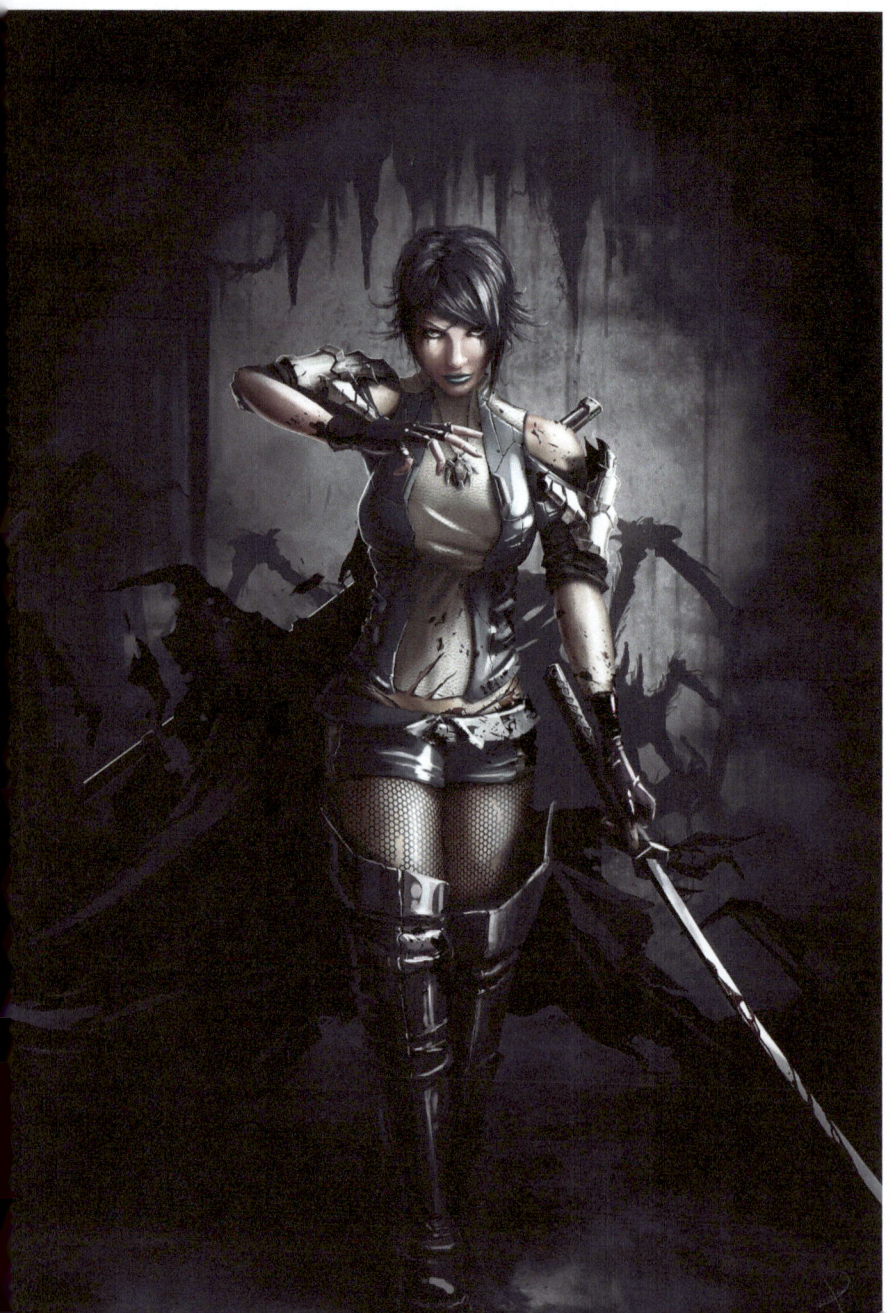

AHMED ALDOORI
Photoshop (USA)
Headquarters

LEFT
VINCENT LEFEVRE
Photoshop (France)
Blue Killers

OPPOSITE TOP
MARCO KUNARDI
Digital (Indonesia/USA)
Styx

OPPOSITE BOTTOM
NIGEL GOH
Photoshop (Singapore)
Factory Terminal

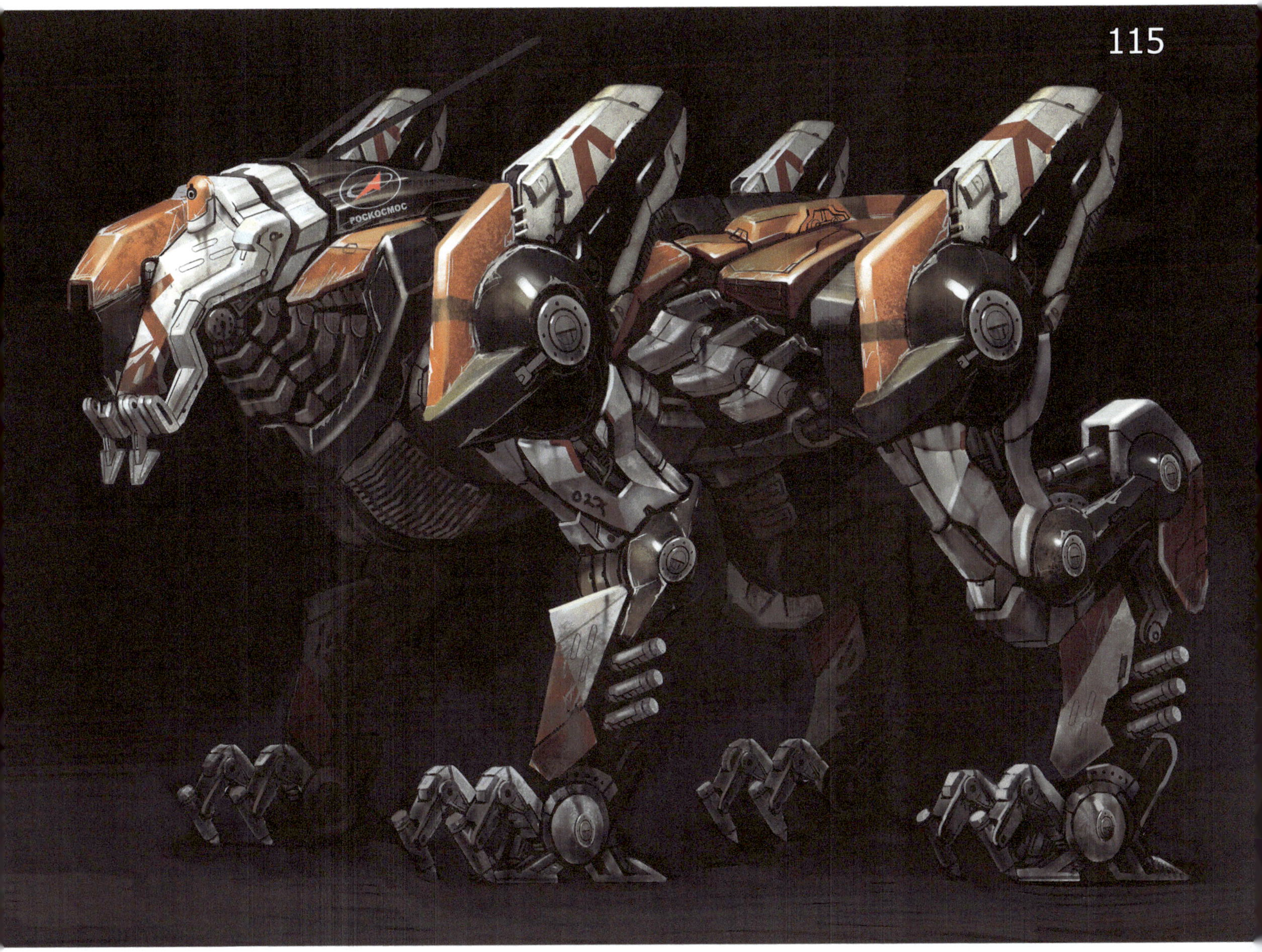

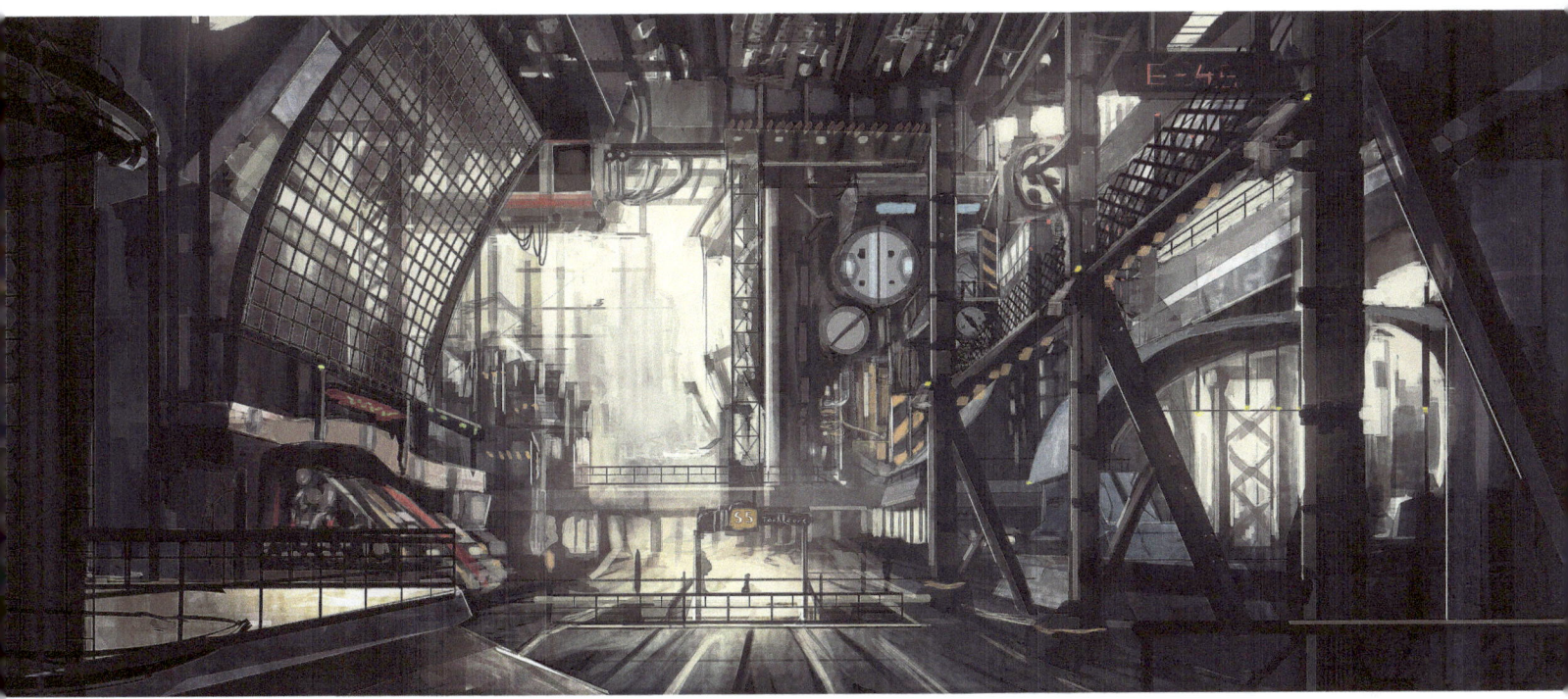

BELOW
MARK REHKOPF
Acrylic (Canada)
Retro Rocket Hero

OPPOSITE TOP
ALEX LYON
Digital (USA)
Space Chimp

OPPOSITE BOTTOM
ANDREA GATTI
Photoshop (Italy)
Hangar

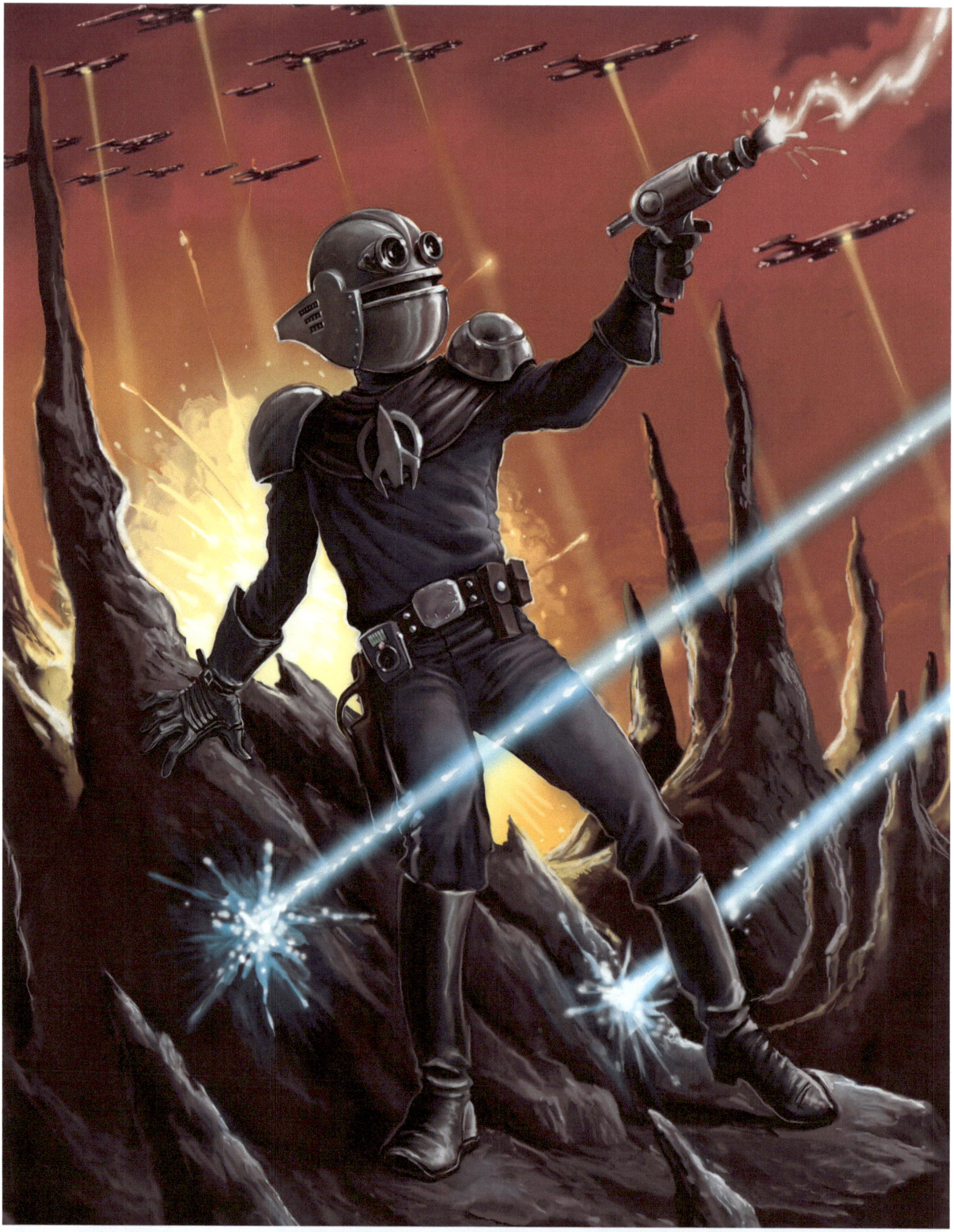

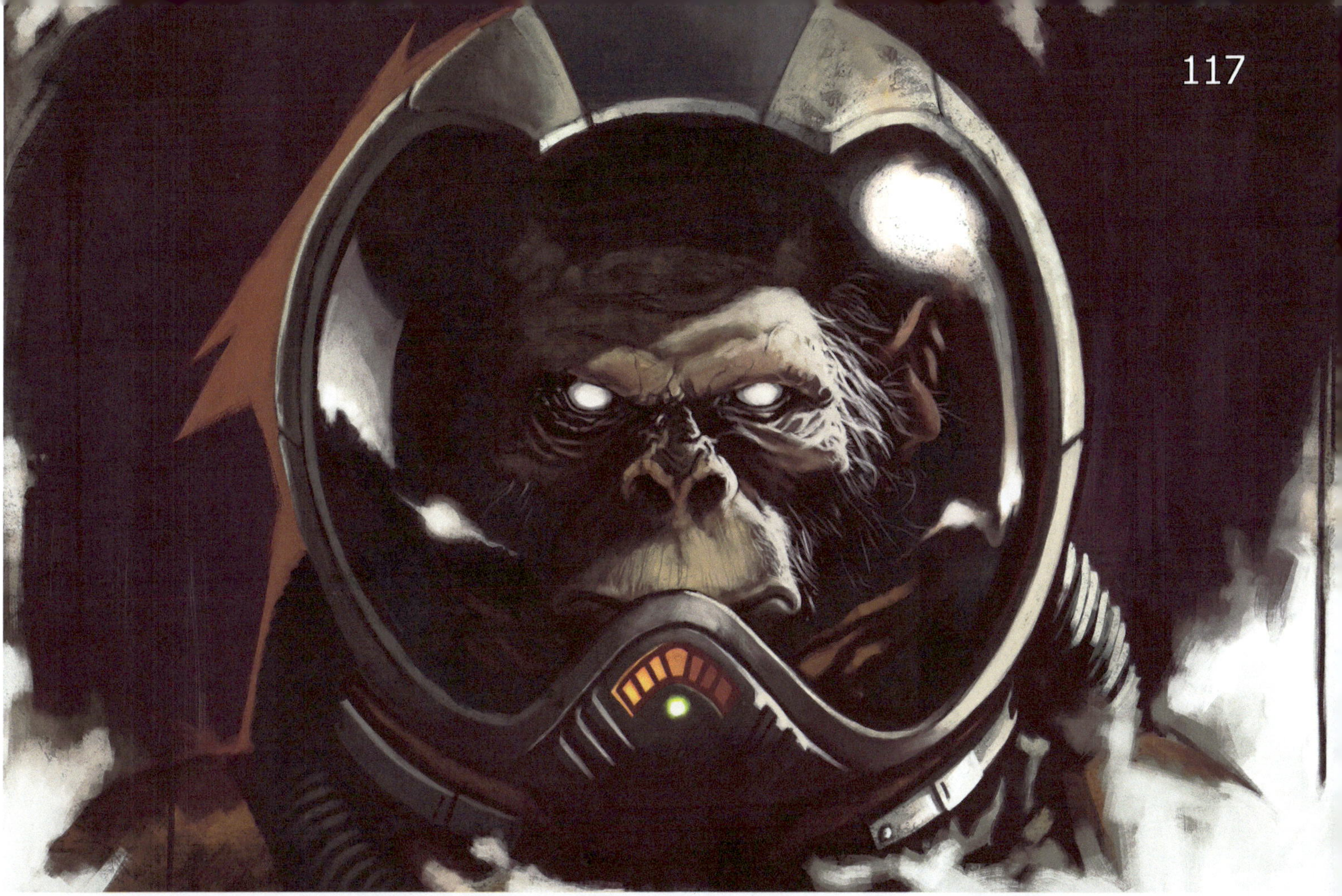

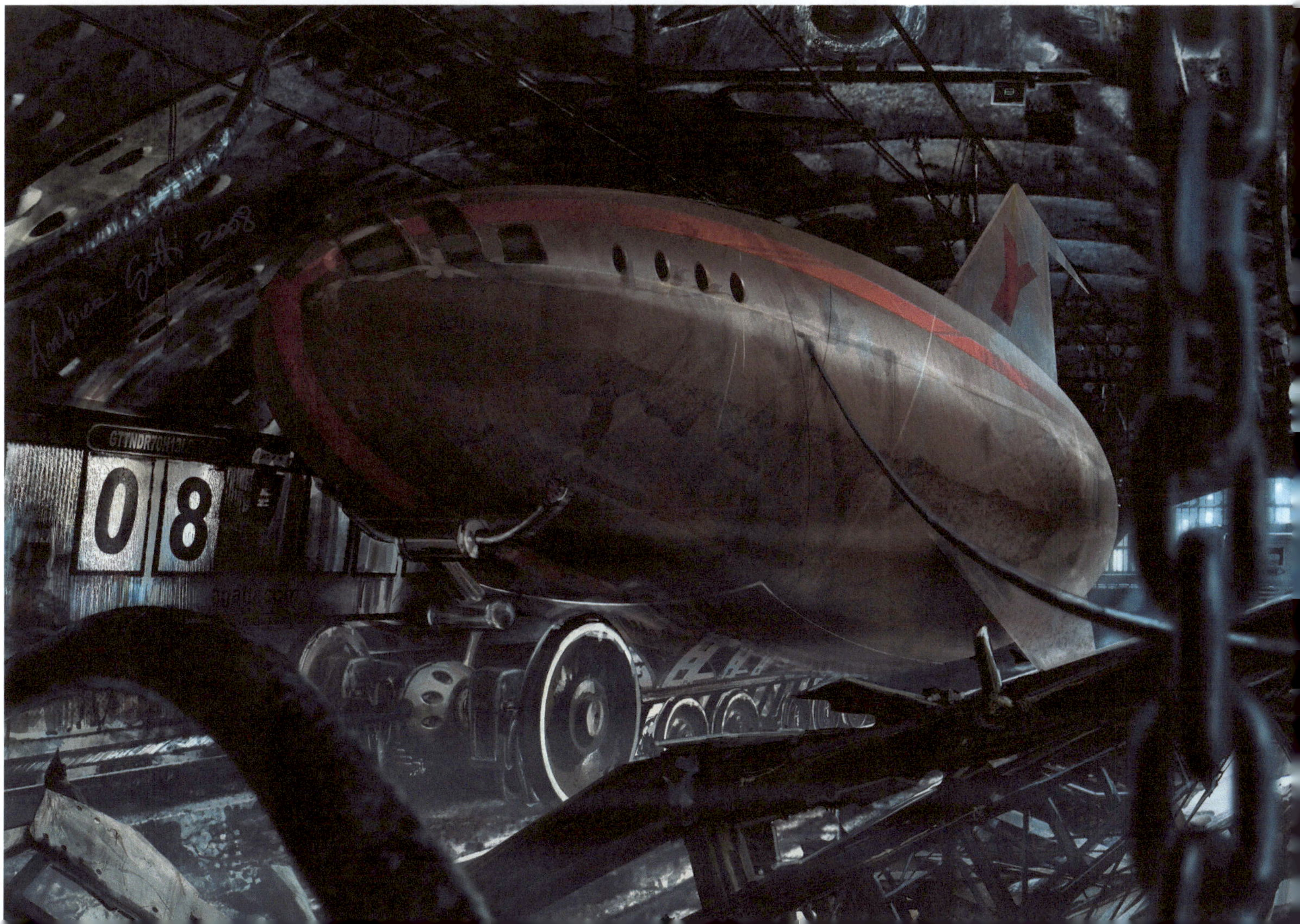
08

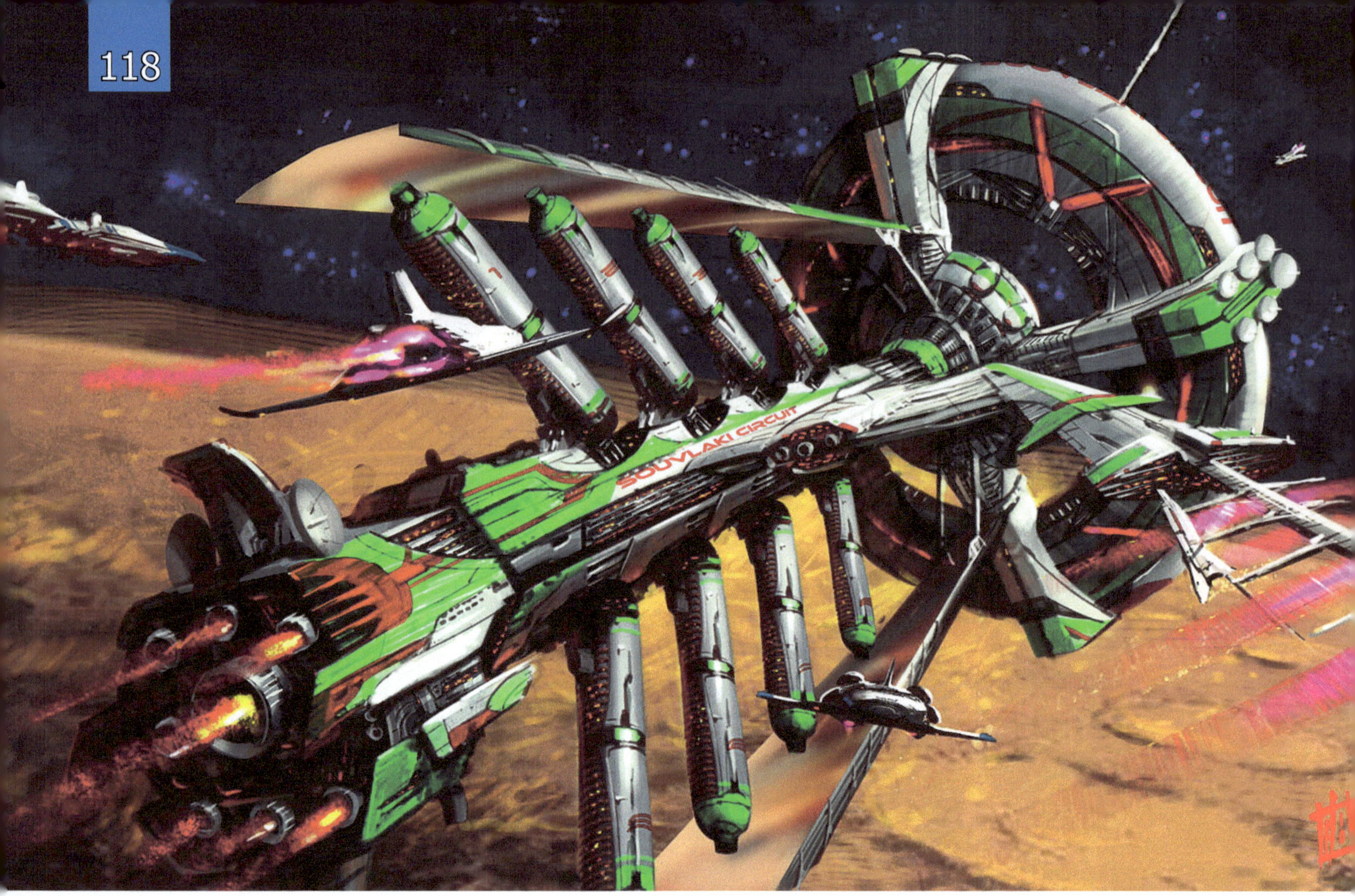
SOUVLAKI CIRCUIT

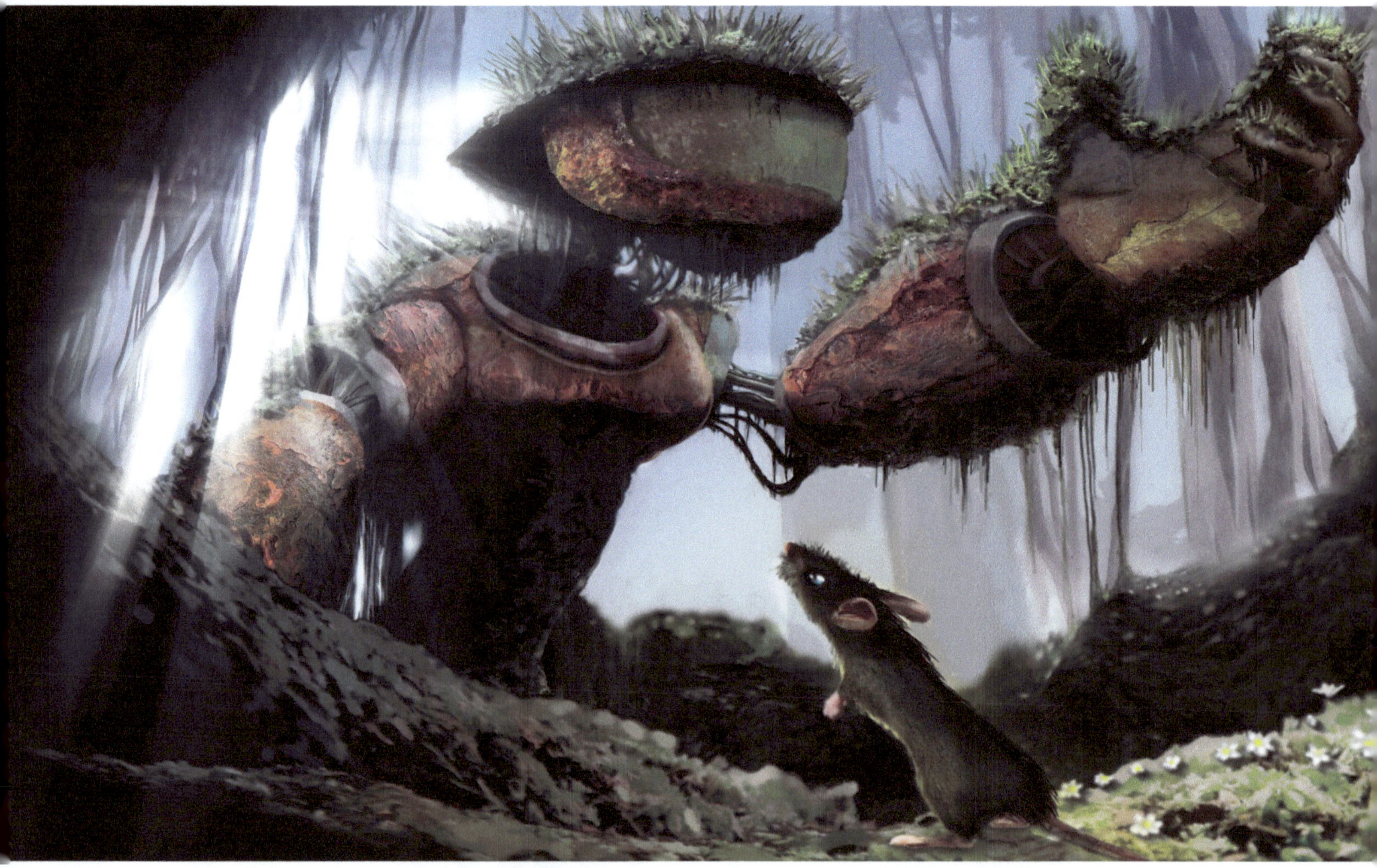

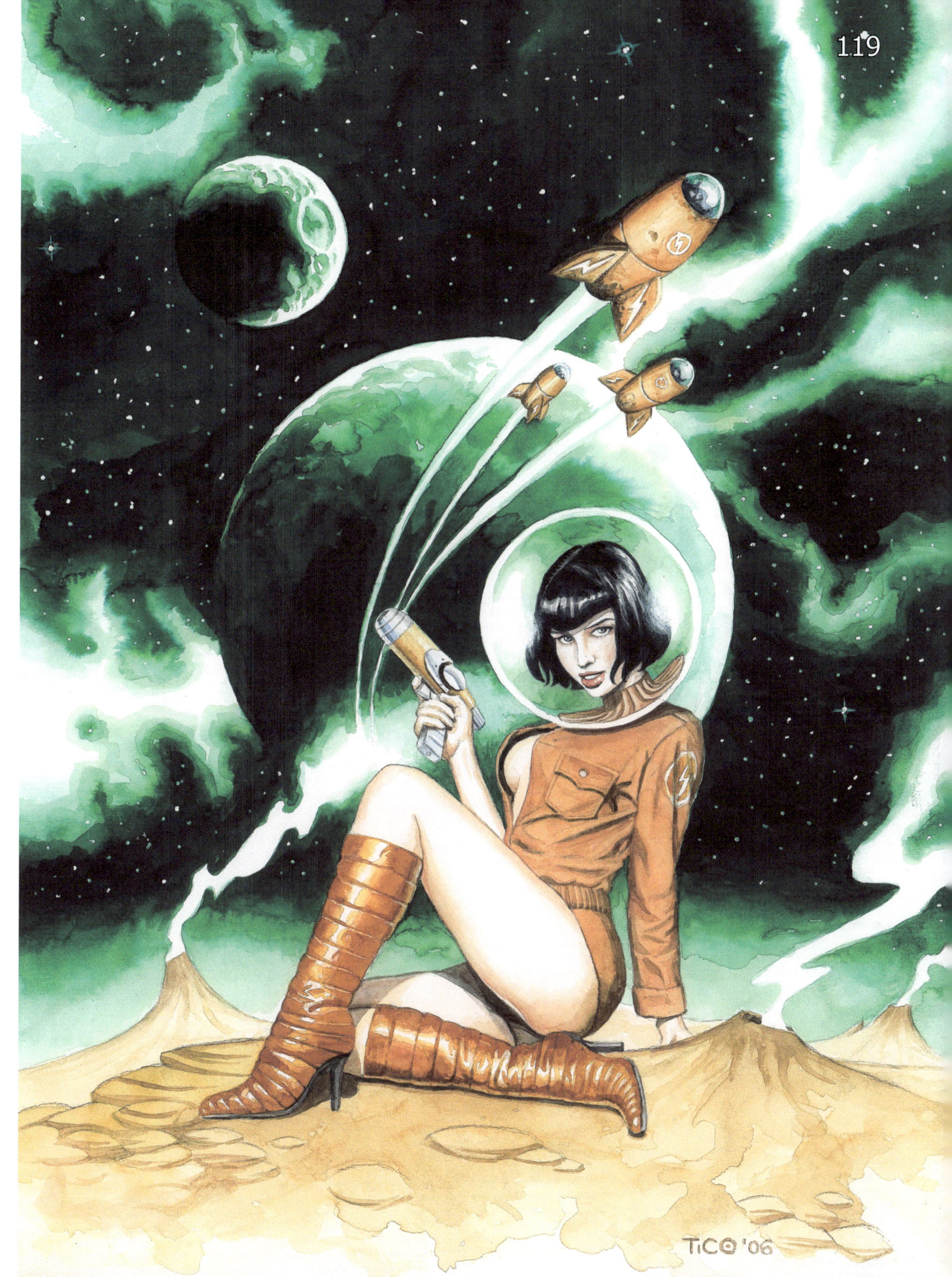

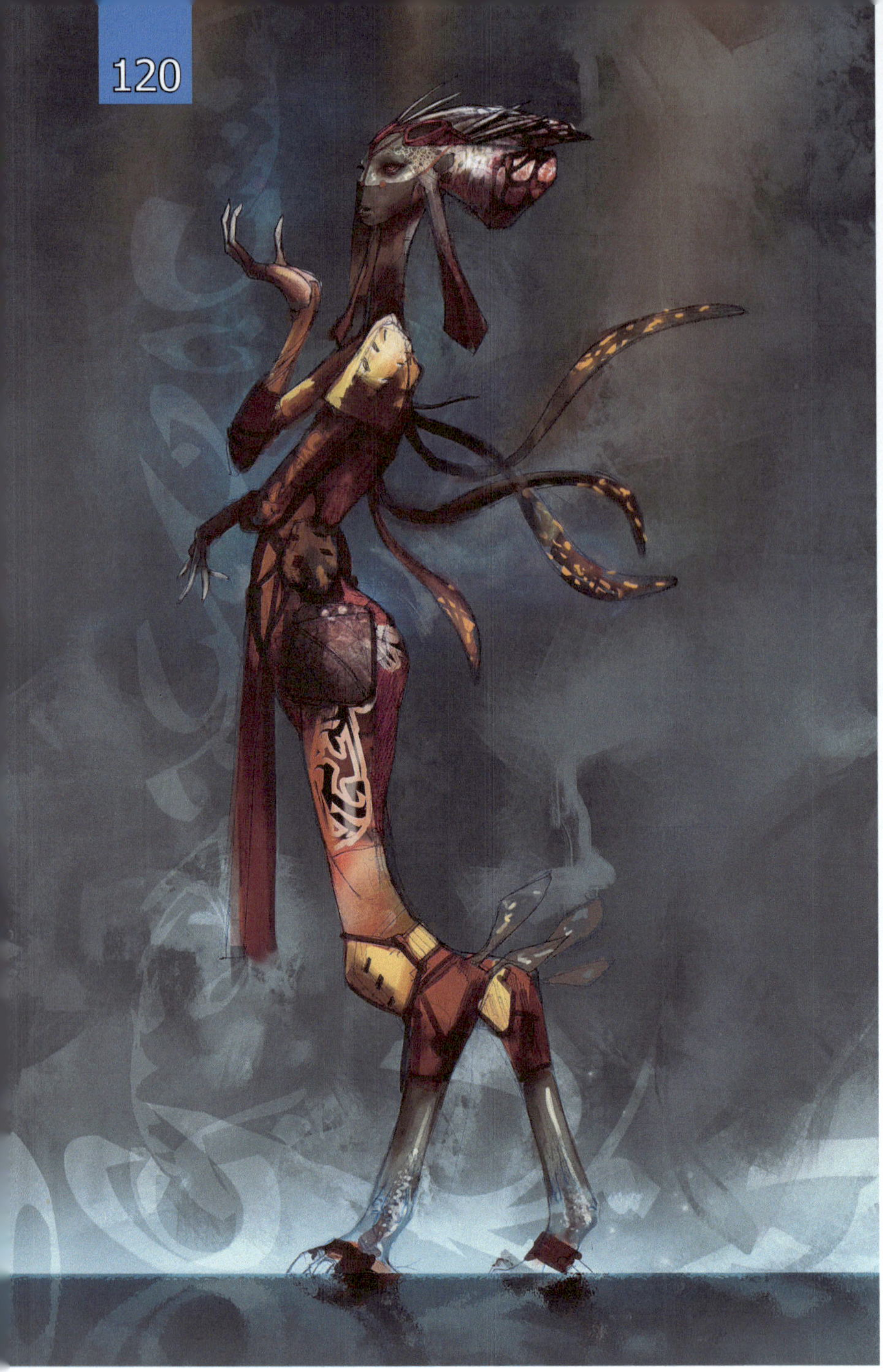

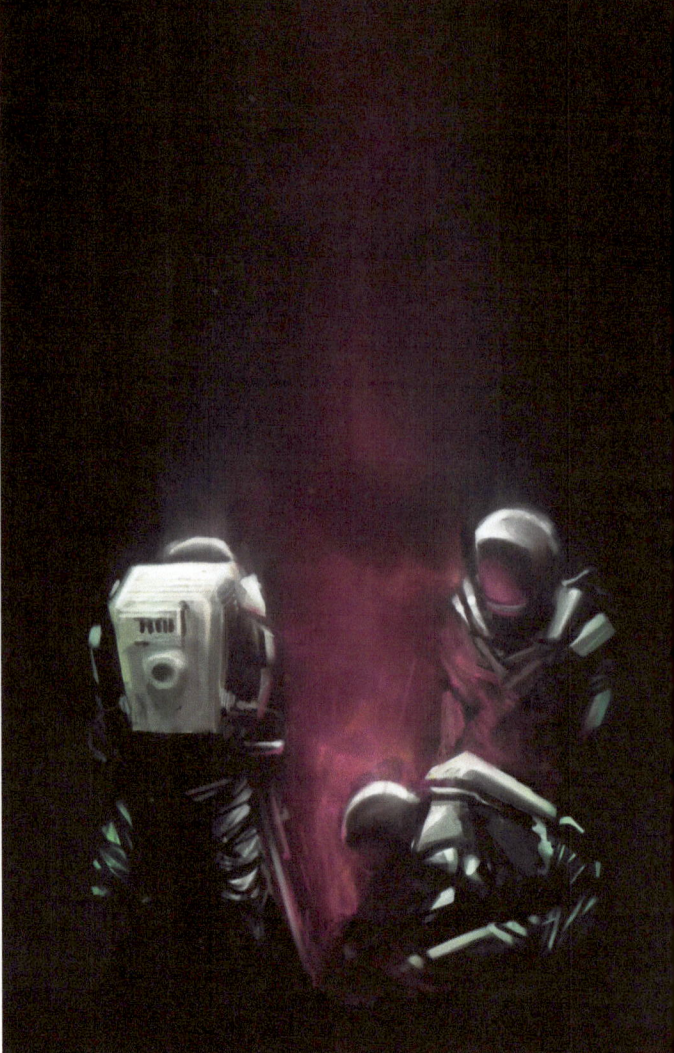

(Current Page)

ABOVE LEFT

AHMED ALDOORI
Photoshop (USA)
Alien Race

ABOVE

FELIPE ESCOBAR
Digital (Chile)
Mineral Search

OPPOSITE TOP

IRENE ZELESKOU
Photoshop (Greece)
Sci-Fi Commander

OPPOSITE BOTTOM

GIA NGUYEN HOANG
Photoshop (VietNam)
SpiderWalker

(Previous)

LEFT PAGE TOP

MARCO KUNARDI
Digital (Indonesia/USA)
Souvlaki Space Colony

LEFT PAGE BOTTOM

DARION LEIGH
Photoshop (UK)
Rusty Robot

RIGHT PAGE

TIHOMIR TIKULIN
Watercolor (Croatia)
Spacegirlt

(Overleaf)

LEFT PAGE TOP

JAKE MURRAY
Painter X (USA)
Evading the Bats

LEFT PAGE BOTTOM

DAVID DEMARET
Digital (France)
The Emperor's Arrival

RIGHT PAGE

CRAIG MUSSELMAN
Photomanipulation (Canada)
Credit: sxc.hu
Industrial Canyon

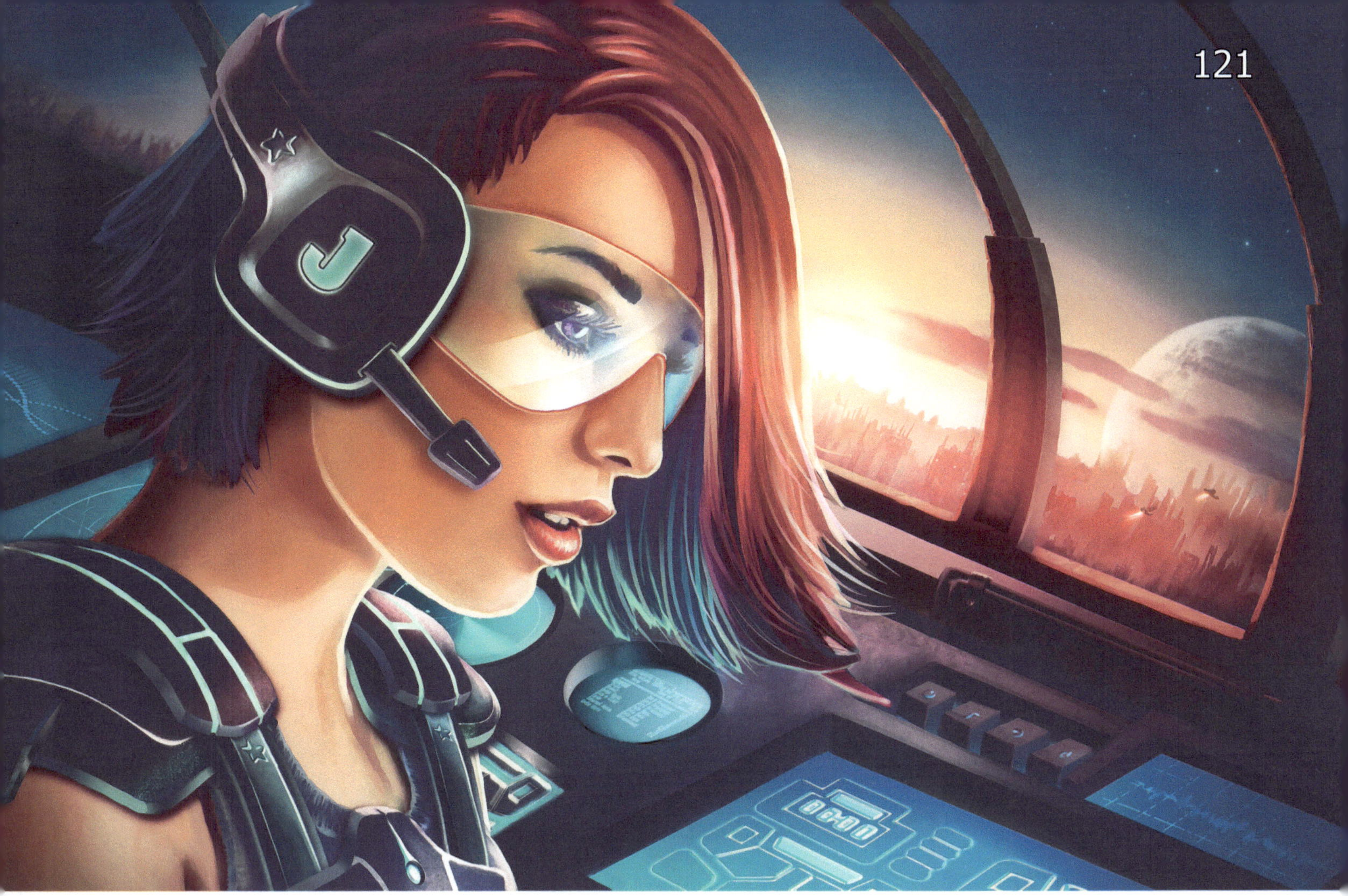

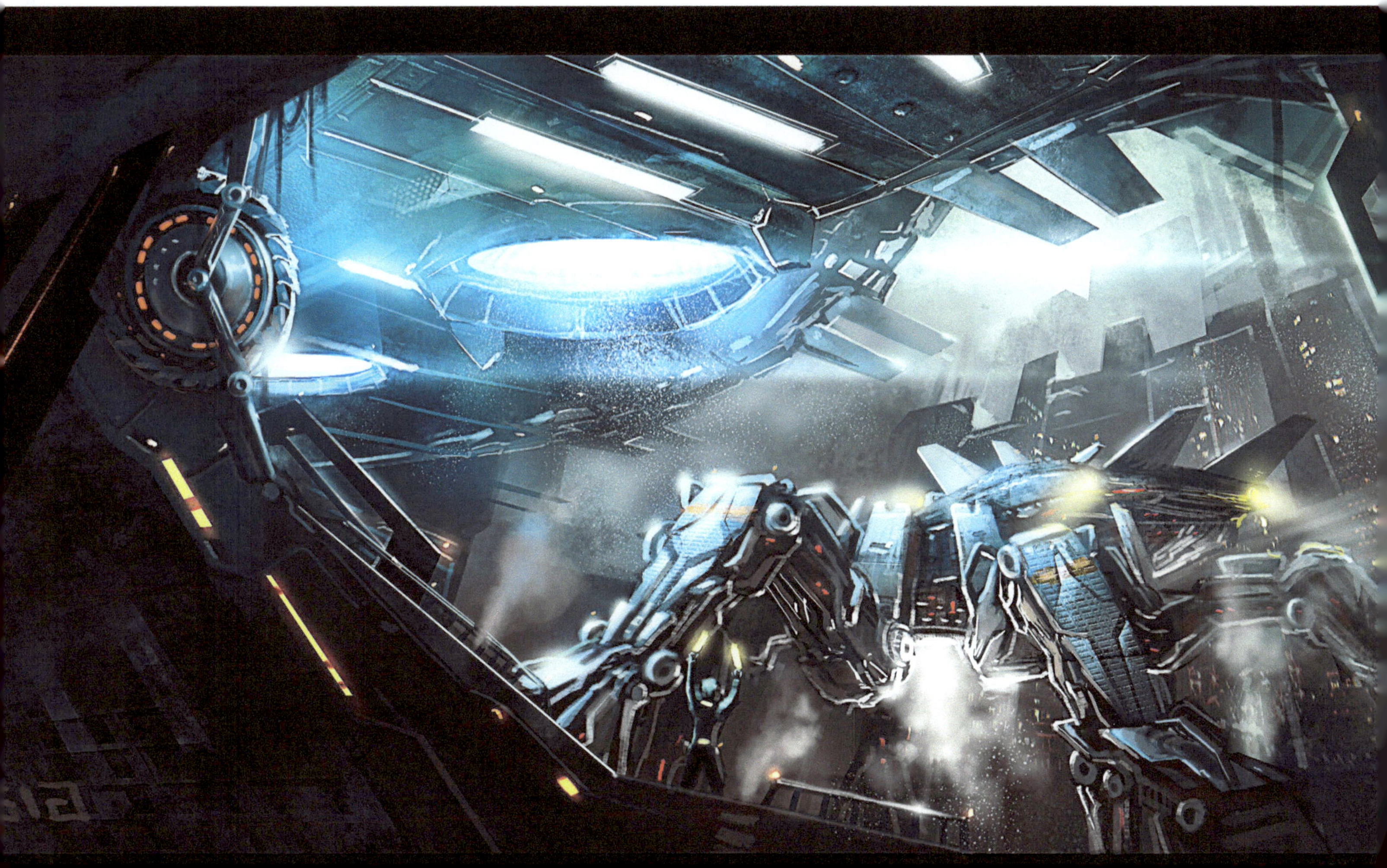

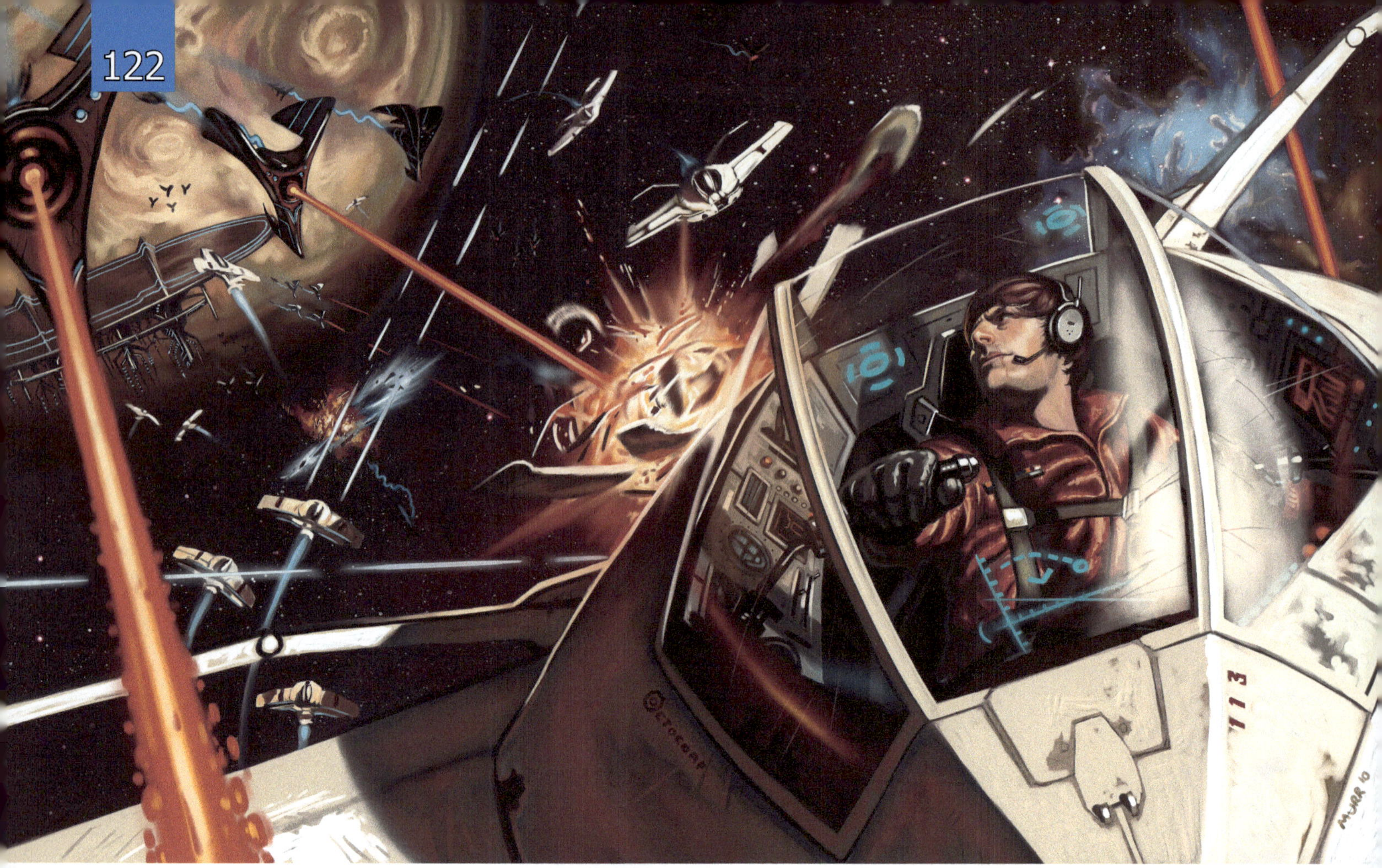

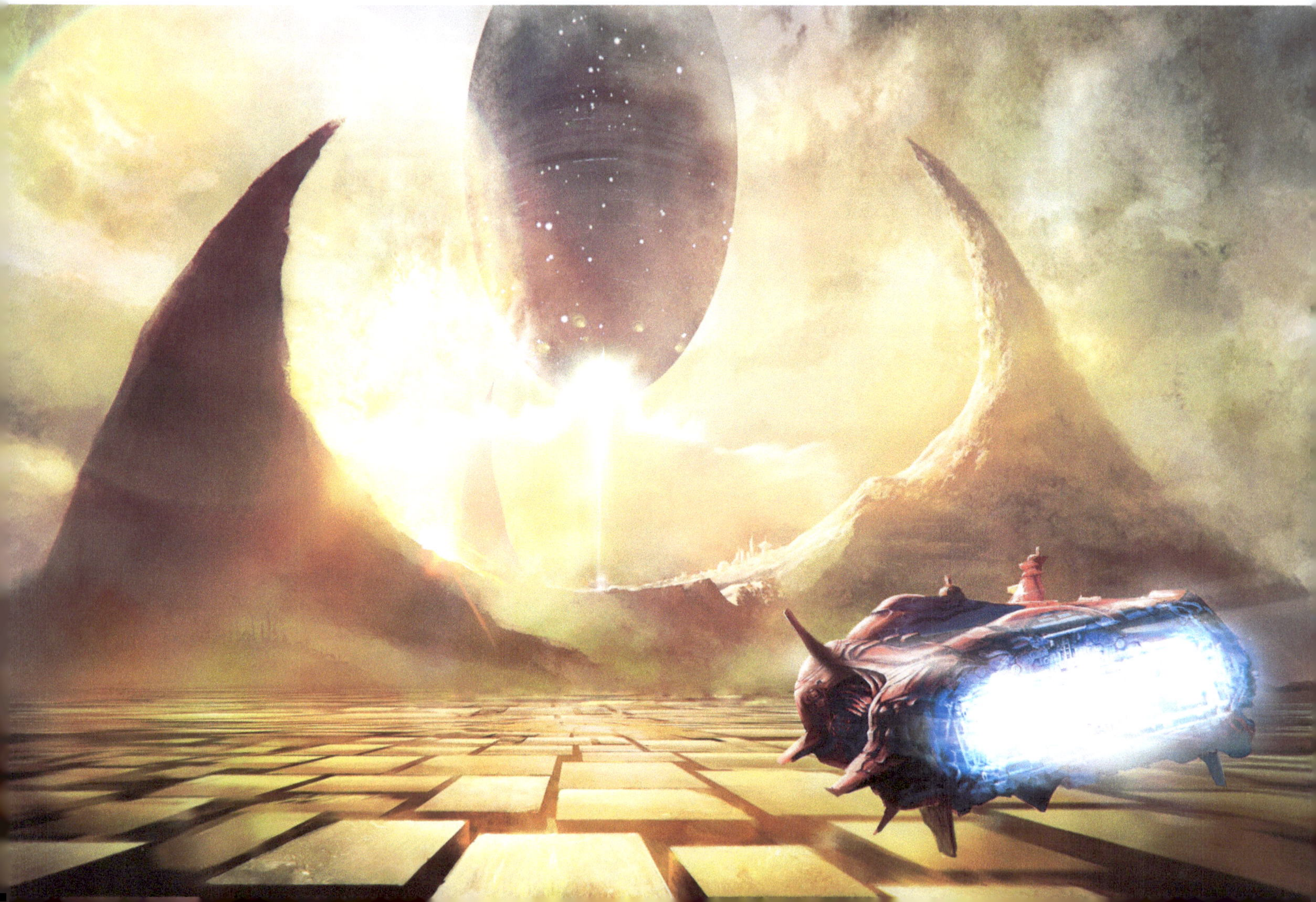

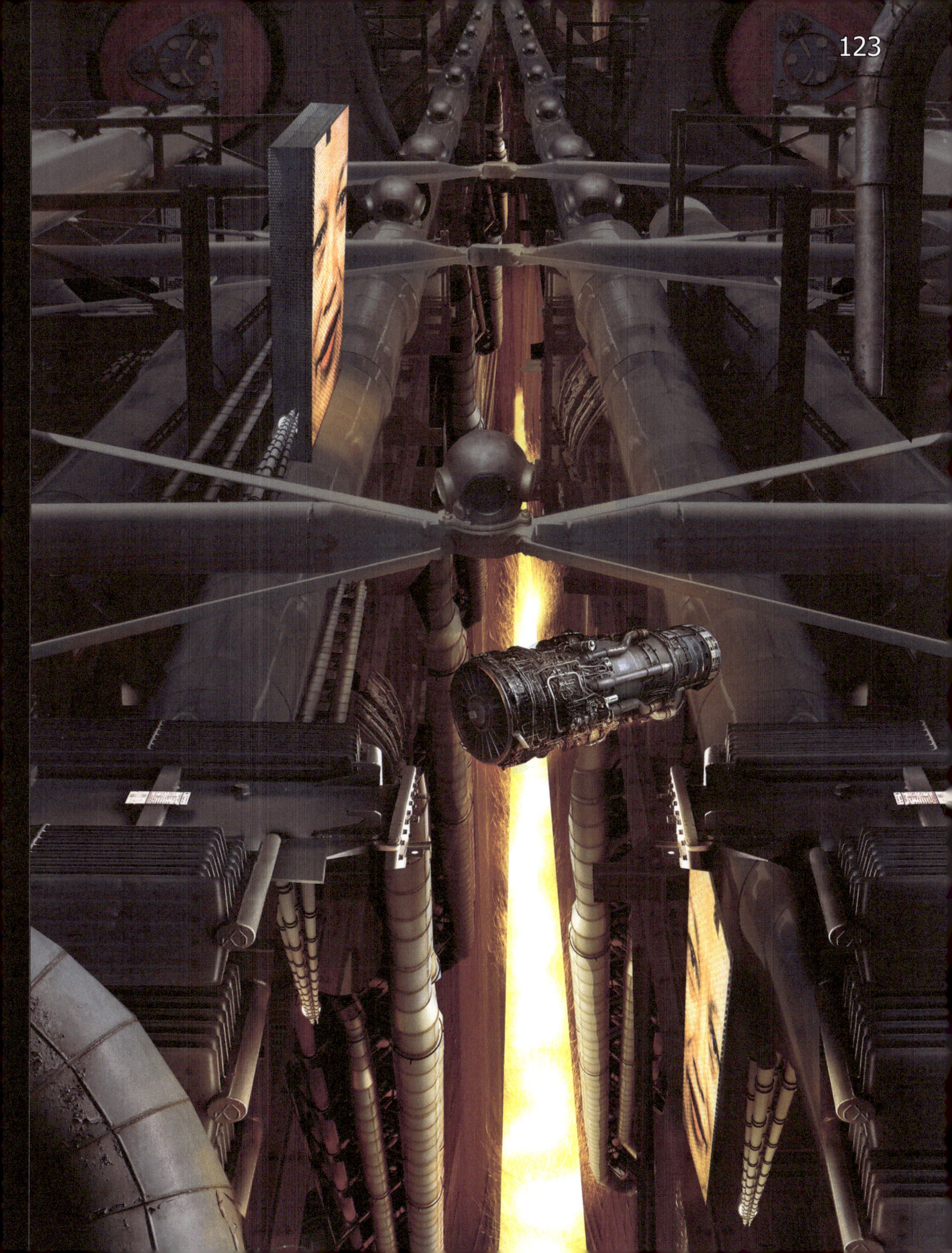

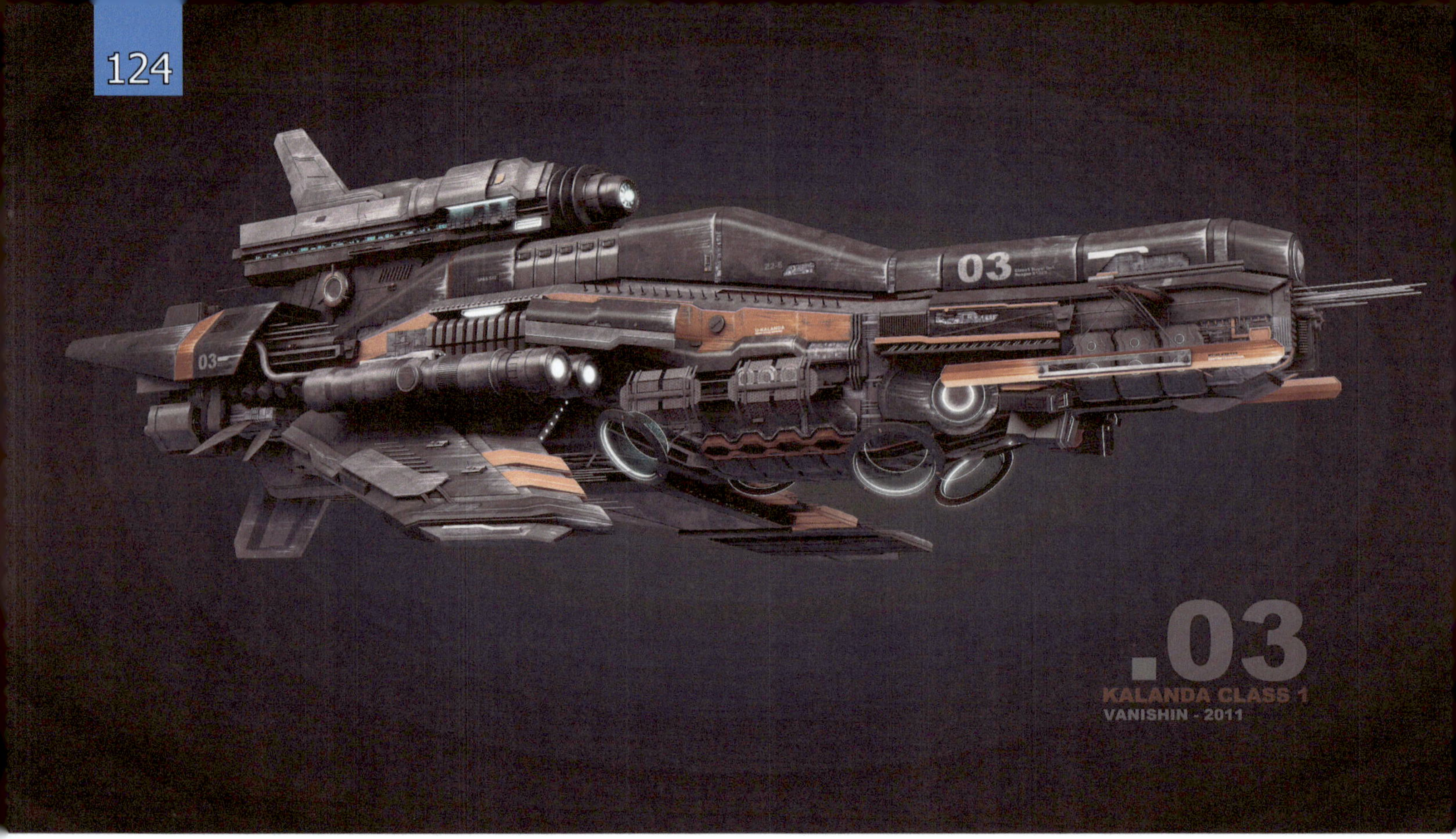

.03
KALANDA CLASS 1
VANISHIN - 2011

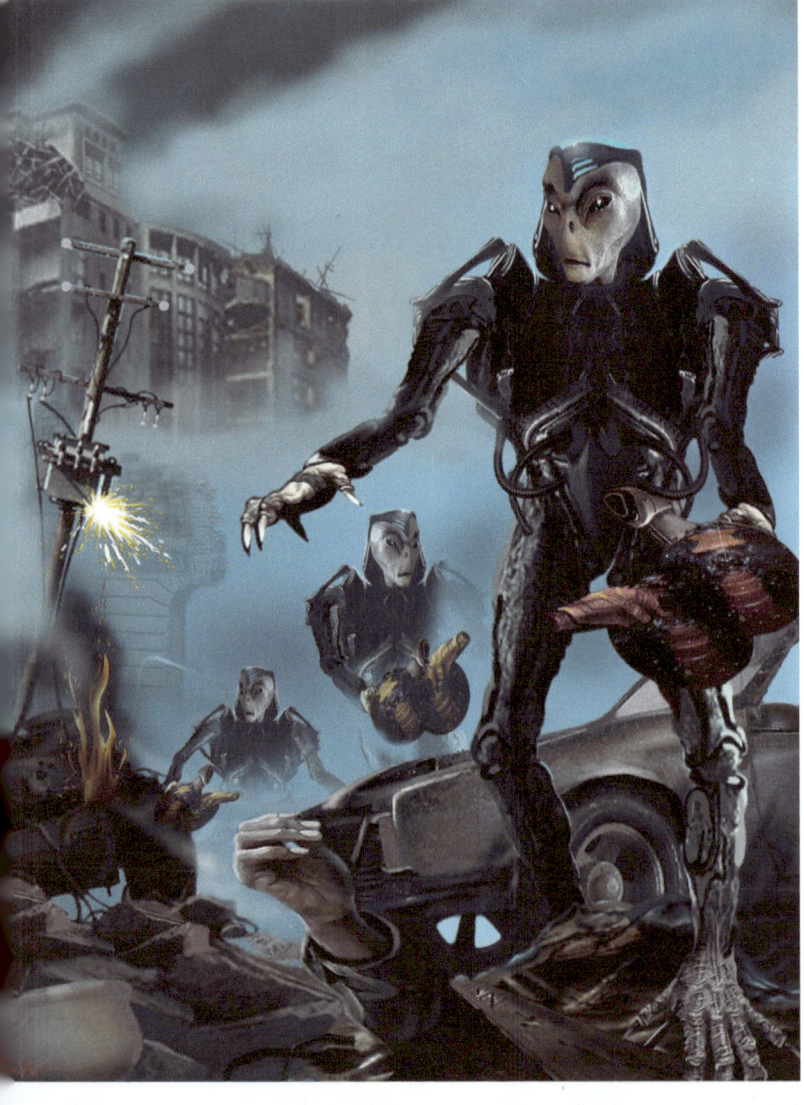

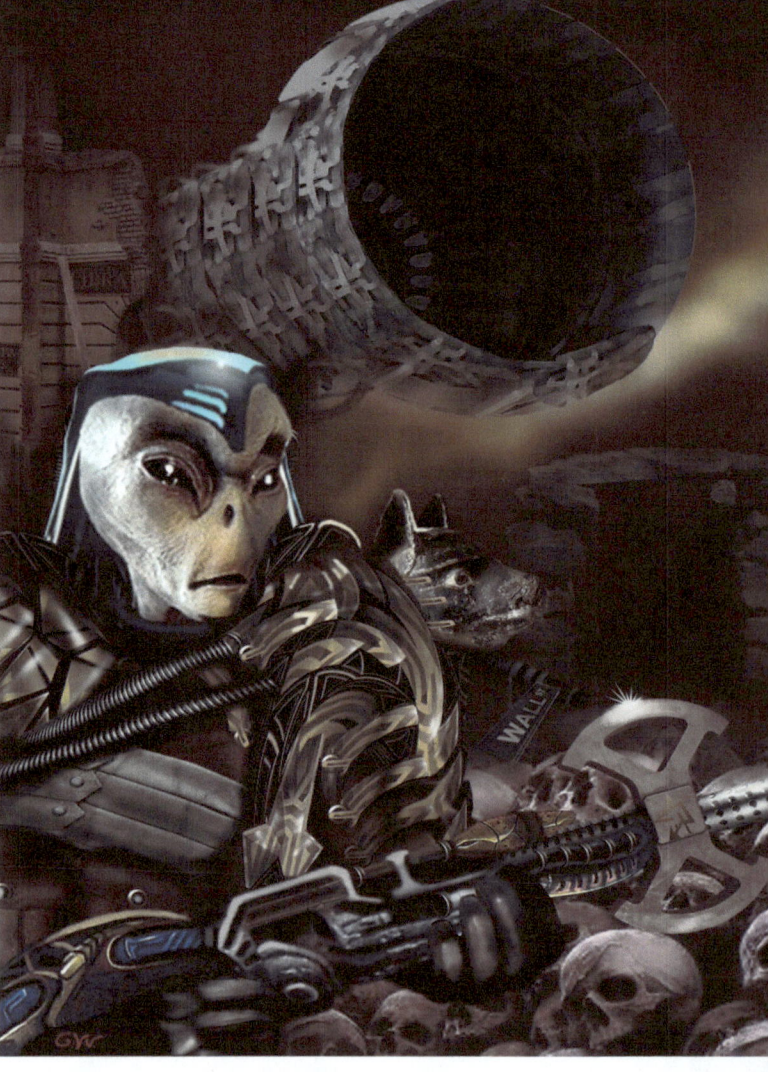

OPPOSITE TOP
Vincent Maréchal
Cinema 4D (France)
U-KALANDA Concept Ship

OPPOSITE BOTTOM LEFT
Gary Woodfield
Acrylic and Photoshop (Australia)
Hadesmen From Deep Space, Secondwave

OPPOSITE BOTTOM RIGHT
Gary Woodfield
Acrylic and Photoshop (Australia)
Hadesmen From Deep Space, Shock Troops

RIGHT
George Patsouras
Photoshop Painting (USA)
Lost

BELOW
Andrea Gatti
Photoshop (Italy)
Deus

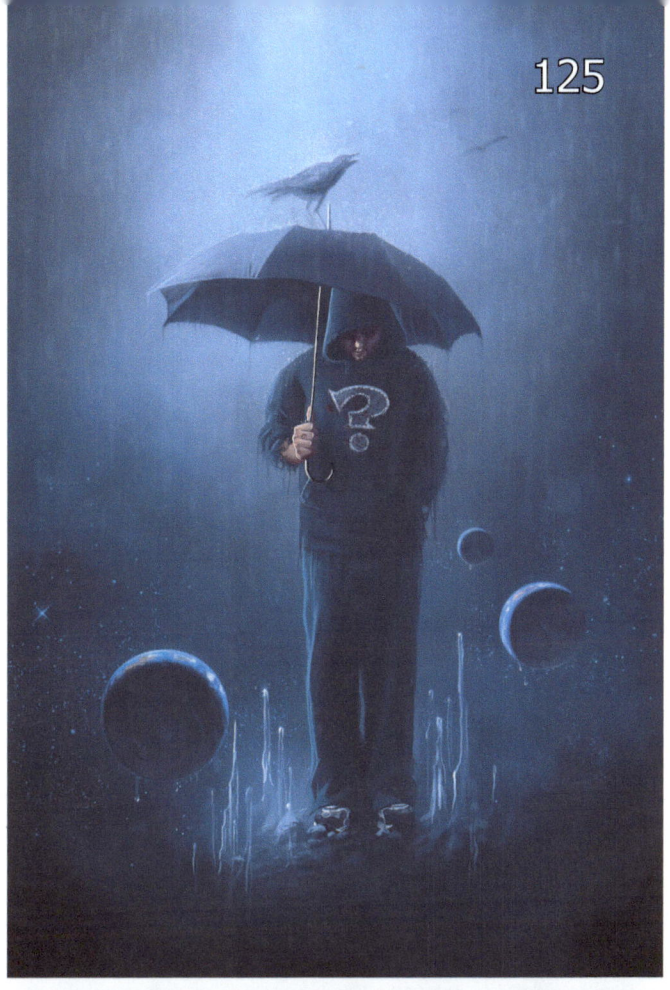

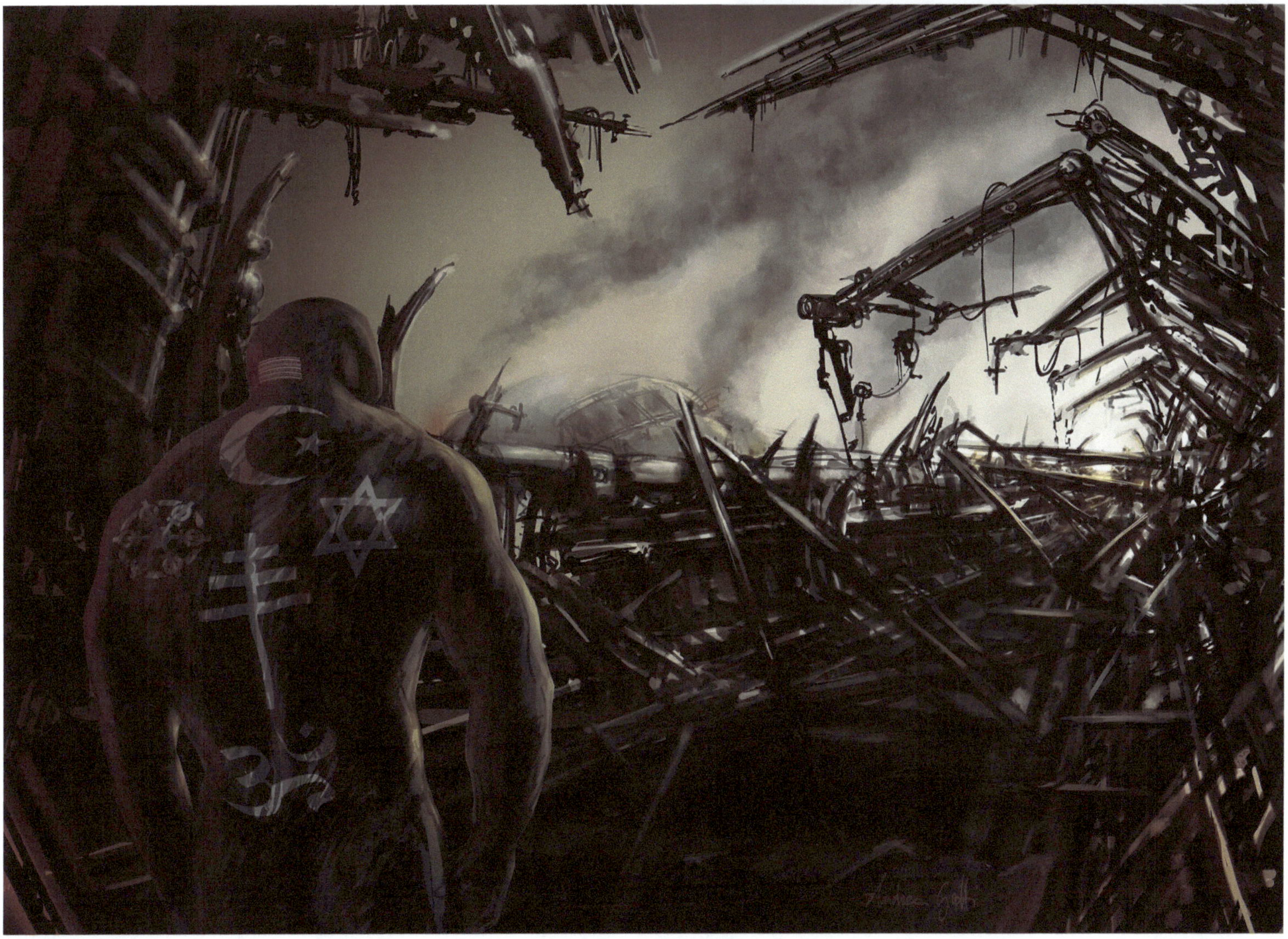

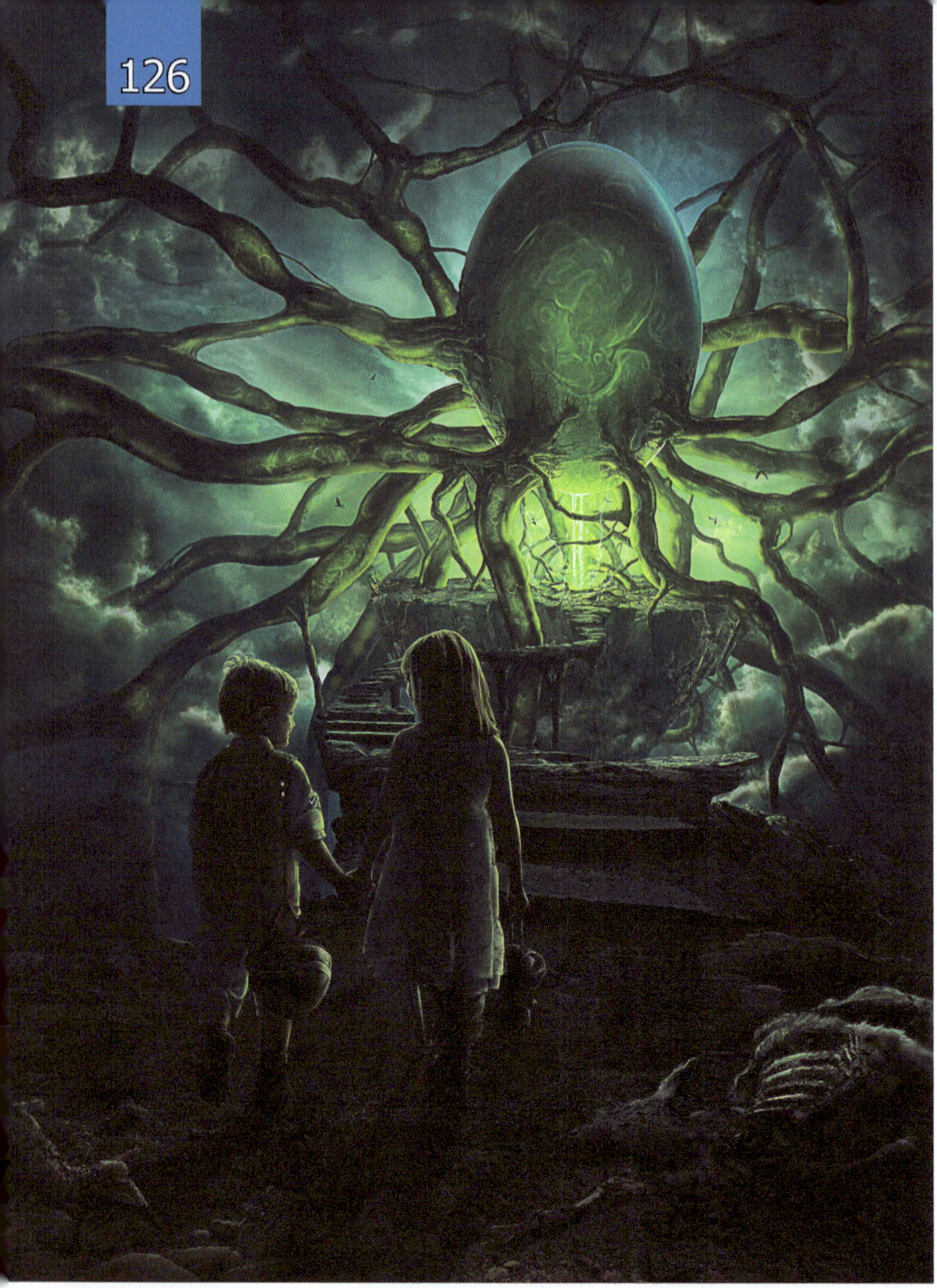

LEFT

GAÉTAN WELTZER
Photoshop (France)
New Era - Ascent

BOTTOM

GIA NGUYEN HOANG
Photoshop (VietNam)
Tree House

CENTRE BELOW

FRANCIS-LEE PIMENTEL
Pencil (England)
Demon I

OPPOSITE

DAVID LECOSSU
Photoshop (France)
Search

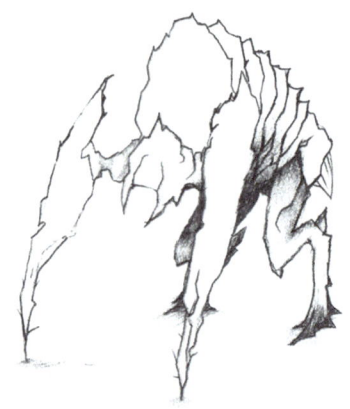

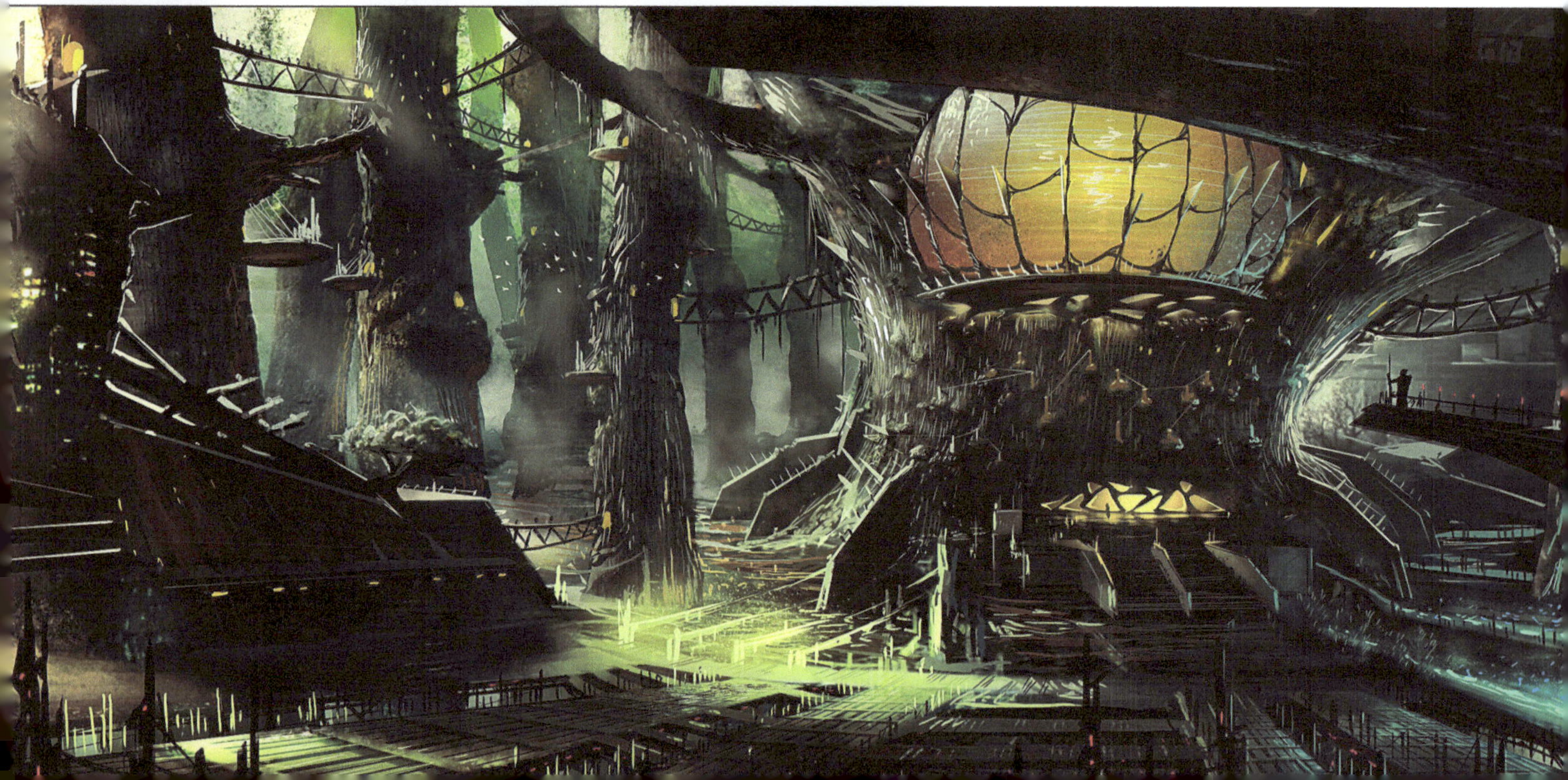

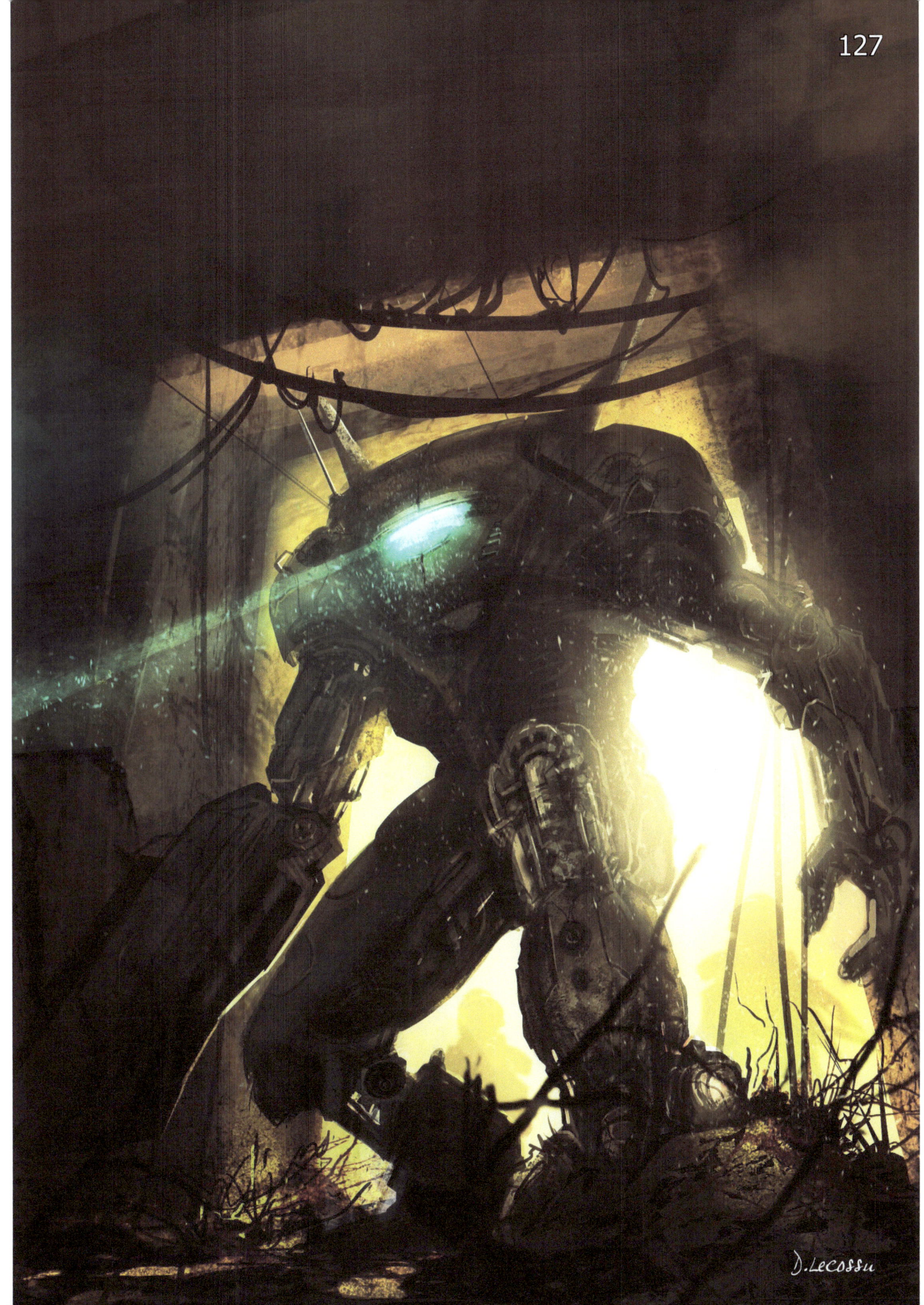

D.Lecossu

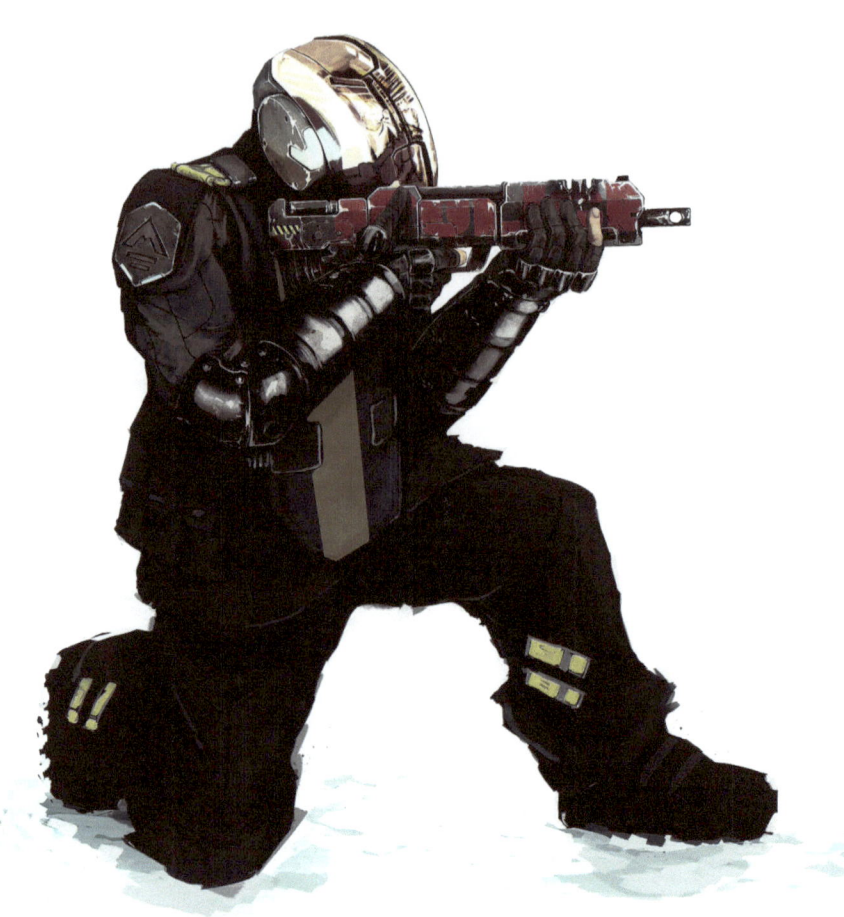

LEFT

Julian Lancaster
Photoshop (Canada)
Sci-fi Police

BELOW

Ahmed Aldoori
Photoshop (USA)
Orange Bot

OPPOSITE TOP

Eko Puteh

Handriyanto
Colour Photoshop (Indonesia)

Garrie Gastonny
Line Art (Indonesia)
The Defenders

OPPOSITE BOTTOM

Ahmed Aldoori
Photoshop (USA)
Chameleon Bot

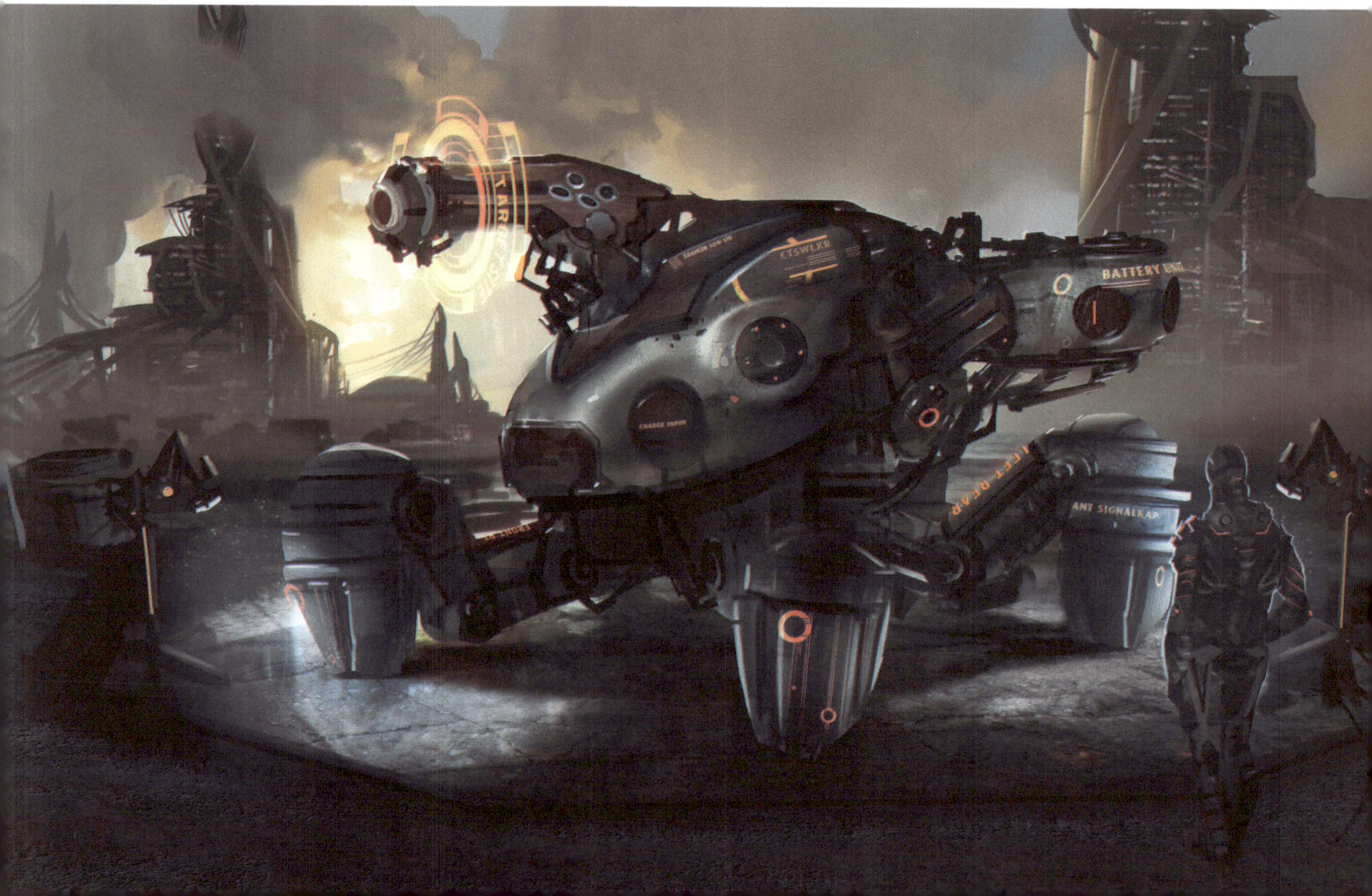

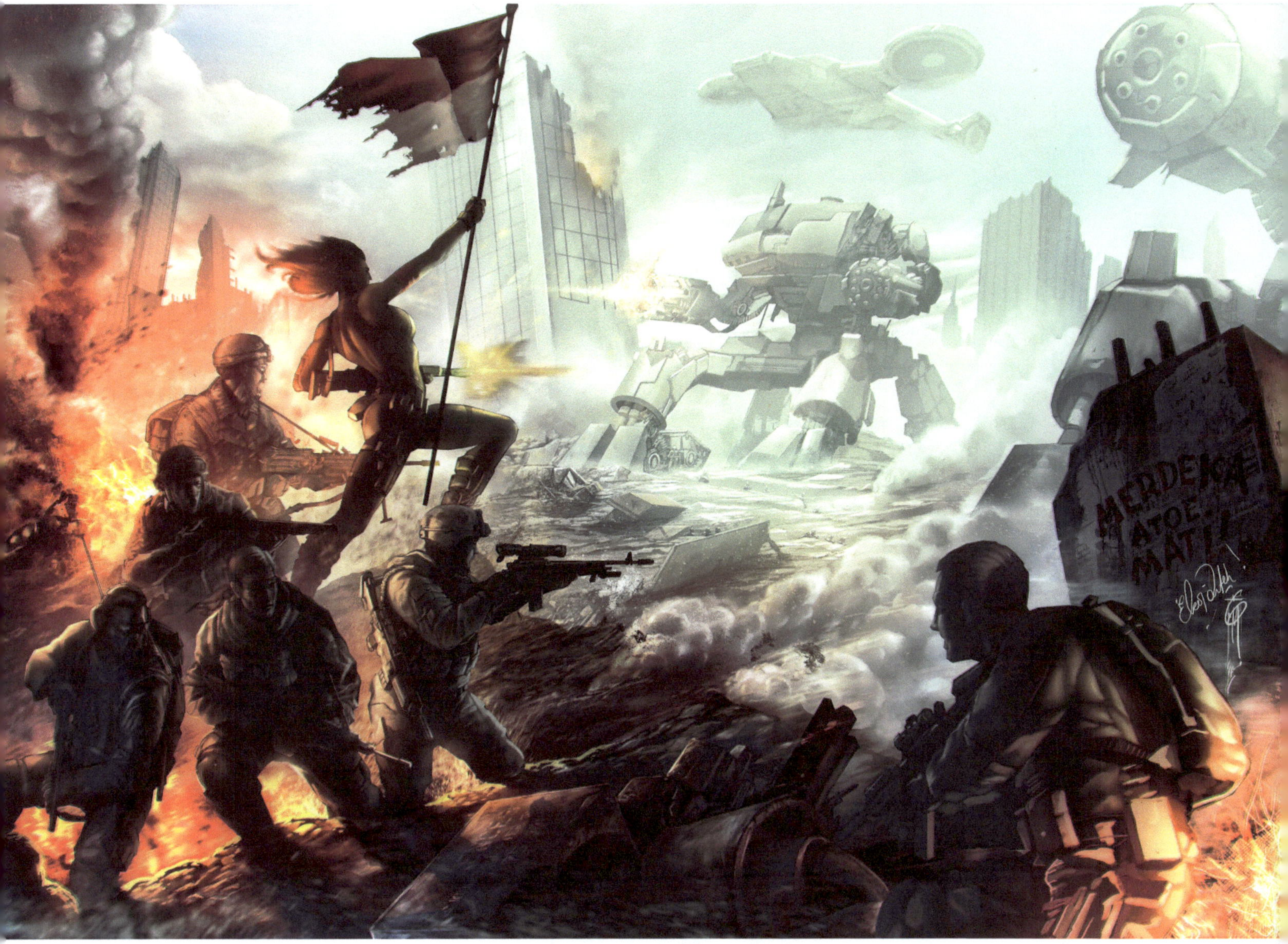

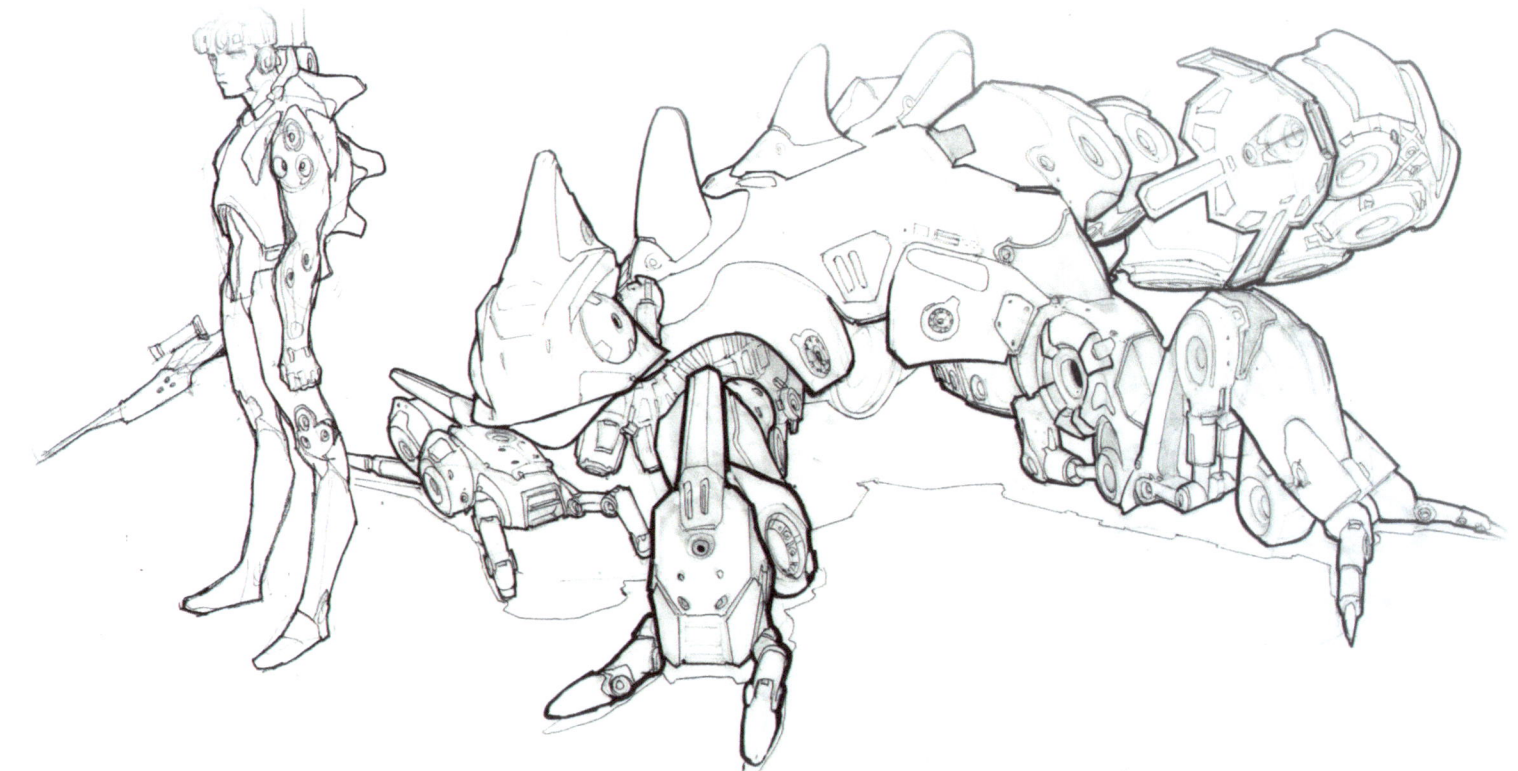

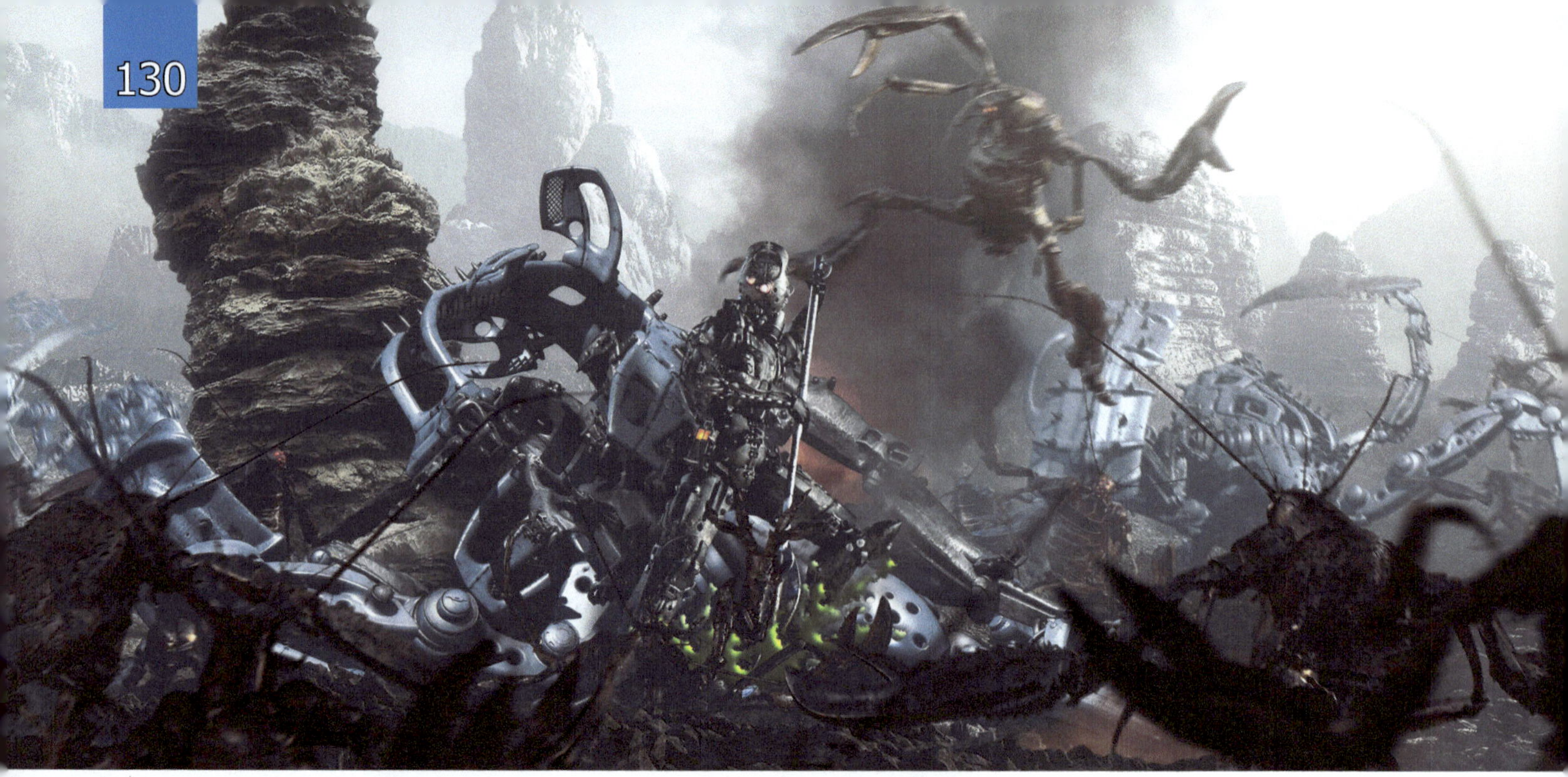

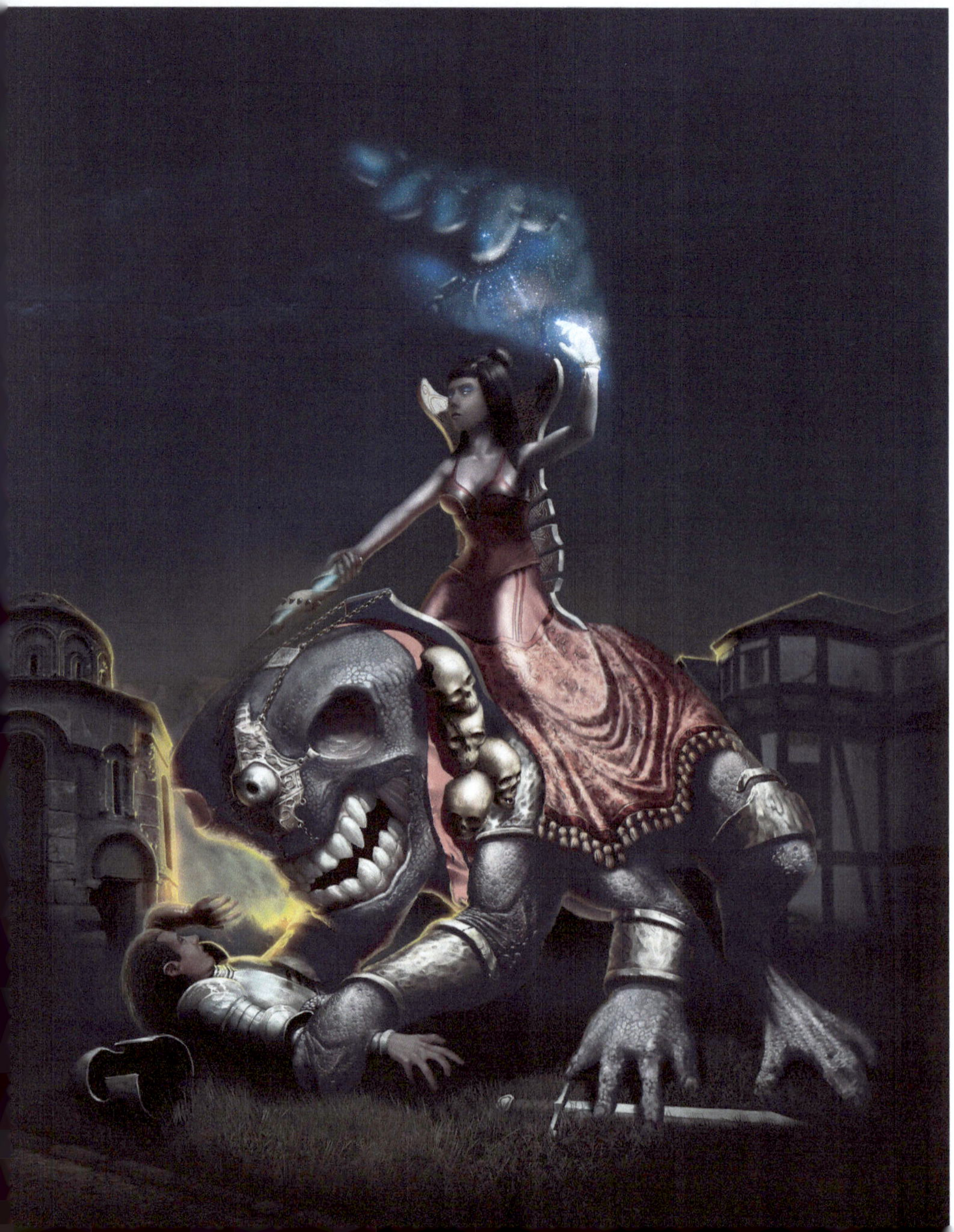

ABOVE

ANGEL ALONSO
Digital 3D (Spain)
Invasion of Chaos

LEFT

BOTOND HARKO
Photoshop (Romania)
Takeover

OPPOSITE TOP

ANGEL ALONSO
Digital 3D (Spain)
Collectors in the Mother City

OPPOSITE CENTRE

ANGEL ALONSO
Digital 3D (Spain)
In Repair

OPPOSITE BOTTOM

ANGEL ALONSO
Digital 3D (Spain)
The Chaos Storm

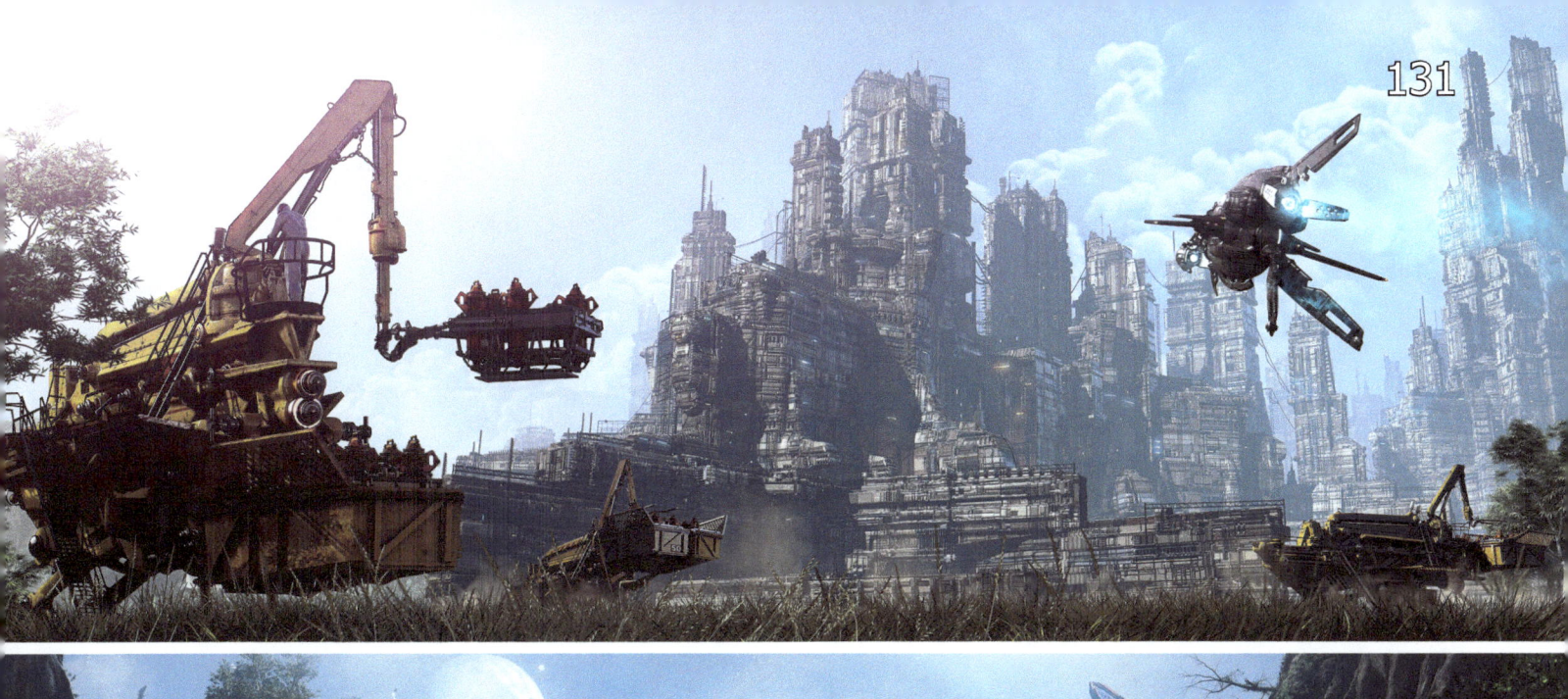

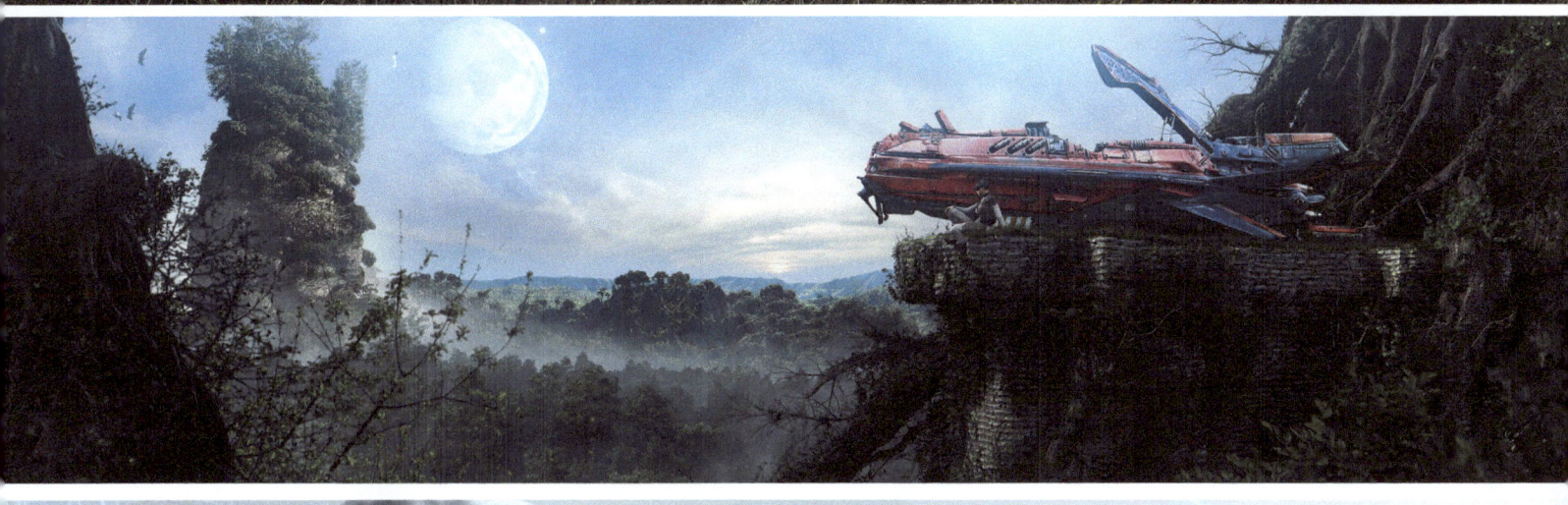

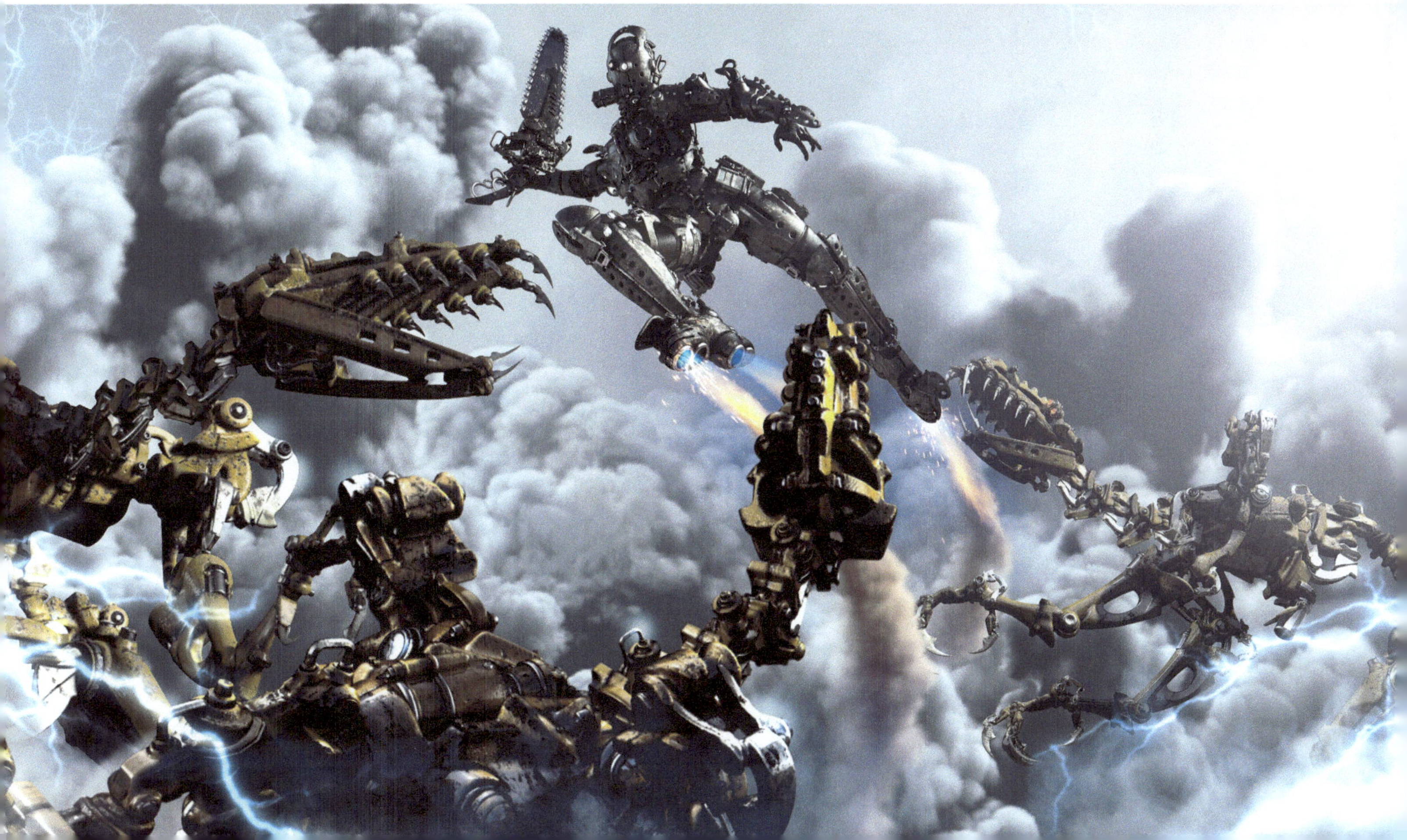

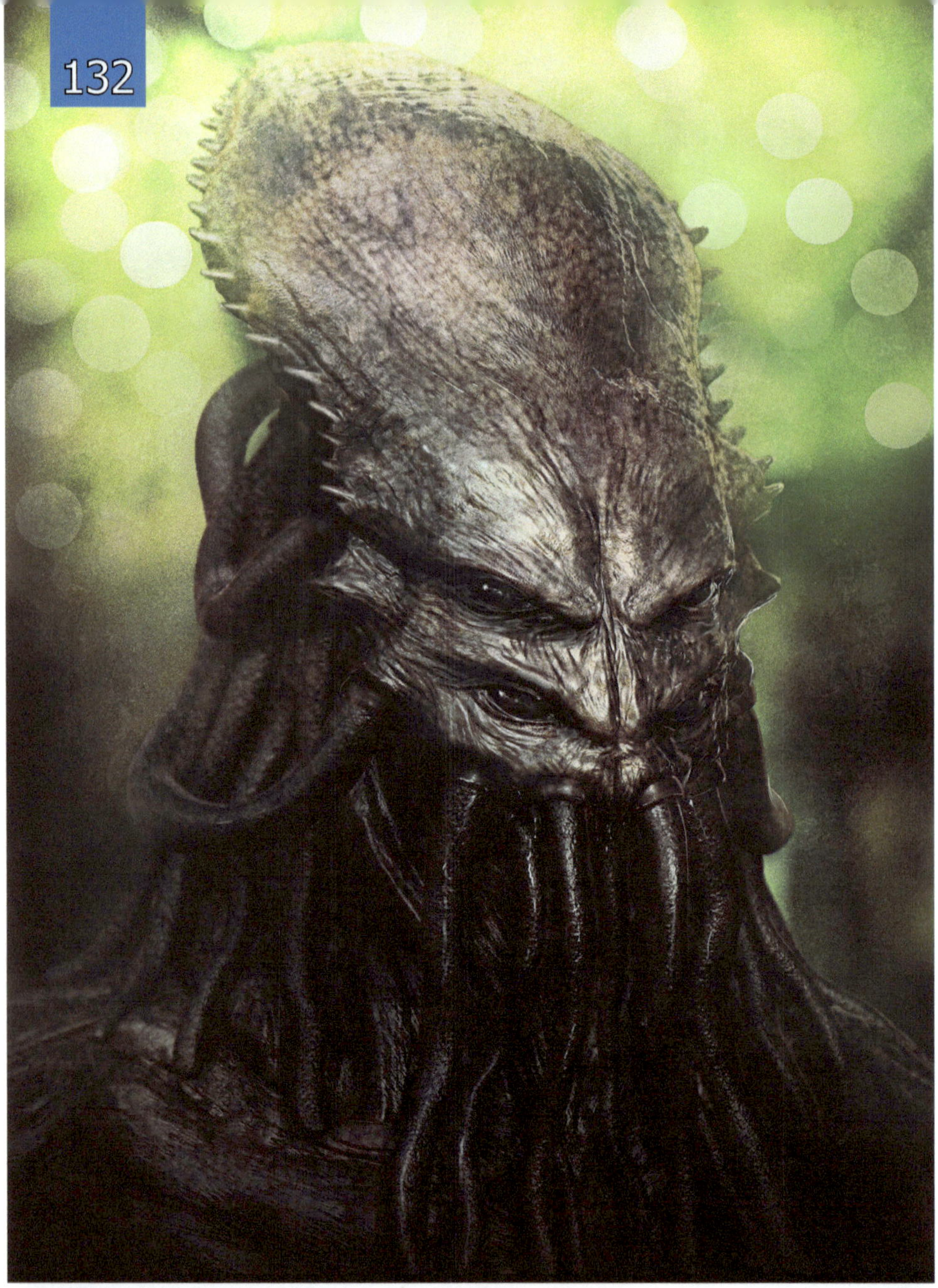

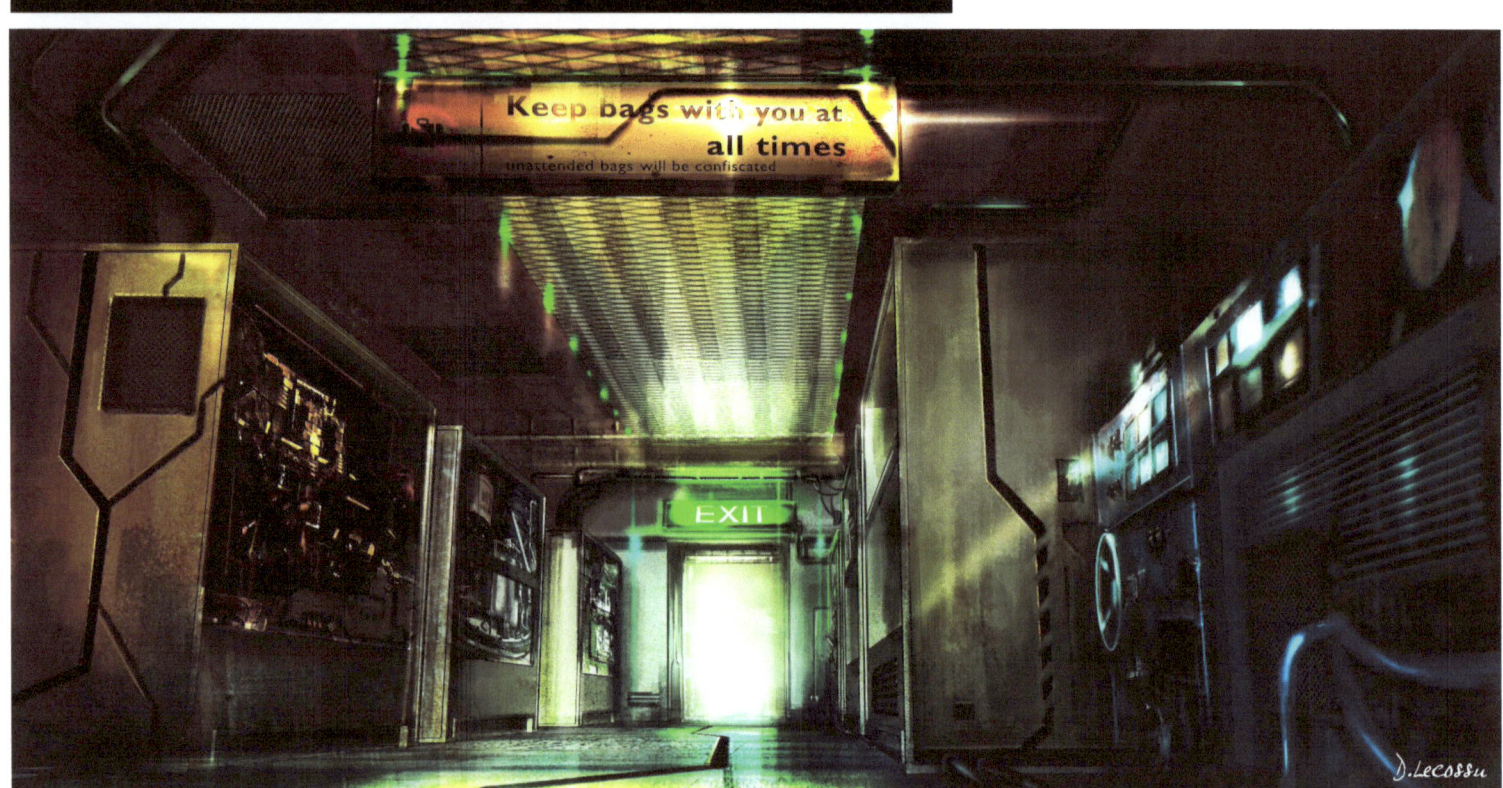

LEFT

RIYAHD CASSIEM
Zbrush and Photoshop (South Africa)
Octohybrid

BELOW

DAVID LECOSSU
Photoshop (France)
Couloir

OPPOSITE TOP

RIYAHD CASSIEM
Zbrush and Photoshop (South Africa)
Mechoid

OPPOSITE BOTTOM

DAVID LECOSSU
Photoshop (France)
The Wood

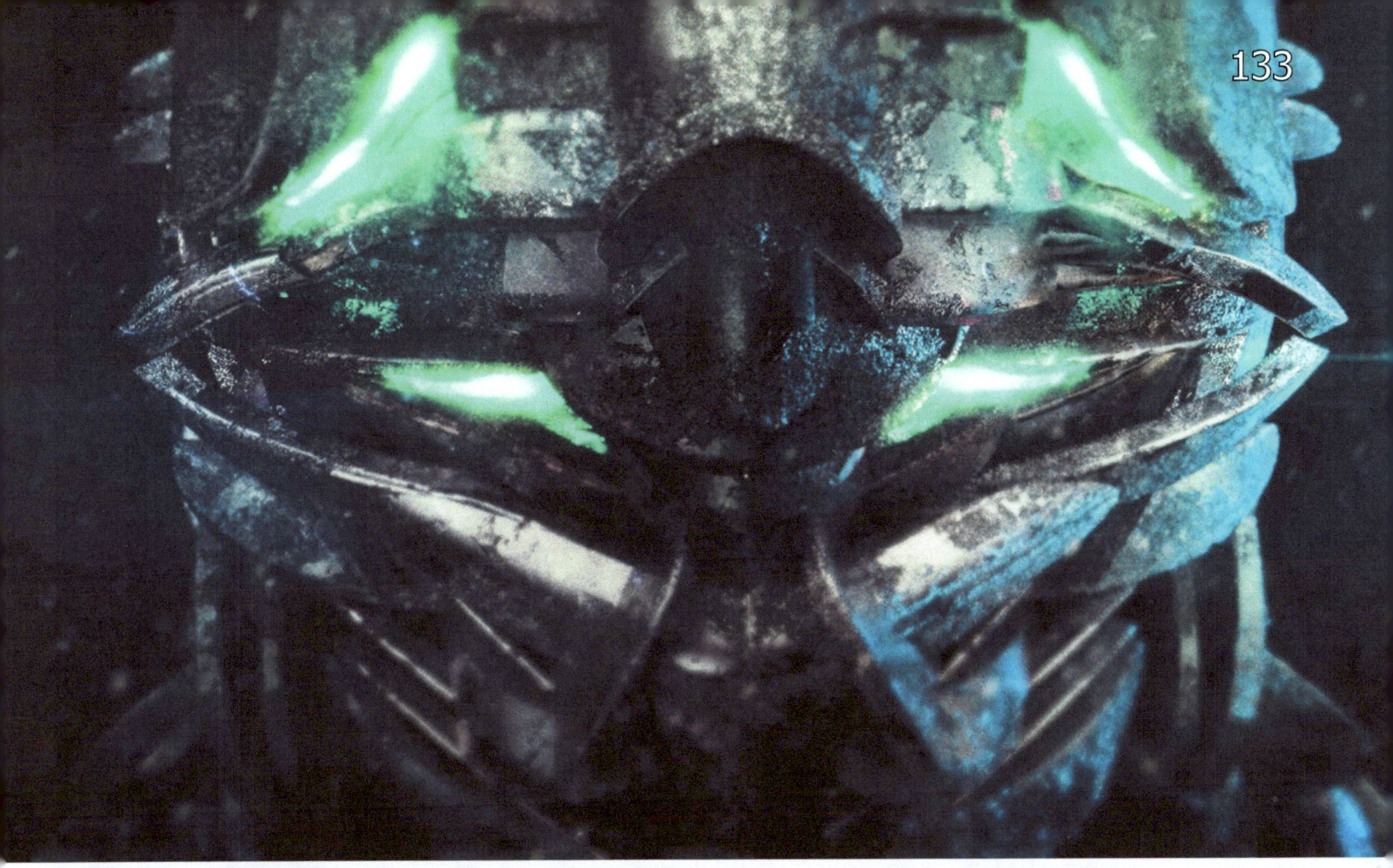

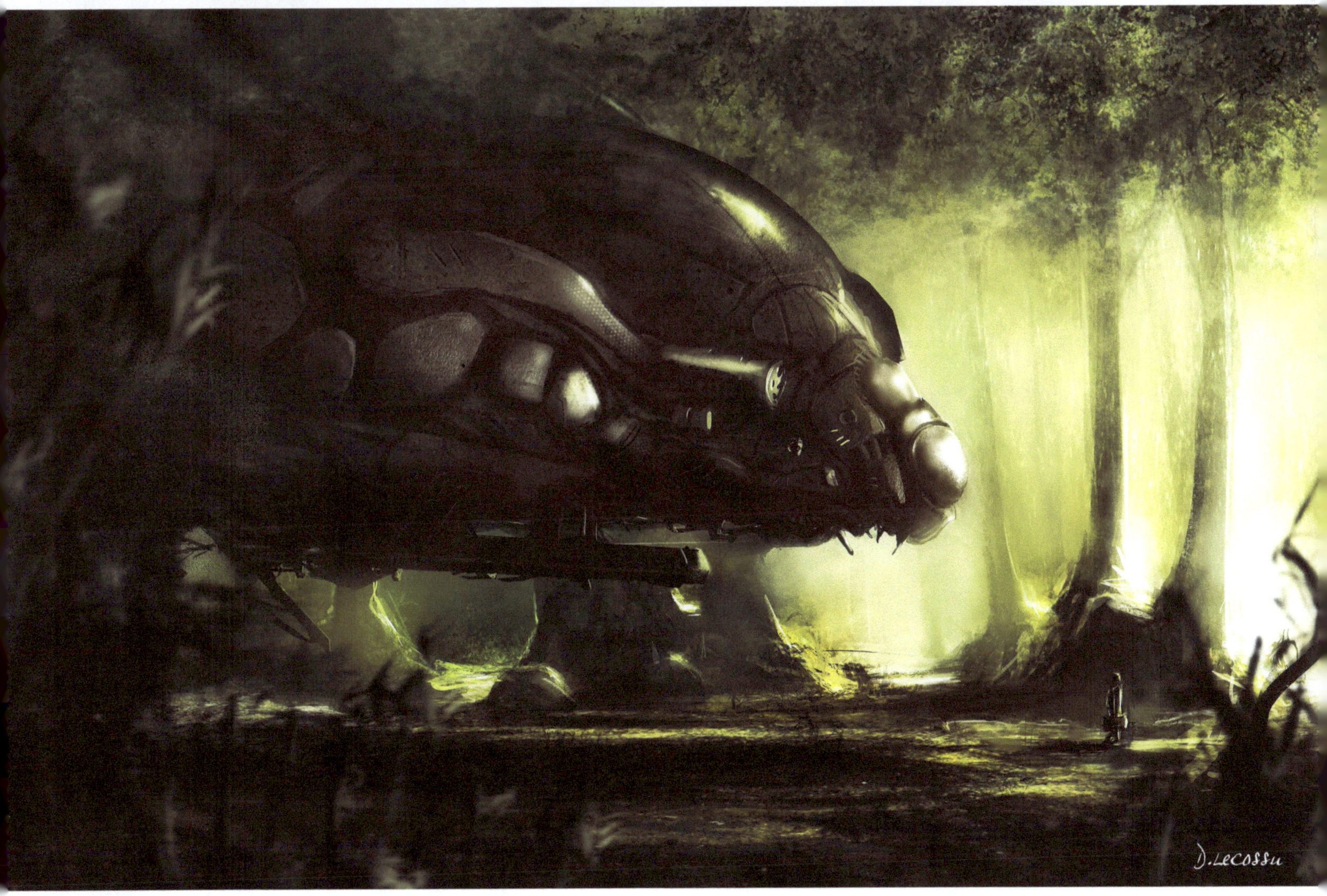

D.Lecossu

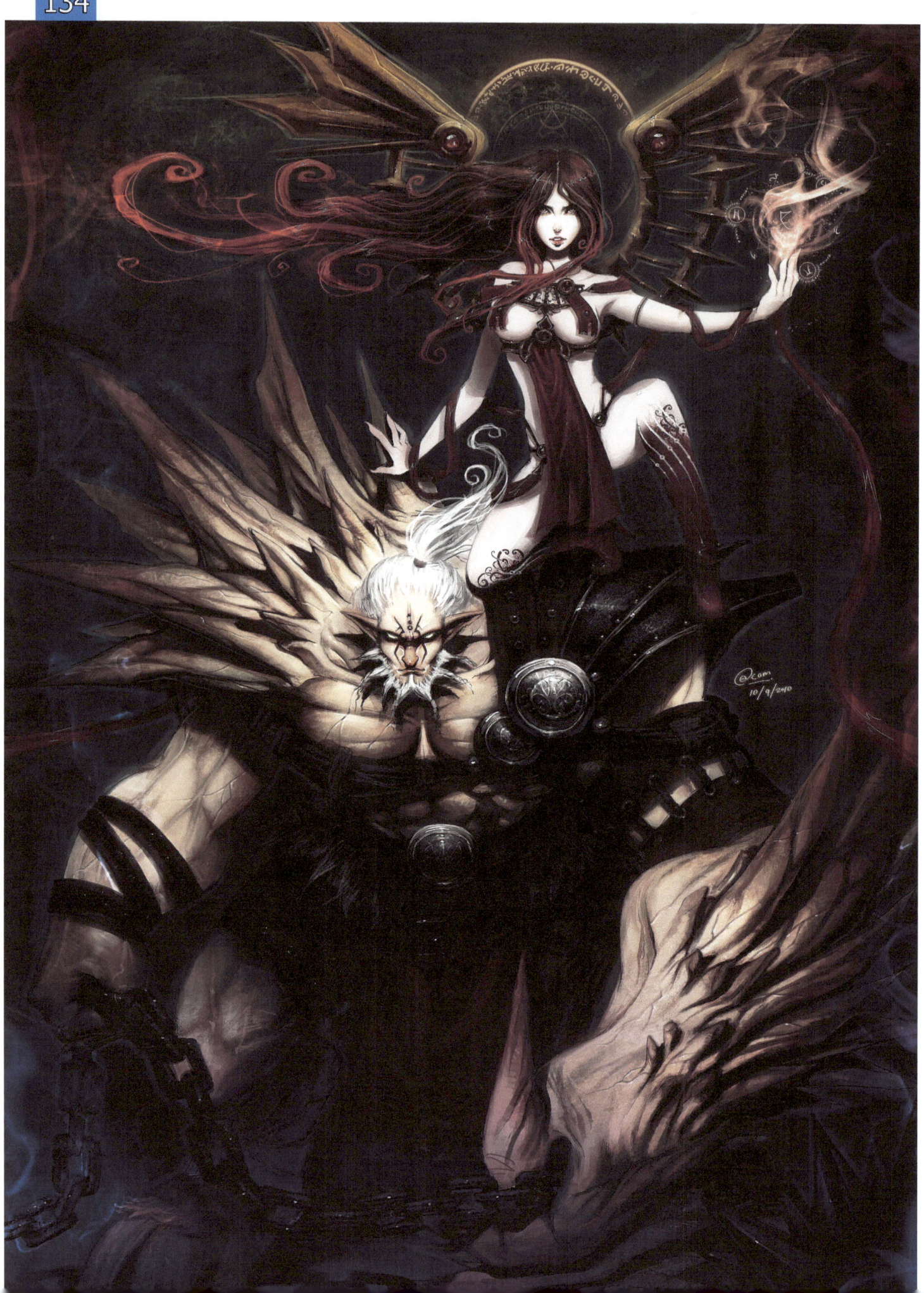

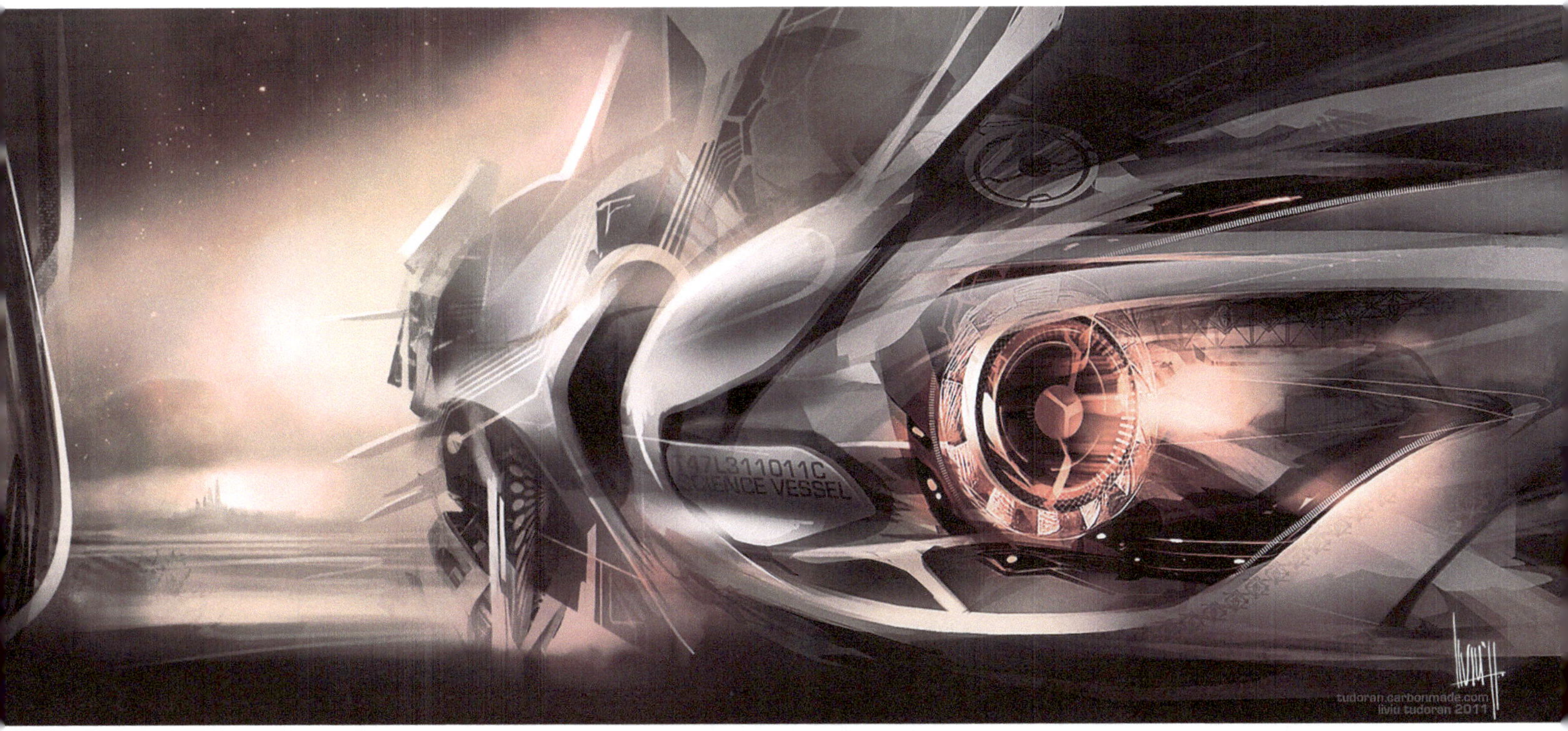
L311011C
VESSEL
tudoran.carbonmade.com
liviu tudoran 2011

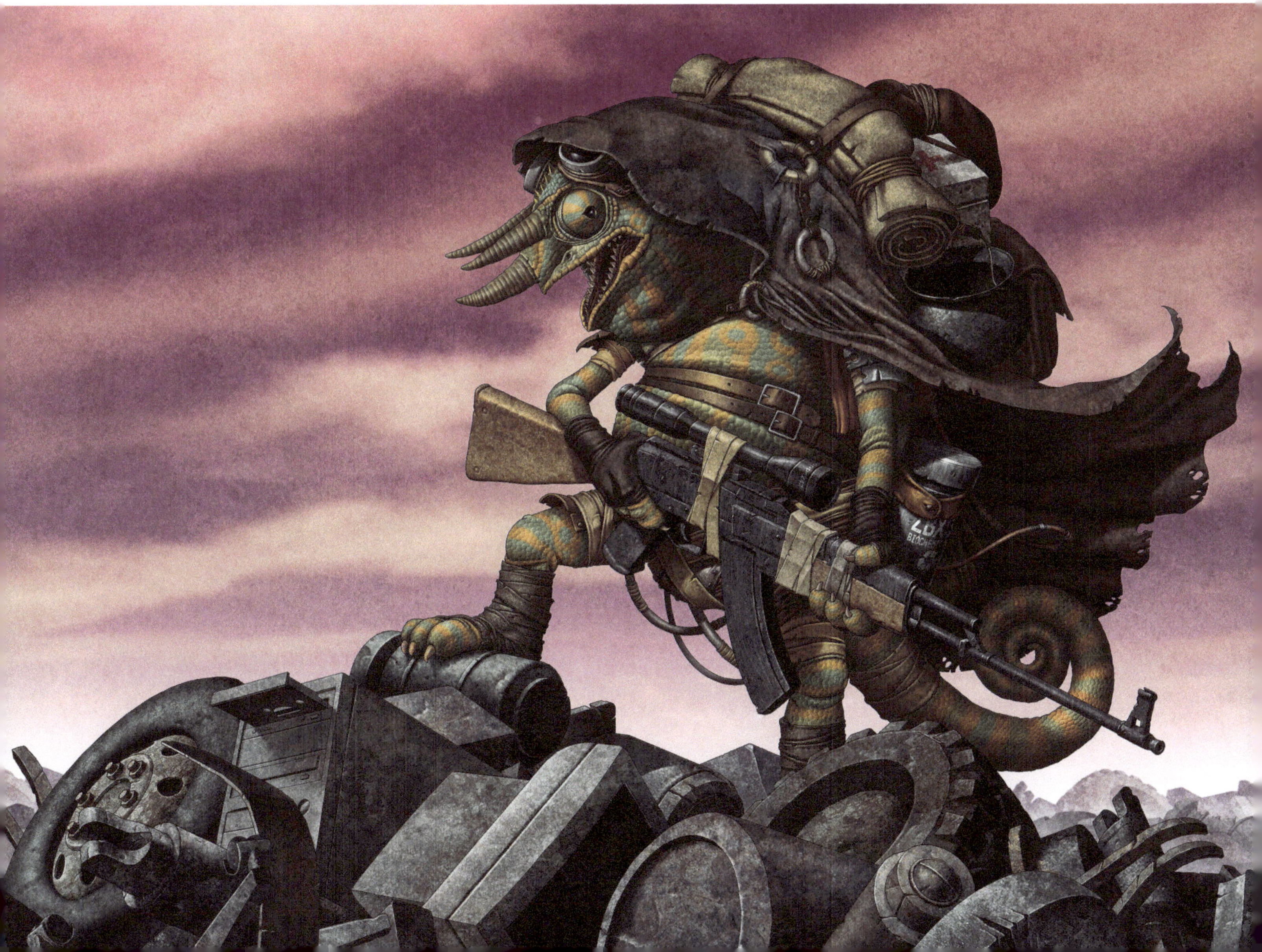

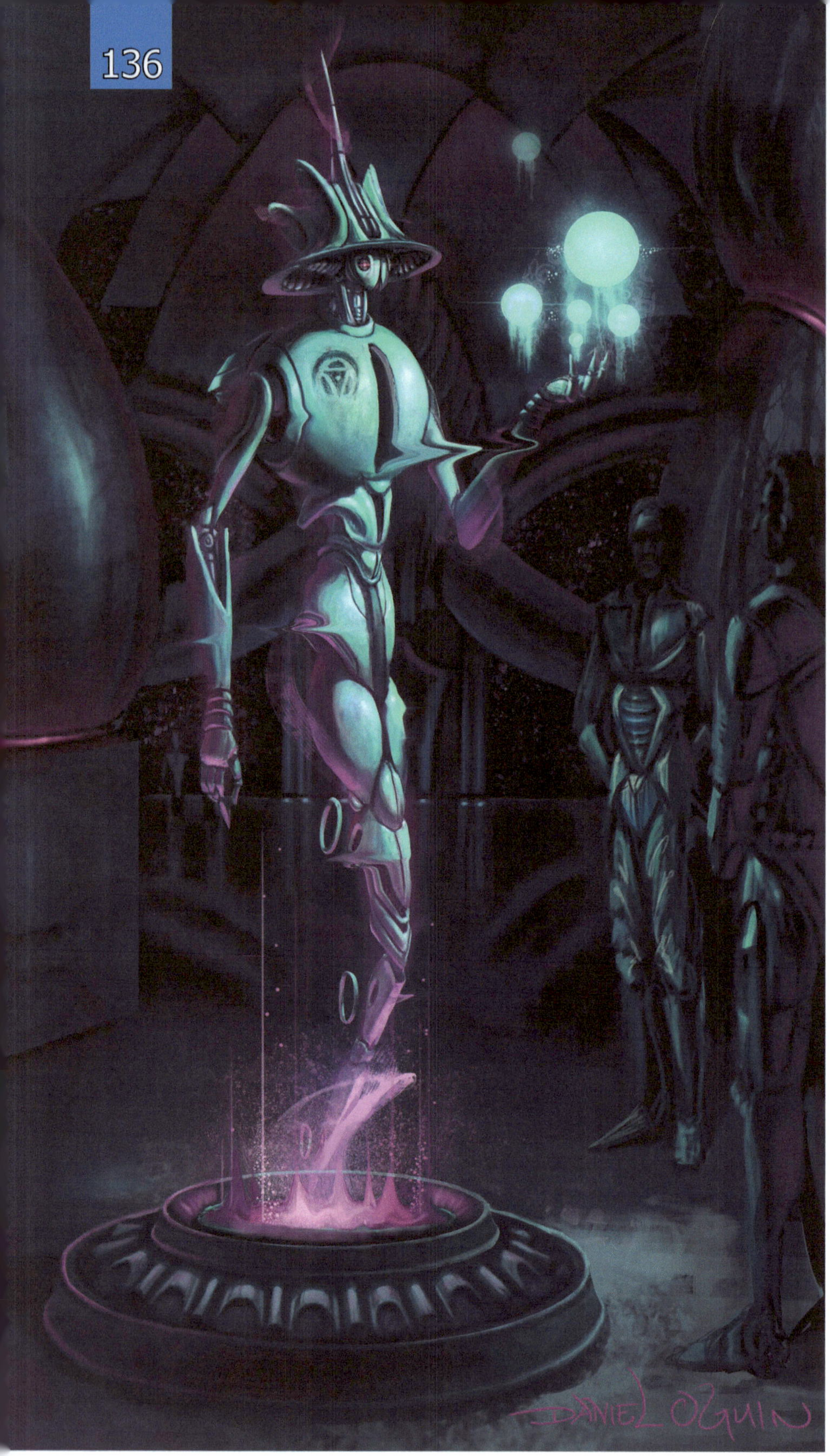

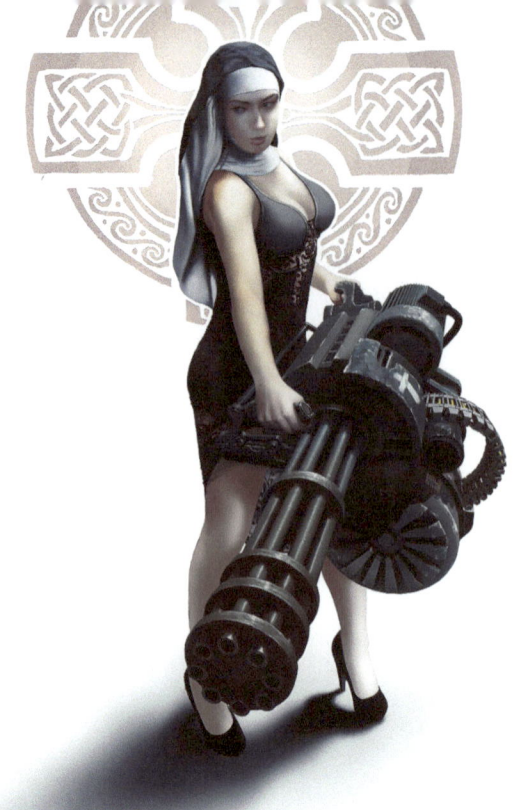

(Previous)

LEFT PAGE

YEE-LING CHUNG
Digital (Malaysia)
Earth and Fire

RIGHT PAGE TOP

LIVIU TUDORAN
Photoshop (Italy)
Science Vessel

RIGHT PAGE BOTTOM

KRISZTIAN BALLA
Digital (Hungary)
Humaleon

(opposite page)

OPPOSITE BOTTOM

LORENZ HIDEYOSHI RU-
WWE
Digital Photoshop (Germany)
Unearthly

OPPOSITE TOP

GAÉTAN WELTZER
(detail) *Photoshop (France)*
Revival of the Death Colossus

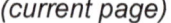

(current page)

ABOVE

DANIEL OGuin
Photoshop (USA)
A.I. Hologram

TOP RIGHT

BOTOND HARKO
Photoshop (Romania)
Nun with a Gun

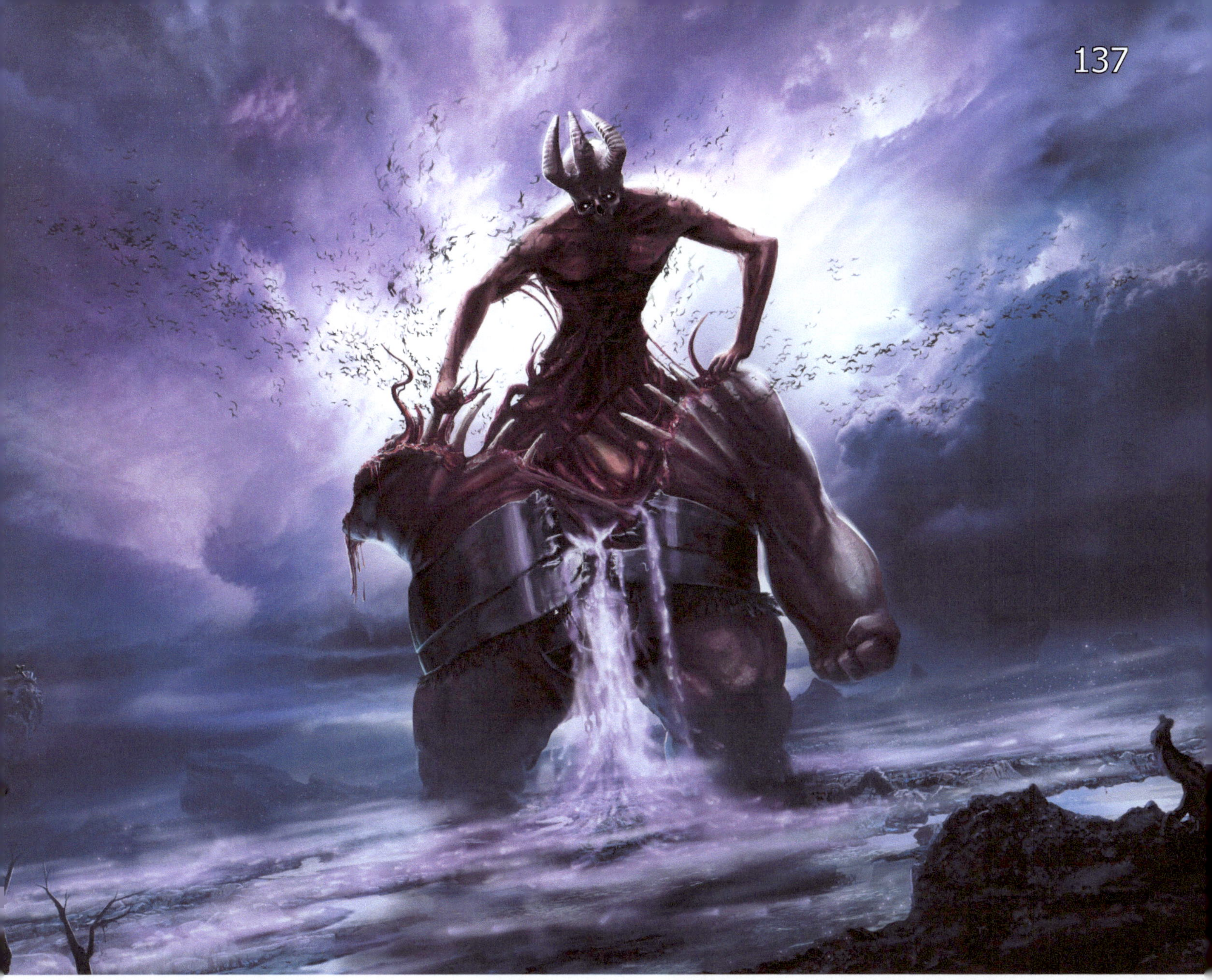

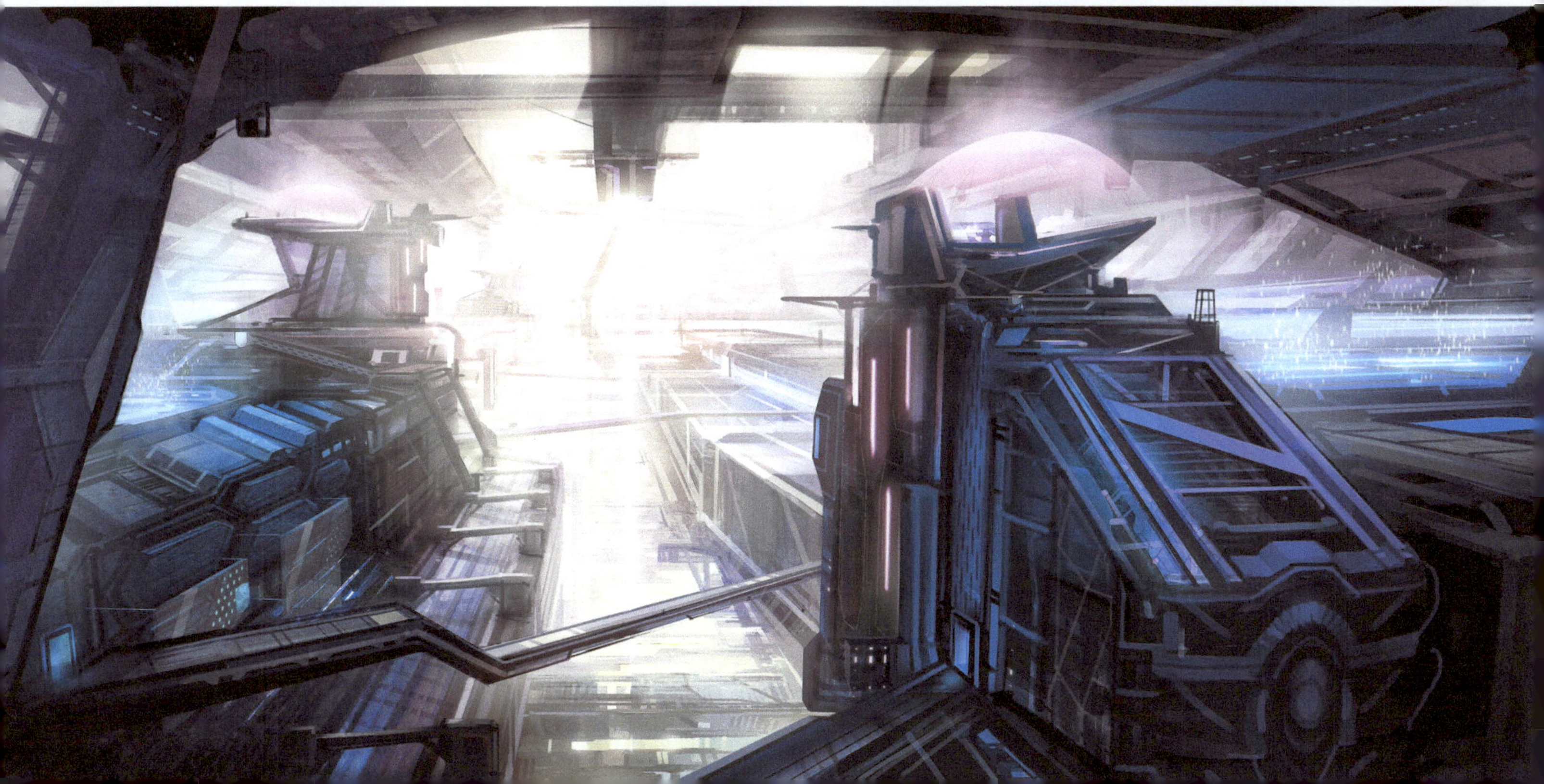

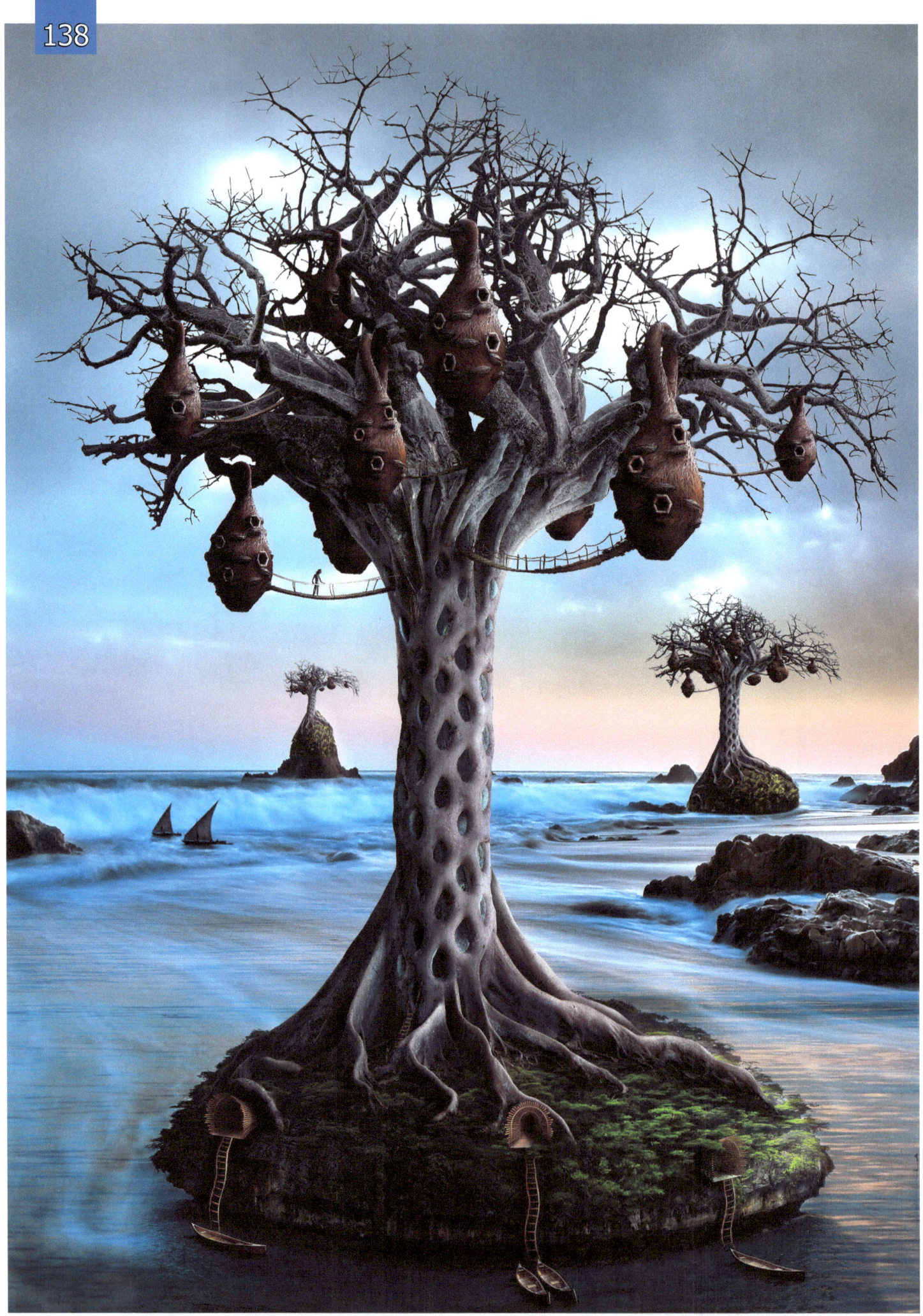

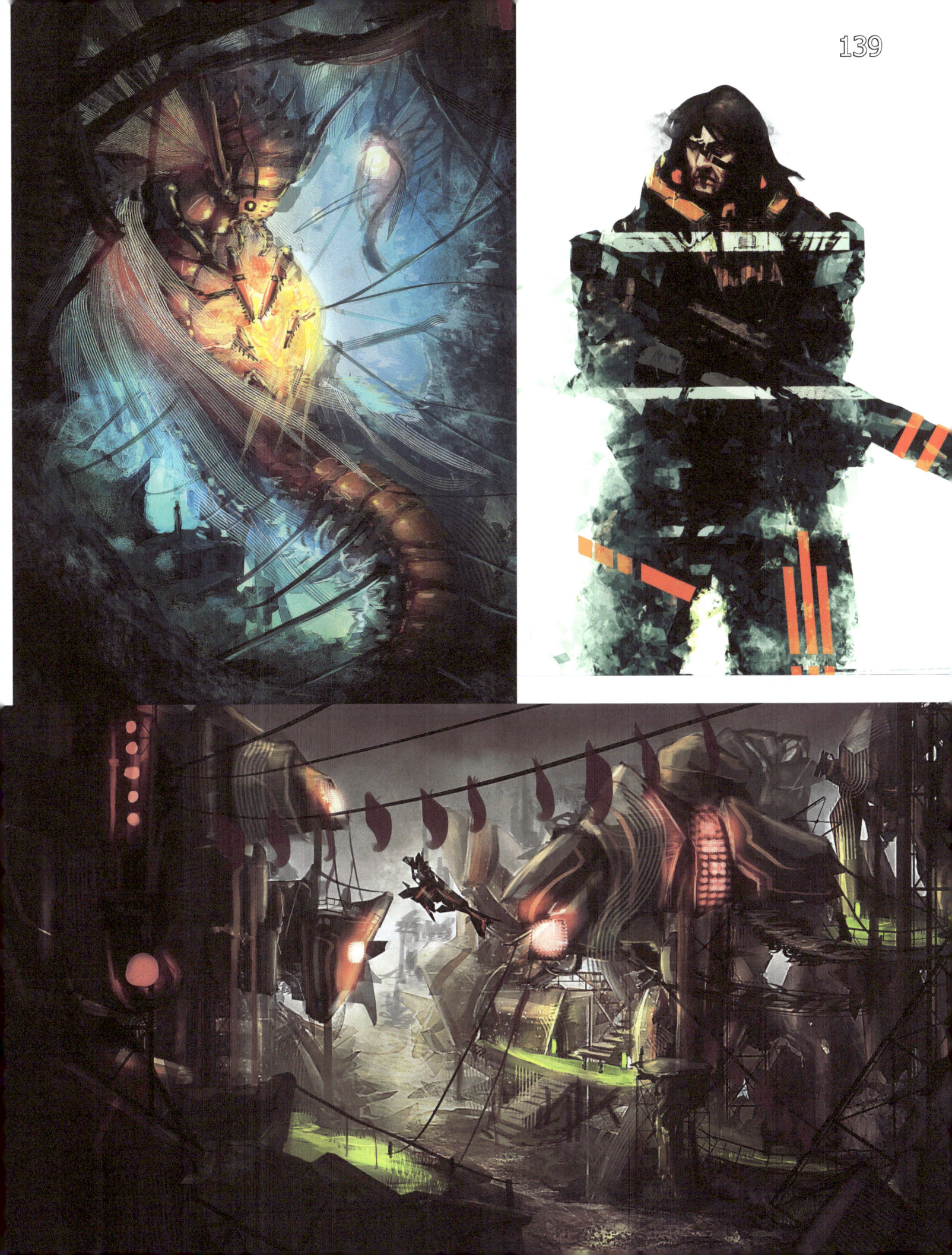

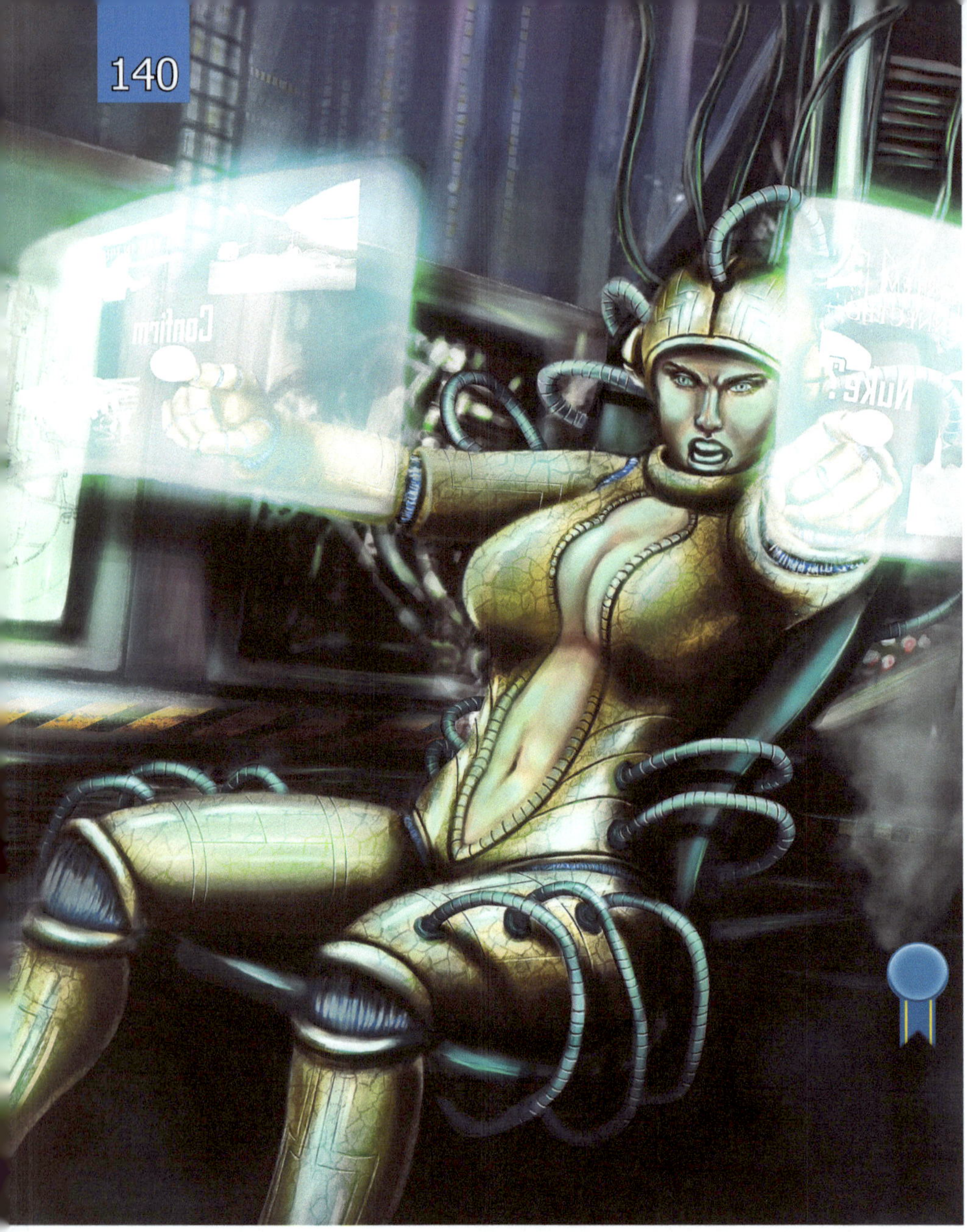

(Previous)

LEFT PAGE

ONA LOOTS
Photomanipulation (South Africa)
Credit: sxc.hu
Arboretum

RIGHT PAGE TOP RIGHT

JULIAN LANCASTER
Photoshop (Canada)
Displacement Suit

RIGHT PAGE TOP LEFT

NIGEL GOH
Photoshop (Singapore)
Nakumata the Giant Fly

RIGHT PAGE BOTTOM

NIGEL GOH
Photoshop (Singapore)
Run Down Sci Town

(Current page)

LEFT

MARKUS STADLOBER
Photoshop and Painter (Austria)
Virtual Field Commander

BELOW

GIA NGUYEN HOANG
Photoshop (VietNam)
Dragon Hatchery

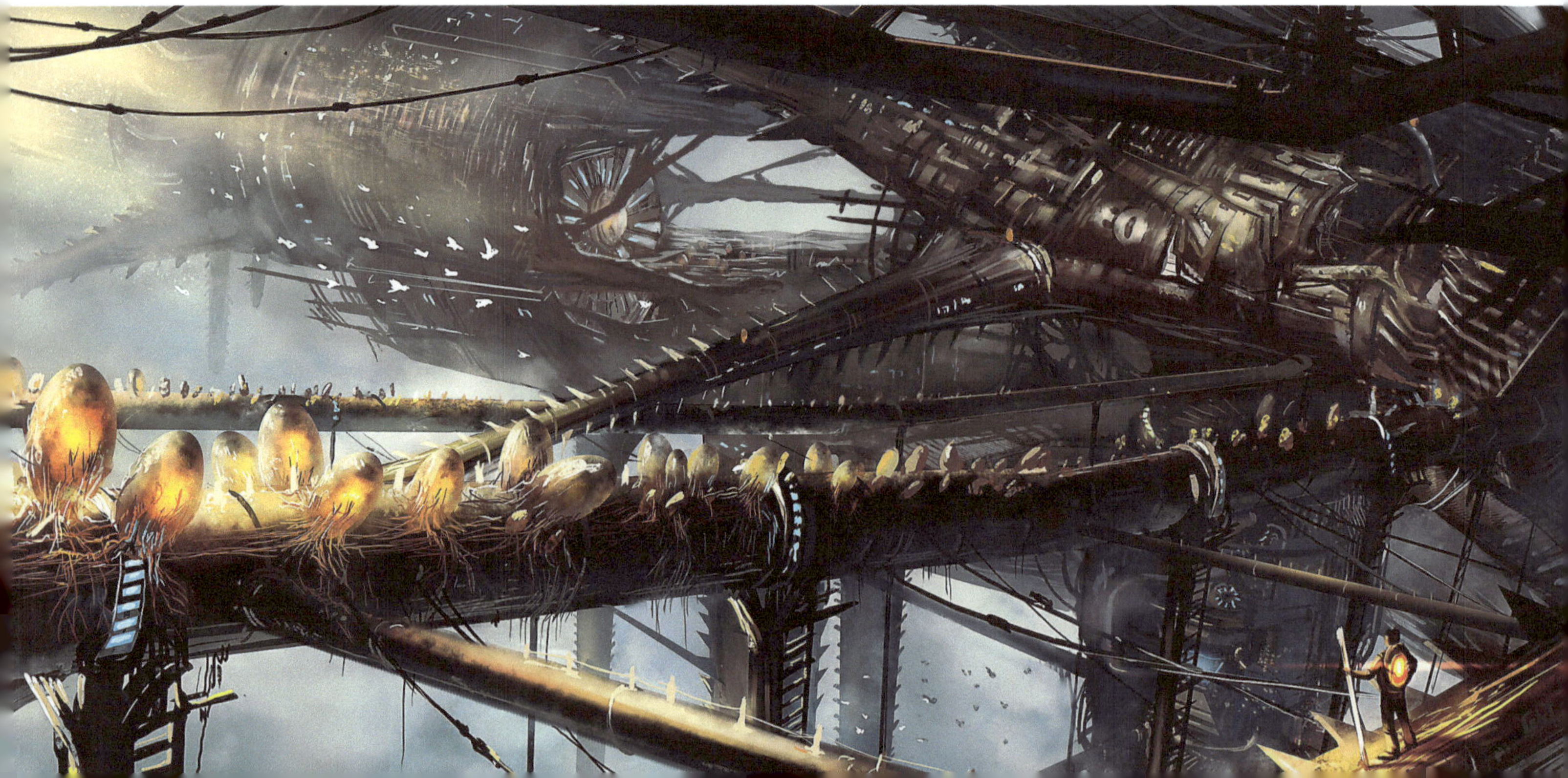

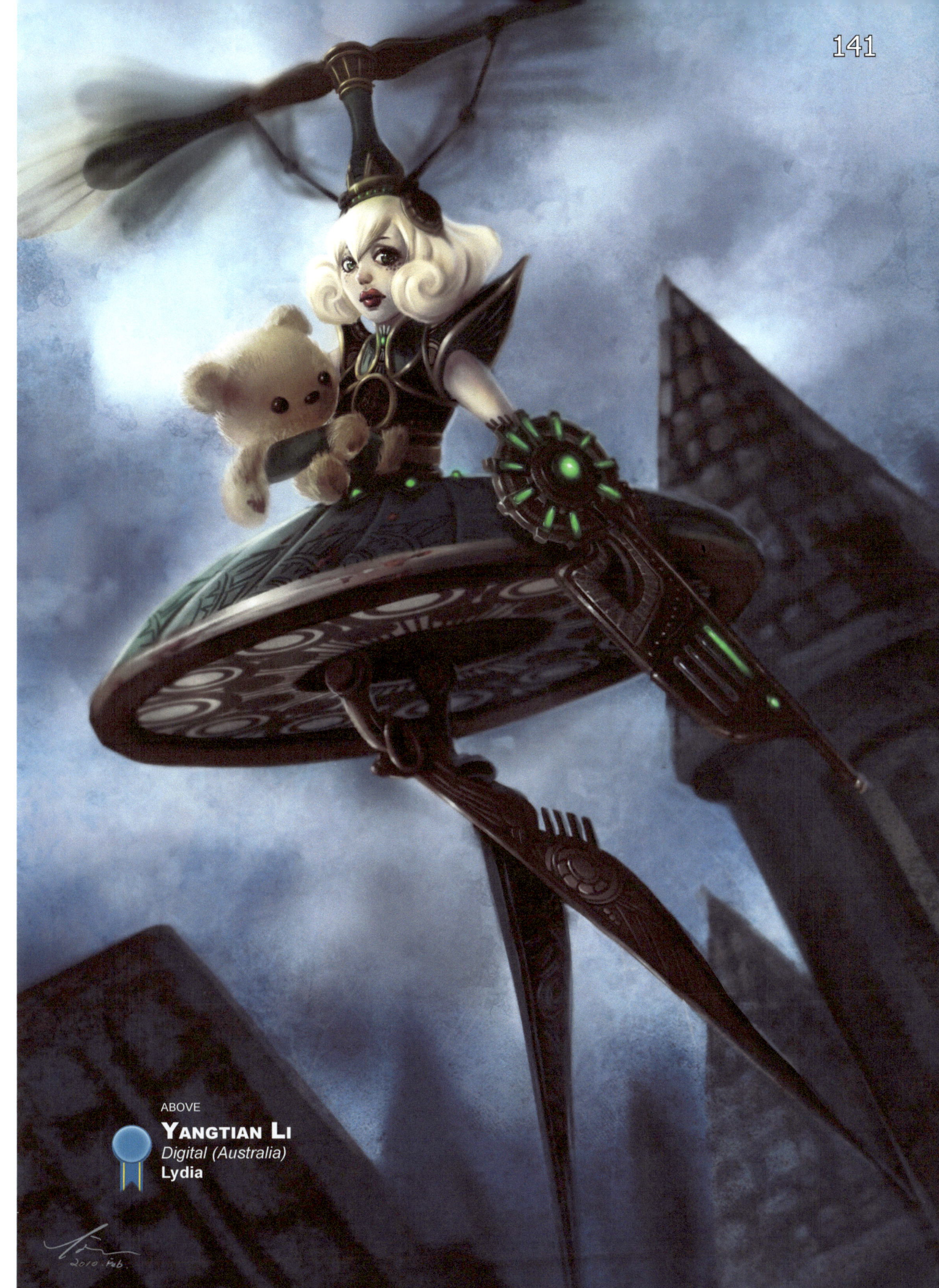

ABOVE
YANGTIAN LI
Digital (Australia)
Lydia

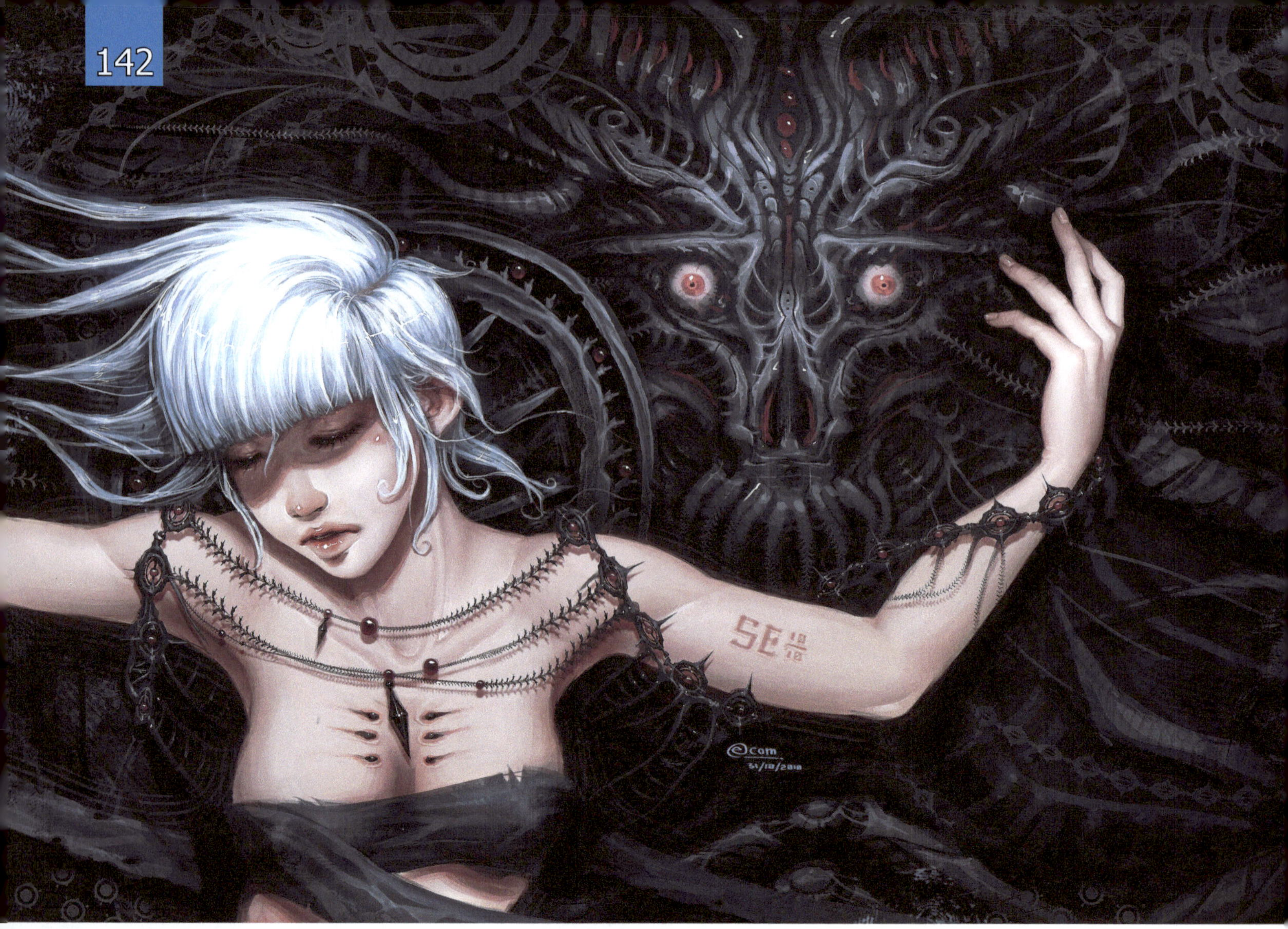

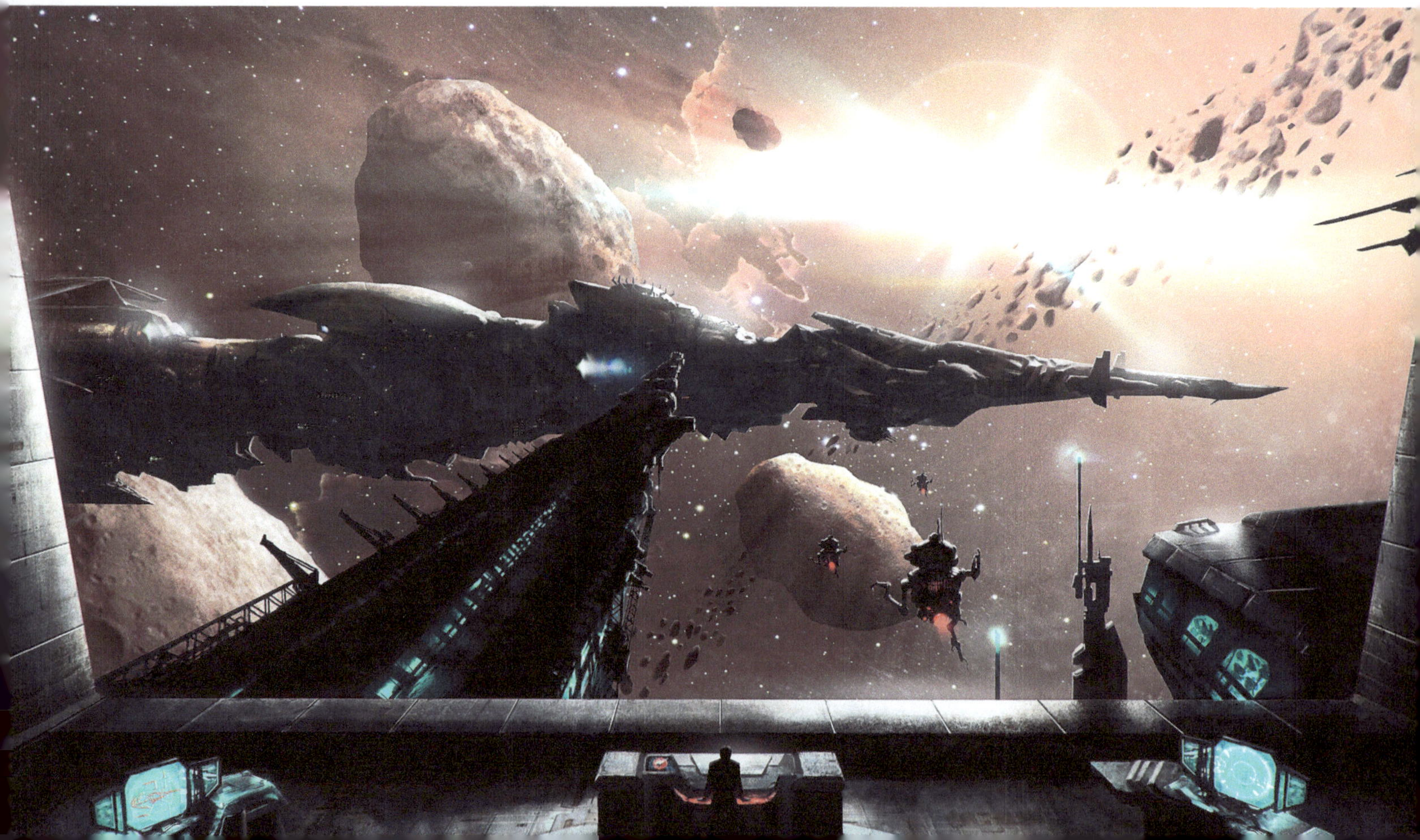

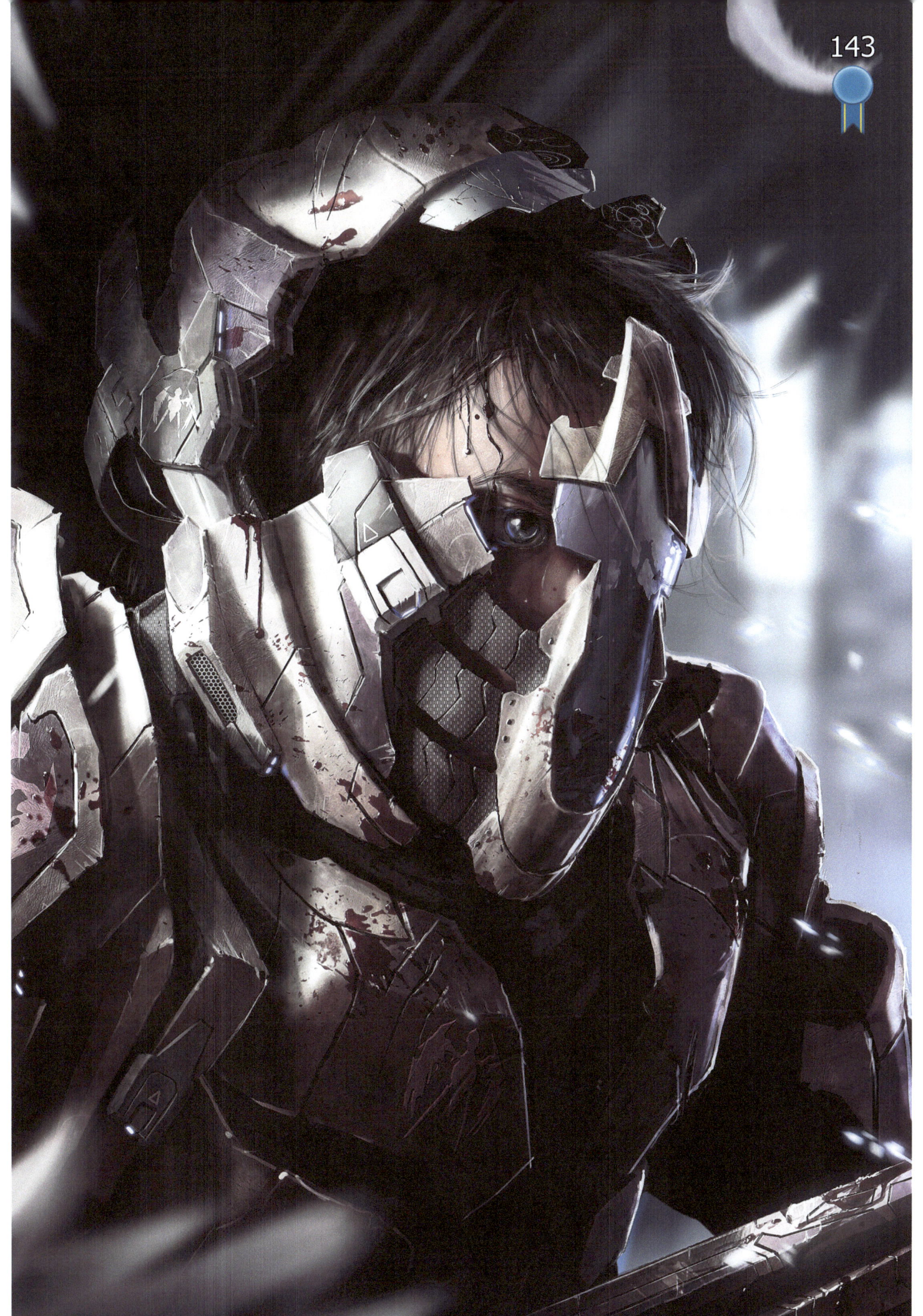

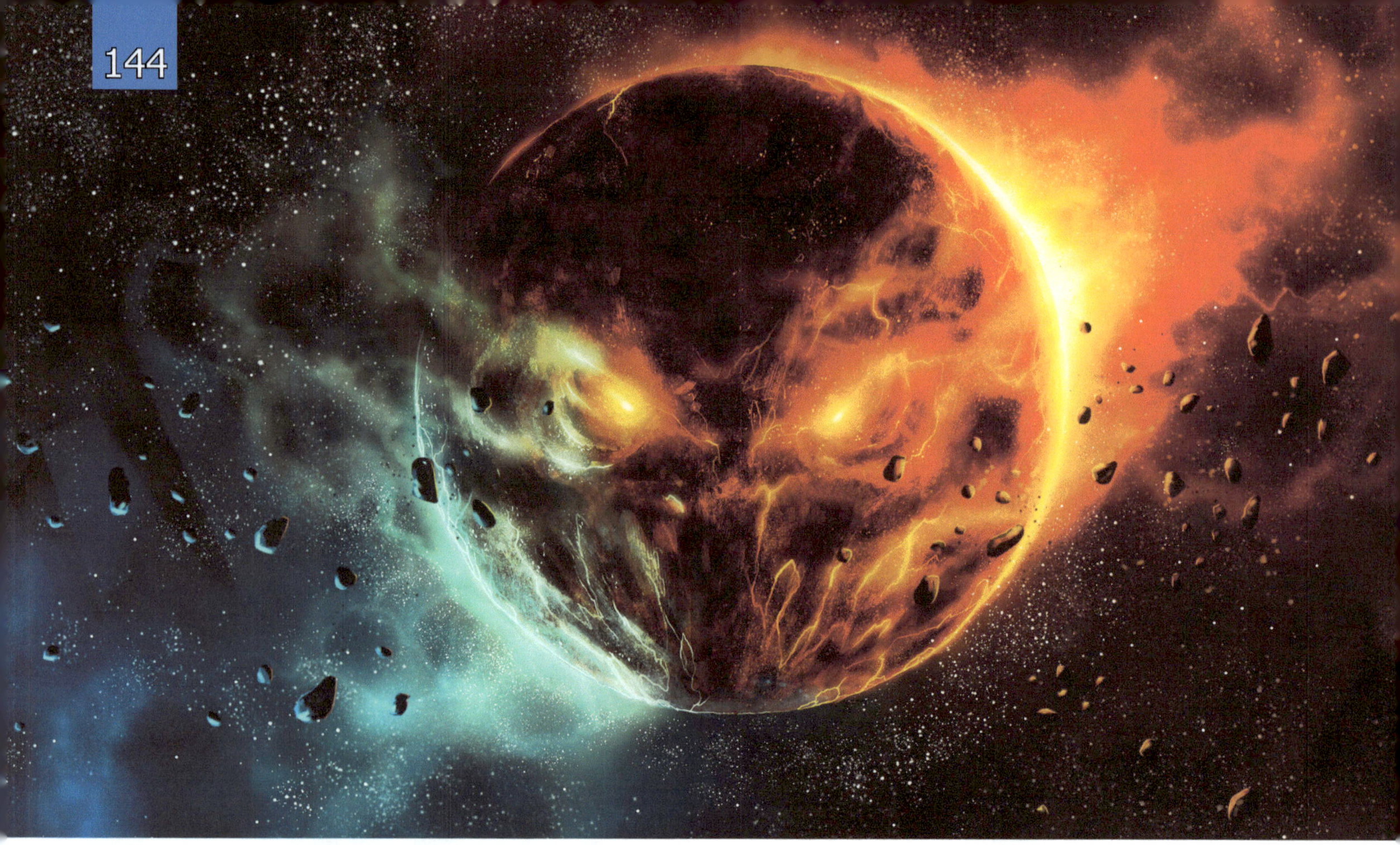

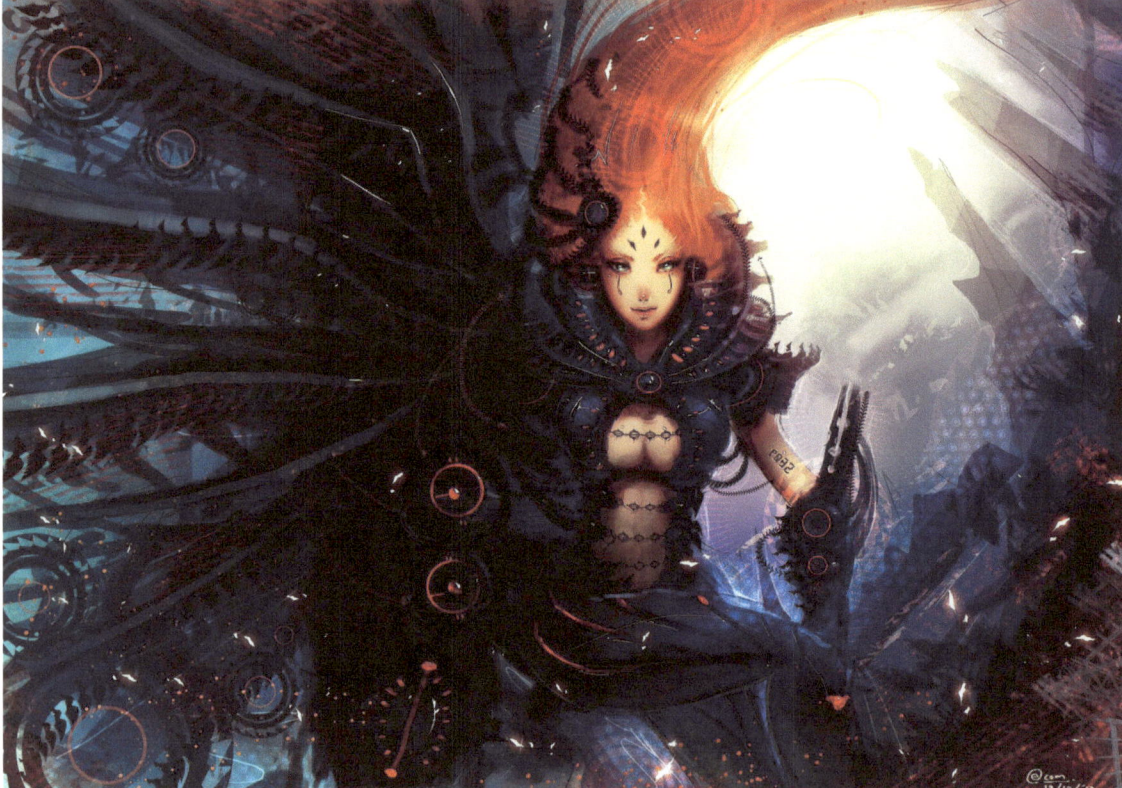

(Previous)

LEFT PAGE TOP
YEE-LING CHUNG
Digital (Malaysia)
Black Matter

LEFT PAGE BOTTOM
DAVID DEMARET
Digital (France)
Black Arrow Destroyer

RIGHT PAGE
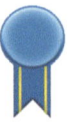
VINCENT LEFEVRE
Photoshop (France)
Bio Paladin

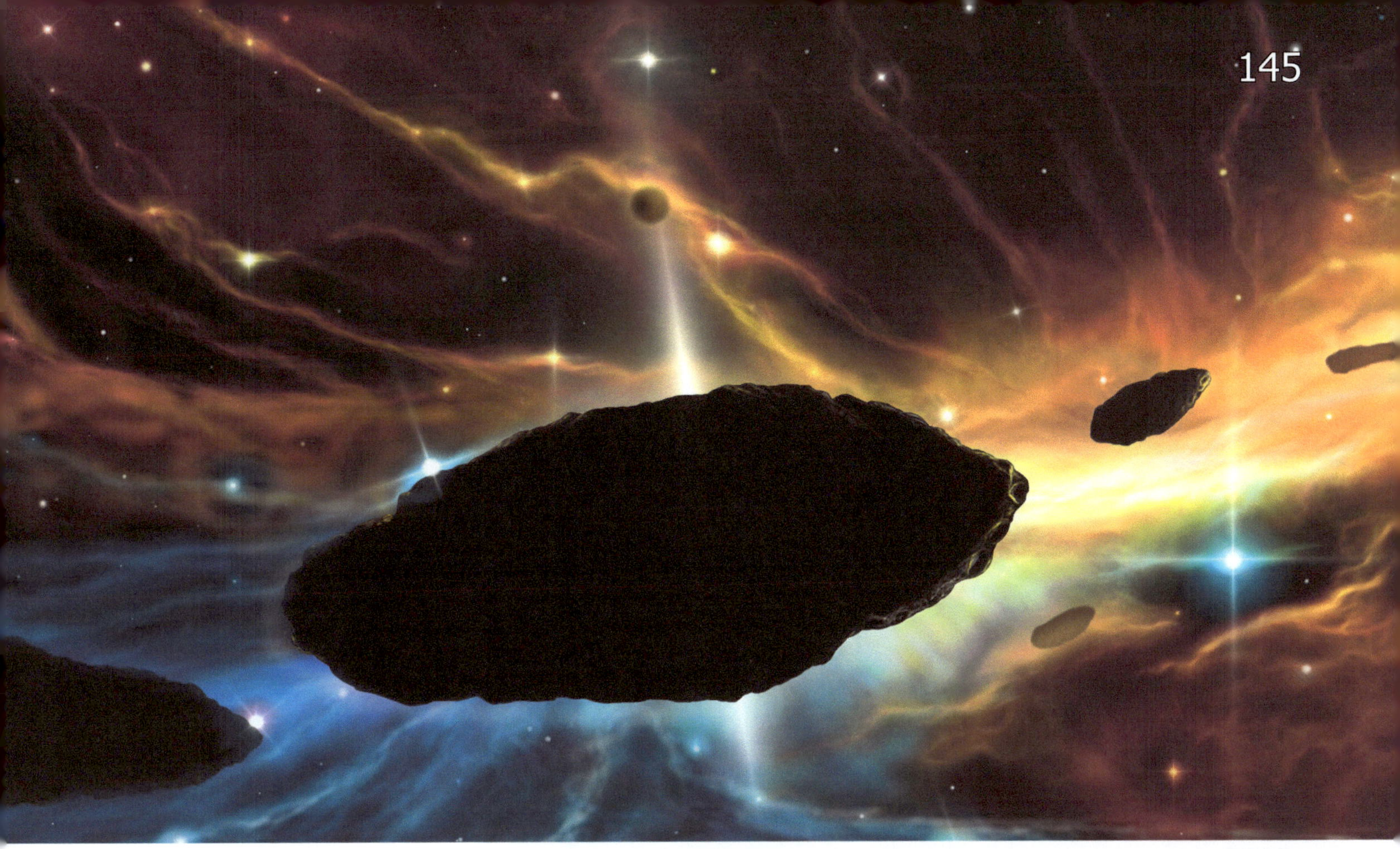

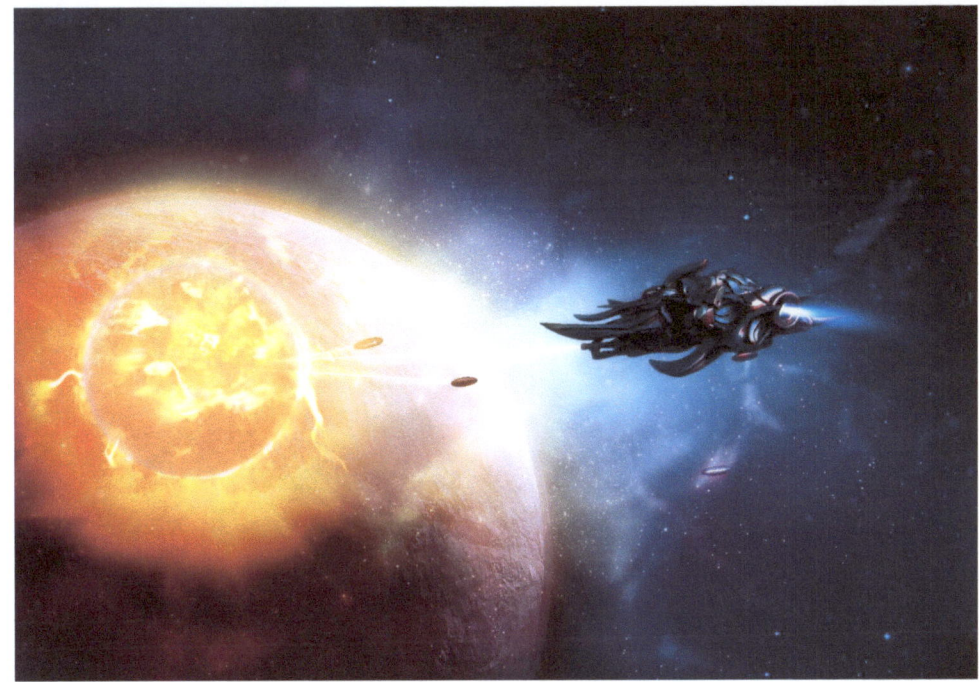

OPPOSITE TOP

FRANCIS-LEE PIMENTEL
Photoshop (England)
Savage Planet

OPPOSITE BOTTOM

YEE-LING CHUNG
Digital (Malaysia)
Digital Era CF2010

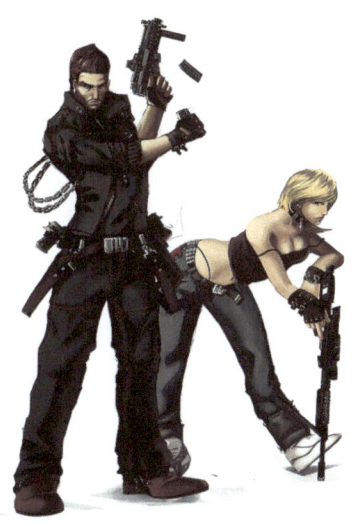

MIDDLE RIGHT

ANTON CHEREVAN
Zbrush and Photoshop (Ukraine)
Octopus

TOP

MICHAEL C. TURNER
Digital(USA)
Cosmic Lighthouses

LEFT

RUI FERREIRA
Sketchbook Pro, Photoshop (Portugal)
Draco & Roz

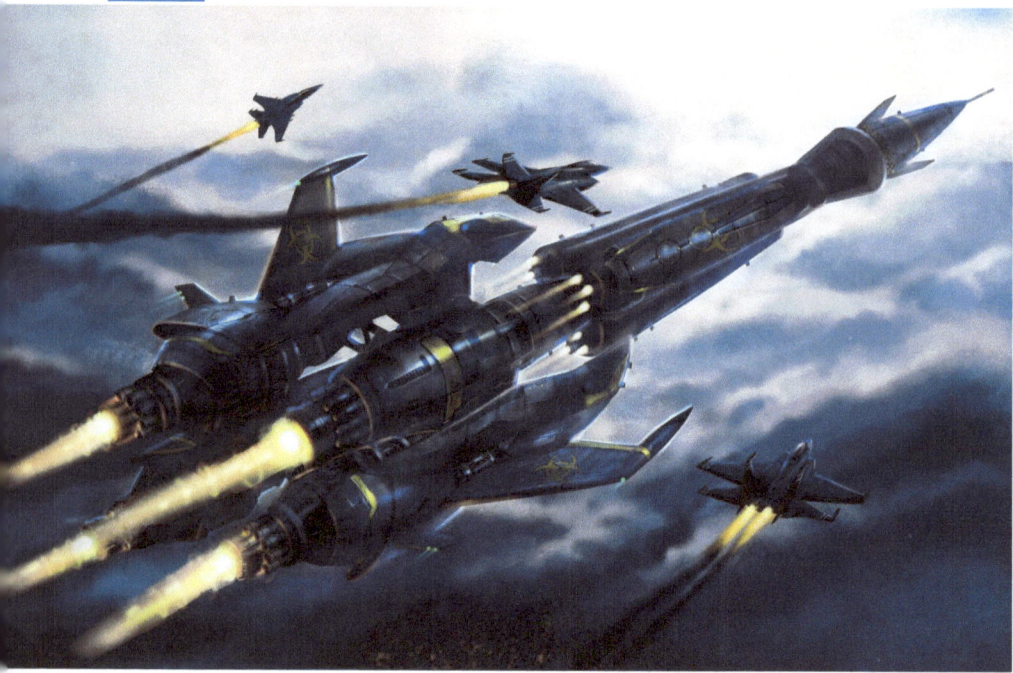

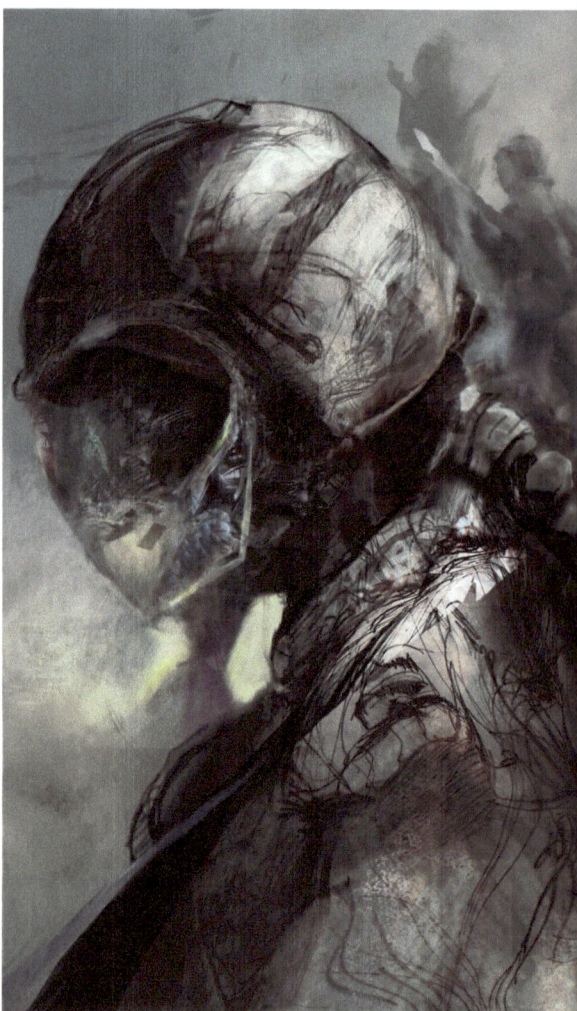

ABOVE

MARCO KUNARDI
Digital (Indonesia/USA)
Behemoth Satellite

BELOW

ANGEL ALONSO
Digital 3D (Spain)
Dystopia

RIGHT

WIL OBERDIER
Pencil/Digital (USA)
Guarding

OPPOSITE

SAM MANLEY
Photoshop (England)
Portal

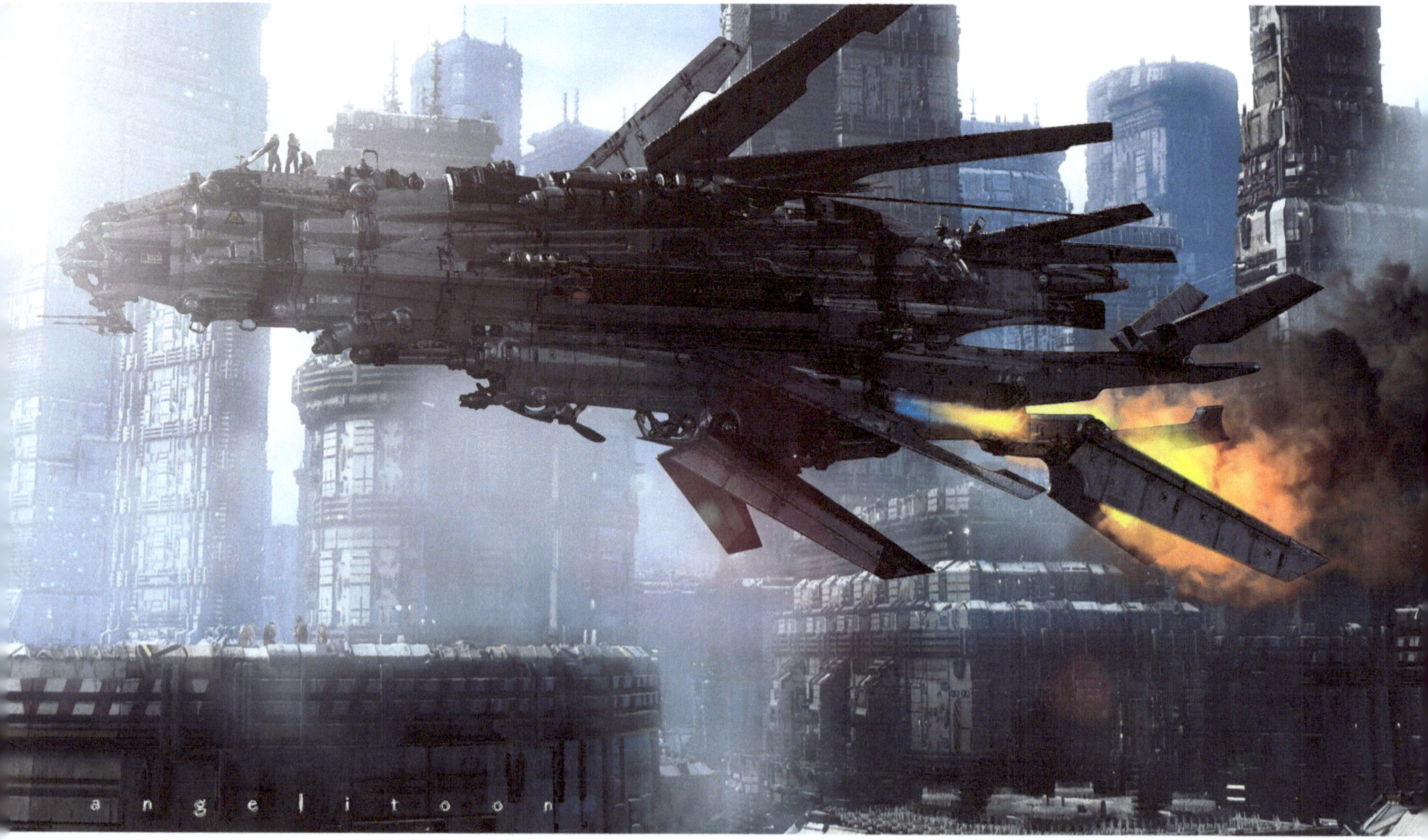

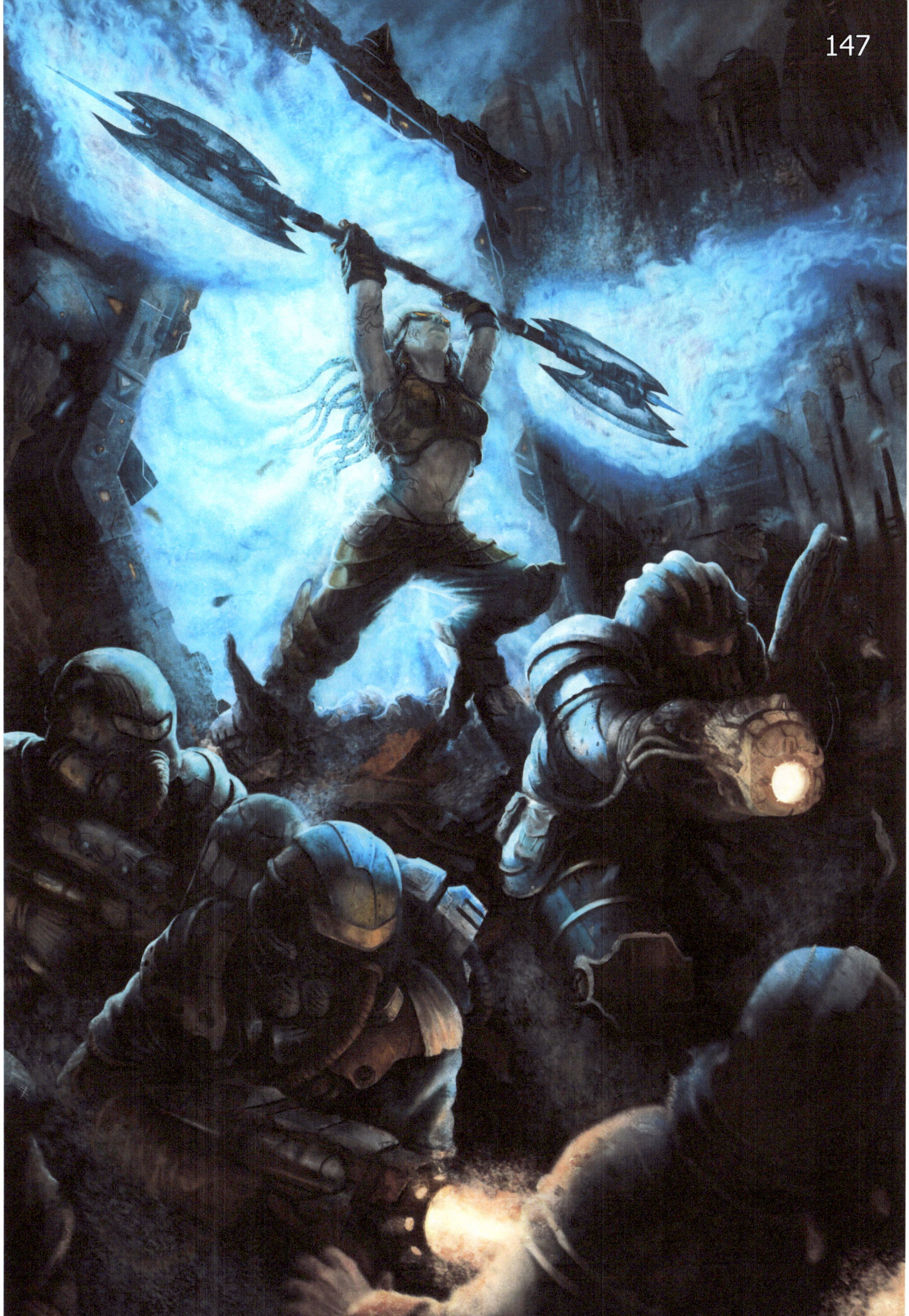

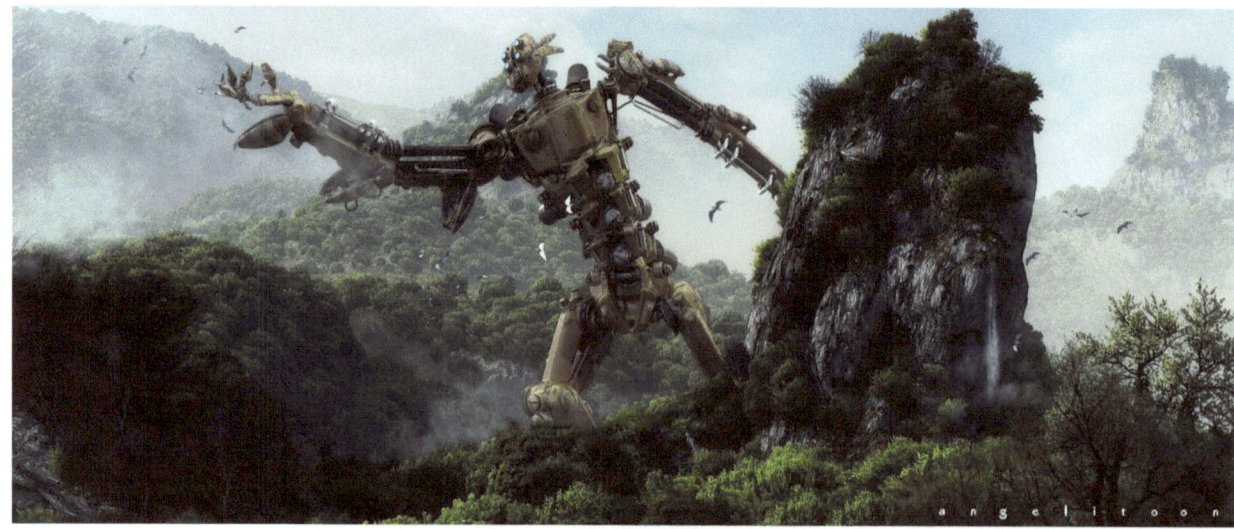

TOP

ANGEL ALONSO
Digital 3D (Spain)
The Lover Life

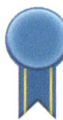

RIGHT

YUKARI MASUIKE
Photoshop (Japan)
Forestgiant

OPPOSITE BOTTOM

CRAIG MUSSELMAN
Photomanipulation (Canada)
Credit: sxc.hu
Cyberpet 3: Mechahopper

OPPOSITE TOP LEFT

OLIVER WETTER
Photoshop (Germany)
Call of Cthulhu

(Overleaf)

LEFT PAGE

GEORGE PATSOURAS
Photoshop Painting (USA)
Self Portrait,

RIGHT PAGE

CRAIG MUSSELMAN
Photomanipulation (Canada)
*Credit: deviantart.com
(skydancer-stock) , sxc.hu*
Dracosteology

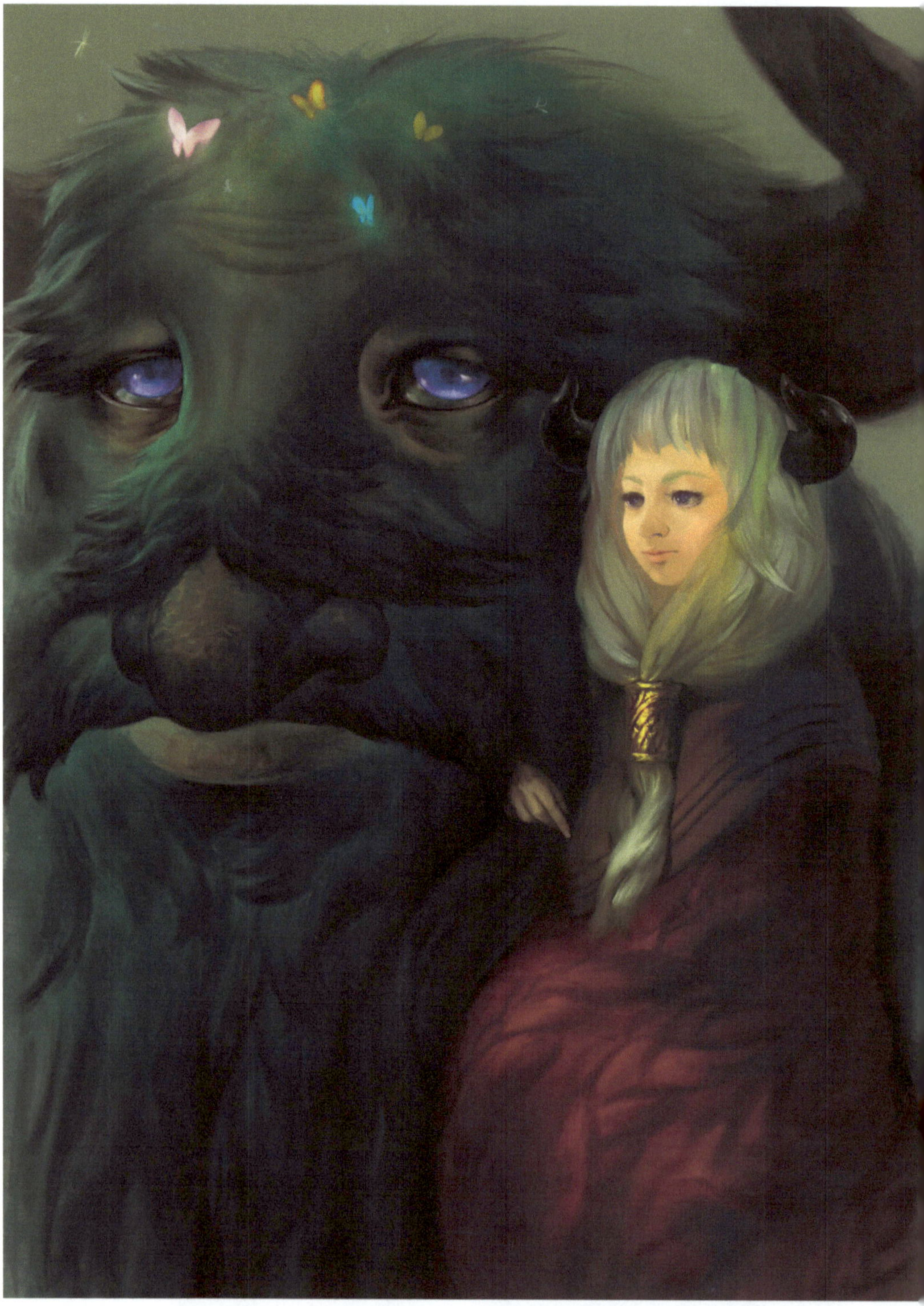

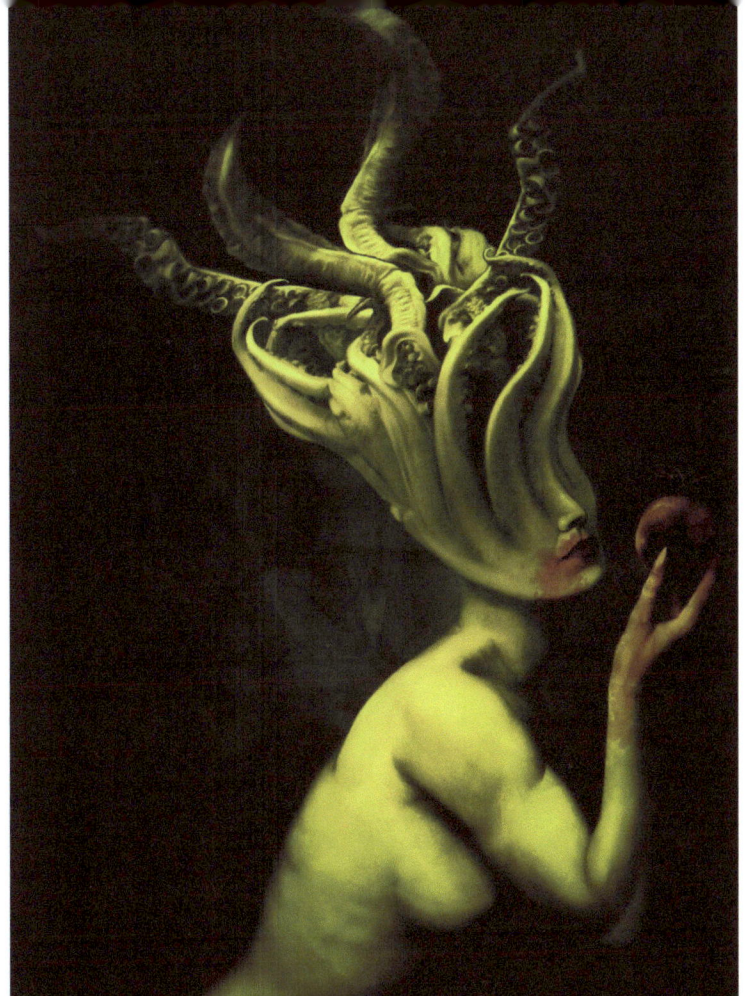

DANILO FERREIRA DA SILVA
Pencil (Brazil)
Alien

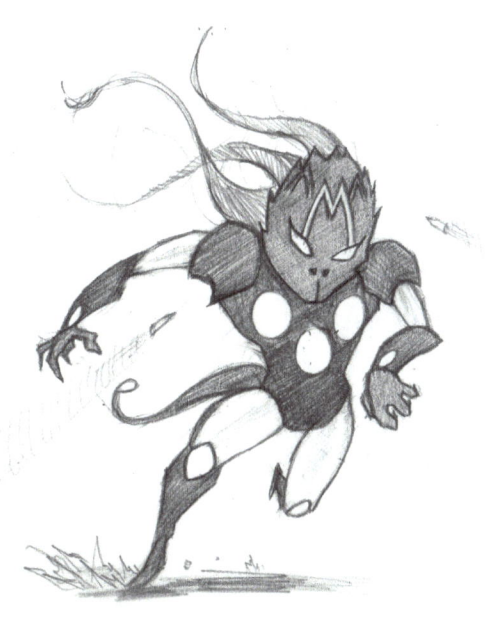

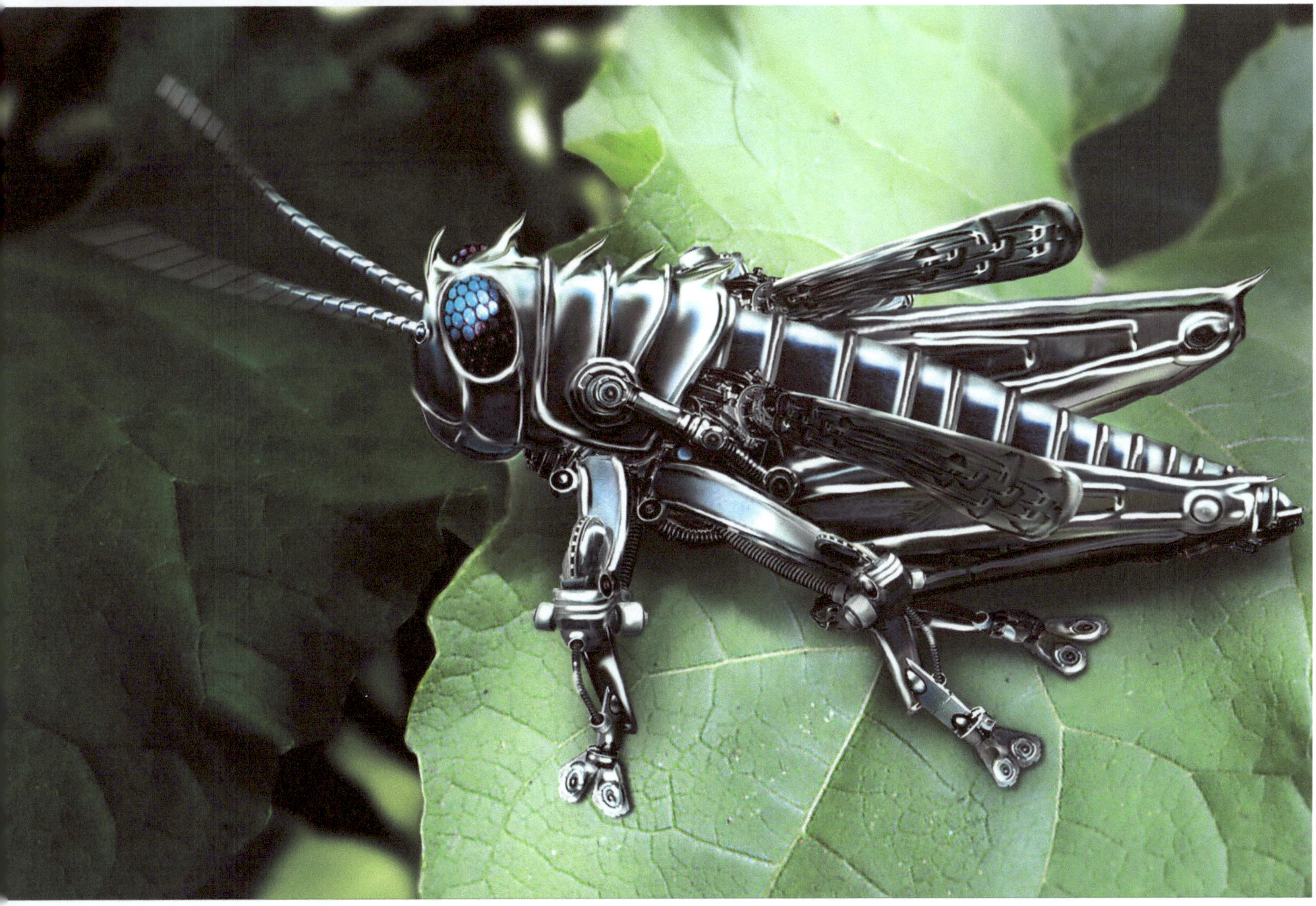

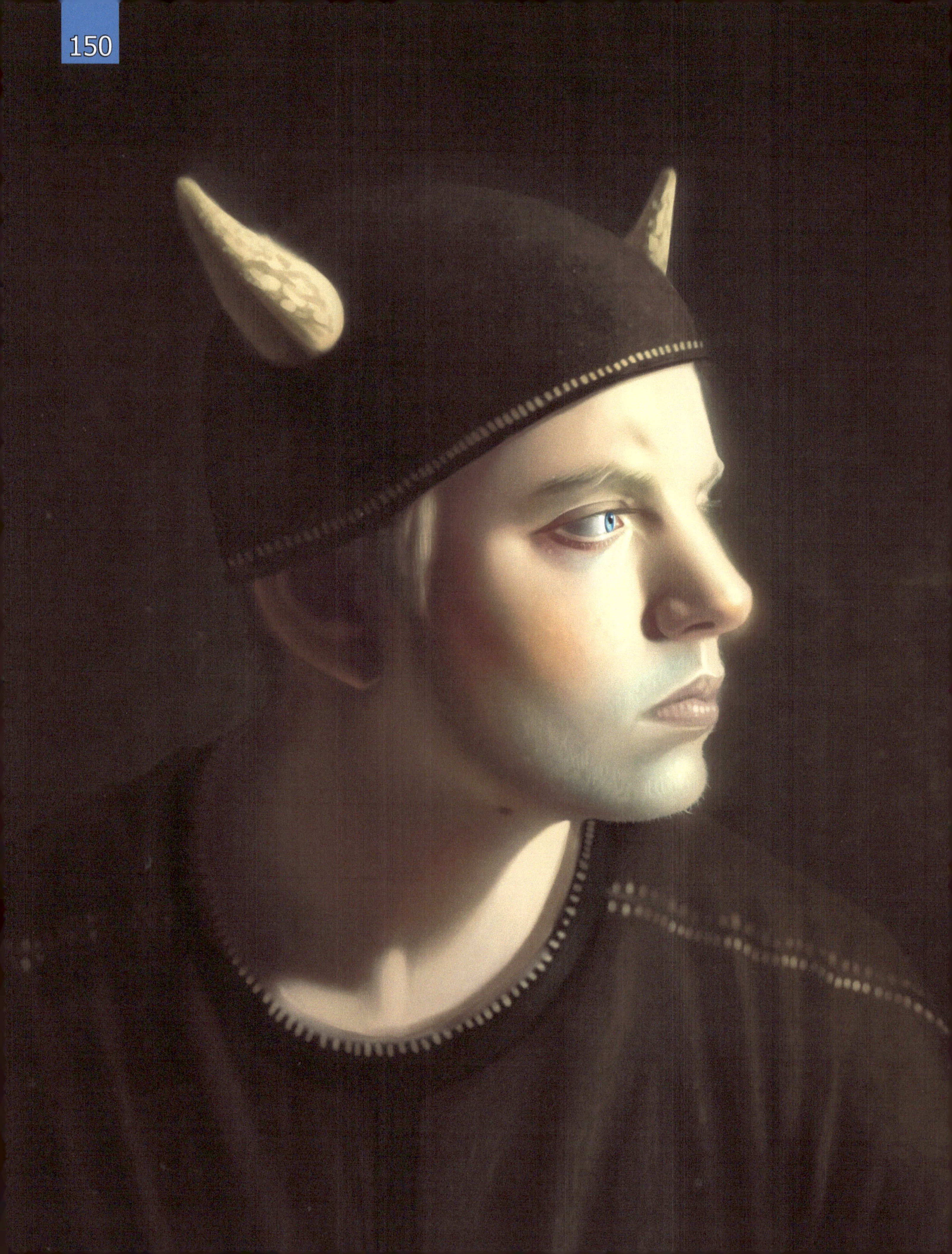

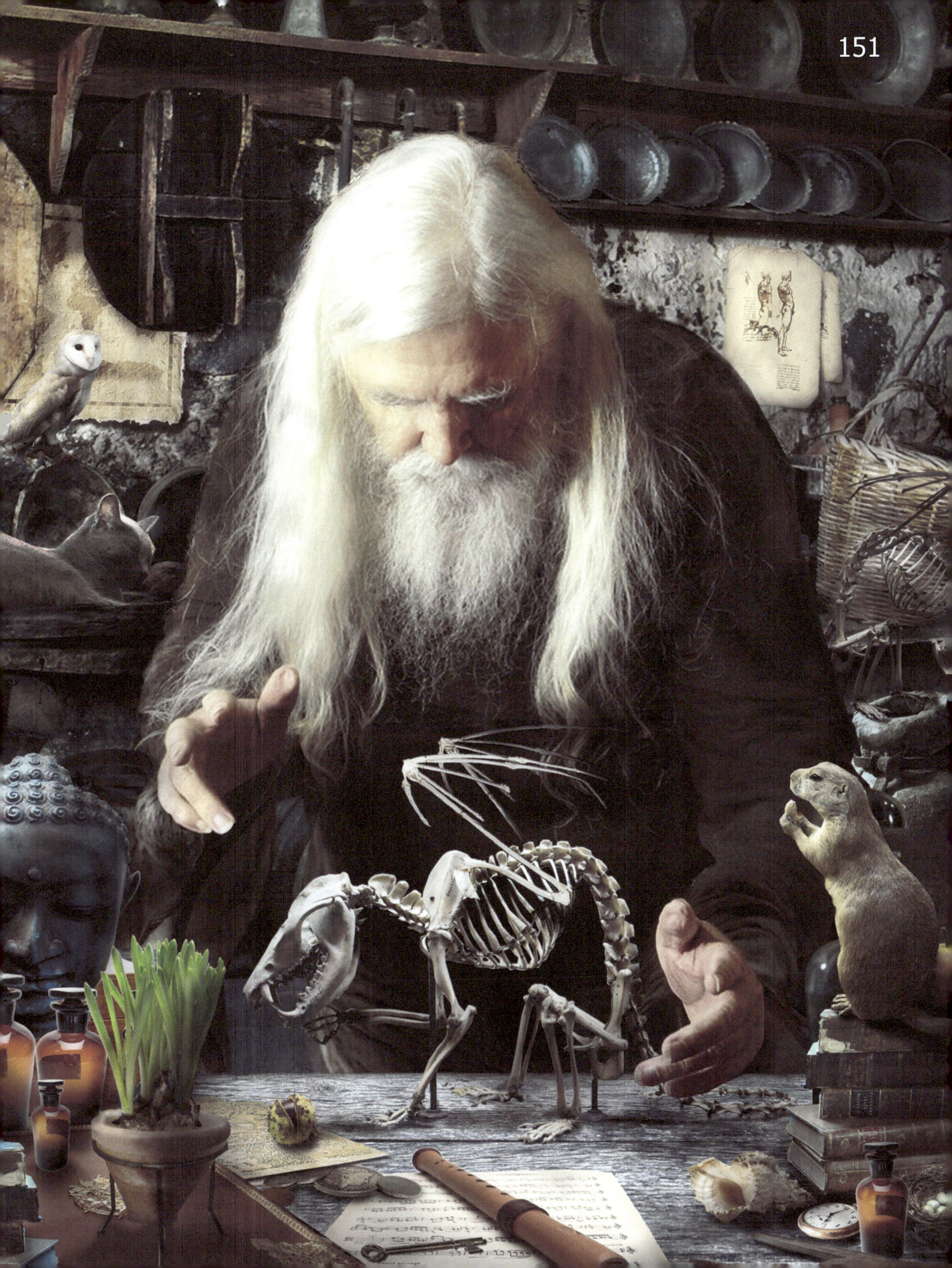

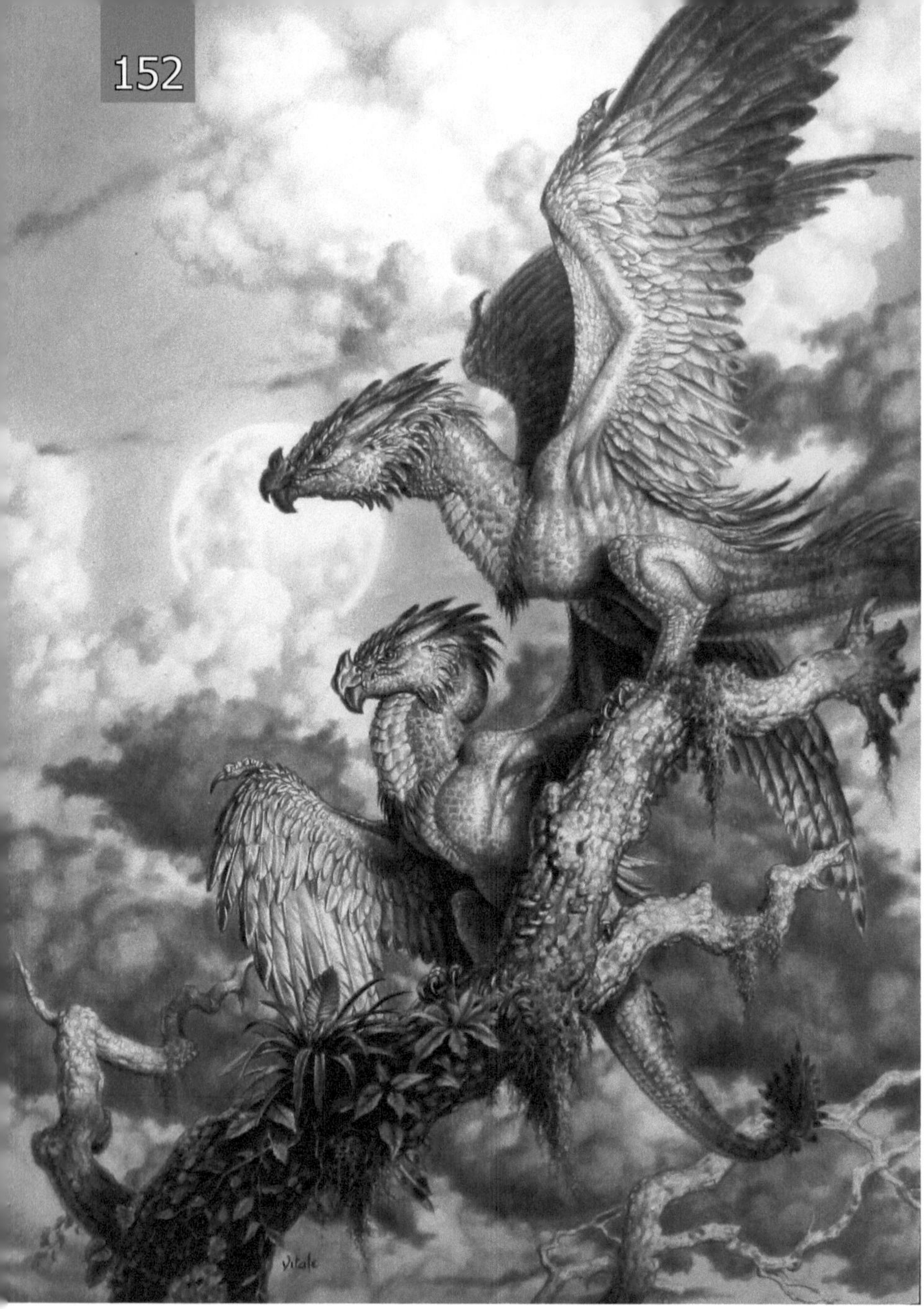

152

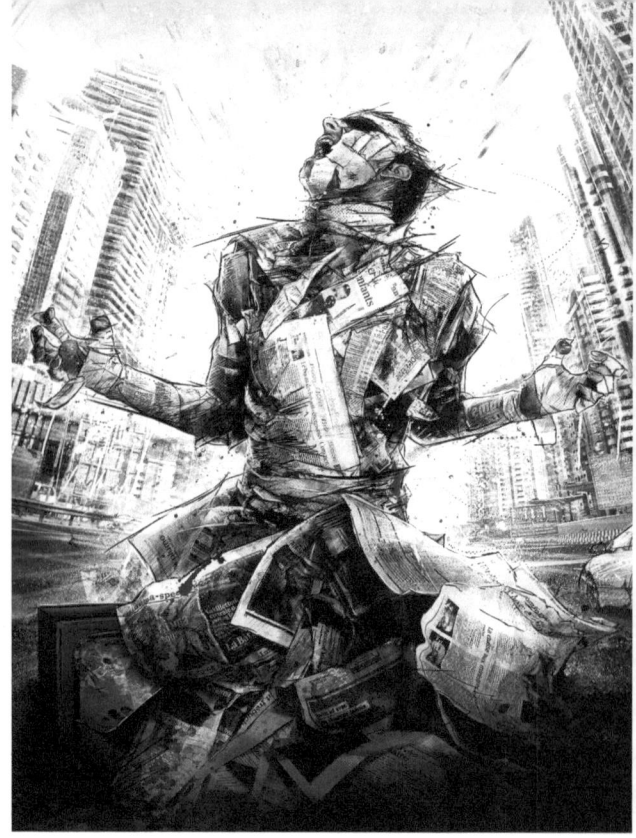

ABOVE

YVAN FEUSI
Photomanipulation (Switzerland)
Media Overdose

LEFT

RAOUL VITALE
Oil on masonite (USA)
Evening Vigil

BELOW

MARCO KUNARDI
Sketches (Indonesia/USA)
Concept Sheet

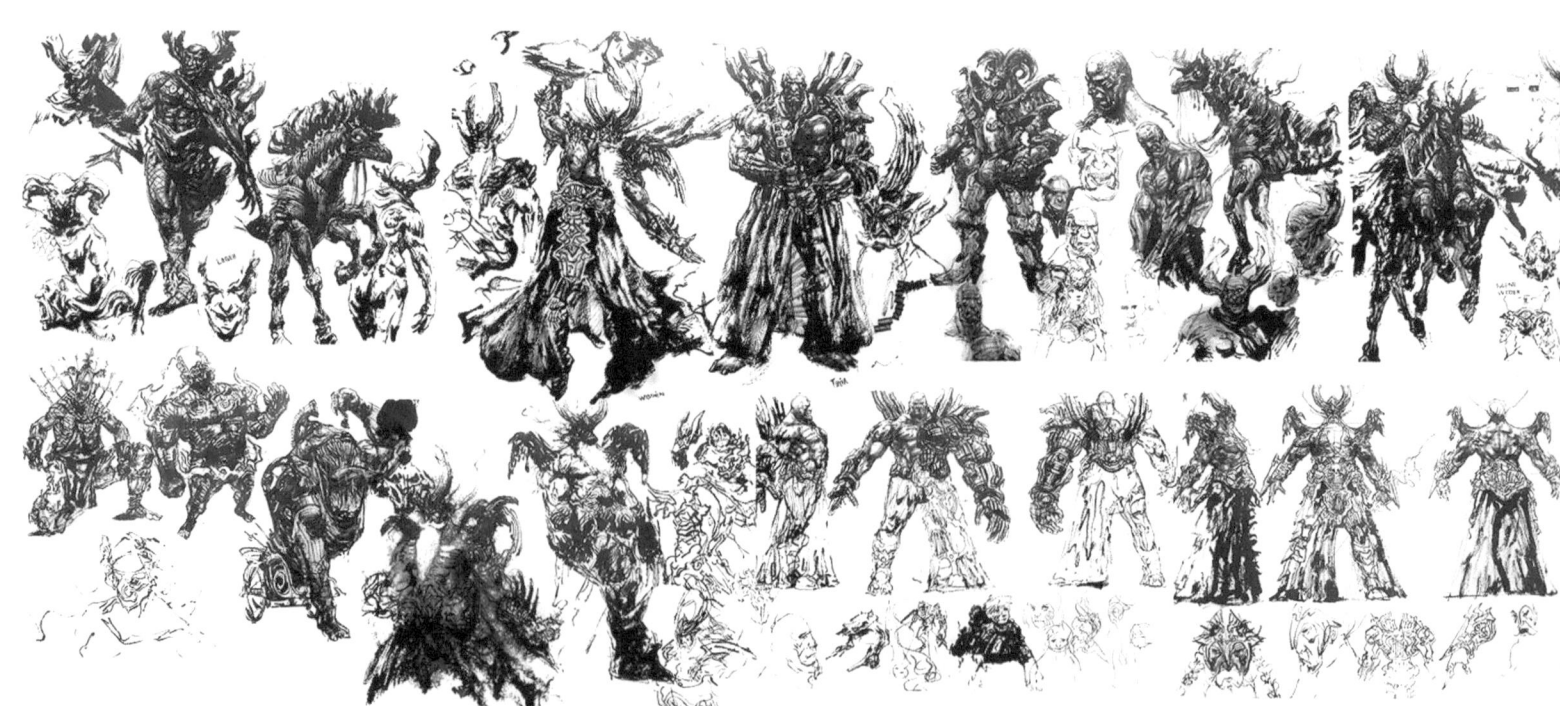

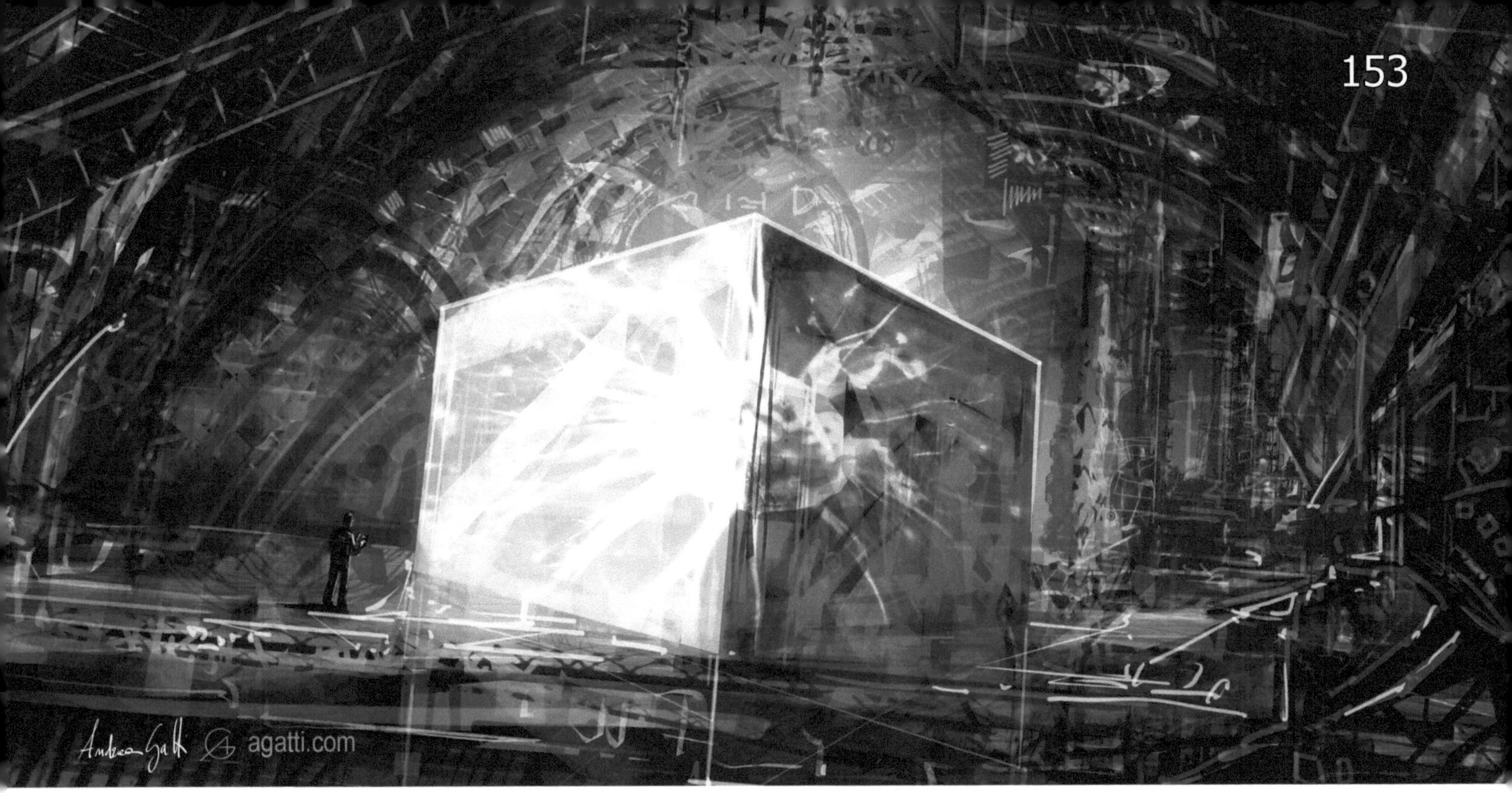

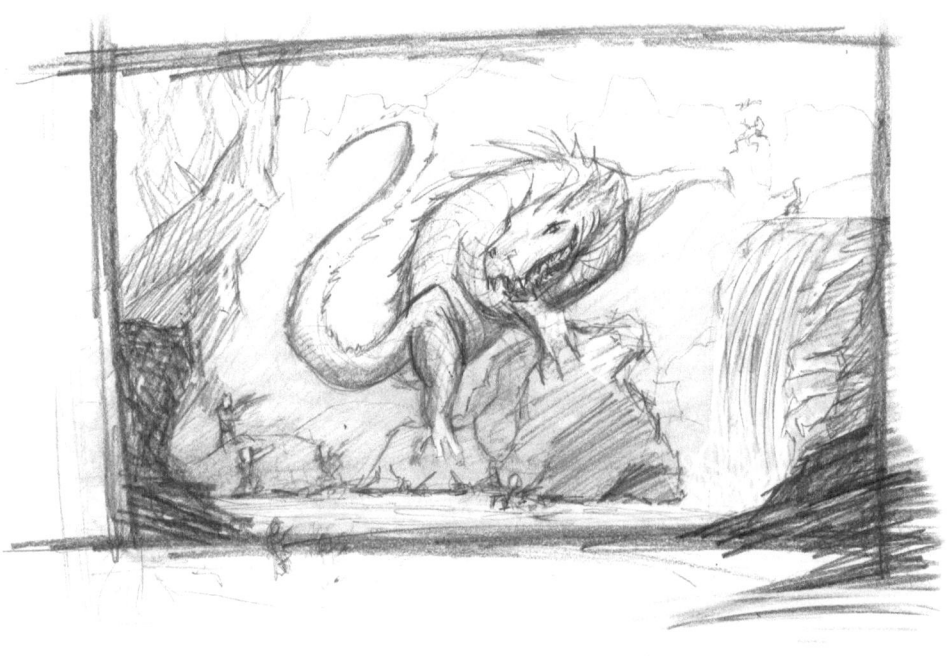

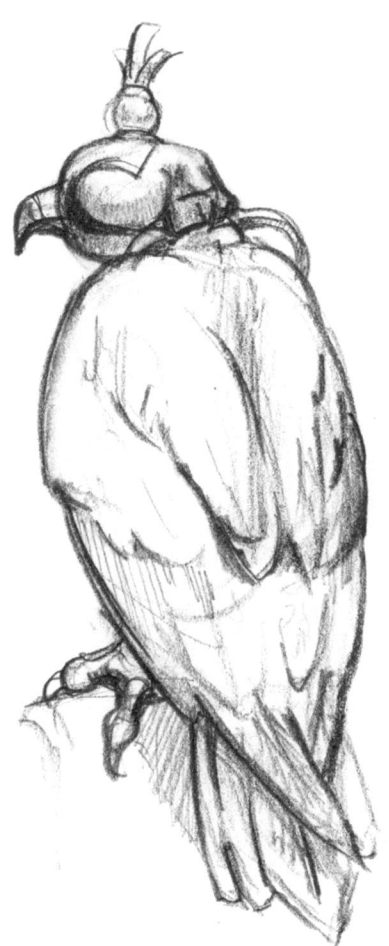

BOTTOM RIGHT

DANILO FERREIRA DA SILVA
Pencil (Brazil)
Dragon

BOTTOM LEFT

JASON MARTIN
Pencil (USA)
Bird Gesture Drawing

TOP

ANDREA GATTI
Photoshop (Italy)
EngineRoom

Contributing Artists

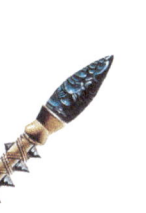

ABOVE
BRUNO MALDONADO TAPIA
Acrylic Airbrush (Mexico)
Dintel 8

MARK REHKOPF
Acrylic (Canada)
Robot Hero

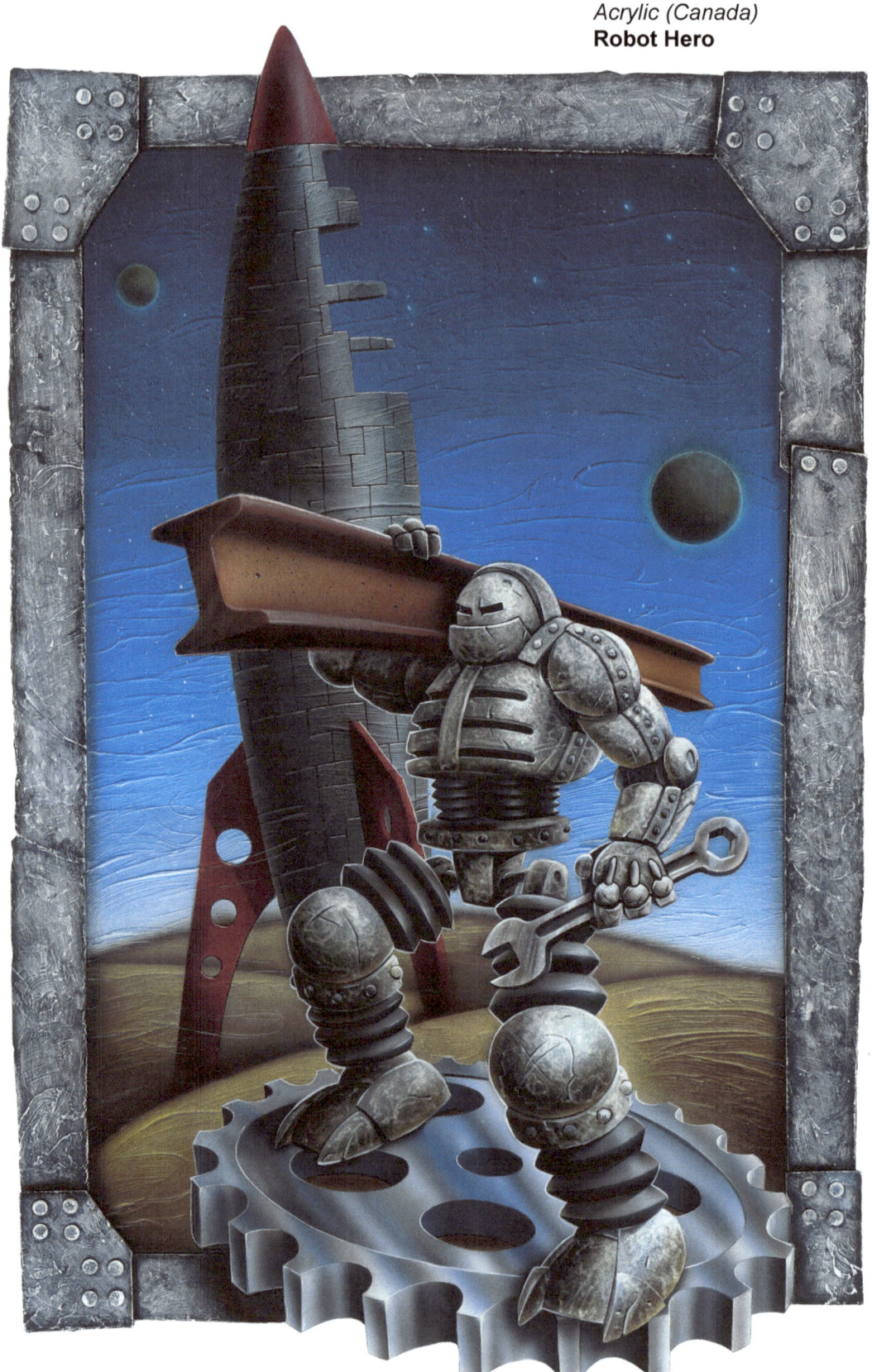

www.ingramcontent.com/pod-product-compliance
Lightning Source LLC
Chambersburg PA
CBHW050715180526
45159CB00003B/1033